AMERICAN FOLK SONGS FOR CHILDREN

American Folk Songs
for Children IN HOME, SCHOOL AND NURSERY SCHOOL

A BOOK FOR CHILDREN,
PARENTS AND TEACHERS

by Ruth Crawford Seeger

ILLUSTRATED BY BARBARA COONEY

Doubleday & Company, Inc., Garden City, New York.

To Michael and Peggy
and Barbara and Penelope

Acknowledgments

I want to thank many more people than can be included on these pages. Traditional singers like Bascom Lamar Lunsford and eighty-year-old Emma Dusenbury. Mothers like Fran Irving and Betty Purcell. An acquaintance who became a friend through the songs, like Rose Alschuler. A personal friend who opened many doors—Vanett Lawler. First, however, my husband, who had talked of gathering together songs like these long before those first weeks at nursery school, back in 1941, when he challenged "Why don't you?" to my hesitation. And the Sandburg family, for my memories of first knowing music like this—memories of spring and fall evenings and a guitar and songs and Lake Michigan below the pine trees. And the Bentons, Tom and Rita, for late hours in their loft down on New York's 8th Street, with harmonicas, guitars, and singing. And with special affection, the Lomax family, for their large part in building and nurturing in me a sense of the variety and aliveness of American folk idioms.

Then, the school in which the book began to grow—the Silver Spring Cooperative Nursery School of Silver Spring, Maryland—for the spirit of adventure with which parents and teachers met the songs and used them. And, at school, Glenore Horne, without whose enthusiasm and instant pleasure in the singing of each new song as it came along, the book might never have been made. And Margaret Fairley, whose thoughts on the delicate balance between tradition and improvisation became so linked with my own that it is hard now sometimes to tell which are hers and which are mine. And Rose Leff Gregg who, knowing how I feel about using the songs, helped and contributed to the writing of several chapters on usage, because she was sure I had not said what I meant to say.

Then my colleague, Laura Pendleton MacCarteney, who gave freely of warm, friendly interest as well as practical professional advice at a time when both were especially needed. And Gertrude Price Wollner, whose pioneer work in music improvisation with children brought us together for long discussions. And Dr. Agnes Greig, for the enrichment of my own insight and for her thoughtful reading of the manuscript. Mary Lemon Lambert, too, for enthusiastic correcting of music proof. And certainly Lilla Belle Pitts, for the picture of herself as a small child running home light-hearted through Mississippi twilight singing "Run, Chillen, Run."

Perhaps most of all, though, the Seeger children Michael and Peggy and Barbara and Penelope, who remember not only singing the songs but numbering pages, punching holes, licking reinforcements, pasting music, typewriting, even proofreading—and finding a sign on the study door when they came home from school: MOTHER WORKING.

And to the following publishers, societies, institutions and individuals, for permission to use the various songs as indicated:

AMERICAN FOLKLORE SOCIETY for "Johnny Get Your Hair Cut" from *Hill Country Tunes* by Samuel Preston Bayard, in the *Memoirs of the American Folklore Society,* Vol. 39; for the following songs from the *Journal of American Folklore:* "Sailing in the Boat" ("Rose in the Garden") from *Song Games from Connecticut* by Emma M. Backus; "Old Mister Rabbit," "Scraping Up Sand in the Bottom of the Sea" ("Shiloh"), and "Yonder She Comes," from *The Missouri Play-Party* by Mrs. L. D. Ames, Vol. 24.

BOTKIN, B. A. for "Buffalo Girls," "Jim along Josie," and "Walk along John" from *The American Play-Party Song,* University of Nebraska Press. Copyright, 1937.

COLLINS, FLETCHER, JR. for "Eency Weency Spider," and "What Shall We Do When We All Go Out?" from *Alamance Play Party Songs and Singing Games,* Elon College, N.C., 1940.

EDDY, MARY O. for "There Was a Man and He Was Mad" from *Ballads and Songs from Ohio,* J. J. Augustin, New York. Copyright, 1939.

FISCHER, CARL for "Turtle Dove" from *30 and 1 Folk Songs from the Southern Mountains,* compiled and arranged by Bascom Lamar Lunsford and Lamar Stringfield. Copyright, 1929.

HARBISON, KATHERINE for "When I Was a Young Maid" from *In the Great Meadow and the Prairie,* in the *Southern Folklore Quarterly,* Vol. II, No. 3.

HARCOURT BRACE AND COMPANY for "By'm Bye" ("Stars Shining"), and "Hanging Out the Linen Clothes" from *The American Songbag* by Carl Sandburg. Copyright, 1927.

HARVARD UNIVERSITY PRESS for "Built My Lady a Fine Brick House," "The Closet Key," "Do, Do, Pity My Case," "Hop Old Squirrel," "Jimmy Rose He Went to Town," "Juba," "Old Aunt Kate," "Old Mister Rabbit," "One Cold and Frosty Morning" ("Old Jessie"), "Lula Gal" ("Tie My Shoe"), "Run, Chillen, Run" ("Run, Nigger, Run"), "Riding in the Buggy, Miss Mary Jane," "This Lady She Wears a

Dark Green Shawl," "Who's That Tapping at the Window," from *On the Trail of Negro Folk Songs* by Dorothy Scarborough. Reprinted by permission of the President and Fellows of Harvard College; for "As I Walked Out One Holiday" ("The Little Boy Threw His Ball So High," or "The Jew's Garden"), "Down by the Greenwood Sidey-o," "Down Came a Lady" ("Lord Daniel's Wife," or "Little Matthew Grove"), "It Rained a Mist" from *Traditional Ballads of Virginia* by Arthur Kyle Davis. Reprinted by permission of the President and Fellows of Harvard College.

INDIANA HISTORICAL COMMISSION for "Such a Getting Upstairs" ("Getting Upstairs") from *The Play-party in Indiana* by Leah Jackson Wolford. Copyright, 1916.

LIBRARY OF CONGRESS, and the collectors and singers of the following songs, transcribed from field recordings in the Archive of American Folklore:

HERBERT HALPERT, collector, for: "Adam Had Seven Sons," "Here Sits a Monkey" ("Here Sits a Lady"), "Oh, John the Rabbit," sung by groups of children in Mississippi.

JOHN A. LOMAX, collector, for: "Baby Dear," sung by Daisy Smith; "Big Old Owl" ("Jim Crack Corn"), sung by Alec Dunford; "Dog Tick," sung by Ray Wood; "How Old Are You" ("Yaddle Daddle"), sung by the Gant family; "I'm Going to Join the Army," sung by J. M. Mullins; "Old Molly Hare," sung by Alec Dunford; "Pretty Little Girl with the Red Dress On" ("Poor Howard"), sung by Leadbelly.

SIDNEY ROBERTSON, collector, for: "Bought Me a Cat," "Did You Go to the Barney," "The Juniper Tree," sung by Emma Dusenbury; "Free Little Bird" and "John Henry," sung by Bascom Lamar Lunsford; "Frog Went a-Courting," "Jesus Borned in Bethlea," sung by S. F. Russell.

CHARLES SEEGER, collector, for: "My Horses Ain't Hungry," "Old Joe Clarke" ("Round and Round"), "Skip-a to My Lou," sung by Rebecca Tarwater.

LOMAX, JOHN A., ESTATE OF, for "All Around the Kitchen" ("Cocky Doodle Doodle Doo"), "Billy Barlow," "Hush Little Baby," "Ducks in the Millpond," "Every Monday Morning" ("John Henry"), "Go to Sleepy," "Going Down to Town" ("Lynchburg Town"), "Have a Little Dog" ("Toll a Winker"), "Little Bird, Little Bird," "The Little Black Train," "Mary Wore Her Red Dress," "Old Blue," "Rain or Shine" ("Doney Gal"), "Sally Go Round the Sunshine" ("Sally Go Round the Moon"), "The Wind Blow East," from *Our Singing Country*, John A. and Alan Lomax, The Macmillan Company. Copyright, 1941; for "Old Molly Hare" and "Pretty Little Girl with the Red Dress On" (see Library of Congress, above).

LUNSFORD, BASCOM LAMAR for "Free Little Bird" and "John Henry," transcribed from recordings made by Sidney Robertson (see Library of Congress, above).

MACCARTENEY, LAURA PENDLETON for permission to adapt "Little Gray Ponies" ("Little Horses") from *Songs for the Nursery School,* The Willis Music Company. Copyright, 1937.

THE MACMILLAN COMPANY for "Goodbye, Julie" ("Miss Julie Ann Johnson") from *Negro Folk Songs as Sung by Leadbelly,* by John A. and Alan Lomax. Copyright, 1936; for "Goodbye, Old Paint," "The Little Pig" ("Tale of a Little Pig"), "Pick a Bale of Cotton," from *American Ballads and Folk Songs* by John A. and Alan Lomax. Copyright, 1934.

MCINTOSH, MR. AND MRS. DAVID S. for "Roll That Brown Jug Down to Town" from *Singing Games and Songs from Southern Illinois.* Cooperative Recreation Service, Delaware, Ohio. Copyright, 1941.

NORTON, W. W. for "Blow, Boys, Blow," and "Fire Down Below" from *Songs of American Sailormen* by Joanna Colcord. Copyright, 1938.

OXFORD UNIVERSITY PRESS, AND MISS MAUD KARPELES for "The Cherry Tree Carol," "What Did You Have for Your Supper" ("Jimmy Randall, My Son"), "Monday Morning Go to School" ("The Two Brothers"), "Rose, Rose and Up She Rises," "Poor Old Crow" ("The Three Ravens"), "What'll We Do with the Baby," from *English Folk Songs from the Southern Appalachians,* collected by Cecil J. Sharp, edited by Maud Karpeles. 1932.

OWENS, WILLIAM A. for "Jingle at the Windows" ("Tideo") from *Swing and Turn: Texas Play-Party Games,* Tardy Publishing Company. Copyright, 1936.

PENN NORMAL, INDUSTRIAL AND AGRICULTURAL SCHOOL, St. Helena Island, N. C. for "I Got a Letter This Morning," "Sweet Water Rolling," "Mary Had a Baby," "When the Train Comes Along," from *Saint Helena Island Spirituals* by N. G. J. Ballanta – (Taylor), G. Schirmer. Copyright, 1925.

SOUTHERN FOLKLORE QUARTERLY for "When I Was a Young Maid" (see Harbison).

TEXAS FOLKLORE SOCIETY for the following songs from the *Publications of the Texas Folklore Society:* "Oh, Oh the Sunshine" ("Oh, Oh You Can't Shine"), "Rain Come Wet Me" from *Old Time Darky Plantation Melodies* by Natalie Taylor Carlisle, Vol. V; two choruses of "Old Joe Clarke" ("Round and Round") from *Some Texas Play-Party Songs* by Dudley and Payne, Vol. I; "Toodala" from *Toodala* by Helen Gates, Vol. XVII.

VIKING PRESS, THE for "Who Built the Ark? Noah, Noah" from *Rolling Along in Song* by J. Rosamond Johnson. Copyright, 1937.

VOSE, ELIZABETH M. for "Hush 'n' Bye" ("All the Pretty Little Horses").

WILKINSON, WINSTON for an excerpt from *Virginia Dance Tunes* in the *Southern Folklore Quarterly,* Vol. 6, No. 1.

Ruth Seeger's songbook is no sudden notion. It represents many years of a rare mother living with her music and her children. Her collection embodies an extraordinary array of time-tested songs for little ones, many of them so old they have been forgotten and now have the freshness of the new.

Carl Sandburg

Preface

Children will take the songs in this book to their hearts, for the young belong to that spiritual fellowship which lives close to the heart of things. On the instant of hearing, children will know that here are songs that will give vitality, beauty, and power to their own emotions, imaginations, and experiences.

Because this is so, *American Folk Songs for Children* is as truly a child's book as it is a book for parents and teachers. For it is made up of songs that have been shaped by folk wisdom. That is, by children and grownups who have been, and continue to be, moved to give voice to what has been felt, heard, seen, and lived through.

Happily, Ruth Crawford Seeger knows in her very bones what folk art *is* and what it *is not*. So the fresh, simple beauty and worth of the material selected have not been spoiled by either an intellectualized attitude or by sophisticated treatment.

As a matter of fact, this is a book, if ever there was one, that has grown out of the very heart of an affectionate and co-operative family and social life. One has to read only the opening chapter—*How the Book Grew*—to feel completely at home, as well as in love, with all who have had a share in its "growing."

What Mrs. Seeger has said in the introductory chapters has all the qualities that make folk songs *good:* freshness, simplicity, human understanding, sincerity, and the rightness of age-old wisdom.

No teacher or parent, interested in making music mean more in the lives of children, can afford to miss the delight that comes from the *rightness* of what is said about the use of these songs in schools and homes. And no teacher who has had misgivings about some of the things done at school in the name of creative expression will fail to gain comfort from the wise counsel to be found in *Improvising on the Words*.

But why go on telling teachers and children and parents why *American Folk Songs for Children* is a treasure? Some of the joy of discovery should be left for the many who have waited a long time for just such a reward.

Whether the takers be young or old—and they are certain to be both—here is a book to warm the hearts of all who are sensitive to the enduring quality of things lovely in themselves.

LILLA BELLE PITTS
Professor of Music Education
Teachers College
Columbia University

Contents

Classified Indices

How the Book Grew

These songs were sung around home with our own children, and at schools with other children of varying ages. They were gathered together and given simple piano arrangements for use in the Silver Spring Cooperative Nursery School of Silver Spring, Maryland, during its initial year, 1941. They have also been used by Laura Pendleton MacCarteney, and myself, at the National Child Research Center, and by me at the Foxhall Nursery School, the Green Acres School, and, with older children, at the Whitehall Country School, the Georgetown Day School and the Potomac School, all of Washington, D.C. or nearby Maryland.

The songs are folk (traditional) songs—tunes and words—current in various parts of North America where the English language is predominant. They are published here as they were found in the collections and folklore journals from which they were taken or on the phonograph recordings in the Archive of American Folklore in the Library of Congress in Washington. The State in which each song was collected is indicated above its notation. Most of the songs are known in other States as well, either in this or in other versions. Except in a few cases and in small details, changes have not been made either in the music or the words: the stanza which appears as part of the music notation, and any stanzas immediately following the music notation, are traditional or folk texts. Suggestions for improvisation are clearly indicated as such, either by explanatory remarks or headings.

To call the collection a book of songs for children, parents, and teachers is to outline doubly the history of its growth—first, through the experience of two parents with their own children, to whom songs like these were almost as natural as speech; second, through the experience of a parent-teacher with a group of thirty-odd mothers and their children, to many of whom native American music idioms were unfamiliar.

Back as far as our own children can remember, our house has been full of the sound of songs like these—ballads, work songs, love songs, prison songs, dance songs, hollers, chants, spirituals, blues. It was part of my job as music editor of a book of American folk music to transcribe several hundred such tunes from phonographic recordings made throughout the country—along roadsides, in valley and mountain homes, in towns and cities, fields and prisons. Our children would hear one of these songs hours on end—slow, fast, loud, soft, a single phrase repeated over and over until a notation could be devised which would show some of the subtle nuances of the melody and still be easy to read. The song would pursue them through open windows on a summer day while they played. It would travel to them through closed doors in winter while they ate or slept or had the measles. Not infrequently the phonograph would be heard all day and far into the night. Of course I also sang the songs myself. I couldn't help singing them. And that was a good way of trying out the singability of my notations.

So by the time three years had passed and the book had gone to press, Barbara and Peggy and Michael (then three and five and seven) had acted as test tubes for many a song of love, woe, or nonsense (three songs apiece each night if they were in bed on time). The phonograph might have played *Ol' Hannah* half a day—but they wanted it sung to them when bedtime came, and again next morning when Ol' Hannah showed her face above a cold winter horizon. Ol' Hannah is the sun.

> *Go down, Ol' Hannah,*
> *Well . . . well . . . well . . .*
> *Don't you rise no more.*
> *If you rise in the mornin'*
> *Set the world on fire.*

Just as Barbara turned four a co-operative nursery school was in process of getting started in Silver Spring. Barbara and I enrolled. Each mother was expected to participate in the school activities one day a week with her child, and was given special duties. The music program fell to me.

After a few weeks some of our family favorites began to be heard at school—songs like *Skip-a to My Lou, Old Joe Clarke, My Horses Ain't Hungry*. The children liked them. And the mothers liked them. They liked them so much that we decided to try an experimental year during which we would sing chiefly American folk songs. I began to cull, from among the songs I knew and from the many collections of American folk music, from folklore journals and phonographic field recordings at the Library of Congress, songs which would fill our needs. And I found plenty of them—plain tunes, melodically simple, rhythmically vital, whose traditional texts possess the spirit of work and play and thought and speech of small children.

Do we want to sing about rain? Here is an old ballad heard in Virginia for generations (*It Rained a Mist*). Or about wind and sunshine? Here is a Bahaman clapping-and-drumming song (*The Wind Blow East*). Or about trains, or hammers, or color, or sleep, or cooking, or buying things, or going upstairs, or tying shoes? Then here is a spiritual (*The Little Black Train*) and a work song (*This Old Hammer*) and a singing game (*This Lady She Wears a Dark Green Shawl*) and a lull-aby (*Go to Sleepy*) and a nonsense song (*Old Aunt Kate She Bake a Cake*) and a dance song (*Going Down to Town*) and a play-party song (*Such a Getting Upstairs*) and another dance song (*Lula Gal*). Do we want to play ball (*Down by the Greenwood Sidey-o*) or turn around and around (*Old Joe Clarke*) or walk or run or skip or jump (*Jim Along Josie*)? Or just sit and count stars (*By'm Bye*)? Here's a song of sailing, and of fire on a ship. Here's a song of a rabbit, a pig, a cat, a free little bird, an old black crow. Here's a song about picking cotton, and selling tobacco, and raising vegetables, and scraping up sand from the bottom of the sea. Here's a family song, with no one left out. And here are songs which can sing about each of us and what he is wearing or seeing or doing or wanting to do—songs which can change with the day and our thoughts.

When the first dozen songs were tentatively selected, a copy was made for each of the two teachers and the six "music mothers" who had volunteered to help with the music on days when I would not be at school. We all met one evening to learn and discuss the new songs, staying till a late hour to swap favorites back and forth to the accompaniment of someone's guitar.

It began to be evident, after that meeting, that the "music mothers" were not the only ones who wanted to sing. Others said: "We like these songs the children are singing; we want to sing them at home. Where are our copies of the music?" So after that we made enough copies for every school mother, with complete text included for adult singing (some stanzas of which might be thought unsuitable for children!). Each new set of a dozen untried songs called for another music meeting: the songs must be learned and their uses discussed from various angles—musical, textual, educational.

To these meetings came a good third of the school mothers, to-gether with teachers and a somewhat reluctant volunteer to stay out-doors with the children while everyone else sang and talked. Thus a fair percentage of the mothers were acquainted with a fair percentage of the songs. And many of the children heard and sang them not only at home but also in the cars en route to and from school.

There were frequent reminders of both adult and child enjoyment. Mrs. Stant would telephone: "Sandra brought home half a new song today. Can you give me the other half? We want to sing it all." Mrs. Weinig would ask with polite impatience: "Where are my new song sheets? Bill's father wants them." Mrs. Irving would telephone excit-edly: "*John Henry* was just sung on the radio. It's a grand song; I'm glad you told us the story of it." Mrs. Jones would report: "Peter broke into *John Henry* fortissimo while he was playing today and sang it clear through—I thought you'd like to know." Mrs. Horne would report: "Raymond won't stop singing *Mary Wore Her Red Dress* until we've clothed all our family and friends and distant acquaintances." Mrs. Fairley would tell how that word "patterroller" had tickled Will's sense of humor and how he went all over the house repeating it and chuckling. I would hear about Jane Irving running up and down the playground bank shouting, "Who moan for me"; about Ann pounding clay with solid satisfaction, chanting, "Juba this and Juba that"; about Janet Gleysteen, "hanging out the linen clothes" each evening in her bath, singing all seven stanzas with washcloth as stage property.

I would hear: "These songs are fresh. We like them. At first we thought some of them a little queer, but now we feel at home with them. And we like them."

The music meetings developed into what one of our visitors called a spontaneous laboratory. A number of questions arose, with the new songs as springboards. They were freely—sometimes hotly—discussed.

One of these concerned dialect pronunciation. Shall we sing "dat" or "that," "de" or "the," in songs which, like *Who Dat Tappin' at de Window*, have been set down by the folklore collector in dialect spelling? Aside from the question as to how consistent various collectors are in the recording of dialect—how important to the song is the pronunciation of the words? What sorts of changes can be allowed without loss of character to the song and without loss to the child of a valuable social and speech experience? Or is this experience valuable? And where shall we draw the line between such expressions as "ain't"—imagine correcting it to "aren't" in *My Horses Ain't Hungry*—and "gwine"—which has come to have undemocratic associations of questionable value? Does the use of such stylized expressions as "de," "dat," "gwine"—especially by the educated city singer, to whom they are not natural modes of expression and to whom they signify lower levels of education than his own—tend to be self-conscious, condescending, precious, "cute"? Shall we perhaps just decide to sing the song in a way natural to each of us—not too carefully or precisely—dropping a few final "g's" from the "ings" when the mood strikes us, but not straining after the picturesque?

More extended was the discussion called forth at a music meeting by the song *Juba*, who "killed a yellow cat" with apparent detachment. Several mothers were seriously concerned. They said: "We are trying to teach our children kindness to animals—why, then, a song about killing?" Someone wanted Juba to chase the cat rather than kill it—and from someone else came the rejoinder that children are more apt to chase than to kill anyway, and that to sing about chasing might therefore be worse because it is more likely to be carried out!

From this whimsical beginning arose a number of more serious basic considerations. Should we try to shield the child from feeling of sadness, of hurting or being hurt, of killing, dying? *Can* we shield him? Such feelings are not unnatural to him; he has them, to a greater or lesser extent, already within himself. It is not unnatural for a child to build fantasies around killing, hurting, destroying even things or people he loves. If he can sing about these things—can take action through song—the deed is done (in fantasy) and the pressure relieved. Can we not say, then, that having songs around which sing of these things may be a means of easing such feelings within himself, and of helping to make him more comfortable with himself as well as with what is around him?

Further, how much of a sense of sadness or cruelty or destruction does the child extract from mention of these concepts in song? A strong contributing factor is the mood of the music itself, considered as a thing apart from the words of the song. In most fine-art ("classical") song-writing the composer seeks a one-to-one relation between the mood of the words and the mood of the music, thus tipping the scales considerably in either one direction or the other. Folk song, on the other hand, usually maintains an enviable emotional balance. A song of tragedy is often sung to a simple, direct tune—and, as often, to a vivacious one. Songs whose words might be considered painful may make the feet want to dance.

The mood of a song depends to a great extent, of course, on the *manner of singing*—and on the manner of singing will depend to a great extent the child's reaction to the actual words of the song. Do we not too often tend to suggest to the child through manner of singing—and even more through manner of speaking or telling a story—what we think the child *ought* to feel? If a song is sung in a simple straightforward manner, without sentimentality, may we not say that whatever concepts it conveys will either be accepted as a part of the pattern of living—often constituting a valuable extension of the child's experience —or passed on like many other mysteries, to be understood later?

This fear of hurting the child through song-content came to me at that time as somewhat of a surprise. I had no ready-made thought-out answers. I could answer that it had seemed to us—to my husband and myself—a natural thing to sing to our children about all sorts of living, and that you cannot separate living and dying. I could say that we had never laid undue stress on songs of "sadness," but that when they came along we passed some of them on to our children as part of what it was our privilege to give them. I could tell how Peggy, when she was two and a half and in the hospital with an infected burn—not allowed to see anyone but nurses and doctors—had sent down the hospital corridors hour after hour, in a clear high voice, the long story of

Barbara Allen, sung to her and Michael during previous months by their father with other ballads night after night by request. I could point to the rollicking story of the old gray mare as a favorite with our children—the old gray mare who lay down in the creek bed and died, contributing her skin through subsequent stanzas to cutting, curing, and shoemaking "to keep my toes from the winter frost." I could point to John Henry's fatal race with the steam drill as another favorite—the graveyard stanza sometimes sung, sometimes omitted. I could speak of other songs covering varying degrees and sorts of feeling: the regretful prison lament with the haunting tune seeming never to end (*I Been a Bad Bad Girl*) and the song of the whaling boat that never returned because the whale "made a flunder with his tale" (*The Whale Get Strike*) and the lilting Bahaman ditty with the taunting line "I'm going to pack up your eyes with sand." And I could quote from a song most loved by our children—the song of the faithful possum-hunting dog, *Old Blue:*

9. *When old Blue died he died so hard*
   He shook the ground in my back yard.

10. *Old Blue died, I laid him in the shade,*
    I dug his grave with a silver spade.

11. *I let him down with a golden chain,*
    Link by link slipped through my hand.

12. *There is only one thing that bothers my mind,*
    Blue went to heaven, left me behind.

13. *When I get there, first thing I'll do,*
    Grab me a horn and blow for old Blue.

When children grow older and read of murders and dying and killing in our outspoken newspapers, will they perhaps remember such a burial scene as that of old Blue? And who can say that Peggy, wondering why her father and mother never came to see her through long seven days, found some indefinable connection between her own hurt and whatever of the hurt she may have felt or drawn from the words and spirit of the song of Barbara Allen? If a child's unexpected hurts can become connected with hurts he has heard about in story or poetry or song—if he can reach back into his experience and tie these individual hurts of his to what one might call group hurts—will he perhaps feel in his own less lonely?

A subject of still more lively and frequent argument was that of concrete meaning. Must all words and phrases of a song be brought within the child's experience? Should they all be capable of conveying concrete meaning to him? In adapting a song to particular uses must there always exist a direct one-to-one relation between the text of the song and the use to which it is being put? Shall we change the phrase "Who moan for me" to "Who'll go with me" just because "who moan" is outside the word-meaning world of these particular children? How about the lure of *unknown* meaning? As I think of two-year-old Penelope, I think of two characteristic gestures. With one hand she is holding a ball or some concrete object she knows about. With the other she is reaching out, fingers spread wide. To Sarah or to me? Not always. Maybe to a bright ball shining through dark leaves of trees at night, or to a sound up in the sky, or to some even less definite something.

And what do we mean by meaning? How about sound-meaning and touch-meaning? The ears and tongue and lips also test words. And those four repetitions of the refrain of *Riding in the Buggy, Miss Mary Jane*—

> *Who moan for me,*
> *Who moan for me,*
> *Who moan for me, my darling,*
> *Who moan for me?*

—always bear a lusty quality when the children sing them, as though twice as many are singing—singing because they can't help singing— singing as though they are tasting the words and finding them as good and solid as a bar of chocolate.

Again and again this discussion was revived by new songs and new uses for songs. *Do, Do, Pity My Case* is given its first singing at a music meeting. Queries one mother: "What can this mean to my child?" Soon after that one of our three-year-olds, who has been singing little either at home or at school, is reported chanting the phrase all day with exceptional relish. And later on the mother who questioned its usefulness names the "Do Do" song in her monthly music report as her child's current favorite.

And Johnny is counting his buttons while we sing—

> *By'm bye*
> *By'm bye*
> *Stars shining*
> *Number, number one,*
> *Number two, number three—*

Surely we need not change "stars" to "buttons" as we sing and count? Why not give the stars and the buttons a chance to play around together? To be bound too closely to the literal—to a hard and fast relation between the song and a particular use of it—is to cramp the imagination of *both child and adult*.

These discussions never reached, during that year or following years, any official conclusion. But in the minds of some of us they crystallized into a general attitude toward the songs and their uses with children. Yes—improvise on the words of the songs, bring them at times completely into the world the children know. But keep alive, too, the traditional words. Remember that apparently meaningless phrases may mean a great deal to the child in abstract sound experience, besides possessing the value of extending his horizon. Strive to maintain a balance between two of the outstanding values which music like this possesses for him—the vigorous beauty of the traditional text, and an inherent fluidity and creative aliveness which invites improvisation as a natural development in the life of the song.

Why American Folk Music for Our Children?

This kind of traditional or folk music is thoroughly identified with the kind of people who made America as we know it. It is a music they liked and still like. They made it and are still making it. Some of it came with them from other countries and has been little changed. Some of it came with them from other countries and has been much changed. Some of it grew here. All of it has partaken of the making of America. Our children have a right to be brought up with it.

If it is one of the aims of education to induct the child into the realities of the culture in which he will live, may we not say that this traditional music and language and ideology, which has not only grown out of but has in turn influenced that culture—and is still influencing and being used by it—should occupy a familiar place in the child's daily life, even though it may not be current in the particular neighborhood in which he happens to be living. Many of us open a savings account at the bank when a child is born, and add layer after layer of small deposits which he can later draw on for a college education. Perhaps a fund of songs might be begun as early, and added to layer after layer—an ever-growing wealth of materials which he can draw on at will and can take along with him as links from himself to the various aspects of the culture he will be going out to meet.

It belongs to our children— it is an integral part of their cultural heritage

This music has been a natural part of work, play, sleep, fun, ridicule, love, death. It has grown out of and passed through many ways of living and doing. Facts and fantasies cling to it from its wandering. It knows and tells what people have thought about the ways of living and the things that happened. Through it one can grow in intimate appreciation of the railroads it helped build, the cotton it helped pick, the ships it helped sail, the land-stretches it made less lonely.

Over a period of months several groups of four-year-olds came close in their own way to the growth of railroading, from the laying of tracks (singing *This Old Hammer*) and the drilling of tunnels (*John Henry*) to the assembling of many sorts of train cars (*The Train Is A-Coming*) and finally to the train in motion, "rumbling through the land" (*Little Black Train*) and arriving at the station (*When the Train Comes Along*). Some mornings all the songs in this little song-story-

It is a bearer of history and custom

drama were "acted out" in free rhythmic play; sometimes one or two song-plays were enough. The entire song sequence grew spontaneously, day by day, out of the singing of a work song to which the children liked to hammer, fist-to-fist.

It gives early experience of democratic attitudes and values

This kind of music has crossed and recrossed many sorts of boundaries and is still crossing and recrossing them. It can give the children a glimpse of ways of life and thought different from their own. It can do this in an unself-conscious way—not as a teacher who comes especially to instruct, but as a traveler dropping by with stories to tell about places he has come from, and with plans, perhaps, about places to which he may be going.

It has grown through being needed and used— it has adapted itself frequently to new surroundings

This music bears many fingermarks. It has been handled roughly and gently. It has been used. It has been sung and resung—molded, modified by generations of singers from Maine to Florida and across the country. Some songs have acquired hundreds of stanzas.

This adaptability and breadth of experience give it special appeal and value to small children. One song can cover a gamut of experiences. New words can grow out of new needs and uses—and the song can come to be an integral part of a child's living. It can be the window through which children look at themselves, their neighbors, their toys, thoughts. The creative process involved in improvising on the pattern of such a song may not be far removed from that involved in making songs of their own.

When this book was about to go to press I came across a paragraph in an old folklore journal which expressed so intimately the spirit which I had drawn from daily use of the songs with children that it seemed as though the words had come straight out of my own experience. In fact, several of the phrases were almost identical with phrases of my own —phrases which I had mulled over and pulled out of singing and growing and living with the songs over a period of years. This paragraph, written by Natalie Taylor Carlisle and published in Volume V of the Publications of the Texas Folk Lore Society, seems to me significant enough for quotation here:

> *. . . The subject matter of the old time . . . song was a part of his (the singer's) daily experience. Furthermore, his peculiar style of music was part and parcel of himself. Whatever he experienced, he sang. Most of his songs had few words because most of them centered upon a single idea or circumstance. However, the song itself might be as long as the individual singer wished to make it, depending entirely upon the mood and occupation of the singer and not upon the number*

of words in it. Sometimes a song was an entire day's length. The following, a great favorite in past times, is said to have had its origin in a path along a riverside where there were both sand and clay-mud. In walking along this path, which led from plantation quarters to a church, the church people constantly warned each other to keep out of the mud and to stay in the sand. From this warning grew the song:

Moderately fast

TEXAS

Take 'em out the mud, Keep your foot in the sand.

After being sung in this order for a long time, the song used to be reversed and sung thus:

> Keep it in the sand,
> Take your foot out the mud.

. . . Thus a song of very few words might become very very long.

Songs like these are not finished in the sense that a piece of fine-art ("classical") music, or even popular music, is finished. They are always ready to grow. They are forever changing, adapting themselves to meet new situations and needs. The traditional singer seldom hands on a song just as he found it: in some way, small or great, he makes the song his own. A single word may change: the soldier's wife and children-twice-three are moved from London to Columbus, or a frog goes courting with a six-shooter instead of sword and pistol. The singer may change many words, or add entire stanzas, or make subtle differences in the tune. Usually such improvisation is spontaneous—the result of mixing a particular person or group, a particular song and a particular occasion or mood.

It is not "finished" or crystallized— it invites improvisation and creative aliveness

No doubt the rhythmic vitality of this music lends ease to the process of improvisation. It gives a basis, a solid structure on which to build. It gives also an impulse to rhythmic activity. Three fourths of the songs in this book are singing games, play-party songs, square-dance tunes, work songs, patting or jigging songs. They are accustomed to action, to being danced to, clapped to, skipped to, worked to. Children listening often start clapping of their own accord, or skipping, or jumping, or kicking their feet, or trying some new motion.

It has rhythmic vitality— it is music of motion

It is a kind of music which everyone can help make— it invites participation

It is within the singing capacity of practically everyone—even small children—yet it is "good" music. It is not a music to be worshiped from afar and performed only by those with special gifts or intensively acquired technique—yet it partakes of the quality of greatness. To enjoy it, one need not dress up either oneself or one's voice. One can sit down with it comfortably, knowing that many parents and children have sat down with it before and tested its goodness—knowing that its value as good music has been democratically determined by general agreement and group acceptance.

It is not just children's music— it is family music

We have said that this music belongs to our children. Perhaps it is even more important to say that it belongs to them as adults. This is not music which they will have to outgrow. It is not a specially prepared baby food, strained and predigested, and administered with an almost unavoidable element of condescension by adults and older brothers and sisters. It need not be discarded along with the kiddy car and the tricycle. Songs like these are sung by all ages. They are family stuff. Fletcher Collins, in his introduction to *Alamance Play-Party Songs and Singing Games,* speaks with conviction:

> *My own experience, and that of collaborating teachers . . . has been that few (such) songs and dances are ever the exclusive property of one age-group, but rather that as the performer's age increases, so also does the range of his appreciation of such songs. And that is, after all, the prime test of a permanent cultural possession, that it means something progressively to every age-level in every country . . .*
>
> *These songs glorify the family as the prime social unit, for they have been raised through many centuries of family life, when everyone from grandfather down to the youngest toddler joined in King William was King George's son.*

Singing the Songs

So often comes from parents the wistful remark: I like music but I can't sing. The speaker usually means one of two things: either he cannot sing the type of music which he has been taught to look up to as good music (fine-art or "classical" music like that of Bach, Beethoven, Schubert, Brahms, Debussy); or he cannot use his voice in the *manner* of singing which is considered good in performing this type of music. And so, feeling that active participation in good music is beyond him, he hides his voice away and says he cannot sing.

Almost a first requisite in singing with small children is the natural and wholehearted pleasure which the singer finds in the song. *It is the song which is important,* to both singer and listener. And often an "untrained" voice (untrained in *bel canto* singing) will convey to the child a greater enjoyment of the song itself than will the voice which has been made to concentrate hour after hour on the manner of singing the song—on the smoothing-out and perfecting of its own quality.

A first requisite to the traditional (folk) singer too, and to his listeners, is this wholehearted pleasure in the song. Here again it is the song itself which is most important. The writings of folklorists and collectors, and the many phonograph recordings of traditional singers, give constant evidence of this. Vance Randolph, for instance, who has listened to hundreds of Missouri singers and recorded their songs, remarks, in his *Ozark Folksongs,* that "there is a singular absence of affectation or self-consciousness about the Ozark minstrel's performance, and in applauding him one says simply, 'That sure is a good song,' without any mention of the singer's talent or ability."

So allow yourself pleasure in the song, and sing it for its own sake. This is music which anyone can sing and feel he has a right to be comfortable with. And do not have contempt for your voice if it is reedy or breathy or splintery or nasal. Remember that some of the finest traditional singers have similar qualities of voice, and that the songs not only are at home with voices like these, they sound well with them.

Sing the songs simply. Do not feel that you must sing "with expression"—that you must slow down when the song is sad and speed up when it is happy, or that you must vary the dynamics (get loud or soft) according to the meaning of the words. And when you get to the end of a song, feel free to "just stop," without the slowing-down which is so customary in fine-art music.

Sing most of the songs with strong accent on the first of the measure. Feel the beat of the song—its pulse—as a thing which continues throughout the singing of all stanzas or repetitions of the song. In $\frac{2}{4}$ meter, for instance, the quarter note is the beat, or pulse; in $\frac{2}{2}$, the half note is the pulse—and so on. If you want to tap the beat with your foot, feel free to do so, even though fine-art musicians frown on such a practice. On one recording made at a folk festival, the singer's foot-tapping recorded so loud that the singing could scarcely be heard!

Remember that most of the songs are used to being sung at a fairly fast speed. As an aid in determining this speed, precise tempo marks have been added to the general speed indications given in the upper left-hand corner of each song. These tempo marks have been given in terms of the metronome— ♩. = 42, ♩ = 60, et cetera. If you have no metronome, the second-hand of your watch can be of help. Thus, ♩ = 60 means that there are sixty quarter notes within the space of each minute. Try to "get the feel" of the pulse in the ♩ = 60 speed— and then relate other speeds to it. A speed of ♩ = 120 will, for instance, be twice as fast. Do not, however, take these tempo marks too literally. They are only a guide to the speed, and so to the spirit, of the song.

Since a singer can destroy the spirit of naturalness through straining after tones which are too high, most of the songs have been set within a pitch range which is conducive to easy, unforced singing for both adult amateur singers and for children (from middle C to the D a ninth above it). In songs of wider range it has seemed better to give preference to the lower register. Do not be concerned if some tones are low for your voice. Traditional singers often dismiss such tones in a half-sung, half-spoken manner. A number of songs containing wide range and unusual intervals have been included in the book, with the conviction that it is important for children to hear songs which they may not be expected to sing. Sing these songs naturally yourself—and you may be surprised someday to hear your three- or four-year-old (especially if he does not know you are around) singing them with gusto. This happened in our school with a number of songs like *Every Monday Morning*. Children sometimes catch easily intervals and rhythms which to us seem strange or difficult.

Do not feel that you must be able to play the piano in order to enjoy singing with children. These songs are used to being sung unaccompanied. This is especially true of singing games and play party songs and, of course, lullabies. In fact, the piano often gives to the tune a sharpness of line, and to the song-experience a finality, which is not fitting to this music. It can even discourage singing. Hearing the tune played so clearly, the singer grows lazy, and lets his ears rather than his voice use the song.

Improvising on the Words

The songs in this book can be enjoyed without reading any suggestions as to using or singing or accompanying them. To those, however, who feel need of help in the folk art of taking a song and making it one's own—yet leaving within the song the essence of its character as a group possession—the following remarks may be of interest. They are suggestions only, not rules.

First become well acquainted with the song as it stands. This means knowing it well enough to sing it without reading the notes. Let the rhythm of the traditional words be something you feel comfortable with. Carry the song around with you, as children do. You will probably find yourself breaking out with it at odd moments, as children do. You may find you are so at home with it that you feel no need to change it.

Let improvisation on the words be as spontaneous as possible. Let it grow out of the moment, the day, the child, and you. Tomorrow something quite different may happen. This is the way many songs like these have grown and changed in the past.

You may be tempted at times to take advantage of the adaptability of a song and twist it in a way unnatural to it. Remember, then, that the changes through which this music has already passed have been gradual, and that improvisation on words has for the most part come from singers brought up with music like it—singers who understood instinctively its nature and habits.

Let improvisation come from the child as much as possible—from things he happens to do or say or sing. Don't hesitate to join in on the fun—but remember that the adult faces numerous pitfalls when "thinking up" words for children, such as affectation or overconscientious attention to particular uses for a song, or preconceived notions as to child speech, understanding, or enjoyment.

Make sure that improvisation of new words does not deprive the child of old traditional words. "This lady she wears a dark green shawl" gives him something quite different in image and sound from the adaptation "This Betsy she wears her light blue dress." Perhaps you might say to him: "This song belongs to many people, and they sing it in different ways." Give the child, too, experience of some of the song titles—as, for instance, the unforgettable *Down by the Greenwood Sidey-o*.

Avoid the feeling that a direct one-to-one relation is essential between the words of a song and the action or use to which it is being momentarily put. It is debatable whether "Let's go hunting" should be changed to "Let's go skipping" just because children are skipping to the music of *Billy Barlow*. There will, of course, be times when the spontaneity of the moment can best be captured through a literal approach. But it should be borne in mind that the integrity and often the beauty of the song-as-a-whole may suffer from too great bondage to the literal.

Remember that the suggested improvisations which accompany many of the songs in this book are given only as springboards. Most of them grew out of some specific moment, motion, word, or wish. With you and your children something quite different may happen.

If, when singing a song like *Mary Wore Her Red Dress*, you ask children what of their own they would like to sing about, you sometimes receive answers which do not fit the rhythm of the song. Traditional singers often insert extra counts to care for such syllables. Children laugh with the pleasure of hearing so many words elbow their way into the middle of a song pattern they know.

Using the Songs at Home

It is a natural thing to pick up the rhythm of a song and carry it around the house, letting it grow out of or into the varied activities and inactivities that are part of a day. One must be careful, of course, not to draw songs in by the hair of their heads (or the tails of their notes) —nor to feel that every time one goes upstairs or downstairs one must sing a song about it. Singing with small children should be casual and unpretentious. For this reason, homemade songs and chants are often better than songs whose patterns you feel are cut and finished. The rhythm and nuances of children's speaking voices are often half over the border to music, and a chance remark or question will suggest a tune. This occurred one morning in our family with a request urgently repeated:

But you need not feel that the "finished" songs are finished. Feel free to use tidbits of songs you know. These also make excellent tone plays. One evening I happened to sing *By'm Bye* to Penelope as I was putting her to bed. A few evenings later, as I was taking her on her customary rounds, we sang good-by to each of the family bedrooms. There was not time to sing the whole *By'm Bye* song—and it would have seemed artificial. So we sang only the beginning interval and its echo. This soon became a ritual. It extended to an accidental peek out the window at the snow (By'm bye, snow), and the snow still later became rain or stars or moon or birds, according to the moment. One evening we saw her slipping into her sisters' rooms and heard *By'm Bye* being sung to all the dolls and animals in their cradles. She sang that simple interval of a fourth as though in it were contained many intangible things.

This using of pieces of songs you know—small motives, or half phrases or phrases—is an excellent springboard toward the making of your own songs. One sure-fire way of getting children upstairs is to sing about it. Start the song *Such a Getting Upstairs,* and the process is accomplished quickly. But at times the singing-through of a complete song at the "appropriate" moment seems too formal and planned, as though the stage had been set in advance. Try, then, letting your voice play around with just part of the song: let it wander off and travel along the path of similar rhythms on different (or the same) pitch levels. Perhaps you will find yourself making variations on the basic motive— but do not think too hard about trying to make a "good tune." The rhythm and spontaneity are more important at first. Your beginning might happen something like this:

The song need not have a formal end—it can just stop.

Many work songs consist chiefly of a small motive repeated over and over, picked up and carried along, sometimes by one person, sometimes by another, to the rhythm of tie-tamping on the railroad, or log chopping or rock splitting. Not unrelated were some of the song experiences which Barbara and I had as we walked a lonely half-mile stretch from school, throwing song phrases back and forth—sometimes our own, sometimes improvisations on songs we knew. And one day when the family was playing Flinch, Peggy drew a Number 1 from the card stack and half sang, half chanted in triumph as she continued to build up the pile of cards:

The rhythm caught and stuck. For months we never played the game without it.

There are times, of course, when entire songs—even extensions of them—fit the pattern of the day informally and without artificiality. Most mothers find some pleasant way of pulling shirts over children's heads. We happened on one, to the tune of *Where, Oh, Where, Is Pretty Little Susie?*

Where oh where is pretty little Penny,
Where oh where is pretty little Penny,
Where oh where is pretty little Penny,
'Way down yonder in the polo shirt.

Come on, girls, let's go find her,
Come on, girls, let's go find her,
Come on, girls, let's go find her,
'Way down yonder in the polo shirt.

And the children did seem to dress faster when we added, stanza by stanza, minute details about *John the Rabbit's* habits of dressing. And was it partly the unendingness of *Mary Had a Baby* which quieted a sick child day after day? It usually began:

Mammy had a baby, aye Lord,
Mammy had a baby, aye my Lord,
Mammy had a baby, aye Lord,
The people keep a-coming and the train done gone.

Baby named Ronnie, aye Lord,
Baby named Ronnie, aye Lord,
Baby named Ronnie, aye Lord,
The people keep a-coming and the train done gone.

Baby had blue eyes, aye Lord, etc.

—but from then on the song was never twice the same.

There is always bedtime. Song singing has one advantage over story reading: the room can be dark, inviting sleep. And darkness, in turn, through depriving the singer of a book to rely on, can encourage the spontaneous making of new stanzas. As to choice of songs, you may find lively ones as quieting as quiet ones. Every night Michael wanted *Turtle Dove* before the door was closed to its inch of crack—but there had usually been a spirited singing session preceding it. And the fast crisp tune of the old minstrel song *Buffalo Girls* lays Penelope's head quiet on the pillow to hear Peggy and Barbara improvise questions-and-answers on any or all of the day's happenings, from dancing by the light of the sun to milk-drinking to tooth-brushing to looking at the stars, and on, until the song sends them one by one away to bed.

Fast

Buf-fa-lo girls ain't you com-ing out to-night, com-ing out to-night, com-ing out to-night,

Buf - fa-lo girls, ain't you com-ing out to-night, to dance by the light of the moon?

Ain't you, ain't you, ain't you, ain't you com-ing out to-night, com-ing out to-night, com-ing out to-night,

Ain't you, ain't you, ain't you, ain't you com-ing out to-night, to dance by the light of the moon?

Certainly music like this is not typical "quiet music." Neither are courting songs like *Cindy*, nor dance songs like *Cripple Creek*, nor spirituals like *Them Bones*, nor ballads like *Black Jack Davy*, nor work songs like *John Henry*, nor song-chants like *John Done Saw That Number*, with such lines as these:

> *God told the angel:*
> *Go down, see 'bout old John.*
> *Angel flew from the bottom of the pit,*
> *Gathered the sun all in her fist,*
> *Gathered the moon all 'round her wrist,*
> *Gathered the stars all under her feet,*
> *Gathered the wind all 'round her waist,*
>
> *Crying Holy, Lord,*
> *Crying Holy, Lord,*
> *Crying Holy, Lord,*
> *Crying Holy.*

You yourself, through singing and using, will find sorts of songs which you and your own children like to sing. It might be of interest to recall the frequent reference in folklore books to ballads of outlawry, sadness, death, even murder, as "a song my mother used to sing me to sleep with."

Using the Songs at School

One thing which impressed me when I started singing and playing with groups of small children was the importance of different sorts of links.

First there was the link between the children and me. To be sure, I had plenty of songs knocking around in my head. But somehow these songs had to meet and get acquainted with embryo songs in the children's heads, and with rhythms knocking around in their feet and arms and bodies. Thus each song-and-action session with the children must be a joint creation of theirs and mine. We were making a sort of musical composition together, in which one song experience grew out of another, and out of that another, and so on.

Sometimes this flow came easy. Sometimes it was hard to follow. Sometimes links had to be searched for—not only links between the children and me but, this time, links from one song to another, or occasionally from one word or motion to another.

Certain songs began to slip into these gaps as link songs. They were usually, I realized later, of the dance or play-party type, like *Old Joe Clarke* or *Jim Along Josie*—songs which were used to being thrown around, played with, joked with. One of these had several hundred stanzas already. No wonder such songs could make us feel at home with ourselves and with each other: they were seasoned travelers. Songs like these could easily take on the color and spirit of any situation. They could, like *Toodala,* keep growing from day to day, become the warp on which the fabric of an entire morning's thoughts and actions and wishes might be woven.

I came to feel that the children's gain, and mine, from such experiences was not just a piece of music—a song. Greater gain was the feeling we had of making something together, of taking a small piece of experience and using it—sometimes just letting it grow, sometimes nurturing it. Such experiencing of a combined individual and group accomplishment can mean a great deal to the individual taking part in it. He has not only made a contribution: he receives a contribution from the group in return. And perhaps here was the most important link of all—the link created from the individual to the group, and vice versa.

Important to the adult guiding such a process of give-and-take is the question of balance, the decision when to follow the child and when to lead. For continuity, one of the basic elements in a creative process, can be lost through lack of selectiveness. In the middle of singing *Hush, Little Baby,* Renny's heels get busy in a fast rhythm-beat on the floor. It is hard to decide whether to complete the experience already begun or to follow Renny on to another. A favorite heel-tapping rhythm play grew from following through just such a "diversion of attention." At the end of an extended session of quiet shoe-tying to the refrain of *Lula Gal,* the stanza was begun—and somebody's feet began kicking up and down. The joyful exhilaration which rose with the layers of noise added by each pair of shoes as it joined the others, made the diversion seem right—a healthy and natural release. So we went on and on with the music, returning finally to the quiet refrain— for the fun of more kicking again. Such a decision may depend on many factors—among them, the diverter's normal attention span. For if he is a habitual interrupter and can be counted on to desert the next activity as soon as it is begun, it is questionable whether his impulse is significant to the group or to himself. Perhaps most of all you will be listening for the group's reaction to the "interruption." Jock jumped up one day while we were singing a quiet song and started turning around and around. We went on singing our quiet song. Barry jumped up to join Jock. We still went on singing. Louis and Lucia jumped up too— and we switched to "Round and round, old Joe Clarke," continuing the lively rhythm of this favorite song by group insistence through many repetitions.

"Adverse" situations or environment can often be used as springboards to new experiences. In one school there were four steps leading to a forbidden area. Adventure always seemed up those steps. With a song about "such a getting upstairs"—which involved stopping at the top and waiting until everyone was ready to sing about "such a gettin' downstairs"—the steps could be enjoyed. Then too there was David, who started pulling Peter's hair. It seemed a natural thing to remember the lines from an old ballad:

> *Brother, comb my sweetheart's hair*
> *As we go marching home.*

As we sang the song over and over, David switched from pulling to combing. Soon everyone was busy combing someone's hair, and another finger play had been "discovered" by the group for itself.

While working with groups of children at various schools over a period of several years, I have from time to time jotted down tentative conclusions as reminders to myself and as possible help to others. They are the product of concrete daily experience with the type of songs contained in this book, but may be found to have general value.

Sing the song first at its natural speed—not too slowly, precisely or carefully. The first singing should give the spirit of the song, an impression of the song as a whole rather than an analysis of it. When a song has only one stanza, sing it over and over, not just once, so that the child not only meets the song but gets a little acquainted before it is gone.

Songs like these should not drag. Remember that most of them are accustomed to a lively speed and a strong metrical accent (on the first beat of each measure). This should be especially borne in mind when using them for rhythmic play.

Sit with the children on the floor when you can, especially with two- and three-year-olds. Getting closer together occasionally can give both adult and children greater confidence. Some "difficult moments" have automatically disappeared when the adult came down off the piano stool.

Do not be concerned if small children do not sing when part of a group. Reports gathered from mothers have frequently shown that children who are not participating at school are singing with gusto at home. Perhaps they may like to tap their feet or clap their hands while others sing. But do not be disturbed if they "just sit." One never knows what they are taking in or when they will start singing.

Longer songs may be simplified at first for smaller children by omitting the words of a refrain (as in *All Around the Kitchen*) or of a stanza (as in *Run, Chillen, Run*). The music of that section may perhaps be played without singing, as an instrumental interlude.

Many of these songs make excellent rhythm band music, especially songs of the dance or play-party type like *Old Joe Clarke, Skip-a to My Lou, Jingle at the Window,* and others. A list of such songs is given in the classified index.

Keep-going-ness is one of the notable characteristics in traditional performance of music like this. Do not hesitate, especially when using the songs for rhythmic activity, to keep the music going through many repetitions—sometimes with singing, sometimes without. Do not fear monotony: it is a valuable quality.

Although most groups of children want and probably need more action songs than "listening" songs, bear in mind too the value of the quiet song, and seek each day what seems the best balance for that day between the two types. The changing needs and moods of the children will be your guide on each occasion. Be ready with quiet music if you see unconstructive wildness growing out of too much activity—but do not force a quiet song just for the sake of variety.

Do not be in a hurry to move from one song or activity to another. Children occasionally derive more pleasure and value from one or two songs or activities which they like than from a variety of half-tasted experiences. One morning a group of children became so enamored of turning around and around to *Old Joe Clarke* that they wanted to do nothing else, and greeted each tentative departure to another song with clamors for return to this momentary favorite. We spent most of a music period turning around and around, one way and another.

It is especially important to feel unhurried with the smallest children. A two-year-old who stands by unmoving through three or four repetitions of a song may be just ready to discover his own way of meeting and enjoying the music during a fifth or sixth repetition. Be patient and wait and watch while the music does the urging—then still be patient and continue the music long enough to allow the children full satisfaction in their discovery before leading on to another.

In singing a new song for the first time to a group of children you will occasionally feel hesitant—even anxious—because you are uncertain of their reaction to it. At such times you may find yourself hurrying on too soon to a well-tried song which you and the children together know better. Try instead, sometimes, keeping the new song going, giving the children plenty of time to become familiar with it, singing it on and on in one uninterrupted song experience—like a train going past station after station rather than a trolley stopping at each street corner. Often a song begun with inner uncertainty but kept going in this way has seemed to gather momentum as it went along, increasing not in speed but in a sense of conviction within both adult and children.

If there is a group teacher, and she remains in the room with the children during the music period, rely on her as little as possible for group control. Establish an understanding with her as to her role and as to your policy and manner of procedure, and ask that she give help only as a last resort (either in control or suggestion or stimulus)—and perhaps only on some predetermined sign from you. And lean on her only when a child's persistent diversion of group attention has proven unusable creatively and destructive of group enjoyment. On a number of occasions a creative moment has been almost lost through overzealous adult attempt to control the attention of everyone in the group. "Now you must all listen to the music"—and the nursery becomes a concert hall.

Have confidence, then, in yourself and the child. Remember that, through fear of losing control of a group, you may also lose what might have been a productive experience. Be ready with a few "link" songs which can always be counted on to draw the children together in case of "emergency"—and then feel free to welcome the unexpected and to follow where it leads.

If a child gets up and leaves a singing group, the adult's first thought may be that he has lost interest and will be a disturbance to others, and that he should therefore either be called back to the group or asked to leave the room. Yet that child at that moment may be finding his way of living-through what the song means for him.

When Carter got up during the first singing of *When the Train Comes Along*—

> *If my mother ask for me*
> *If my mother ask for me*
> *I'm going to meet her at the station*
> *When the train comes along*—

it was not clear whether he had lost interest and was wandering off to some other activity. His actions were vague, he sauntered a roundabout way hither and yon in apparently lackadaisical fashion. The group watched him while we went on singing, but nobody joined him. I was uncertain whether to continue the new song or to drop it and return to it another day. But we kept our eyes on Carter and went on singing the stanza over and over—

> *If my mother ask for me*
> *If my mother ask for me*——

After a while Carter paused over by the door, went through a few mysterious motions, then came a straight way back to the group and sat down. "I met my mother at the station," he explained.

Listen to the child, then, and wait and watch and be ready for him without hurry—and think occasionally of that perky phrase from the Bahaman song—

Don't you   hur-ry wor-ry with me,

And give to the child, rather than to the piano, your eyes and attention. Remember that the smallest movement of his fingers may be a thread to follow—a link from one song to the next, or from him to you, or from him to the group—and so from the group back to him again.

Tone Play and Phrase Repetition

Children who are shy about singing (and many of them are, especially when they think someone is listening) will sometimes join in on a single tone when they would not think of tackling a whole row of them. This single tone is a thing they can identify and pin to—somewhat as, in a street of row-houses all alike, they might feel comforted to see a flag flying from their own window.

Use of tone-play should be as spontaneous as possible. Folk songs, especially of the work-song or "response" type, provide made-to-order tone-plays. The single-tone response is, of course, the simplest. Children join in on the "yes ma'am's" of *Did You Go to the Barney?* or *Oh, John the Rabbit* without invitation, and long before they sing the whole song.

A final tone, as in *Down Came a Lady*, or a repeated initial tone, as in *Oh, Oh, the Sunshine*, also provides natural tone-play material.

Two-tone tone-play is only a little less simple. The echoed interval of a fourth in *By'm Bye* is easy to sing.

Nonsense refrains are time-honored tone-plays. *The Little Pig* contains one of the simplest. *Bought Me a Cat* presents a wide variety.

oink   oink   oink

Dog went boo,   Duck went slish - y,   slosh - y,

Cat went fid - dle - i -   fee,   fid - dle - i -   fee.

Songs like *There Was a Man and He Was Mad* and *Hush, Little Baby* invite children to supply rhyming words at the end of the stanza—and tones as well.

pud- ding bag.   mock- ing bird.

Responses at different pitch levels within the same song, as in *I Got a Letter, Miss Julie Ann Johnson,* and *The Train Is A-Coming,* make slightly more advanced tone-plays.

Oh,   yes,   Oh,__ yes,   o - ho,   o - ho!

oh, yes,   oh, yes,   oh, yes.

And even small children purse their lips to make a try at whistling the refrain of *Have a Little Dog.*

(Whistle_____)

A sort of extended tone-play occurs when the singer for one reason or another repeats a phrase or part of a phrase within the fabric of a song. Such repetition gives the child more to hold on to in getting acquainted with the song than does the shorter tone-play. It also adds a feeling of elasticity to the singing experience, even approaching at times the nature of the creative process, though no new music or words be added. Often too, it seems, through its very monotony and stubborn repetition of beat, to increase the impulse to rhythmic motion.

40

Round and round
(And round and round
And round and round
And round and round), old Joe Clarke,
Round and round I say,
Round and round, old Joe Clarke,
I ain't got long to stay.

The number of repetitions of such key phrases is never twice the same. It follows the children's individual needs and reactions. Slow or shy children may require the encouragement of many repetitions before joining the others in turning around or scraping up sand.

Scraping up sand
(And scraping up sand
And scraping up sand
And scraping up sand
And scraping up sand
And scraping up sand
And scraping up sand) in the bottom of the sea,
Shiloh, shiloh,
Scraping up sand in the bottom of the sea,
Shiloh, Liza Jane.

There may be two shoes to tie today, and ten tomorrow.

Lula gal, Lula gal,
Lula gal, Lula gal,
Tie my shoe, boy, tie my shoe,
Tie my shoe, boy, tie my shoe,
(Tie my shoe, boy, tie my shoe,
Tie my shoe, boy, tie my shoe).

And there is no telling from day to day how long it will take to hang out the clothes, or bring them in, or mend them.

'Twas on a Tuesday morning
The first I saw my darling
A-hanging out the linen clothes,
A-hanging out the linen clothes,
(A-hanging out the linen clothes,
A-hanging out the linen clothes,
A-hanging out the linen clothes).

When singing with larger groups of children, repetition of this sort is also useful as a means of shortening songs which would normally devote an entire stanza or line to each child.

Goodbye, Kathy, o-ho!
Goodbye, Jimmy, o-ho!
Goodbye, Richard,
(And Vivian
And Marjory
And Alice
And George
And Sue
And Kiki
And Lynne
And Marna) o-ho!
Goodbye, Abigail, o-ho!

Accompanying the Songs

These songs do not need any instrumental background. Most of them are used to being sung without accompaniment. When accompanied, the most usual instruments are the guitar, autoharp, mandolin, banjo, accordion, and harmonica. If you can play any of these, use them freely. Since, however, the piano is the instrument most frequently found in town and city homes and schools, the following suggestions are chiefly concerned with this instrument as background to songs and activities for small children, and with its use in as easy and natural a manner as possible.

One trouble with the piano as an accompanying instrument in singing with small children is that the children are more likely to see the pianist's back than his face. Make sure you are giving most of your attention to the child rather than to the piano. If the written accompaniment keeps your eye on the page, abandon it. Try letting the left hand play the tune along with the right, an octave below. Or if playing with two hands keeps your eye on the piano keys, try playing the tune with one hand. Certainly an unaccompanied tune played with convincing and regular rhythmic beat has more meaning than an accompanied tune whose rhythmic outline is blurred through hesitation.

A strongly rhythmic accompaniment can, however, influence noticeably the reaction of a group to a song, especially when the song is used for rhythmic play. It can provide a rhythmic framework for the tune. It can and should emphasize the pulse of the tune. It can give variety in rhythmic experience yet be of simplest harmonic structure.

You may find that "chording" by ear allows you to provide a more natural and rhythmic accompaniment than reading by note, even if you are a fairly good note reader. You may find, too, that chording a tune is easier than you think. Chord letters have been placed above each staff line, as aid not only to players of traditional instruments like the guitar, but also to pianists who want to try making their own accompaniments. These chord letters represent, in all but a few songs, a simplification of the harmonies underlying the written accompaniments.

Look over the songs and see how few chords you need to know. Most songs require only the three common chords or triads of the key in which the song is set. These are built up, in intervals of a 3rd, on the first, fourth, and fifth tones or steps of the scale. The scales most used in this book, and the three common chords of each scale, are given below. The seventh chord (formed by placing another interval of a 3rd on top of a triad) is included for completeness, since a number of chord letters in the songs call for seventh chords. In chording, however, the triad can always be substituted for the seventh if the latter is too difficult to play—G for G⁷, D for D⁷, etc.

Scales most used, and the common chords of each

Scales less used, and the common chords of each

In the six most used scales there are altogether only eight triads to learn: C, G, D, A, F, B♭, E♭, A♭. Try acquainting your left hand (and your right) with these chords. Play them in a few simple rhythmic patterns until you are so at home with them that you can establish a pattern and keep it going with little or no attention. Think more in terms of motion than of richness. Think of keeping the tune moving along, of giving it legs to walk or run on rather than a plush chair to sit in. If all three tones of a chord sound too "thick" when played close together, try thinning the chord, either by omitting one of the tones, or by changing the position or order of the tones, or by playing the chord-tones separately in any of a number of patterns. Just moving a chord an octave higher sometimes helps. The following example gives a few simple patterns of tone-arrangement possible in the use of any one triad.

Do not feel obliged to make frequent change back and forth from one chord to another (C to F, F to C, et cetera). Seek simplicity rather than variety of harmonic structure. Traditional guitar and banjo players are not in a hurry to move from one basic harmony to another. In a song like *Down Came a Lady,* for instance, they would probably stay on the F chord until the next to last measure—and some players would not change chord at all. In *Old Molly Hare* the traditional player would be apt to omit the added IV chord. In *Skip-a to My Lou* and *Billy Barlow,* on the other hand, the chord-tones are clearly outlined by the tune itself. This is true of a great many of these songs.

Sometimes a single song can follow or lead the children through a variety of experiences by means of a few simple changes in type of accompaniment. The accompaniment can be varied in *rhythmic pattern* (for running, walking, skipping, etc.); in *arrangement of tones* (close together, far apart, all high, all low, etc.); in *quality of tone* (smooth, roughly picked, lightly picked, dull and heavy, etc.); in dynamics, or *amount of tone* (loud, soft, medium loud, medium soft, etc.). Sometimes chording by ear makes easier this adapting of types of accompaniment to types of activity—gives the player more freedom to move from one rhythmic pattern to another, allows him to follow more spontaneously when a new mood or motion appears. The variations included with the song *Jim Along Josie* give an idea of the ease with which this can be done. The same basic chords are used throughout the variations. Accompaniments to many other songs can be as easily varied.

Remember, in changing the dynamics from one rhythmic activity to another (soft for tiptoe, loud for jumping, medium loud for walking, hopping, skipping, etc.), not to feel you must vary the loudness or softness *within* any one variation. Do not try to play with "expression" or shading. Play simply. Bring the song into the room in natural straightforward manner, as an old friend with whom you feel comfortable.

Avoid especially, in most songs, a heavy left hand. Chording will usually sound best when played with varying degrees of staccato, or picked, "popcorn" tone—sometimes light, sometimes brittle, sometimes half-staccato, but seldom wooden or plodding. And take care not to play with excessive loudness, unless for particular effect. Older children of seven or eight have come troubled to the piano, saying: "You are playing so loud, I can't hear the words." Younger children seldom voice such helpful reminders.

Remember, too, when playing for rhythmic activity, to give vigorous metrical accent on the first beats of measures—to feel the pulse of the song. And keep the music going; do not stop playing any one song too soon. Repeat it over and over, without pausing between repetitions, for if you pause between you are apt to lose the pulse and the keep-going-ness. Words of songs may be omitted entirely for rhythmic play or may be alternately sung and omitted. Traditional banjo pickers often do this, playing intricate variations on a tune for several minutes, then laying the words of a single stanza on top of the playing, then more playing, then another stanza, and so on ad lib. The banjo does not stop playing, from beginning to end of the performance. There is no break in pulse or continuity.

Explore the wide pitch-span of the piano, low to high. You may be inclined at first to stay safely at home near middle C, since pioneering into the outer octaves draws the hands away from each other. Yet the same song played in various octave combinations can give quite different effects. Get used to playing all over the piano. Try moving a chord or a tune or part of a tune around among the seven octave positions. Take the C chord, for instance, and learn to move it quickly from one octave to the next. Take a tune in the key of C and learn to play it from the same tone of each octave. Then see how many different octave combinations the two hands can find—playing sometimes two octaves apart, or three, or four, or both very high or very low. Over a score of such octave combinations are possible, only a few of which are included among the *Jim Along Josie* variations.

Do not feel you must be prepared with a specific song to match every possible request. When Jock comes up to the piano with his body full of angles, wanting to be a tiger, it would be a shame to postpone his urge because you cannot remember a ready-made tiger song in a hurry. He will be glad to show you his way of being a tiger, and you can make your own tiger music—with your eyes more on Jock than on the piano keys. Perhaps you may establish the beat or pulse of the music with some easy figure in the left hand—the warp of the music you are about to weave. With that continuing, you are free to let the right hand travel in and out among dissonances and consonances, looking sometimes for a tune, sometimes for a rhythm. Do not be afraid of wrong notes. You may find, if you come back again and again to a so-called wrong (or rough) note, that it sounds right—that it "belongs" and you like it. If not, you can try sliding your finger from the rough note to a "smoother" one close by. You may even find yourself experimenting with the sound of adjacent tones (half and whole steps) played simultaneously—and liking them too. Perhaps most important is the feeling that each tone or interval which you play *pulls* to another. Listen for this pull. See if your fingers can get the feel of it without help from your eyes—for Jock and the other tigers who have joined him are vital threads in the musical cloth you are weaving.

Nonsense

One sturdy element has been left out of the preceding chapters. It was left out because it belonged in all of them. It was present at all the music meetings and during the earnest telephone discussions on the meaning of meaning. It is certainly one of the basic values to children in music like this. It should be a live ingredient in the process of improvisation, whether at home or at school, and can even make itself heard in the playing of the music. It is the homely yeast and soda in the process of song mixing—its immediate momentary bubbling will appear artificial only to those who forget how heavy the bread can be without it.

This element is—a sense of humor. An appreciation of nonsense. A willingness to lay logic aside, to respect the ridiculous.

Children like nonsense. They come asking fondly for "that silly old song" (*Old Aunt Kate*). They wait through five stanzas of *The Little Pig* to laugh loud at "the woman, the man, and the little piggee" all lying on the shelf ("on the *shelf!*" they repeat with superior scorn for such foolishness—then ask for the song all over again).

The sense of the funny need not obtrude. One can simply be ready to welcome it when it appears, as an old friend dropping in for a chat rather than as a formally invited guest. The adult must take care, while playing around with songs and having fun with them himself, not to thrust unduly on children his own concepts of nonsense. If he does, he may find himself falling into the snare of being "cute" instead. He should not, on the other hand, always hold back, waiting for the child to take the lead. Part of what he can contribute is the sense of adventure, of discovering something together.

Children often find fun in corners where adults would overlook it. When Tony first heard *She'll Be Coming Round the Mountain When She Comes*, he gave a man-size shout. "She'll be *comin'* when she comes!" he repeated with delight, then turned to include me in his discovery: "That's another foolish one, isn't it!" And would you think of a song like *Hush 'n' Bye* as foolish?

> *Hush 'n' bye, don't you cry,*
> *Go to sleep, you little baby,*
> *When you wake you shall have some cake*
> *And all the pretty little horses.*

Yet, the day after we had sung it for the first time, someone begged for "that new foolish song"—and I floundered until he explained: "You know—the song where the *baby* eats *cake*."

American folklore is, of course, full of rugged humor. The girls poke fun at the boys—

> *Old Dan Tucker was a mighty man,*
> *He washed his face in a frying pan,*
> *Combed his hair with a wagon wheel,*
> *And died with a toothache in his heel.*

—and the boys poke fun at the girls—

> *I went down to Cindy's house,*
> *She was standing in the door,*
> *Her shoes and stockings in her hand*
> *And her feet all over the floor.*

—and fibbing fun is everywhere. Darby's ram has horns that reach up to the moon ("a man went up in January and never got down till June"); the boll weevil cannot be frozen by ice nor burned by fire ("Here I are, here I are, this'll be my home"); the elephant jumps over the fence so high that he clears the sky ("never came back 'til the Fourth of July"). Not so far from the spirit of this is the child who sings about the rain raining all over the piano instead of the grass, or John the Rabbit eating nails and splinters instead of carrots, or the man who was so mad that he jumped into a dog's bark.

THE SONGS

Yonder She Comes

Moderately fast ♩=120

MISSOURI

Yon - der she comes And it's how-dy how-dy do, Oh,

where have you been since the last that I met you?

2. Rise you up, my lady (or gentleman),
Present to me your hand,
I know you are a pretty girl (or handsome man),
The prettiest in the land.

Down Came a Lady

LORD DANIEL'S WIFE

VIRGINIA

Moderately fast ♩ = 120

Down came a la-dy, Down came two,

Down came Lord Dan'-l's wife And she was dressed in blue.

Ending

IMPROVISATION and RHYTHMIC PLAY: *In one school the steps were steep, and each person's coming down was an event to sing about.*

Down came a lady,
Down came two,
Down came Miss Peggy Smith
And she was dressed in blue.

The lady (or gentleman) may be doing other things—coming in, jumping up, dancing away. Several children may be included in one stanza:

In came Matthew,
Jeremy too,
In came Marianne
And she was dressed in blue.

TONE PLAY:

Adult: And she was dressed in . . .
Child: . . . . blue.

51

Who's That Tapping at the Window?

VIRGINIA

Moderately fast ♩ = 88

Who's that tap-ping at the win-dow? Who's that knock-ing at the door?

Mam - my tap-ping at the win-dow, Pap - py knock-ing at the door.

NAME PLAY and FINGER PLAY:

Who's that tapping at the window?
Who's that knocking at the door?
Danny tapping at the window,
Mika knocking at the door.

If there are many children, the music of the last two lines can be extended to include them all. Tapping may be light; knocking, heavy.

Tony tapping at the window,
Gary knocking at the door,
Mora tapping at the window,
Maggie knocking at the door,
and so on.

Such a Getting Upstairs

INDIANA

Fast ♩ = 120

Such a get-ting up-stairs I nev-er did see,

Such a get-ting up-stairs it don't suit me.

Repeat ad lib

This is a favorite going-up-to-bed song. It can be a getting-down-stairs song as well. It is the refrain of a play-party tune whose second section can be whistled or hummed or played, or sung with varying words like the following from Virginia:

Some love cof - fee, some love tea, But I love the pret-ty girl that winks at me,

The folklorist Winston Wilkinson notes the similarity of a Virginia version of this tune to that of an old English Morris Dance tune, and points further to the rites of the old processional dance, in which the performers danced down the streets, and into the village houses, and up the stairs and down again.

53

Toodala

Moderately fast ♩ = 120

Might-y pret-ty mo-tion, too-da-la, too-da-la, too-da-la,

Might-y pret-ty mo-tion, too-da-la, too-da-la-la la-dy.

2. Rock old Soni, toodala, toodala, toodala,
   Rock old Soni, toodala, toodala-la-lady.

3. Right back this way, toodala, toodala, toodala, etc.

4. Swing your partner, toodala, toodala, toodala, etc.

Toodala parties used to be held frequently in Texas. The dancing was usually outdoors; entire families came, from babies to old men, and the young people danced. Words were improvised during the dancing, which was in the manner of square dancing.

IMPROVISATION and RHYTHMIC PLAY: *This dance song sings easily over and over without stopping—picking up whatever things are happening, repeating in unbroken flow words or phrases the children are saying, noticing new toys, bright colors, the weather. For instance:*

(The children are coming in from outdoors, and no child's name is left out of the song)

Good morn-ing to you, too-da-la, too-da-la, too-da-la,
Good morn-ing to Bill, too-da-la, too-da-la, too-da-la,
"I can take my hat off," too-da-la, too-da-la, too-da-la,

Good morn-ing to you, too-da-la, too-da-la-la-la-dy.
Good morn-ing to Bob-by, too-da-la, too-da-la my dai-sy.
"I can take my coat off," too-da-la, too-da-la my dai-sy.

Good morning to Sam, toodala, toodala, toodala,
He takes his hat off, toodala, toodala my daisy.

Here comes Joanna, toodala, toodala, toodala,
She has her coat on, toodala, toodala my daisy.

She can pull it off now, toodala, toodala, toodala,
She can do it herself, toodala, toodala-la-lady.

(Each laborious detail becomes part of the growing song)

Pulled off my rubbers, toodala, toodala, toodala,
They're hard to pull off, toodala, toodala-la-lady.

Take off my leggings, toodala, toodala, toodala,
Can do it myself, toodala, toodala my daisy.

I unbutton my coat, toodala, toodala, toodala,
I can do it myself, toodala, toodala-la-lady.

Has lots of buttons, toodala, toodala, toodala,
One, two, three, four, five, toodala, toodala-la-lady.

It hangs up high, toodala, toodala, toodala,
Hang it up myself, toodala, toodala my daisy.

(The children gather around one by one, waiting for the song to tell more about what they are doing or saying or hearing or holding in their hands. Any line may be sung once or twice or many times.)

I'm ready now, etc.
I'm singing now.
See my new shoes.
My new brown shoes.
I have a blue sweater.

I have red pants.
See Dicky's flower.
I have one too.
A silver bell.
Let's hear it ring.

The sun is shining.
The grass is wet.
I heard a robin.
The birds are singing.
I'm singing too.

(Perhaps someone starts turning around or running or jumping)

I'm turning round, etc.
Around and around.
Now turning the other way.
Around and around.
Jumping up and down now.

Running around now.
Sit down awhile.
And I lie down awhile.
I can close my eyes.
I can go to sleep.

Wake up now.
Open my eyes.
Stretch my toes.
Jumping up and down again.
Running around again.

55

How Old Are You?

I'LL BE SIXTEEN THIS SUNDAY

TEXAS

Moderately fast ♩ = 120

"How old are you, my pret-ty lit- tle miss? How old are you, my hon- ey?"

She an-swered me with a tee hee hee, "I'll be six-teen this Sun - day."

REFRAIN (may be omitted)

The yad-dle lad-dle lad- dle um dai - sy, The yad-dle lad-dle lad- dle um,

Yad-dle lad-dle lad-dle um, Yad-dle lad-dle lad-dle um dai - sy.

2. Where are you going, my pretty little miss?
   Where are you going, my honey?
   She answered me with a tee hee hee,
   "I'm looking for my mummy."
   Refrain:

3. Where do you live, my pretty little miss? etc.
   "I live on the hill with mummy."
   Refrain:

4. What can you do, my pretty little miss? etc.
   "I can put on bread for mummy."
   Refrain:

IMPROVISATION: Children can seldom wait beyond the second line to tell how old they are, or where they live, or what they can do.

How old are you, my pretty little miss (or good old man)?
How old are you, my honey?
"I'm four-and-a-half, I'm four-and-a-half,
I'm four-and-a-half this Sunday (or Monday or Tuesday, etc.)."

Jimmy Rose He Went to Town

Jim-my Rose he went to town, Jim-my Rose he went to town,

Jim-my Rose he went to town To 'com-mo-date the la-dies.

IMPROVISATION and RHYTHMIC PLAY: Jimmy Rose—or Raymond Horne or Paul Gregg or Timmy Wright—may be going away, or outdoors, or to rest, to lunch, to play, to school, to the store. Or he may be running around, or skipping, hopping, walking, jumping up and down, washing his hands, combing his hair, drinking his juice, "to commodate the ladies."

ACCOMPANIMENT: Speed and type of accompaniment may be adapted to the rhythmic play.

What Shall We Do When We All Go Out?

Moderately fast ♩ = 96

NORTH CAROLINA

What shall we do when we | all go out, | All go out, | all go out,

What shall we do when we | all go out, When we | all go out to | play?

IMPROVISATION and RHYTHMIC PLAY: Children have
suggested many things, in song and motion.

1. We will ride our three-wheel bikes,
   Three-wheel bikes, three-wheel bikes,
   We will ride our three-wheel bikes
   When we all go out to play.

2. We will slide on the sliding board, etc.
3. We will see-saw up and down, etc.
4. We will pull our wagons 'round, etc.
5. We will climb the jungle-jim, etc.
6. We will dig in the sandpile, etc.
7. We will watch the beans grow, etc.
8. We will look for frogs' eggs, etc.
9. We will see the leaves fall, etc.

Goodbye, Julie

MISS JULIE ANN JOHNSON

Moderate ♩ = 112

Miss Ju- lie Ann John- son, o - ho!

Miss Ju- lie Ann John- son, o - ho!

Good - bye, _____ Ju - lie, o - ho!

Good - bye, _____ Ju - lie, o - ho!

2. Oh, where's my Julie? o-ho!
    Oh, where's my Julie? o-ho!
    She's gone to Dallas, o-ho!
    She's gone to Dallas, o-ho!

3. Going to catch that train, boys, o-ho!
    Going to catch that train, boys, o-ho!
    Going to find my Julie, o-ho!
    Going to find my Julie, o-ho!

4. Going to hug my Julie, o-ho!
    Going to hug my Julie, o-ho!
    Miss Julie Ann Johnson, o-ho!
    Miss Julie Ann Johnson, o-ho!

NAME PLAY: Each child likes to hear his name sung.

Goodbye. Robin, o-ho!
Goodbye. Eric, o-ho!
Goodbye. Connie, o-ho!
Goodbye. Karen, o-ho!

TONE PLAY:

Adult: Goodbye. Julie . . .
Child: . . . . o-ho!

Goodbye, Old Paint

Moderate ♩. = 60

REFRAIN

Good - bye, old Paint, I'm a - leav - ing Chey - enne,

Good - bye, old Paint, I'm a - leav - ing Chey - enne.

STANZA (*may be played without singing, as piano interlude*)

Old Paint's a good po - ny. He runs when he can, ____

D.C. al fine

Good morn - ing young la - dy, My po - ny won't stand. ____

REFRAIN:

Goodbye, old Paint,
I'm a-leaving Cheyenne,
Goodbye, old Paint,
I'm a-leaving Cheyenne.

2. I'm a-riding old Paint,
   I'm a-leading old Fan,
   Goodbye, little Annie,
   I'm off for Montan'.
   Refrain:

3. Oh, hitch up your horses,
   And feed them some hay,
   And seat yourself by me
   As long as you stay.
   Refrain:

4. My horses ain't hungry,
   They'll not eat your hay,
   My wagon is loaded
   And rolling away.
   Refrain:

It is said that this song was often used as a "Home, Sweet Home"
at the end of a cowboy dance—but as long as someone could remember
or improvise another stanza, the dance would go on.

Oh, Oh, the Sunshine

OH, OH, YOU CAN'T SHINE

Very Free

TEXAS

Oh, oh, the sun - shine!

Oh, oh, the sun - shine!

Oh, oh, the sun - shine!

Sal - ly's got a red dress, but - toned be - hind,

Sal - ly's got a red dress, but - toned be - hind.

1. Oh, oh, the sunshine!
   Oh, oh, the sunshine!
   Oh, oh, the sunshine!
   Susan's got blue overalls, buckled in front,
   Susan's got blue overalls, buckled in front.

or

2. Frankie's got brown shoes, laced on top, etc.
3. Jane's got a blue ribbon, tied in a bow, etc.
4. Anne has long hair, braided behind, etc.
5. Bruce has red socks, don't button at all, etc.

Sweet Water Rolling

SOUTH CAROLINA

Moderately slow ♩ = 60

Sweet wa-ter roll-ing, Sweet wa-ter roll,

Roll-ing from the foun-tain, Sweet wa-ter roll.

The Wind Blow East

NASSAU, BAHAMAS

Moderately fast ♩ = 132

Oh, the wind blow east,
The wind blow west,
The wind blow the *Setting Star*
Right down in town.
Refrain:

IMPROVISATION: The wind blows many things down into town —snowflakes, raindrops, autumn leaves, red leaves, yellow leaves, thunderclouds.

ACCOMPANIMENT: Clapping or drumming, or both, makes a natural accompaniment. In the Bahamas the song is accompanied with intricate and lively clapping, and the refrain is repeated as many as a dozen times.

Sunshine and Setting Star are names of two ships which were blown "right down in town" during a hurricane in the Bahamas.

Rain, Come Wet Me

TEXAS

Free

Rain, come wet me. Sun, come dry me.

Keep a-way, pret-ty girls, Don't come a-nigh me.

67

It Rained a Mist

Moderate ♩.=60   VIRGINIA

It rained a mist, it rained a mist,

It rained all o-ver the town, town, town,

It rained all o-ver the town. It

2. And all the boys went out to play
   A-tossing their ball around, round, round,
   A-tossing their ball around.

3. At first they tossed their ball too low,
   And then they tossed it too high, high, high,
   And then they tossed it too high.

4. They tossed it into a lady's garden
   Where roses and lilies lie, lie, lie,
   Where roses and lilies lie.

IMPROVISATION: Children sing about many objects it rains or snows over—the school big tree, the grass, the roof, even odd things like the piano, the floor, or "me, me, me."

Rain or Shine

DONEY GAL

Slow ♩. = 42

Refrain: It's rain or shine, sleet or snow,
Stanza: We'll ride the range from sun to sun,

For a Me and my Don - ey gal are on the go,
cow - boy's work is__ nev - er done,

Yes, rain or shine, sleet or snow,
He's up and gone at the break of day,

Me and my Don - ey gal are bound to go.
A - driv - in' the do - gies on their wea - ry way.

A cowboy's life is a dreary thing,
For it's rope and brand and ride and sing,
Yes, day or night in the rain or hail,
He'll stay with his dogies out on the trail.
Refrain:

We whoop at the sun and yell through the hail,
But we drive the poor dogies down the trail,
And we'll laugh at the storms, the sleet and snow,
When we reach the little town of San Antonio.
Refrain:

One Cold and Frosty Morning

OLD JESSIE

Moderately fast ♩ = 96

ALABAMA

One cold and frost-y morn-ing Just as the sun did rise,

The poss-um roared, the rac-coon howled,'Cause he be-gan to freeze,

He drew him-self up in a knot, With his knees up to his chin,

And ev'-ry-thing had to clear the track When he stretched out a-gain.

REFRAIN

Old Jes-sie was a gen-tle-man A-mong the old-en times.

This is said to have been sung before the Civil War. One singer recalled that his father used it as a waking-up song for his children.

By'm Bye

STARS SHINING

TEXAS

Very Free

By'm bye, By'm bye. Stars shin - ing,

Num - ber, num - ber one, num - ber two, num - ber three, Good Lawd, by'm

bye, by'm bye, Good Lawd, by'm bye.

FINGER PLAY: "Number, number one, number two, number three"—continuing on up to five or ten or more, if desired—may be used as a finger play. Many things may be counted aside from stars and fingers, such as buttons on clothing, or children, or stair steps, or foolish things like shoes untied.

TONE PLAY: Children echo By'm Bye without being asked, and like to join in on the numbering phrase, especially if it is extended through a growing series of numbers.

Jim Along Josie

Moderately fast

Hey jim a- long, jim a-long Jo - sie, Hey jim a - long, jim a- long Jo.

Hey jim a - long, jim a-long Jo - sie, Hey jim a -long, jim a- long Jo.

2. Walk jim along, jim along Josie,
   Walk jim along, jim along Jo. (*Repeat*)

3. Hop jim along, jim along Josie,
   Hop jim along, jim along Jo. (*Repeat*)

IMPROVISATION and RHYTHMIC PLAY: Josie may have thoughts or motions other than those in the traditional text given above.

4. Run, jim along, jim along Josie, etc.
5. Jump, jim along, jim along Josie, etc.
6. Tiptoe along, jim along Josie, etc.
7. Crawl along, jim along, jim along Josie, etc.
8. Swing along, sing along, jim along Josie, etc.
9. Roll, jim along, jim along Josie, etc.

An invitation is sometimes appreciated:

Let's go walking, jim along Josie, etc.
Let's go running, jim along Josie, etc.
Let's sit down now, jim along Josie, etc.

For rhythmic play the music should be repeated many times without stopping. The words will probably be sung only once, or not at all.

ACCOMPANIMENT: *Speed and type of accompaniment may be adapted to the various rhythmic activities. The sample variations which follow are suggestions only. Do not use them if you can make your own. In all of them the chordal basis is the same.*

The simple dance-song Jim Along Josie *is said to be based on an old minstrel song. It is widely known, especially as a game or play-party song. In some versions* Josie *appears to be the dance itself:*

Hold my mule while I dance Josie.

In a very old one, still sung, "Josie" is something to wear:

Who's been here since I been gone?
Pretty little girl with a josey on.

"Hey jim along" is also sung "Hey get along," "Hi come along," "Hey jam along," "Come-a-get along," "Come-a-high, jim along."

In skipping, time, bright

10 *mf*

Moderate, quiet

11 *p*

Let's sit down now, jim a-long Jo - sie, Let's sit down now, jim a-long Jo.

There Was a Man and He Was Mad

OHIO

Moderately fast ♩ = 104

There was a man and he was mad, And he jumped in-to the pud-ding bag.

2. The pudding bag it was so fine
   That he jumped into a bottle of wine.

3. The bottle of wine it was so clear
   That he jumped into a bottle of beer.

4. The bottle of beer it was so thick
   That he jumped into a walking stick.

5. The walking stick it was so narrow
   That he jumped into a wheel barrow.

6. The wheel barrow it did so crack
   That he jumped onto a horse's back.

7. The horse's back it did so bend
   That he jumped into a taching end.

8. The taching end it was so rotten
   That he jumped into a bag of cotton.

9. The bag of cotton it set on fire
   And blew him up to Jeremiah.

   (*spoken*)
   Pouf! Pouf! Pouf!

IMPROVISATION: Children as well as adults like to make new stanzas for this song. One mother and her child improvised a dozen couplets around the house. And a group of four-year-olds were so bowled over by the beer-bottle jump that they followed through, one morning, with hilarious adventures of their own—bubbles that wouldn't stop bubbling, a cork popping, an explosive flight skyward, and a long series of impractical encounters with airplanes.

RHYTHMIC PLAY: Various jumping plays are improvised during the singing of the song. Sometimes children like to take turns jumping over a stick held a few inches from the floor.

TONE PLAY:

Adult: And he jumped into the . . .
Child: . . . . pudding bag.

Riding in the Buggy, Miss Mary Jane

SOUTH CAROLINA

Moderately fast ♩= 104

Rid-ing in the bug-gy, Miss Ma - ry Jane, Miss Ma - ry Jane, Miss Ma - ry Jane,

Rid-ing in the bug-gy, Miss Ma - ry Jane, I'm a long ways from home.

REFRAIN

Who moan for me? Who moan for me?

Who moan for me, my darl-ing, Who moan for me?

2. Sally's got a house in Baltimore,
   In Baltimore, in Baltimore,
   Sally's got a house in Baltimore
   And it's full of chicken pie.
   Refrain:

3. I've got a girl in Baltimore,
   In Baltimore, in Baltimore,
   I've got a girl in Baltimore,
   And she's sixteen stories high.
   Refrain:

4. Fare you well, my little bitty Ann,
   My little bitty Ann, my little bitty Ann,
   Fare you well, my little bitty Ann,
   For I'm going away.
   Refrain:

IMPROVISATION and RHYTHMIC PLAY: *Miss Mary Jane may ask to ride in a car, or on a trolley, an airplane, a camel, an elephant. The accompaniment can be adapted accordingly. This is a favorite car riding song while going to and from school.*

Billy Barlow

Moderately fast ♩. = 96

"Let's go hunt-ing," says Risk-y Rob,

"Let's go hunt-ing," says Rob-in to Bob,

"Let's go hunt-ing," says Dan'l to Joe,

"Let's ___ go hunt-ing," says Bil-ly Bar-low.

2. "What shall I hunt?" says Risky Rob,
   "What shall I hunt?" says Robin to Bob,
   "What shall I hunt?" says Dan'l to Joe,
   "Hunt for a rat," says Billy Barlow.

3. "How shall I get him?" says Risky Rob,
   "How shall I get him?" says Robin to Bob,
   "How shall I get him?" says Dan'l to Joe,
   "Go borrow a gun," says Billy Barlow.

4. "How shall I haul him?" etc. (3 times)
   "Go borrow a cart," said Billy Barlow.

5. "How shall we divide him?" etc. (4 times)

6. "I'll take shoulder," says Risky Rob,
   "I'll take side," says Robin to Bob,
   "I'll take ham," says Dan'l to Joe,
   "Tail bone mine," says Billy Barlow.

7. "How shall we cook him?" etc. (4 times)

8. "I'll broil shoulder," says Risky Rob,
   "I'll fry side," says Robin to Bob,
   "I'll boil ham," says Dan'l to Joe,
   "Tail bone raw," says Billy Barlow.

This is favorite skipping or skating music. Dramatic play may grow out of it with older children.

The Juniper Tree

ARKANSAS

Moderately fast ♩.= 96

O sis - ter Phoe - be, how mer - ry were we, The

night we sat un - der the jun - i - per tree, The

jun - i - per tree, Hi - o, hi - o, The

jun - i - per tree, Hi - o.

2. Put this hat on your head to keep your head warm
   And one or two kisses will do you no harm,
   Will do you no harm, I know, I know,
   Will do you no harm, I know.

3. Go choose you a partner, go choose you a one,
   Go choose you the fairest that ever you can,
   Now rise you up, sister, and go, and go,
   Now rise you up, sister, and go.

RHYTHMIC PLAY and GAME: Small children like most to skip around freely to this music. Older children sometimes play the traditional singing game. During the first stanza they form a circle around a center child and skip or walk around him. During the second stanza someone from the circle puts a hat on his head. The center child then chooses another from the circle to take his place in the center, and the game is repeated. The third stanza may be omitted with small children.

Old Joe Clarke

ROUND AND ROUND

TENNESSEE

Fast ♩ = 132

REFRAIN

Round and round, old Joe Clarke, Round and round, I say,

Round and round, old Joe Clarke, I ain't got long to stay.

STANZA (*may be played without singing, as piano interlude*)

Old Joe Clarke he had a house, Six - teen sto - ries high,

Ev' - ry sto - ry in that house Was full of chick - en pie.

D.C. al fine

Old Joe Clarke is a well-known square-dance tune. All the traditional refrains lend themselves to free rhythmic play. This song has often drawn a group of children together when nothing else would.

84

OTHER REFRAINS:

Rock-a-rock, old Joe Clarke,
Rock-a-rock, I'm gone;
Rock-a-rock, old Joe Clarke,
And goodbye, Susan Brown.

Fly around, old Joe Clarke,
Fly around, I'm gone;
Fly around, old Joe Clarke,
With the golden slippers on.

Row around, old Joe Clarke,
Sail away and gone;
Row around, old Joe Clarke,
With golden slippers on.

Roll, roll, old Joe Clarke,
Roll, roll, I say;
Roll, roll, old Joe Clarke,
You'd better be gettin' away.

OTHER STANZAS:

Old Joe Clarke he had a dog
As blind as he could be;
Chased a redbug 'round a stump
And a coon up a hollow tree.

I went down to old Joe's house,
Never been there before,
He slept on the feather bed
And I slept on the floor.

If you see that girl of mine,
Tell her if you can,
Before she goes to make up bread
To wash those dirty hands.

When I was a little boy
I used to play in ashes
Now I am a great big boy
Wearing Dad's mustaches.

IMPROVISATION and RHYTHMIC PLAY: Children have always been fond of turning around and around until they are dizzy, then falling down.

REFRAIN:

Round and round, old Joe Clarke,
Round and round, I say,
Round and round, old Joe Clarke,
I ain't got long to stay.

STANZA:

Round and round and round, I turn,
Round and round, I say,
Round and round and round I turn
And . . .

> (*spoken*)
> NOW FALL DOWN!

And . . .

> NOW UP AGAIN!

And . . .

REFRAIN (*singing again*):

> Round and round, old Joe Clarke,
> Round the other way, etc.

Clap Your Hands

Moderately fast ♩ = 108

Clap, clap, clap your hands, Clap your hands to - geth - er,

Clap, clap, clap your hands, Clap your hands to - geth - er.

INTERLUDE (*children continue rhythmic play*)

IMPROVISATION and RHYTHMIC PLAY: *This entire song has been adapted from the dance song* Old Joe Clarke *(page 84). Many of the motions came first from the children: in the middle of a song someone would start tapping toes or stamping feet.*

2. Stamp, stamp, stamp your feet,
   Stamp your feet together,
   Stamp, stamp, stamp your feet,
   Stamp your feet together.

3. Tap, tap, tap your toes, etc.
4. Nod, nod, nod your head, etc.
5. Shake, shake, shake your hands, etc.
6. Stretch, stretch, stretch up high, etc.
7. Wheels, wheels going round, etc.
8. Dig, dig, dig the ground, etc.
9. See, see, see the moon, etc.
10. Sing, sing, sing a song, etc.

Down by the Greenwood Sidey-o

One day I was sit-ting in my fa-ther's hall, I saw three babes a-play-ing ball.

All day long and I love you all, Down by the green-wood sid-ey-o.

A ball may be rolled back and forth to the rhythm of singing. The song should be sung with strong accent, but smoothly. "Babes" may be changed to "children."

Roll That Brown Jug Down to Town

ILLINOIS

Fast ♩ = 120

Roll that brown jug down to town, Roll that brown jug down to town,

Roll that brown jug down to town, So ear-ly in the morn - ing.

2. Big 'tatoes grow in sandy land,
   Big 'tatoes grow in sandy land,
   Big 'tatoes grow in sandy land,
   Way down in Alabam'.

3. Sift that meal and save the bran, etc.

IMPROVISATION and RHYTHMIC PLAY: A ball-rolling game is fun, the children sitting either in a line or a semicircle, and the adult rolling the ball to each in turn.

Roll that red ball down to town,
Roll that red ball down to town,
Roll that red ball down to town,
So early in the morning.

The song can also roll on through endless series of variations. Chuck kept it going one day through a dozen or more.

1. Ride that big bike down to town.
2. Jump that little Jack down to town.

3. Walk that little dog home again.
4. Roll your little self down to school, *and so on.*

And when one of the children didn't want to go to bed, a never-stopping song about each process made her laugh out loud. It began downstairs:

Roll that little girl up the steps,

and continued through each piece of clothing
Pull that blue shirt over your head,

and ended with bed
Roll that little girl into bed.

As I Walked Out One Holiday

A LITTLE BOY THREW HIS BALL SO HIGH

Moderate ♩. = 60

VIRGINIA

1. As I walked out one hol - i - day, The flakes of snow did fall,
2. A lit-tle boy threw his ball so high, He threw his ball so low,

And all the chil - dren in the school Were out a - play - ing ball.
He threw it in a dusk - y gar-den A - mong the blades of snow.

3. Out came the neighbor's youngest daughter
   All dressed in fairy green.
   "Come in, come in, my lad," she said,
   "You may have your ball again."

She'll Be Coming Round the Mountain When She Comes

2. She'll be driving six white horses when she comes,
   She'll be driving six white horses when she comes,
   She'll be driving six white horses,
   She'll be driving six white horses,
   She'll be driving six white horses when she comes.

3. Oh, we'll all go out to meet her when she comes, etc.

4. Oh, we'll all have chicken and dumplin's when she comes, etc.

Juba

Fast ♩ = 120

light staccato throughout

Ju - ba this and Ju - ba that, Ju - ba killed a yel - low cat,

Ju - ba up and Ju - ba down, Ju - ba run - ning all a - round.

Juba may have, or see, or find, or chase the yellow cat, and jump, hop, dance, clap hands, pat knees.

Juba is an old "patting" song and dance which is still known and danced by all ages. It is often half sung, half spoken, to the accompaniment of fast clapping and patting of the knees and, occasionally, intricate footwork.

Run, Chillen, Run

Fast ♩ = 120
REFRAIN

Run, chil-len, run, the pat-ter-roll-er catch you, Run, chil-len, run, it's al-most day.

light staccato throughout

Run, chil-len, run, the pat-ter-roll-er catch you, Run, chil-len, run, it's al-most day.

STANZA *(if too high for easy singing, the words can be spoken or the tune whistled, while playing.)*

That child ran, and that child flew, That child lost his Sun-day shoe.

REFRAIN:

Run, chillen, run, the patterroller catch you,
Run, chillen, run, it's almost day.
Run, chillen, run, the patterroller catch you,
Run, chillen, run, it's almost day.

2. Jumped the fence and ran through the pasture,
   First ran slow and then he ran faster.
   Refrain:

3. Let me tell you what I'll do,
   I'm going to find me a Sunday shoe.
   Refrain:

4. Let me tell you where I'll be,
   I'm going to hide behind that tree.
   Refrain:

A patterroller was a patrolman whose job it was, in pre-Civil-War days, to patrol plantation borders. In some localities the workers were allowed to visit neighboring plantations but had to be back before daybreak.

All Around the Kitchen

COCKY DOODLE DOODLE DOO

Fast ♩=84

ALABAMA

All a-round the kitch-en, Cock-y doo-dle doo-dle doo, All a-round the kitch-en, Cock-y doo-dle doo-dle doo, Now

REFRAIN *(may be played over and over without singing, for free rhythmic play)*

stop right still, Cock-y doo-dle doo-dle doo, Put your
hand on your hip, Cock-y doo-dle doo-dle doo, Let your
right foot slip, Cock-y doo-dle doo-dle doo, Then
do like this, Cock-y doo-dle doo-dle doo, Then
do like this, Cock-y doo-dle doo-dle doo. ——

Ending

RHYTHMIC PLAY: Children react to this perky song with various sorts of body play, especially if the music is repeated many times without stopping. In one room there were four tall posts. Someone started going around one of them—and soon each post was the center of an orbit.

GAME: Older children may like to play the game as it was played in Alabama. The children form a circle around a center child and "march or skip" while singing. Then they stand still while the singer in the center "makes a motion," as her ingenuity dictates. She may kneel, prance, bow, dance a jig, or otherwise cavort. Sometimes the player chooses the motion and the others must follow her example, must "do it like this."

I'm Going to Join the Army

Moderately fast ♩ = 104

KENTUCKY

vamp ad lib

I'm going to join the ar-my, I'm going to vol-un-teer,

I'm going to be a sol-dier Be-fore an-o-ther year.

2. May I go with you, Johnny?
   I'll travel by your side,
   And when the battle's over
   You'll make me your bride.

3. Yes, come go with me, Sally,
   And travel by my side,
   And when the battle's over
   I'll make you my bride.

Scraping Up Sand in the Bottom of the Sea

SHILOH

MISSOURI

Fast ♩ = 126

Scrap-ing up sand in the bot-tom of the sea, Shi-loh, Shi-loh,

Scrap-ing up sand in the bot-tom of the sea, Shi-loh, Li-za Jane.

REFRAIN

Oh, how I love her, Oh, Li-za Jane,

Oh, how I love her, Good-bye, Li-za Jane.

2. Black those shoes and make them shine,
   Shiloh, shiloh,
   Black those shoes and make them shine,
   Shiloh, Liza Jane.
   Refrain:

3. A hump-back mule I'm bound to ride, etc.
   Refrain:

4. Hopped up a chicken and he flew upstairs, etc.
   Refrain:

RHYTHMIC PLAY and FINGER PLAY: Dredging machines—and whales—scoop up sand from the bottom of the sea. Steam shovels scoop it up from the vacant lot down the street where a new house is being built. Small garden shovels scoop it up to make the ground ready for seeds. Fingers scoop up sand too, scrape it and sift it through endless repetitions of the first two lines of this song.

Old Mister Rabbit

Moderately fast ♩= 100

MISSISSIPPI

Old Mis - ter Rab - bit, You've got a might- y hab - it Of jump-ing in the gar - den And eat - ing all my cab - bage.

IMPROVISATION and RHYTHMIC PLAY: Old Mister Rabbit may eat all sorts of vegetables. And of course he will jump all over the garden.

TONE PLAY:

Adult: And eating all my . . .
Child: . . . . cabbage.

ACCOMPANIMENT: The chords may be arpeggiated if desired:

Old   Mis -ter   Old   Mis -ter

Old Molly Hare

Very fast ♩ = 120

Old Mol-ly Hare, _____ What you do-ing there?_____

Run-ning through the cot-ton patch As fast as I can tear.

2. Old Molly Hare,
   What you doing there?
   Sitting in my fireplace
   A-smoking my cigar.

3. Old Molly Hare,
   What you doing there?
   Sitting on a haystack
   A-shooting at a bear.

4. Old Molly Hare,
   What you doing there?
   Sitting on a butter-plate
   A-picking out a hair.

5. Old Molly Hare,
   Your tail's too short,
   Yes, doggone it,
   I can tuck it out of sight.

6. Dogs say "boo"
   And they bark too,
   I haven't got the time
   For to talk to you.

7. Riding of a goat
   And leading of a sheep
   I won't be back
   Till the middle of the week.

99

Oh, John the Rabbit

Moderately fast ♩ = 88   MISSISSIPPI

Oh, John the Rab-bit, Yes ma'am,

Got a might-y hab-it, Yes ma'am,

Jum-ping in my gar-den, Yes ma'am,

Cut-ting down my cab-bage, Yes ma'am,

My sweet po-ta-toes, Yes ma'am,

My fresh to-ma-toes, Yes ma'am,

And if I live, — Yes ma'am, To see next fall, — Yes ma'am,

I ain't gon-na have, Yes ma'am, No cot-ton at all, Yes ma'am.

IMPROVISATION: The list of vegetables may be extended. Or other habits may be sung about, with details changing from day to day. John does many things in the morning. The music for lines 3 to 7 below may be repeated with as many new words as the children can think of, before finishing the song.

Oh, John the Rabbit, Yes ma'am,
Got a mighty habit, Yes ma'am,
Jumping up in the morning, Yes ma'am,

Putting on his clothes, Yes ma'am,
His socks and shoes, Yes ma'am,
His shirt and pants, Yes ma'am,

And if he's ready, Yes ma'am,
By half-past eight, Yes ma'am,
He can go to school, Yes ma'am,
And he won't be late, Yes ma'am.

The Little Pig

TEXAS

Moderately fast ♩ = 104

There was an old wom-an and she had a lit-tle pig, — Oink, oink, oink,

There was an old wom-an and she had a lit-tle pig,

It did-n't cost much and was-n't ver-y big, — Oink, oink, oink.

2. That little pig did a heap of harm,
   Oink, oink, oink,
   That little pig did a heap of harm
   A-rooting 'round the old man's farm,
   Oink, oink, oink.

3. The little pig died for want of breath, etc.
   Now wasn't that an awful death! etc.

4. The little old woman, she sobbed and she sighed, etc.
   Then she lay right down and died, etc.

5. The old man died for want of grief, etc.
   Wasn't that a great relief! etc.

6. There they lay all one two three, etc.
   The man and the woman and the little piggee, etc.

7. There they lay all on the shelf, etc.
   If you want any more you can sing it yourself, etc.

RHYTHMIC and DRAMATIC PLAY: The first two stanzas lend themselves to free rhythmic play. The singing of the entire song may call forth simple dramatic play. Or out of some child's action or word may grow—sometimes expanding or changing from day to day—an unexpected play sequence. This happened one morning when a "pig" lay down and "went to sleep."

2. Those little pigs curled up in a heap,
       Oink, oink, oink,
   Those little pigs curled up in a heap,
   They shut their eyes and went to sleep,
       Oink, oink, oink.

3. They slept and slept and slept and slept,
       Sh—sh—sh—
   They slept and slept and slept and slept
   And slept and slept and slept and slept—
       Sh—sh—sh—

4. The farmer woke them one by one
       Oink, oink, oink,
   The farmer woke them one by one
   And then they rolled out in the sun
       Oink, oink, oink.

5. They rolled and rolled and rolled and rolled, etc.
   The music of this stanza may be repeated ad lib—and then:

6. Those little pigs rolled back in their pen
       Oink, oink, oink,
   Those little pigs rolled back in their pen
   And then they went to sleep again
       Oink, oink, oink.

Bought Me a Cat

ARKANSAS

Fast ♩ = 108

1. Bought me a cat, the cat pleased me, Fed my cat un-der yon-ders tree,

Cat went fid-dle-i-fee, fid-dle-i-fee.

2. Bought me a hen, the hen pleased me, Fed my hen un-der yon-ders tree,

Hen went chip-sy chop-sy, Cat went fid-dle-i-fee, fid-dle-i-fee.

3. Bought me a duck, the duck pleased me, Fed my duck un-der yon-ders tree.

Duck went slish - y slosh-y.
Hen went chip - sy chop-sy, Cat went fid - dle - i - fee, fid - dle - i - fee.

4. Bought me a goose, the goose pleased me, Fed my goose un-der yon - ders tree.

Goose went qua, Duck went slish - y slosh-y.
Hen went chip - sy chop-sy, Cat went fid-dle-i- fee, fid-dle-i- fee.

105

5. Bought me a dog, the dog pleased me, Fed my dog un-der yon-ders tree.

Dog went boo,
Goose went qua,
Duck went slish-y slosh-y,
Hen went chip-sy chop-sy,
Cat went fid-dle-i-fee, fid-dle-i-fee.

6. Bought me a sheep, the sheep pleased me, Fed my sheep un-der yon-ders tree.

Sheep went baa,
Dog went boo,
Goose went qua,
Duck went slish-y slosh-y
Hen went chip-sy chop-sy, Cat went fid-dle-i-fee, fid-dle-i-fee.

7. Bought me a cow, the cow pleased me, Fed my cow un-der yon-ders tree,

Cow went moo,
Sheep went baa,
Dog went boo,
Goose went qua,
Duck went slish-y slosh-y
Hen went chip-sy chop-sy, Cat went fid-dle-i-fee, fid-dle-i-fee.

8. Bought me a horse, the horse pleased me, Fed my horse un-der yon-ders tree,

Horse went neigh,
Cow went moo,
Sheep went baa,
Dog went boo,
Goose went qua,
Duck went slish-y slosh-y,
Hen went chip-sy chop-sy, Cat went fid-dle-i-fee, fid-dle-i-fee.

Hop, Old Squirrel

Moderately fast ♩ = 112

VIRGINIA

Hop, old squirrel, ei-dle-dum, ei-dle-dum, Hop old squirrel, ei-dle-dum dum,

Hop, old squirrel, ei-dle-dum, ei-dle-dum, Hop, old squirrel, ei-dle-dum dee.

The following traditional words can form a basis of selection for various games. One group of children, many years ago in Virginia, were seen running from tree to tree singing some of them.

1. Hide, old squirrel, eidledum, eidledum, etc.
2. Hunt for the squirrel, etc.
3. Peep, little squirrel, etc.
4. Find the old squirrel, etc.
5. Run, old squirrel, etc.
6. Chase the old squirrel, etc.
7. Catch the old squirrel, etc.
8. Bring in the old squirrel, etc.

RHYTHMIC PLAY:

1. Hop, little bird, eidledum, eidledum, etc.
2. Hop (or leap) old frog, etc.
3. Hop on one foot, etc.

My Horses Ain't Hungry

TENNESSEE

INTRODUCTION (may be omitted)

(The horses are in the barn, eating hay)

etc. ad lib

Moderately fast ♩. = 60

My hors - es ain't hun - gry, They won't eat your hay,

So I'll get on my po - ny, I'm go - ing a - way.

INTERLUDE (faster, for rhythmic play)

Repeat ad lib

2. I know you're my Polly,
   I'm not going to stay,
   So come with me, darling,
   We'll feed on our way.

3. With all our belongings
   We'll ride till we come
   To a lonely little cabin,
   We'll call it our home.

RHYTHMIC and DRAMATIC PLAY: Various rhythmic, dramatic, and finger plays grow out of singing this much-loved song. One of the simplest involves the first stanza only: choosing a barn, quiet waiting for the song to begin, extended galloping when the music goes faster—and then, usually, returning to the barn for repetition of the game. Four- and five-year-olds sometimes like to go on to the second and third stanza, discover a cabin, and set up housekeeping.

IMPROVISATION: An adaptation based on Laura Pendleton MacCarteney's Little Gray Ponies *is liked by very small children:*

1. Little horses, little horses,
   Come out of your barn,
   The door is wide open,
   The sunshine is warm.

   Interlude (same music played faster ad lib, for galloping)—then:

2. Little horses, little horses,
   Come back to your barn,
   The door is wide open,
   Your blankets are warm.

Did You Go to the Barney?

Free

ARKANSAS

Did you go to the barn-ey? Yes ma'am.

Did you see my mu-lie? Yes ma'am.

Did you ride my mu-lie? Yes ma'am.

And how did he ride? *smooth*

REFRAIN (may be played over and over for rhythmic play)

He rocked just like a cra-dle, He rocked just like a cra-dle.

112

2. Did you go to the barney? Yes ma'am.
   Did you see my mulie? Yes ma'am.
   Did you feed my mulie? Yes ma'am.
   And what did you feed him?
   I fed him corn and fodder,
   I fed him corn and fodder.

3. Did you go to the millie? Yes ma'am.
   Did you get any flour? Yes ma'am.
   Did you bake any cakes? Yes ma'am.
   And why did you bake them?
   Oh, I'll marry next Thursday morning,
   Oh, I'll marry next Thursday morning.

IMPROVISATION and RHYTHMIC PLAY: Children ask to ride or feed other animals and things—ponies, elephants, bicycles, ice skates. They want to sing about going to the firehouse, to the store, to the zoo. The questions and answers make new stanzas.

Did you go to the firehouse? Yes ma'am.
Did you see my fire engine? Yes ma'am.
Did you ride my fire engine? Yes ma'am.
And how did it ride?

The rest of the music may be played over and over without singing, for free rhythmic play.

Did you go to the zoo? Yes ma'am.
Did you see my tiger? Yes ma'am.
Did you feed my tiger? No ma'am.
And why didn't you feed him?
He slept up on the shelf,
He slept up on the shelf.

TONE PLAY:

Adult: Did you go to the barney? . . .
Child: . . . . Yes ma'am.

Sometimes "No ma'am" is answered with a glint in the eye, and a whole group becomes imbued with the fun of saying it.

Have a Little Dog

TOLL-A-WINKER

TEXAS

Fast ♩=100

Have a lit-tle dog and his name is Don *(whistle_____)*

Have a lit-tle dog and his name is Don,

His legs go to feet and his bod-y goes to tongue,

Toll-a-wink-er, toll-a-wink-er, tum tol-ly-aye.

2. Have a little box about three feet square (*whistle*)
   Have a little box about three feet square,
   When I go to travel I put him in there,
   Toll-a-winker, toll-a-winker, tum tolly-aye.

3. When I go to travel I travel like an ox, (*whistle*) (*2 times*)
   And in my vest pocket I carry that box, etc.

4. Had a little hen and her color was fair, (*whistle*) (*2 times*)
   Sat her on a bomb and she hatched me a hare, etc.

5. The hare turned a horse about six feet high, (*whistle*) (*2 times*)
   If you want to beat this you'll have to tell a lie, etc.

OTHER STANZAS:

1. I had a little mule and his name was Jack.
   I rode him on his tail to save his back.

2. I had a little mule and his name was Jay,
   I pulled his tail to hear him bray.

3. I had a little mule who was quite slick,
   I pulled his tail to see him kick.

4. This little mule he kicked so high,
   I thought that I had touched the sky.

5. I had a little mule he was made of hay,
   First big wind come along and blowed him away.

Frog Went A-Courtin'

VIRGINIA

Moderately fast ♩ = 112

F ... **C7** ... **F**

Frog went a-court-in' and he did ride,___ M-hm,

Frog went a-court-in' and he did ride,___ M-hm, **C7**

F

Frog went a-court-in' and he did ride,___

B♭ ... **C7** ... **F**

Sword and pis-tol by his side,___ M-hm.

2. Rode right up to Miss Mouse's door, M-hm,
   Rode right up to Miss Mouse's door, M-hm,
   Rode right up to Miss Mouse's door,
   Gave three raps and a very loud roar, M-hm.

3. Said he, "Miss Mouse, are you within?" M-hm, etc.
   "Yes, kind sir, I sit and spin, M-hm."

4. He took Miss Mousie on his knee,
   Said, "Miss Mouse, will you marry me?"

5. "Without my Uncle Rat's consent,
   I wouldn't marry the President."

6. Uncle Rat he laughed and shook his fat sides,
   To think his niece would be a bride.

7. Uncle Rat went a-running down to town
   To buy his niece a wedding gown.

8. "Where shall the wedding supper be?"
   "Way down yonder in the hollow tree."

9. "What shall the wedding supper be?"
   "A fried mosquito and a black-eyed pea."

10. First to come in was a flying moth,
    She laid out the table cloth.

11. Next to come in a Juney bug,
    Carrying a water jug.

12. Next to come in was a bumberly bee,
    Set his fiddle on his knee.

13. Next to come in was a broken-backed flea,
    Danced a jig with the bumberly bee.

14. Next to come in was Missus Cow,
    Tried to dance but didn't know how.

15. Next to come in was a little black tick,
    Ate so much it made him sick.

16. Next to come in was Doctor Fly,
    Said Mister Tick would surely die.

17. Next to come in was a big black snake,
    Ate up all the wedding cake.

18. Next to come in was an old gray cat,
    She swallowed the mouse and ate up the rat.

19. Mister Frog went a-hopping over the brook,
    A lily-white duck came and swallowed him up.

20. Little piece of cornbread lying on the shelf,
    If you want any more you can sing it yourself.

Little Bird, Little Bird

Very fast ♩ = 112

SOUTH CAROLINA

Lit-tle bird, lit-tle bird, go through my win-dow,

Lit-tle bird, lit-tle bird, go through my win-dow,

Lit - tle bird, lit-tle bird, go through my win-dow, And buy mo-lass-es can-dy.

REFRAIN

Go through my win - dow, my su-gar lump, Go through my win - dow, my su-gar lump,

And buy mo-lass-es can-dy.

118

Blue bird, blue bird,
Fly through my window,
Blue bird, blue bird,
Fly through my window,
Blue bird, blue bird,
Fly through my window,
And buy molasses candy.

REFRAIN:

Fly through my window,
My little bird,
Fly through my window,
My little bird,
And buy molasses candy.

RHYTHMIC PLAY: This song lends itself to free rhythmic play as well as to simple game playing.

TWO GAMES:

Two children join hands and hold arms high to form an arch. The others pass beneath, one by one.

All the children except one form a circle with hands joined and arms arched to form windows. The remaining child goes in and out the windows.

Free Little Bird

Very fast ♩ = 144

light staccato throughout

I'm as free a lit-tle bird as I can be, I'm as

free a lit-tle bird as I can be,___ I'll___

build my nest in the sour ap - ple tree, Where those

bad boys will nev-er both-er me.

2. Oh, who will shoe your little foot,
   And who will glove your little hand,
   And who will kiss your sweet rosy cheeks
   When I'm gone to that far distant land?

3. Oh, it's mama will shoe my little foot,
   And it's papa will glove my little hand,
   And it's you shall kiss my sweet rosy cheeks
   When you come from that far distant land.

4. Take me home, little birdie, take me home,
   Take me home by the light of the moon,
   With the moon a-shining bright and the stars a-giving light
   Take me home to my mama, take me home.

120

Poor Old Crow

THE THREE RAVENS

Moderately slow ♩= 60   VIRGINIA

Three old crows sat on a tree, Just as black as crows could be.

Poor old crow, poor old crow, Just as black as a crow could be.

The old he-crow says to his mate: "What shall we do for meat to eat?"

Poor old crow, poor old crow, Just as black as a crow could be.

Ducks in the Millpond

Fast ♩=112   VIRGINIA

Ducks in the mill - pond, a - geese in the clo - ver, a -

Fell in the mill - pond, a - wet all o - ver.

REFRAIN

Lawd, Lawd, _____ gon-na get on a rink - tum,

Lawd, Lawd, _____ gon-na get on a rink - tum.

2. Ducks in the millpond, a-geese in the clover,
   Jumped in the bed, and the bed turned over.

   REFRAIN:

   Lawd, Lawd, gonna get on a rinktum,
   Lawd, Lawd, gonna get on a rinktum.

3. Monkey in the barnyard, a-monkey in the stable,
   Monkey get your hair cut as soon as you're able.
   Refrain:

4. Had a little pony, his name was Jack,
   I put him in the stable and he jumped through a crack.
   Refrain:

5. Ducks in the millpond, a-geese in the ocean,
   A-hug them pretty girls if I take a notion.
   Refrain:

Jim Crack Corn

BIG OLD OWL

Moderately fast ♩=112

VIRGINIA

Big old owl with eyes so bright, On man-y a dark and star-ry night,

I've of-ten heard my true love say, "Sing all night and sleep all day."

REFRAIN

Jim ___ crack corn, I don't care, Jim ___ crack corn, I don't care,

Jim ___ crack corn, I don't care, Old Mas-ter's gone a-way.

124

2. Said the blackbird to the crow:
   Down to the cornfield let us go;
   Pulling up corn has been our trade,
   Ever since Adam and Eve was made.
   Refrain:

3. Said the sheldrake to the crane:
   When do you think we'll have some rain?
   The farm's so muddy and the brook so dry,
   If it wasn't for the tadpoles, we'd all die.
   Refrain:

4. When I was a boy I used to wait
   On Master's table and pass the plate,
   Hand round the bottle when he got dry,
   And brush away the blue-tail fly.
   Refrain:

This version of the well-known minstrel song Jim Crack Corn *was notated from a phonograph recording of the singing of an old man, who states on the record that he in turn learned it from an aged banjo picker when he himself was a small boy.*

Eency Weency Spider

NORTH CAROLINA

Moderately fast ♩.= 104

Een - cy ween - cy spi - der went up the wa - ter spout,

Down came the rain_____ and washed the spi - der out,

Out came the sun_____ and dried up all the rain,

Now een - cy ween - cy spi - der went up the spout a - gain.

This is a favorite finger play.

Dog Tick

LOUISIANA

Dog tick, dog tick, dog tick, 'bac - co worm,

Why can't a dog tick dance ___ like a 'bac - co worm?

Dog tick, dog tick, dog tick, 'bac - co worm,

Why can't a dog tick dance ___ like a 'bac - co worm?

Who Built the Ark? Noah, Noah

Built it out of a hick-o-ry bark, — 2. He
Plenty of room for the large — and small, — 3. He
gan to cut and be-gan — to hew, — 4. And
No-ah shout and-a No - ah sing. — *D.C. al fine.*

5. Now in come the animals two by two,
   Hippopotamus and kangaroo,

6. Now in come the animals three by three,
   Two big cats and a bumble bee,

7. Now in come the animals four by four,
   Two through the window and two through the door,

8. Now in come the animals five by five,
   Four little sparrows and the redbird's wife,

9. Now in come the animals six by six,
   Elephant laughed at the monkey's tricks,

10. Now in come the animals seven by seven,
    Four from home and the rest from heaven,

11. Now in come the animals eight by eight,
    Some were on time and the others were late,

12. Now in come the animals nine by nine,
    Some was a-shouting and some was a-crying,

13. Now in come the animals ten by ten,
    Five black roosters and five black hens,

14. Now Noah says, go shut that door,
    The rain's started dropping and we can't take more.

Return to Refrain

Mary Wore Her Red Dress

TEXAS

Moderately fast ♩ = 112

Ma - ry wore her red dress, Red dress, red dress,

Ma - ry wore her red dress All day long.

2. Mary wore her red hat,
   Red hat, red hat,
   Mary wore her red hat
   All day long.

3. Mary wore her red shoes, etc.
4. Mary wore her red gloves, etc.
5. Mary made a red cake, etc.
6. Where'd you get your shoes from, etc.
7. Got them from the dry goods, etc.
8. Where'd you get your butter from, etc.
9. Got it from the grocery, etc.
10. Mary was a red bird, etc.

IMPROVISATION and NAME PLAY: When you ask children what piece of clothing they want to sing about, you get a wide assortment of answers. Even the most cumbersome can be fitted to the tune by the traditional practice of inserting extra beats for the extra syllables (see page 28).

Sing about my new dirty brown shoes.
Sing about my red-dress-with-green-and-yellow-flowers.
Sing about my very old overalls.
Sing about my knees.
Sing about my head.
Sing about my red-and-blue-and-black-and-white-striped socks.
Sing about the yellow-sweater-my-mommy-brought-me-from-
    New-York.

Out of daily incidents or a word or a motion arise other things to sing about. Brennan appears with a red ball or a fresh bandage on her finger, Philip has been dyeing Easter eggs yellow, Chris sees a caterpillar and starts crawling, Louis looks out the window and sees snow falling.

COLOR GAME: A color-guessing game is fun. It helps children to notice and to listen.

Who wore a pink dress,
Pink dress, pink dress,
Who wore a pink dress
All day long?

Elsa wore a pink dress,
Pink dress, pink dress,
Nancy wore a pink dress
All day long.

Pretty Little Girl with the Red Dress On

Moderately fast ♩ = 120

Poor old How-ard's dead and gone, Left me here to sing this song,
Who's been here since I been gone? Pretty little girl with the red dress on,

REFRAIN

Pret-ty lit-tle girl with the red dress on,

Pret-ty lit-tle girl with the red dress on,

Pret-ty lit-tle girl with the red dress on, who knows,

Pret - ty lit - tle girl with the red dress on.

This Lady She Wears a Dark Green Shawl

Moderately fast ♩ = *80*

GEORGIA

This la - dy she wears a dark green shawl, A dark green shawl, a dark green shawl,

This la - dy she wears a dark green shawl, I love her to my heart.

This too is a favorite name, color and clothing song. The remaining traditional stanzas are really singing-game directions:

2. Now choose you a partner, honey my love,
   Honey my love, honey my love,
   Now choose you a partner, honey my love,
   I love you to my heart.

3. Now dance with your partner, honey my love, etc.

4. Farewell to your partner, honey my love, etc.

Walk Along, John

Moderately fast ♩= 88

OKLAHOMA

Come on, boys, and hush your talk-ing,

All join hands and let's go walk-ing.

REFRAIN

Walk a-long, John, with your pa-per col-lar on,

Walk a-long, John, with your pa-per col-lar on.

IMPROVISATION and RHYTHMIC PLAY: One by one, a group of walkers may be drawn together.

Come on, Bill, and hush your talking,
Let's join hands and go a-walking,
Walk along, Bill, with your blue pants on,
Walk along, Bill, with your blue pants on.

If there are many children, the refrain may be repeated over and over with only an occasional return to the beginning.

Walk (or come) along, Judy, with one shoe on,
Walk along, Janet, with your hair falling down,
Walk along, Mike, with your dad's old hat,
                    and so on.

In one section of the country this song is said to have been sung as a corn shucking song, with the following refrain:

Shock along, John, shock along,
Shock along, John, shock along.

Do, Do, Pity My Case

Moderately fast ♩ = 88

LOUISIANA

Do, do, pi-ty my case, In some la-dy's gar - den,

My clothes to wash when I get home, In some la - dy's gar - den.

IMPROVISATION and DRAMATIC PLAY: Children have carried through in free rhythmic play the activities of an entire afternoon. The accompaniment may be adapted accordingly. Many of the activities—such as sewing or washing hands—become finger plays. Such stanzas as the following have been improvised; they change from day to day.

1. Do, do, pity my case,
   In some lady's garden,
   My hands to wash when I get home,
   In some lady's garden.

2. My cat to feed when I get home, etc.

3. To set the table when I get home, etc.

4. To have some cake when I get home, etc.

5. My nap to take when I get home, etc.

6. To see my dad when I get home, etc.

7. To dig my garden when I get home, etc.

8. To watch the robins when I get home, etc.

Hanging Out the Linen Clothes

2. 'Twas on a Tuesday morning, the first I saw my darling
   A-hanging out the linen clothes, a-hanging out the linen clothes

3. 'Twas on a Wednesday morning, the first I saw my darling
   A-taking in the linen clothes, a-taking in the linen clothes.

4. 'Twas on a Thursday morning, the first I saw my darling
   A-ironing of the linen clothes, a-ironing of the linen clothes.

5. 'Twas on a Friday morning, the first I saw my darling
   A-mending of the linen clothes, a-mending of the linen clothes.

6. 'Twas on a Saturday morning, the first I saw my darling
   A-folding of the linen clothes, a-folding of the linen clothes.

7. 'Twas on a Sunday morning, the first I saw my darling
   A-wearing of the linen clothes, a-wearing of the linen clothes.

Sometimes the last line of each stanza is sung over and over until the clothes are thoroughly "washed" or "ironed" or "mended."

137

Lula Gal

TIE MY SHOE

Moderately fast, accented ♩ = 96

Lu - la gal, Lu - la gal, Lu - la gal, Lu - la gal,

Tie my shoe, boy, tie my shoe, Tie my shoe, boy, tie my shoe.

REFRAIN—*faster (may be played over and over, without singing, for rhythmic play)*

Jaw-bone walk and a jaw-bone talk, Jaw-bone eat with a knife and fork,

Left my jaw-bone in the cor-ner of the fence, And I have not seen my jaw-bone since.

Old Aunt Kate

Moderately fast ♩=112

Old Aunt Kate she bake a cake, She bake it 'hind the gar - den gate,

She sift the meal, she gim-me the dust, She bake the bread, she gim-me the crust,

She eat the meat, she gim-me the skin, And that's the way she took me in.

What Did You Have for Your Supper?

JIMMY RANDALL, MY SON

Moderate ♩. = 60

NORTH CAROLINA

It's what did you have for your sup-per, ___ Jim-my Ran-dall, my son?

Oh, what did you have for your sup-per, ___ my ___ own lit-tle one?

Sweet milk and sweet par-snips, Mo-ther, make my bed soon,

For I'm tired at the heart and I want to lie down.

Baby Dear

SOUTH CAROLINA

Moderate ♩=80

Ba - by dear, ba - by dear, Don't you cry,

Fa - ther will come to you Bye and bye,

Mo - ther is bak - ing you Cakes to eat.

Inclusion of friends and relations can make this a song without end.

Johnny Get Your Hair Cut

HEY BETTY MARTIN

PENNSYLVANIA

INTERLUDE I (may be played or whistled)

*Return to the beginning or
continue to Interlude II*

INTERLUDE II

D.C. al fine

2. Johnny get your gun and your sword and your pistol,
   Johnny get your gun and come with me.

3. Hey Betty Martin, tiptoe, tiptoe,
   Hey Betty Martin, tiptoe fine.

143

I Got a Letter This Morning

SOUTH CAROLINA

Moderately fast ♩ = 88

I got a let-ter this morn - ing, oh, yes,

I got a let-ter this morn - ing, oh, yes.

IMPROVISATION: Many new stanzas grow out of singing this song with children. Some may be used as finger plays. Others suggest simple dramatic play.

1. I wrote a letter this morning, oh, yes,
   I wrote a letter this morning, oh, yes.

2. I mailed a letter this morning, etc.

3. Who brought a letter this morning? etc.

TONE PLAY:

Adult: I got a letter this morning . . .
Child: . . . . oh, yes.

Rose, Rose, and Up She Rises

KENTUCKY

Moderately fast ♩ = 100

Rose, Rose, and | up she ris - es, | Rose, Rose, and | up she ris - es,

Rose, Rose, and | up she ris - es So | ear - ly in the | morn - ing.

2. I wonder where Maria's gone,
I wonder where Maria's gone,
I wonder where Maria's gone,
So early in the morning.

IMPROVISATION: A waking-up song may grow out of stanza 1:

What shall we do with the sleepy Jackie? (3 times)
So early in the morning?

Wake him up and shake him up, (3 times)
So early in the morning.

Hoo-ray and up he rises, (3 times)
So early in the morning.
and so on.

An absence song may stem from stanza 2:

I wonder where Joanne has gone,
I wonder where has Arnold gone,
I wonder where Susanna's gone,
So early in the morning?

145

What'll We Do With the Baby?

KENTUCKY

Moderately fast ♩ = 84

What'll we do with the ba - by? What'll we do with the ba - by?

What 'll we do with the ba-by? Oh, we'll wrap it up in cal - i - co,

Wrap it up in cal - i - co And send it to its pap- py -o.

146

Hush, Little Baby

ALABAMA

Fast ♩ = 120

F   C7   F

Hush, lit-tle ba- by, don't say a word, Ma - ma's going to buy you a mock-ing bird.

2. If that mocking bird won't sing,
   Mama's going to buy you a diamond ring.

3. If that diamond ring turns brass,
   Mama's going to buy you a looking glass.

4. If that looking glass gets broke,
   Mama's going to buy you a billy goat.

5. If that billy goat won't pull,
   Mama's going to buy you a cart and bull.

6. If that cart and bull turn over,
   Mama's going to buy you a dog named Rover.

7. If that dog named Rover won't bark,
   Mama's going to buy you a horse and cart.

8. If that horse and cart fall down,
   You'll still be the prettiest girl in town.

TONE PLAY:

Adult: Mama's going to buy you a . . .
Child: . . . . mocking bird.

Pick a Bale of Cotton

Fast ♩=144

TEXAS

E min.

B

Stanza: Well me ____ and my part - ner Can pick a bale of cot - ton,
Refrain: Oh, pick a bale a - pick a bale A - pick a bale of cot - ton,

E min.

B

E min.

Well, me ____ and my part - ner Can pick a bale a day.
Oh, pick a bale a - pick a bale A - pick a bale a day.

2. I can jump-a down and turn around
   And pick a bale of cotton,
   I can jump-a down and turn around
   And pick a bale a day.
   REFRAIN:

3. I had a little girl
   Could pick a bale of cotton,
   I had a little girl
   Could pick a bale a day.
   Refrain:

4. I'm on my way to Texas
   To pick a bale of cotton
   I'm on my way to Texas
   To pick a bale a day.
   Refrain:

REFRAIN:

Oh, pick a bale a-pick a bale
A-pick a bale of cotton,
Oh, pick a bale a-pick a bale
A-pick a bale a day.

IMPROVISATION: Someone started singing one morning:

Well, me and my partner
Can put away our shovels,
Well, me and my partner
Can put them all away.

Oh, pick 'em up and pick 'em up
And pick 'em up together,
Oh, pick 'em up and pick 'em up
And put them all away.

This Old Hammer

2. Well don't you hear that
   Hammer ringing?
   Drivin' in steel, boys,
   Drivin' in steel.

3. Can't find a hammer
   On this old mountain.
   Rings like mine, boys,
   Rings like mine.

4. I've been working
   On this old mountain
   Seven long years, boys,
   Seven long years.

5. I'm going back to
   Swannanoa Town-o,
   That's my home, boys,
   That's my home.

6. Take this hammer,
   Give it to the captain,
   Tell him I'm gone, boys,
   Tell him I'm gone.

RHYTHMIC and DRAMATIC PLAY: This Old Hammer and the John Henry songs are favorites for hammering. They may also form part of a railroad song-and-story sequence (see page 21).

The Train Is A-Coming

Moderate ♩=60

The train is a-com-ing, oh, yes, Train is a-com-ing, oh, yes,

Train is a-com-ing, train is a-com-ing, Train is a-com-ing, oh, yes.

2. Better get your ticket, oh, yes,
   Better get your ticket, oh, yes,
   Better get your ticket, better get your ticket,
   Better get your ticket, oh, yes.

3. Room for a-many more, oh, yes.

4. Jesus is conductor, oh, yes.

5. Train is a-leaving, oh, yes.

6. I'm on my way to heaven, oh, yes.

*IMPROVISATION and RHYTHMIC PLAY: Children like to play
train. Sometimes they are cars—*

1. Steve is the engine, oh, yes, etc.
2. Joan is the coal car, oh, yes, etc.
   *(and so on, through all the
   kinds of cars that make up
   freight or passenger trains)*

—and sometimes they are trainmen—

3. Jock is the engineer, oh, yes, etc.
4. Pete is the brakeman, oh, yes, etc.
5. Barry is conductor, oh, yes, etc.
6. Patsy is a passenger, oh, yes, etc.

The train whistles before it starts:

(*Piano or children or both, on any one, two or three tones*)

And the engine eases the train out of the station, slow at first, then
faster—and on around the countryside—perhaps to the music of The
Little Black Train (*page 152*). Usually the train comes back safe and
whole to the station. Sometimes it cannot resist running away to a
wreck.

The Little Black Train

KENTUCKY

Very fast ♩ = 104–144

vamp | *ad lib*

staccato throughout

There's a lit-tle black train___ a - com - ing,

Get all your busi - ness right,___

There's a lit-tle black train___ a - com - ing,

And it may be here to - night.

Ending

2. Oh, the little black train is a-coming,
   It's coming 'round the bend,
   You can hear those wheels a-moving
   And rattling through the land.

3. Oh, the little black train is a-coming,
   It's coming 'round the curve,
   A-whistling and a-blowing
   And straining every nerve.

When the Train Comes Along

When the train comes a - long, When the train comes a - long,

I'm going to meet you at the sta-tion When the train comes a - long.

2. If my mother ask for me,
   Tell her death done summon me,
   I'm going to meet her at the station
   When the train comes along.

3. If my father ask for me, etc.

4. If my brother ask for me, etc.
   and so on.

When Jock's father left by plane for Mexico we sang about meet-ing him at the airport "when the plane comes along."

If my father ask for me
Tell him, look around for me,
I'm going to meet him at the airport
When the plane comes along.

John Henry

* *Beginning with stanza 3, omit this tone and substitute a quarter rest.*

When John Henry was about three days old,
A-sittin' on his pappy's knee,
He gave one loud and lonesome cry:
"The hammer'll be the death of me,
The hammer'll be the death of me."

Well, the captain said to John Henry one day:
"Gonna bring that steam drill 'round,
Gonna take that steam drill out on the job,
Gonna whop that steel on down,
Gonna whop that steel on down."

John Henry said to the captain:
"Well, the next time you go to town
Just bring me back a twelve-pound hammer
And I'll beat your steam drill down, etc."

John Henry said to the captain:
"Well, a man ain't nothin' but a man,
And before I let a steam drill beat me down
Gonna die with the hammer in my hand."

John Henry went to the tunnel,
And they put him in the lead to drive,
The rock so tall and John Henry so small,
He laid down his hammer and he cried.

John Henry said to his shaker:
"Shaker, why don't you sing?
For I'm swingin' twelve pounds from the hips
    on down,
Just listen to that cold steel ring."

John Henry told his captain:
"Look-a yonder what I see—
Your drill's done broke and your hole's done
    choke',
And you can't drive steel like me."

Well, the man that invented the steam drill,
He thought he was mighty fine,
But John Henry drove his fifteen feet,
And the steam drill only made nine.

John Henry looked up at the mountain,
And his hammer was striking fire,
Well, he hammered so hard that he broke his
    poor old heart,
He laid down his hammer and he died.

They took John Henry to the graveyard,
And they laid him in the sand,
Three men from the east and a woman from
    the west
Came to see that old steel-drivin' man.

They took John Henry to the graveyard,
And they laid him in the sand,
And every locomotive comes a-roarin' by
Says: "There lies a steel-drivin' man."

Every Monday Morning

MORE ABOUT JOHN HENRY

ARKANSAS

Moderately fast ♩=72

Well, ev' - ry___ Mon - day___ morn - ing,

When the blue-birds be - gin to sing, —

You can hear those ham - mers a mile or ___ more,

You can hear John Hen- ry's ham-mer ring, oh Lawd - y,

Hear John Hen- ry's ham-mer ring.

This tune and first stanza are different from that of most John Henry songs. The stanzas below have been culled from several traditional sources.

2. When John Henry was a little boy,
   He was on his way to school,
   Well, he looked at the teacher and this is what he said:
   "I want to learn how to hammer too, oh Lawdy,
   Want to learn how to hammer too."

3. John Henry had a little woman,
   And her name was Polly Ann,
   When John Henry was sick and a-lying in his bed,
   Polly drove steel like a man, oh Lawdy,
   Polly drove steel like a man.

4. John Henry had a little woman,
   Named Mary Magdalene,
   She would go to the tunnel and sing for John,
   Just to hear John Henry's hammer ring, oh Lawdy,
   Hear John Henry's hammer ring.

5. John Henry had a little woman,
   And the dress she wore was blue,
   Well, the very last words I heard her say:
   "John Henry, I've been true to you, oh Lawdy,
   John Henry I've been true to you."

6. John Henry told his little woman,
   "Will you fix my supper soon?
   Got ninety miles of track I've got to line,
   Got to line it by the light of the moon, oh Lawdy,
   Line it by the light of the moon."

7. John Henry had a little baby,
   Held him in the palm of his hand,
   Well, the last words I heard that poor boy say:
   "My dad is a steel-driving man, oh Lawdy,
   Daddy is a steel-driving man."

8. Some say John Henry come from England,
   And some say he's from Spain,
   But I say he's nothing but a Louisiana man,
   Just the leader of a steel-driving gang, oh Lawdy,
   Leader of a steel-driving gang.

Going Down to Town

LYNCHBURG TOWN

Moderately fast ♩=120

KENTUCKY

Refrain: I'm go-ing down to town, I'm go-ing down to town, I'm
Stanza: Times a-get-ting hard, Mon-ey get-ting scarce,

go-ing down to the Lynch-burg town To take my to-bac-co down.
Pay me for them to-bac-co, boys, And I will leave this place. D.C.

2. Master had an old gray horse,
   Took him down to town,
   Sold him for a half a dollar
   And only a quarter down.
   Refrain:

3. Old Eli was a rich old man,
   He was richer than a king,
   He made me beat the old tin pan
   While Sary Jane would sing.
   Refrain:

4. Old Eli brought a little girl,
   He fetched her from the South,
   Her hair was wrapped so very tight
   That she couldn't shut her mouth.
   Refrain:

REFRAIN:

I'm going down to town,
I'm going down to town,
I'm going down to the Lynchburg town
To take my tobacco down.

5. Once I had an old black hen,
   She laid behind the door,
   Every day she laid three eggs,
   And Sunday she laid more.
   Refrain:

6. Oh, I went down to town,
   And went into the store,
   And every pretty girl in town
   Came running to the door.
   Refrain:

DRAMATIC PLAY: Children often draw on the tobacco story for dramatic play. Sometimes they use the refrain as a shopping song—going down to town, play-shopping from store to store, then returning to tell or sing about each thing they have bought.

1. I'm going down to town,
   I'm going down to town,
   I'm going down to Silver Spring
   To get my shopping done.

The music may be played ad lib until someone is ready to sing about coming home again.

2. I'm coming home from town, etc.
   I've got my shopping done.

Sailing in the Boat

Moderately fast ♩=80

Sail - ing in the boat when the tide runs high,

Sail - ing in the boat when the tide runs high,

Sail - ing in the boat when the tide runs high,

Wait - ing for the pret - ty girls to come by'm bye.

Here she comes so fresh and fair,
Sky-blue eyes and curly hair,
Rosy in cheek, dimple in her chin,
Say, young man, but you can't come in.

RHYTHMIC PLAY: Children find different ways of sailing in the boat. One boy was careful to moor himself to the dock when he got back. Several others thought of returning with cargoes. Others arched their arms to make drawbridges.

Blow, Boys, Blow

Moderate ♩=72

A yan-kee ship came down the riv-er, Blow, boys, blow,

Her masts and spars they shone like sil-ver, Blow, my bul-ly boys, blow.

2. Who do you think is the captain of her?
Blow, boys, blow;
Why, Bully Hayes is the captain of her,
Blow, my bully boys, blow.

3. And what do you think they've got for dinner? etc.
Pickled eel's feet and bullock's liver, etc.

4. And how do you know she's a Yankee liner? etc.
The Stars and Stripes float out behind her, etc.

Fire Down Below

Moderate ♩=120

There's fire in the low - er deck, Fire down be - low,

Fire in the main - well, The cap - tain did - n't know.

CHORUS

Fire! Fire! Fire down be - low,

It's fetch a buck-et of wa - ter, girls, There's fire down be - low.

2. There's fire up aloft,
   There's fire down below,
   Fire in the galley,
   The cook didn't know.
   Chorus:

3. There's fire in the forepeak,
   Fire down below,
   Fire in the chain-plates,
   The bo'sun didn't know.
   Chorus:

Penelope likes, too, to sing of fire in other places besides ships—in the fireplace, the kitchen stove, the toaster, a cigarette.

Sally Go Round the Sunshine

Moderately fast ♩=120

Sal - ly go round the sun, Sal - ly go round the moon,

Sal - ly go round the sun - shine Ev' - ry af - ter - noon, Boom Boom!

Children join hands, form a circle. The circle may move to the left (the sun), to the right (the moon), to the left again (the sunshine) and fall down at "Boom Boom."

164

This Old Man

NEW YORK

Moderately fast ♩=100

This old man, he played one, He played knick knack on his thumb, Knick knack pad-dy whack, give your dog a bone, This old man came roll-ing home.

2. This old man, he played two,
   He played knick knack on his shoe,
   Knick knack, paddy whack, give your dog a bone,
   This old man came rolling home.

3. This old man, he played three,
   He played knick knack on his knee.

4. This old man, he played four,
   He played knick knack on the floor.

5. This old man, he played five,
   He played knick knack on his hives.

6. This old man, he played six,
   He played knick knack on his sticks.

7. This old man, he played seven,
   He played knick knack up to heaven.

8. This old man, he played eight,
   He played knick knack on his pate.

9. This old man, he played nine,
   He played knick knack on his spine.

10. This old man, he played ten,
    He played knick knack now and then.

Skip-a to My Lou

SHOO-LI-LOO

TENNESSEE

Lit-tle red wag-on, paint-ed blue, Lit-tle red wag-on paint-ed blue,

Lit-tle red wag-on paint-ed blue, Skip-a to my lou, my darl - ing.

REFRAIN

Lou, lou, skip-a to my lou, Lou, lou, skip-a to my lou,

Lou, lou, skip-a to my lou, Skip-a to my lou, my darl - ing.

WAGONS

2. Pull her up and down in the little red wagon,
   Pull her up and down in the little red wagon,
   Pull her up and down in the little red wagon,
   Skip-a to my lou, my darling.
   Refrain:

3. Teeter up and down in the little red wagon, etc.

ANIMALS

4. Pig in the parlor, what'll I do? etc.
5. Cat in the buttermilk, lapping up cream, etc.
6. Rats in the bread tray, how they chew, etc.
7. Chickens in the garden, shoo shoo shoo, etc.
8. Rabbit in the cornfield, big as a mule, etc.
9. Cow in the kitchen, moo cow moo, etc.
10. Hogs in the potato patch, rooting up corn, etc.

GOING TO MARKET

11. Going to market two by two, etc.
12. Dad's old hat and Mama's old shoe, etc.
13. Back from market, what did you do? etc.
14. Had a glass of buttermilk, one and two, etc.

SKIPPING AND CATCHING

15. Skip skip, skip-a to my lou, etc.
16. Skip a little faster, that won't do, etc.
17. Going to Texas, come along too, etc.
18. Lost my partner, what'll I do? etc.
19. I'll get another one prettier than you, etc.
20. Catch that red bird, skip-a to my lou, etc.
21. If you can't get a red bird, take a blue, etc.
22. If you can't get a blue bird, black bird'll do, etc.

REFRAIN:

Lou, lou, skip-a to my lou,
Lou, lou, skip-a to my lou,
Lou, lou, skip-a to my lou,
Skip-a to my lou, my darling.

IMPROVISATION: This song has hundreds of stanzas and is always picking up new ones. One collector alone gives 150, from which the above 22 were selected as encouragement to further improvisation. The phrase "skip-a to my lou" has numerous variants, such as skip to ma lou, skip to my lula, skip come a lou, shoo li loo, shoo la lay.

GAME: "Skip-a to My Lou" can be played in many ways. The following is one of the simplest: The children form a circle with a child in the center. They clap and sing while he skips around. At the refrain "Lou lou," he chooses a child from the circle to skip with him. At the end of the refrain the first child returns to the circle and the second child repeats the game pattern while a new stanza is sung.

Still simpler game patterns can be used.

When I Was a Young Maid

HA HA, THIS-A-WAY

KENTUCKY

Moderately fast ♩ = 112

When I was a young maid, young maid, When I was a young maid, then, oh, then, It was

ha ha, this-a-way, ha ha, that-a-way, This-a-way, that-a-way, then.

Children's choice of occupation shows wide range—they are carpenters, shoemakers, bricklayers, hairdressers, taxi drivers, firemen, animals, insects. Sometimes they form a circle, with center player changing from stanza to stanza and initiating in pantomime his choice of activity for the circle to imitate. The song is, however, especially liked when acted out simply, in free unpatterned play.

168

The Closet Key

Moderate ♩=88

I've lost the clos-et key In that la-dy's gar - den,

I've lost the clos-et key In that la-dy's gar - den.

2. Help me to find the closet key,
   In that lady's garden,
   Help me to find the closet key,
   In that lady's garden.

3. I've found the closet key
   In that lady's garden,
   I've found the closet key
   In that lady's garden.

Very small children use this easily chanted song for informal hiding-and-finding play. Older children may like to play it as indicated in the folklore collection in which it was found:

The children form a ring, as in "dropping the handkerchief," but with hands behind them. One child with a key walks around the ring and places the key in someone's hands. The walker leads the singing of stanzas 1 and 2 (with all children joining in). The child to whom the key was given then leads the singing of stanza 3 (with all children joining in). He then proceeds to walk around the ring himself, singing stanza 1, and the whole process is repeated.

Built My Lady a Fine Brick House

Moderately fast ♩=108

TEXAS

Built my la-dy a fine brick house, Built it in a gar-den, I

put her in but she jumped out, So fare ye well, my darl-ing.

REFRAIN (*may be omitted*)

Oh, swing a la-dy ump - tum, swing a la-dy round,

Swing a la-dy ump - tum and prom-e-nade a-round.

RHYTHMIC PLAY: In one room there was a low bench under a long row of windows. Children stood on it to look outdoors. They liked to sing this song while they jumped off (or were jumped) one by one. If there were many children, we sang the jumping phrase over and over without finishing the song—until the last child was off the bench—

I put him in but he jumped out,
I put her in but she jumped out,
and so on.

Someone always climbed up again to try for a second turn.

GAMES: Any number of simple game patterns may be improvised. One group of children joined hands in a ring and all jumped in toward the center, then back out again. Another group formed a ring around a center child, who listened for the words "but she jumped out" and jumped out of the ring. At another time the center child jumped "out" in front of some child in the ring, who then took her place in the center for a repetition of the game.

171

Where Oh Where Is Pretty Little Susie?

PAWPAW PATCH

Moderately fast ♩=120

light staccato throughout

1. Where oh where is pret-ty lit-tle Su-sie? Where oh where is pret-ty lit-tle Su-sie?
2. Come on, boys, let's go find her, etc.

Where oh where is pret-ty lit-tle Su-sie? Way down yon-der in the paw-paw patch.

2. Come on, boys, let's go find her,
   Come on, boys, let's go find her,
   Come on, boys, let's go find her,
   'Way down yonder in the pawpaw patch.

GAME: Even two-year-olds like to make a hiding game of stanzas 1 and 2. One child hides during stanza 1 while the others cover their eyes. At "Come on, boys," the group runs to find him. Sometimes an improvised third stanza brings everyone back again.

3. Come on, boys, bring her back again (3 times),
   Way down yonder in the pawpaw patch.

Jingle at the Windows

TIDEO

TEXAS

Moderately fast ♩ = *120*

Skip one win-dow, Ti - de - o, Skip two win - dows, Ti - de - o,

Skip three win - dows, Ti - de - o, Jing-le at the win - dows, Ti - de - o.

Jing-ling jing - ling jing-ling Jo, Jing-le at the win - dows, Ti - de - o.

At Christmas time this old play-party song becomes a companion to the favorite Jingle Bells. *Various game patterns may be improvised if desired, but free rhythmic play—with or without bells on ankles or wrists—is perhaps most loved.*

173

Adam Had Seven Sons

MISSISSIPPI

Moderately fast ♩=120

Ad - am had sev - en sons, Sev - en sons had Ad - am,

And they all were bright and gay, And they did what Ad - am say,

"Let's all do this, Let's all do this," says Ad - am.

In Mississippi the game is played as a circle game, with Adam in the center. At "Let's all do this," Adam makes any sort of motion he wishes, and the circle imitates him.

174

Here Sits a Monkey

MISSISSIPPI

Moderate ♩ = 120

Oh, here sits a mon-key in the chair, chair, chair, She
lost all the true loves she had last year, So
rise up-on your feet and greet the first you meet, the
pret-ti-est girl I know

GAME: *The children form a circle around a center child, who sits in a chair or on the floor. They march or skip around her, singing. At the proper time she rises and chooses someone from the circle to take her place in the chair, and the game is repeated. Each new center child may be a different animal or thing—giraffe, zebra, snake, worm. One child wanted to be a piano. It is easier to remember to rise and choose if the circle stops marching at "So rise upon your feet" and starts clapping while continuing to sing.*

Go to Sleepy

SOUTH CAROLINA

Moderate ♩.= 88

1. Go to sleep - y, ba - by, bye, ____
2. Bye - o ba - by, bye, ____

Go to sleep - y, ba - by, bye, ____
Bye - o ba - by, bye, ____

Ma - ma's gone to the mail - boat, Ma - ma's gone to the mail - boat,
Fa - ther's gone to the mail boat, Fa - ther's gone to the mail - boat,

Ending

Bye. ____
Bye. ____

Monday Morning Go to School

THE TWO BROTHERS

NORTH CAROLINA

Moderate ♩ = 76

Mon-day morn-ing go to school. Fri-day eve-ning home,

Bro-ther, comb my sweet-heart's hair As we go march-ing home.

Brother, will you play me a game of ball?
Brother, will you toss a stone?
Brother, will you play another game
As we go marching home?

177

Hush 'n' Bye

ALL THE PRETTY LITTLE PONIES

Moderate $\quad \downarrow = 60$

SOUTH CAROLINA

Hush 'n' bye, don't you cry Oh, you pret-ty lit-tle ba - by,

When you wake you'll have sweet cake, And all the pret-ty lit-tle pon - ies, A

brown and a gray and a black and a bay, And all the pret-ty lit-tle pon-ies.

When we sang a song from Alabama about "all the pretty little ponies," Virginia Vose's mother remembered a similar song which her nurse had sung to her when she was a child in South Carolina. She sang us her version, and we all liked it so much that we learned it. It became a favorite.

Turtle Dove

Poor lit-tle tur-tle dove, sit-ting in a pine,

Mourn-ing for its own true love, and why not me for mine, for mine, And why not me for mine?

2. Hogs in the pen, and corn to feed them on,
   All I want is a pretty little girl to feed them when I'm gone, oh gone,
   To feed them when I'm gone.

3. I went up on the mountain to give my horn a blow,
   And every girl in the valley said, "Yonder comes my beau, oh beau,
   Oh, yonder comes my beau."

4. I'm not going to marry in the fall, I'm going to marry in the spring,
   I'm going to marry a pretty little girl that wears a silver ring, oh
        ring,
   That wears a silver ring.

Mary Had a Baby

Moderately slow ♩=60

SOUTH CAROLINA

Ma-ry had a ba-by, Aye, Lord,

Ma-ry had a ba-by, Aye, my Lord, Ma-ry had a ba-by, Aye, Lord, The

peo-ple keep a-com-ing and the train done gone.

2. What did she name him? Aye, Lord.
   What did she name him? Aye, my Lord.
   What did she name him? Aye, Lord.
   The people keep a-coming and the train done gone.
3. Named him Jesus, etc.
4. Where was he born?, etc.
5. Born in a stable, etc.
6. Where did they lay him?, etc.
7. Laid him in a manger, etc.

A group of older children carried the song on and on through all the details they knew, from the shepherds and the star to the flight into Egypt.

Jesus Borned in Bethlea

VIRGINIA

Moderate ♩=60

Je - sus borned in Beth - lea, Je - sus borned in Beth - lea,

Je - sus borned in Beth - lea, and in the man - ger lay, And

in the man - ger lay, and in the man - ger lay,

Je - sus borned in Beth - lea, and in the man - ger lay.

Children have improvised with ease many new stanzas out of their knowledge of the Christmas story. Only two unrhymed lines are needed.

The Cherry Tree Carol

Moderate ♩ = 120

KENTUCKY
(composite of two versions)

As Ma-ry and Jo-seph were a-walk-ing the green,

There were ap-ples and cher-ries a-plen-ty to be seen,

There were ap-ples and cher-ries a-plen-ty to be seen. 2. Then me.

2. Then Mary spoke to Joseph,
    So meek and so mild,
    "Joseph, gather me some cherries
    For me and my child.
    Joseph, gather me some cherries
    For me and my child."

3. Lord Jesus spoke a few words
   All down unto them:
   "Bow down, you lofty cherry tree,
   Let my mammy gather some."

4. The cherry tree bowed low down,
   Low down to the ground,
   And Mary gathered cherries
   While Joseph stood around.

5. Then Joseph took Mary
   All on his right knee:
   "Pray tell me, little baby,
   When your birthday will be?"

6. "On old Christmas morning
   My birthday shall be
   When the hills and high mountains
   Shall bow unto me."

Classified Indices

186

RHYTHMIC INDEX

Other Indices

Many songs can be used as tone plays and finger plays. The following are good examples.

Index of Song Titles and First Lines

Page numbers of the songs are indicated in **bold figures.**

THE VERDICT IS IN:

EATING ATKINS-STYLE IS THE WAY TO GO FOR GOOD HEALTH AND PERMANENT WEIGHT CONTROL!

"In a head-to-head comparison . . . the Atkins diet trimmed significantly more pounds and body fat in obese but otherwise healthy women than a traditional low-fat diet, according to a report released last week at the annual meeting of The American Dietetics Association."

—*The Washington Post*

"Low-carb principles have been embraced with new fervor."
—*The New York Times*

"Well-organized book . . . Packed with recipes and daily menus with varying amounts of carbohydrates."
—*USA Today*

"This guide is a comprehensive overview for dieters who are ready to embrace the Atkins philosophy."
—*Publishers Weekly*

"Should knock all other diet books off the charts."
—*Newark Star-Ledger*

ATKINS LIFE
FOR

The Complete Controlled Carb Program for
Permanent Weight Loss and Good Health

ROBERT C. ATKINS, M.D.

St. Martin's Paperbacks

To my loving and lovely wife, Veronica, who has unfailingly provided me with emotional, intellectual, spiritual, and controlled carbohydrate nourishment

The information presented in this work is in no way intended as medical advice or as a substitute for medical counseling. The information should be used in conjunction with the guidance and care of your physician. Consult your physician before beginning this program as you would any weight-loss or weight-maintenance program. Your physician should be aware of all medical conditions that you may have as well as the medications and supplements you are taking. Those of you on diuretics or diabetes medication should proceed only under a doctor's supervision. As with any plan, the weight-loss phases of this nutritional plan should not be used by patients on dialysis or by pregnant or nursing women.

ATKINS FOR LIFE

Copyright © 2003, 2004 by Robert C. Atkins, M.D.

ISBN: 0-312-99007-3
EAN: 80312-99007-7

Printed in the United States of America

St. Martin's Press hardcover edition published 2003
St. Martin's Griffin edition / May 2004
St. Martin's Paperbacks edition / January 2005

St. Martin's Paperbacks are published by St. Martin's Press, 175 Fifth Avenue, New York, NY 10010.

10 9 8 7 6 5 4 3 2 1

Contents

Acknowledgments

I'm proud to say that writing this book was a team effort, led by Michael Bernstein, senior vice president of Atkins Health & Medical Information Services at Atkins Nutritionals, Inc. Olivia Bell Buehl, the company's editorial director, collaborated with me on several chapters and supervised the entire project from beginning to end. Without her contributions this book would not have seen the light of day.

Nutritionist Colette Heimowitz, M.S., director of education and research at Atkins Health & Medical Information Services, and Jacqueline Eberstein, R.N., director of medical education of The Atkins Center for Complementary Medicine, pored over every word to ensure the accuracy of the nutritional information. Nutritionists Valerie Berkowitz, M.S., R.D., C.D.E., and Eva Katz, M.P.H., R.D., reviewed scientific studies to make sure our references are in tip-top shape. Food scientist and vice president for product development at Atkins Nutritionals Matt Spolar patiently clarified the intricacies of food science.

Freelance writers Sheila Buff and Lynn Prowitt-Smith contributed their literary talents to collaborate on portions of the copy. Atkins staffer Rebecca Freedman searched far and wide to find an interesting array of Atkins followers who wanted to share their stories and worked with writers Catherine Censor, Janet Blake, and Mary Selover to craft the case studies.

Two of my physician peers were enormously helpful in reviewing the manuscript. Eric Freedland, M.D., made numerous insightful comments and additions. Stuart Lawrence Trager, M.D., orthopedic surgeon and triathlete, reviewed the fitness sections and offered valuable suggestions.

Heartfelt thanks to Kathy Maguire, who was always there to sweet-temperedly do whatever needed to be done. A special thanks goes to Paul D. Wolff, the chief executive officer of our company, and Scott Kabak, the chief operating officer, for assembling this great team.

Key to this book are the mouthwatering low carbohydrate recipes and ingenious meal plans that will demonstrate once and for all that eating the Atkins way—for life—is wonderfully varied and flexible. Atkins Nutritionals food editor Stephanie Grozdea spearheaded the recipe and meal plan portion of the book, assisted by recipe developers Cynthia DePersio and Wendy Kalen. Grady Best served as our recipe tester. Food writer Martha Schueneman, C.C.P., was also a valuable contributor.

Finally, this project would not have occurred had it not been for the superb efforts of senior editor Heather Jackson and her team at St. Martin's.

Introduction

It's a Lifestyle . . .

You probably bought this book either because you want to slim down or you want to stay slim forever. Both are admirable goals, and I trust that *Atkins for Life* will help you achieve them. Atkins and successful weight loss are virtually interchangeable. Millions of people—perhaps you are one of them—have experienced just how effective doing Atkins can be.

But millions more have not yet gotten the message. The most recent figures released in October 2002 by the *Journal of the American Medical Association* reveal that the number of Americans who are overweight has jumped from 55.9 percent in 1994 to 64.5 percent in 2002. Of those, 30.5 percent are now considered obese (defined as 30 percent or more above a healthy weight), compared to 22.9 percent just eight years earlier. According to the Surgeon General, each year an estimated 300,000 deaths in the United States are associated with obesity. Despite this crisis of obesity—and although it may sound surprising coming from me—to focus *only* on weight is to miss the proverbial forest for the trees.

There is another vitally important reason to read this book and follow its advice. Although I am often regarded as a "diet doctor," in reality, over the last thirty-five years I have specialized in complementary medicine, which requires me to handle a full spectrum of health conditions. It also allows me to use all the healing arts and not only drugs but also natural treatments. At The Atkins Center for Complementary Medicine in New York City, we saw patients with unstable blood sugar, diabetes, syndrome X, cardiovascular disease, high blood pressure, arthritis, hormonal imbalances, and osteoporosis, among other conditions. I have always been

struck by how many of these health issues come from or are
exacerbated by excessive insulin production, which is likely
the result of excessive carbohydrate intake.

According to the Centers for Disease Control, the diagno-
sis of diabetes among American adults increased by a stag-
gering 49 percent between 1990 and 2000. The number of
adults diagnosed in the United States increased by 61 percent
since 1991. About one-third of persons with diabetes are
unaware they have the disease and 41 million Americans are
prediabetic, meaning the severity of the epidemic is even
greater. Moreover, according to a panel of doctors represent-
ing several mainstream medicine groups, one-third of Americans are insulin resistant. Also known as syndrome X, this
condition means a person is incapable of managing his or her
insulin balance, increasing the risk of diabetes, heart disease,
high blood pressure, polycystic ovary syndrome, and perhaps
some cancers, including colon and ovarian cancer.

With all this worrisome data in mind, it is crystal clear
that people need to understand that what they eat has implications beyond pounds and inches. Once you understand
that consuming excess carbohydrates elevates insulin levels
and, conversely, restricting carbohydrates induces weight
loss, you will realize that our approach to weight control is
not just about looking slim—it is perhaps the most significant tool you have to influence your overall health and
enhance your chances for a long and vigorous life. If you
recognize yourself in one or more of these descriptions, this
book is written for you:

- You've lost weight following Atkins and want to maintain
  that loss.

- You've lost weight by doing Atkins but see that it is
  beginning to creep back on.

- You want to stop yo-yo dieting once and for all.

- You want to forestall a future weight problem.

- You want to instill in your family eating habits that will forestall health and weight problems.

- You are questioning the healthfulness of the typical American diet.

- You have a genetic predisposition to weight gain, blood sugar imbalances, or cardiovascular problems.

- You are often hungry again not long after you eat and may also have dips in energy, trouble concentrating, or feel irritable, light-headed, or unable to concentrate when you are hungry—all symptoms of a blood sugar disorder.

- You are a woman with polycystic ovary syndrome.

- You have Type 2 diabetes or are prediabetic.

Let me emphasize that this book is not primarily about *losing* weight. It is about *maintaining* a healthy weight. (If you have more than a few pounds to lose, I suggest that you first read *Dr. Atkins' New Diet Revolution*, which focuses on my four-phase weight-loss program.) Compared to maintaining, losing weight is relatively easy. Unfortunately, most people see it as a short-term effort. But if you are unwilling to accept that you will have to make permanent changes in how you eat, weight loss is rarely permanent. When I see patients, I say, "If you are here only for the purpose of losing weight, then both of us will wind up unhappy. Your real objective should be maintaining the weight you lose and maintaining a level of health far beyond that with which you started." Lab tests showing their changed blood sugar, cholesterol, and triglyceride levels will be tangible evidence of that improvement. But equally important is quality of life. Fortunately, when you do Atkins for life, you do not have to eat tiny portions, count calories, or deprive yourself of tasty, fulfilling food.

Instead, *Atkins for Life* will help you incorporate healthy carbohydrates along with protein and fat into a nutrient-rich, varied, and delectable way of eating for a lifetime. You will learn how to distinguish between "good" and "bad" carbs so that you can select those foods that are lower in carbs and have a more moderate impact on your blood sugar, allowing you to cruise along at a steady, energetic pace instead of sending you into blood sugar overdrive.

Although we will spend a lot of time talking about good nutrition, *Atkins for Life* does not offer a dreary list of dietary "shoulds" and "should nots." Instead, it is a manual for success: success in meeting and maintaining your goals concerning your health and the health of your loved ones, success in taking charge of your life, and, yes, success in attaining the body you've always dreamed of. And although we will not specifically discuss fulfillment in relationships, business, athletic prowess, and other important markers of happiness, I'll wager that you'll find that the sense of accomplishment that you experience by taking control of your health—and therefore your future—spills over into every aspect of your life.

Doing Atkins allows you enormous variety in the kinds of foods you can eat. With the exception of added sugars, bleached white flour, other refined carbs, junk food snacks, and hydrogenated or partially hydrogenated oils, you can eat most everything else in moderation *if your individual metabolism permits*. Whether you're interested in losing a few pounds or maintaining your present weight, we'll help you identify your ACE™ (Atkins Carbohydrate Equilibrium™), the number of grams of Net Carbs you can eat, all other things being equal, while neither gaining nor losing weight. Then we'll help you further individualize your program. Perhaps you're happier and less hungry eating five or six small meals instead of three larger ones. Or perhaps you are willing to step up your exercise regimen. You'll learn how you can make such choices and still keep your weight under control. It is this individualization and variety that makes it easy and enjoyable to do Atkins for life.

In addition to a host of strategies for success and the

words of people who've adopted the Atkins lifestyle, you'll find an extensive meal planning section with 125 recipes and 200 meal plans at various levels of carbohydrate intake. The recipes look delicious when you read them, but sampling them will convince you once and for all that controlling carbs need not compromise great taste. Also included are self-tests to keep you on the straight and narrow and numerous lists and tips to make doing Atkins—for life—pleasurable and easier than ever. Finally, we'll help you learn how to make doing Atkins second nature.

Backed by Research

I would like to make a few comments about scientific research, because I feel very strongly that there is important information you need to bear in mind as you read this book. Critics of Atkins like to say that there is no scientific research to support my nutritional philosophy. How wrong they are!

The first published documentation of the success of a controlled carbohydrate dietary regimen appeared in the 1800s, but we needn't go back that far. It was after reading a scientific study on the effectiveness of several low carbohydrate weight-loss programs in the October 1963 issue of the *Journal of the American Medical Association* that I decided to put a similar approach into practice.

We now have, on our Web site at www.atkins.com, summaries of close to eight hundred scientific studies that support the principles upon which the controlled carbohydrate nutritional approach is based. Included in this database are several pivotal studies published and/or publicly presented in the past two years that provide convincing evidence that controlling carbohydrate intake is more effective for weight loss and weight maintenance than low-fat approaches. Perhaps even more important is the fact that these studies also show that many of the participants saw improvements in both their cholesterol and triglyceride profiles.

Respected scientists at Harvard, Stanford, the University of Pennsylvania, Duke, the University of Cincinnati, Tufts, the University of Connecticut, Washington University, the University of Colorado, the Philadelphia Veterans Administration Hospital, and other institutions have acknowledged that the controlled carbohydrate approach to weight control and healthy living is a subject that—based on the very positive results of recent studies—bears further study. I have no doubt that long-term clinical studies will yield results similar to those of recently completed studies. Meanwhile, the assumption put forth by the low-fat philosophy that a calorie is a calorie is a calorie is firmly grounded in scientific research has been dealt a serious blow. After hundreds of millions of dollars of marketing to support the low-fat approach and years of information dissemination, including the Food Guide Pyramid, it is clear that low-fat programs have *not* proved to help most Americans enjoy an optimal weight and improved health.

I am very proud to tell people that my medical practice is my primary life commitment and the nutritional information we provide is based upon sound, published scientific research backed up by my own decades of clinical experience. I am equally proud to say that in 1999 my wife, Veronica, and I established the private, nonprofit Dr. Robert C. Atkins Foundation. The foundation is dedicated to improving the way medicine is practiced in the United States by scientifically validating the safety and efficacy of complementary and alternative medicine approaches. As of this writing we have provided more than three million dollars of funding to the foundation and have made grants to support more than ten independent scientific studies. This funding complements grants for controlled carbohydrate research provided by academic institutions themselves, by organizations such as the American Heart Association, and by the National Institutes of Health.

I have absolutely no doubt that the Atkins Nutritional Approach™ should be the treatment of choice for weight management, good health, and disease prevention for the vast majority of people. I will go out on a limb to state that we are now about to witness a sea change in what is considered a healthful way to eat. With more and more studies comparing low carbohydrate to low-fat dietary approaches under way, I predict that we'll increasingly see recommendations to reduce the intake of added sugars, bleached white flour, and other refined carbohydrates. I also predict that the phobia about all fats will be replaced by an understanding that many fats are good for you. I'll even go so far as to say that the Food Guide Pyramid will undergo a serious remodeling. I welcome the day when a *truly* balanced diet becomes the norm.

In the chapters that follow, as well as in this introduction, I've made some bold statements and they are at the heart of the title *Atkins for Life*. I mean the word *life* in the broadest sense: your physical life—your health and your life span—as well as a life full of gratification and meaning, making every day an adventure and a joy.

—Robert C. Atkins, M.D.

Foreword

A Lifestyle Approach

Dr. Atkins worked tirelessly to help others understand how to implement his teachings in their lives. While he loved working one on one with individual patients, his vision was vastly larger: He wanted to change the way the world eats to promote good health. And so he has. Today estimates of the number of Americans who claim to be watching their carbohydrate intake is anywhere from 30 million to more than 50 million. Dr. Atkins' legacy also lives on not only in the more than a dozen books he has authored, and in the research the Dr. Robert C. Atkins Foundation continues to support, but also in the spirit and energy of all who have benefited from his innovative thinking. Controlling carbohydrates is more than a nutritional strategy, it is an integral part of a lifestyle that is helping millions of people begin the process of taking control of their often-overwhelming lives. This is what *Atkins for Life* can do for you.

CARRYING THE MESSAGE FORWARD

At the time this edition went to press, thirty-three recent independent studies conducted at prestigious research institutions have confirmed that the Atkins Nutritional Approach™ (ANA) is safe and effective. These studies have consistently shown improvement in risk factors for heart disease. (To review these studies, go to **http://atkins.com/science/researchsummaries/index.html.**) Now that Atkins has become mainstream, there seems to be no end to the list of so-called authorities trying to capitalize on the low carb phenomenon. Each and every one of these johnny-come-latelies share the same agenda—presenting themselves as "the next Dr. Atkins." In truth, their "new" ideas are nothing more than reiterations of the approach that Dr. Atkins championed for decades. Because he is sadly no longer here to set the record straight himself, as the chairperson of the Atkins Physicians Council, I have taken that job upon myself.

Try as they may, neither these latter-day Atkins copycats nor the media intent on stirring up debate can rewrite history. Since the publication of *Dr. Atkins' Diet Revolution* in 1972, the ANA has always advocated controlling both the quality and quantity of carbohydrates, teaching people how to make better food choices. Knowledge is power, and, with a better understanding of how different foods impact our bodies, millions of Atkins followers have taken control of their weight, their health, and, yes, their very lives.

The Right Stuff

Over the years, misrepresenting the ANA as the "red meat diet" has sold newspapers. But the ANA has never been about eating only beef, or any meat, for that matter. Dr. Atkins always recommended a balance of protein and fat sources, including fish, shellfish, poultry, and pork. Nor has "doing Atkins" ever been an excuse to overindulge or a recommendation to gorge. Instead, following the program has always been about controlling carbohydrates—omitting those that are refined and devoid of nutrients and concentrating instead on appropriate amounts of vegetables and other nutrient-rich choices—and eating a healthy balance of fat and proteins.

The millions of people who have read Dr. Atkins' books and followed his teachings properly have benefited by slimming down, lowering their blood pressure and blood sugar, and improving cardiac indicators such as lowered cholesterol and triglycerides. They have moved through the four phases of the program, Induction, Ongoing Weight Loss, Pre-Maintenance, and Lifetime Maintenance, which culminate in a lifelong way of eating, and have learned how to individualize Atkins to their own tastes and needs. Over and over again, as the members of the Atkins Physicians Council we hear how Atkins followers have successfully added a fitness regimen to their lives as they come to grips with their weight and health issues. Likewise, we repeatedly hear from individuals who tell us how their success doing Atkins has led to greater self-confidence, which in turn often leads to new jobs, new opportunities, and new relationships.

Ongoing Education

While Dr. Atkins was busy writing this book as well as seeing patients four days a week, it was my privilege to take some of the public role off his shoulders. Part of my job was to educate other physicians, the public, and the media about the ANA. Now, in addition, I gladly take on a new responsibility. While others have attempted to capitalize on the new awareness of the role that excessive and poor-quality carbohydrates play in causing the twin epidemics of obesity and diabetes, it is crucial that we not forget the final lesson offered by this true innovator. *Atkins for Life* provides the road map for long-term success, and is integral to understanding Dr. Atkins' intentions and the evolution of his thinking. Though life is complicated, Dr. Atkins believed that eating should not be. *Atkins for Life* is an indispensable manual for anyone interested in enjoying the lifelong benefits of controlled carbohydrate nutrition, and answers many of the questions now being raised about this approach. It would be naive to think we know all there is to know about controlled carbohydrate nutrition, and with cooperation rather than criticism, with investigation rather than instigation, we can make great gains.

As with his appreciation of the impact of nutrient-deficient carbohydrates on the obesity epidemic, the need to eliminate manufactured trans fats, and to revise the Food Guide Pyramid, it would appear that Dr. Atkins also anticipated the need to make sure that his message would not be misconstrued. Publishing *Atkins for Life* in January 2003, just four months before his death, he was intent on clarifying his message that losing weight is easy, but keeping it off for life is the real challenge.

Moreover, he firmly believed that shedding pounds was not first and foremost about vanity but about good health and disease prevention. Read this book carefully and you will find in it all you need to combat the public misconceptions about Dr. Atkins' approach and prevent his powerful tool from being used incorrectly. Focusing on the principles of carbohydrate awareness, as well as other lifestyle modifications for improved health, this book will teach you how to stop "dieting" and begin the process of *taking control* of your life. Dr. Atkins clearly and purposefully addresses the individualized nature of the Atkins Nutritional Approach, whether you are a college athlete or a postmenopausal woman, with the concept known as your Atkins Carbohydrate Equilibrium (ACE™), the number of grams of Net Carbs you can eat without gaining weight. The hundreds of meal plans in this book at various ACE levels (and delicious recipes) provide practical assistance.

Dr. Atkins also spent considerable attention looking at how various carbohydrate-rich foods differ with regard to their impact on blood sugar. While he found both the glycemic index and the glycemic load helpful in making food selections, he understood that most non-nutritionists found these concepts difficult to implement. So he came up with the Atkins Glycemic Ranking™ (AGR), a simple way to judge the impact on your blood sugar of common foods. They are placed in three categories: Eat Regularly, Eat in Moderation, and Eat Sparingly. What could be simpler! Like the concept of Net Carbs—basically subtracting fiber and other components that don't impact blood sugar from total carbs—which he also devised, the AGR makes it easier to select the right foods. Finally, Dr. Atkins originated the idea of "good carbs," those full of nutrients and fiber, as opposed to "bad carbs," like added sugars, bleached white flour, sugary soft drinks, and most packaged foods. Don't be fooled by others who are trying to take credit for making this distinction. The chapters that follow clearly lay out all this information. This book presents a lifelong strategy, including exercise and meal plans that incorporate a wide range of foods, and takes the first step in showing you how to gain the Atkins advantage, a tool that can change your life.

Dr. Atkins was always open to new ideas and his thinking evolved as a result of both new science and his own clinical observations. In the year and a half since this book was originally published, there has been a tremendous growth in the number of food products created for people controlling their carbohydrates. In the spirit of helping people enjoy healthier lives, we have reworked some of the Atkins Glycemic Ranking charts to reflect these advances in food science. Also, we have decided that it is important to distinguish between the trans fats that occur naturally in small quantities and the dangerous hydrogenated and partially hydrogenated trans fats that are used in many packaged foods.

A Case in Point

The true value of a tool can only be appreciated through use, and I have gained tremendous insight into the incredible power of the Atkins Nutritional Approach as I have incorporated it into my own life. In doing so, I have experienced firsthand what gaining control feels like and how it can impact your response to all of life's challenges. As a physician—and a recreational athlete—I could not imagine that controlling carbohydrates would work for me, but after struggling to manage my weight even while running forty miles a week, I decided to give it a try. Twenty pounds lighter, having clipped thirty minutes from my best time running a marathon, and in training for my first Ironman triathlon, I decided it was time to learn more about the Atkins program. I went right to the source himself. After spending time with Dr. Atkins there was nothing left to decide. This approach was working, and as I trained up to eighteen hours a week for my Ironman competition, I continued controlling my carbohydrates—and my life. I have now completed eight Ironman events (which consist of swimming 2.4 miles, riding a bicycle 112 miles, and then running a full marathon), including two trips to the World Championships in Kiahlua Kona, Hawaii.

Although many would argue that exercise alone, or exercise and calorie reduction combined, is the key to weight loss, I know how difficult this can be. When it takes thirty-five miles of running to burn one pound of body fat, it is simply no wonder that many become discouraged with exercise for weight management. Add to this the self-deprivation associated with low-calorie, reduced-fat dietary approaches, and the energy depletion that occurs with caloric restriction, and it becomes easy to understand why so many people—including me—find Atkins to be a better way.

In addition to sharing my personal experience with exercise and the ANA, I have also had the opportunity to work with researchers in this field, gaining an even greater understanding of how this innovative strategy can help people not only fight obesity, but live healthier, more fulfilling lives. In my role as chairperson of the Atkins Physicians Council, I have testified at Senate hearings regarding the revision of the Food Guide Pyramid, lectured at the American College of Cardiology, and appeared on countless television and radio broadcasts.

Dr. Atkins spent his life breaking down barriers and establishing the framework for the continuance of his life's work. The ANA has always stressed education, and with this book the process continues. The lesson plan has been written, and it is here for us to follow. We live in a complicated world, filled with many things that are beyond our control. I doubt that many people share my desire to swim, bike, and run 140 miles in one day (at least not without a nap!), but I am confident that, like me, you want to take control of your life. Controlling carbohydrates served as the first step in gaining control of my life. I have every confidence that it can help you too begin the path to taking control of your future and reaching your true potential.

—Stuart Lawrence Trager, M.D.
Medical Director for Atkins Nutritionals
and Chairperson, Atkins Physicians Council

PART ONE

A Lifetime Plan

1 | The Atkins Advantage

It really comes down to this: How would you prefer to spend the rest of your life:

A. Munching celery sticks, weighing your portions, and never feeling really satisfied with your food?
B. Eating a wide variety of delicious foods in satisfying amounts—and enjoying every bite?

Why would any sane person not choose answer B? Here's another question: Of the choices above, which one will allow you to achieve and maintain a healthy weight, enhance your health and sense of well-being, and provide you with the satisfaction of being in control of your life? Did you choose answer A? If you did, we have a big surprise for you—the correct answer is B.

> **TIP**
> Team up with an Atkins "buddy," whether a friend, office mate, or your spouse, for psychological support.

This is not a trick question. When you do Atkins, you really do get to eat all kinds of delicious, healthful foods and you never need to go hungry. If your goal is to slim down, your weight will go down—steadily, easily, and for good. If your goal is good health and disease prevention, your energy level will go up—dramatically—and your risk parameters for a myriad of health problems will decline. So say farewell to the daily struggle of a restrictive diet and get ready to embark on doing Atkins for life!

Controlling Carbs for Life

When you follow the Atkins Nutritional Approach™, you simply control the amount of carbohydrates you eat. Much depends upon your metabolism, gender, age, and activity level. As you do Atkins over time, you'll learn your own threshold for carbohydrate consumption, which is the amount of Net Carbs you can eat each day while neither gaining nor losing weight. We call that your Atkins Carbohydrate Equilibrium™, or ACE™ for short. ACE is the place you are aiming for. But first, if you still have a roll around your waist—or other excess baggage to shed—you'll learn to determine how many carbs you can consume each day to achieve your goal weight.

In the weight-loss phases of Atkins (see The Four Phases of Atkins on page 6), your objective will be to eat as many "good" carbs as you can handle and to cut out virtually *all* "bad" carbs. This means no conventional bread, baked goods, and pasta and nothing made with added sugar. Even nutritious carb foods, such as brown rice, lentils, and sweet potatoes will be off the menu until you are close to your goal weight, when most people can reintroduce a surprising variety to their diet. Does this mean going hungry? Absolutely not, because during weight loss you replace those empty calories with a wide assortment of delicious, nutrient-dense, and fiber-rich vegetables and protein-packed foods such as poultry, eggs, fish, meat, and cheese.

Once you have achieved and are maintaining a healthy weight, you will be able to enjoy many of those formerly

---

Controlled Carb Eating Is Healthy Eating

Here's what you get when you eat the Atkins way:
- nutrient-dense meals rich in fiber
- lots of vitamins, minerals, and phytochemicals (plant nutrients)
- appropriate amounts of protein
- a balance of natural fats

Here's what you don't get:
- added sugars
- bleached white flour
- hydrogenated or partially hydrogenated vegetable oil

forbidden foods, so long as you proceed with moderation. The Atkins
difference is quality. Instead of empty
carbohydrates in the form of worthless bleached white flour and sugar,
you'll be eating highly nutritious

> **TIP**
>
> Commit to a real
> lifestyle change. This is
> a healthier way of life,
> not a diet.

fruits such as strawberries, blueberries, and kiwifruit; nuts
and seeds; virtually all veggies; and even moderate portions of beans and whole grains.

In fact, when you are doing Atkins for life, things aren't
as black-and-white as they were in the initial phases of the
program. Instead of "good" and "bad" carbs, you'll learn
more subtle distinctions that will guide you in your food
choices. You'll find that some carbohydrate foods are more
favorable than others. Not surprisingly, the more favorable a
carb food, the more frequently you'll be able to eat it. Eating
the controlled carbohydrate way will almost certainly lead to
weight loss if you're overweight, but Atkins is hardly a fad
or crash diet. In fact, it's just the opposite. Doing Atkins is a
lifetime commitment to good nutrition and improved health,
one that works easily in the "real" world of family meals,
social and business activities, eating in restaurants, and traveling. Not only do you slim down if you need to, but you'll
be able to keep off those unwanted pounds for life. (If you
have a lot of weight to lose, we advise you to begin the
Atkins program with its first phase, called Induction.)

Why It Works

When you do Atkins for life, you don't count calories, nor do
you deprive yourself of a variety of wholesome foods. Instead, you enjoy great, low carb food in satisfying portions.
Why does this lead so easily to weight loss, and then to
weight maintenance and better health? According to the conventional wisdom about dieting, just the opposite should
happen. To answer that essential question, let's take a closer
look at exactly what's in your food.

The Four Phases of Atkins

The Atkins Nutritional Approach™ is a safe, effective way to lose weight steadily and easily. But even more important, it allows you to achieve your goal weight—permanently. Understanding the four phases of doing Atkins is crucial to your success. Here's a quick summary of how they work:

- **Phase 1: Induction.** To get your weight-loss program off to a fast start, you limit your carbohydrate intake to about 20 grams of Net Carbs a day for a minimum of two weeks. (Net Carbs are the only carbs that have a noted impact on blood sugar and will be discussed in detail in chapter 3.) During this time, you satisfy your appetite with fish, poultry, eggs, beef, and other foods high in protein and good fats, such as olive oil. You may also eat 4 cups of salad greens (dressed with your favorite low carb dressing) or 3 cups of salad and a cup of fresh, nonstarchy veggies such as broccoli or zucchini each day. After two weeks, you can add an ounce of nuts or seeds to your daily intake of carbs if they don't interfere with weight loss.

- **Phase 2: Ongoing Weight Loss (OWL).** During OWL, you continue to eat high-quality protein and fat, along with your salad greens and vegetables. Week by week, you add back nutrient-rich carbohydrates such as more veggies, berries, nuts, and seeds—and for some people, even legumes. You do this by adding just 5 grams of Net Carbs per day in weekly increments until weight loss ceases. So you go from 20 to 25 grams per day one week, then to 30 grams daily the next week, and so forth. Once you stop losing weight, drop back 5 grams and you've discovered the amount of carbs you can eat while still losing weight. For most people, that amount is somewhere between 40 and 60 grams daily. Continue until you are within 5 to 10 pounds of your goal weight.

- **Phase 3: Pre-Maintenance.** With your goal in sight, you'll want to slow your weight loss to an almost imperceptible rate so that your good eating habits become ingrained. Each week, you'll now add another 10 grams of daily Net Carbs to your program—or treat yourself to an extra 20 to 30 grams of nutrient-dense foods twice a week—so long as you continue to lose. If your weight loss stops, cut back 5 or 10 grams until you resume gradual weight loss. This is your revised level for carb consumption, at which you will continue until you reach your target.

- **Phase 4: Lifetime Maintenance.** Now that you've achieved your goal weight, you can start enjoying an even wider range of delicious foods. You still need to keep an eye on your carb intake, of course. Is that hard to do? No. Just skip the junk food and use your carb grams on nutrient-rich foods such as whole, unrefined grains and a variety of fruits and vegetables. Most people find that they can maintain their weight by consuming somewhere between 45 and 100 grams of Net Carbs a day. Someone who is fit and exercises an hour or more daily may be able to go even higher. This individualized number is your Atkins Carbohydrate Equilibrium™ (ACE™), the number of grams of Net Carbs you can eat without gaining or losing weight. This is your equilibrium zone in which you'll maintain your weight effortlessly while eating a satisfying, healthful diet.

Basically, everything you eat is made up of some combination of three components: protein, fat, and carbohydrates, along with some water and ash (mineral content), as well as vitamins, and other nutrients.

- Protein. Proteins are made of long, complex chains of amino acids, which in turn are the basic building blocks of your body. You need protein to build and maintain your muscles, bones, organs, and other tissues and to keep your body functioning. In fact, aside from your bones and water, your body is made up almost entirely of protein. Complete dietary protein, meaning it contains all of the essential amino acids, is found in meat, poultry, eggs, fish, shellfish, and dairy products and other animal foods. Plant foods such as seeds, nuts, beans, and whole grains also contain some protein, but these proteins aren't complete—they're missing some of the essential amino acids neces-

> **TIP**
> Add variety to your life with new foods, new recipes, or new activities. All help avoid boredom, making it easier to stay with the program.

sary for good health. Soybeans are the most complete vegetable source, missing only the essential amino acid methionine. (The high heat required to process some soy foods destroys some of these essential amino acids.)

- Fat. Also known as lipids, dietary fats are complex molecules that don't dissolve in water. There are different kinds of fat—some that are really good for you, especially essential fatty acids, and others, such as hydrogenated or partially hydrogenated oils that you should avoid at all costs. Oils are dietary fats that are liquid at room temperature. You'd never know it from the fat phobia that surrounds us, but your body absolutely must have fat for many vital purposes, including making hormones, building cell walls, and storing energy. Dietary fat comes from animal foods and dairy products, including fish and butter. It also comes from such plant sources as olive oil, safflower oil, canola oil, and so on. Nuts, seeds, and a few fruits such as olives and avocados are naturally high in oil.

- Carbohydrates. Carbohydrates are made from long chains of carbon, hydrogen, and oxygen atoms. In general, simple carbohydrates are sugars such as sucrose (table sugar) and fructose (the sugar in fruit). Complex carbohydrates are found in all vegetables, grains, and legumes. When your body digests complex carbohydrates, including starches such as grains, however, it breaks them down into simple carbs—so in the end, many complex carbs become simple sugars. Fiber is one class of complex carbohydrates that your body cannot digest, making it a valuable ally in your weight control efforts. (More on this in chapter 3.)

Okay, chemistry class is dismissed, but now it's time for one more lesson. You need to understand what happens when you eat foods made from proteins, fats, and carbohydrates.

New Name, Same Concept

In the past, we've called the level of Net Carb consumption that allows you to maintain a constant weight your Critical Carbohydrate Level for Maintenance (CCLM). In this book, however, we want to encourage you to think in terms of balance, both in terms of permanent weight control and overall health. So we are introducing terminology that stresses the equilibrium essential for this lifetime level. Instead of CCLM, we would like you to think of your Atkins Carbohydrate Equilibrium™, your ACE™, as the "magic" number that keeps your weight—and the rest of your life—in balance.

The Insulin-Glucose Connection

Whenever you consume carbohydrates (or, to a much smaller degree, protein), your body turns it into glucose, also known as blood sugar, the primary fuel for energy. (Fat is your backup fuel supply.) Your body also produces insulin, a substance that's sometimes called the master hormone. Basically, insulin's job is to transport the glucose from your bloodstream into your cells. It also prevents body fat from being released and burned as fuel.

Your body needs glucose, but it's necessary to keep the level of glucose in your bloodstream within a fairly narrow range. If you eat a lot of carbs, however, you raise your blood sugar to a higher level than your body needs. To clear all that extra glucose out of your bloodstream, your pancreas has to produce an extra spurt of insulin to transport the blood sugar to your cells, where it can be stored for later use. The form in which the excess blood sugar is stored is body fat. That's why insulin is also known as the "fat hormone."

When you eat a food that's mainly rapidly absorbed carbohydrates—a candy bar, for instance, or a slice of white bread—glucose enters your bloodstream very quickly.

> **TIP**
>
> Always weigh yourself at the same time, preferably first thing in the morning. Your weight can fluctuate up to five pounds in a day so weighing in at the same time gives a more accurate comparison.

TIP

Post a photo of yourself at your most fabulous on the refrigerator door, just in case you feel tempted to lose sight of the big picture.

Your body must make insulin and clear that glucose away just as quickly: This process is known as an insulin response. That spike in your blood glucose level gives you a quick energy boost. But the resultant spike in insulin can overshoot, dropping your blood sugar level too low, which then leads to an energy slump. This, in turn, stimulates cravings to eat more carbohydrates.

The insulin response happens mostly when you eat high carb, rapidly absorbed foods. Consuming foods that are mostly protein or fat requires your body to produce far less insulin because it doesn't have to deal with sudden overloads of glucose. Protein also stimulates glucagon, a hormone that counteracts some of the effects of insulin. (It is important to note that if you eat more protein than your body requires—especially *with* high carb foods—it too can convert to glucose.) When your insulin mechanism is not overstimulated, your blood-sugar levels do not fluctuate wildly and along with it, your energy level remains constant. The same applies to your weight, if it's already within a normal range. If you're overweight, cutting down on carbs helps you trim down because eating this way flips the metabolic switch. You go from burning carbs for energy to burning your stored fat instead, which is a perfectly normal and safe process. But because you're cutting carbs, while still eating satiating foods, you aren't hungry—even as you continue to lose weight steadily.

Atkins for You

The flexibility of Atkins means that you can easily personalize the approach to suit your particular needs, both during weight loss and for permanent weight maintenance. If you have just a bit of weight to lose (perhaps up to 10 pounds if you're a postmenopausal woman or up to 20 extra pounds if

Barriers to Success!

Controlling your carbohydrate intake is usually enough to help you manage your weight. But what if you're following the same controlled carb approach that's allowed you to slim down and maintain your weight in the past, and all of a sudden the pounds are piling on? Assuming you're not stuffing yourself, are being mindful of carb intake, and haven't stopped or cut back on your fitness program, there are still some situations that can undermine all your good efforts. Check the list below to see what could be interfering with your success:

- **Medications.** A number of widely prescribed drugs can slow or prevent weight loss. Have you started taking?

  - Diuretics (water pills)

  - Beta blockers

  - Diabetes medications such as insulin, sulfonylureas, and thiazolidinedione; Metformin, on the other hand, can assist with weight management

  - Estrogen and synthetic hormone replacement therapy (HRT)

  - Anti-arthritis drugs, nonsteroidal anti-inflammatories (NSAI)

  - Birth control pills

  - Antidepressants such as selective serotonin reuptake inhibitors (SSRIs), including fluoxetine and paroxetine and tricyclics such as doxepin, and lithium

  - Steroids such as prednisone

By now you should have discussed your commitment to doing Atkins with your doctor at least once. If you have not already done so, go back and discuss the effects of these medications on weight gain. (Note: Some medications for insulin resistance, such as Metformin, will not interfere with weight loss or cause weight gain.)

- **Thyroid problems.** About a quarter of all adults have low thyroid function, known as hypothyroidism, which slows the metabolism and causes weight gain. It is also associated with elevated cholesterol. Hypothyroidism can be especially problematic in peri- and postmenopausal women. If you are entering this phase of your life, you may experience weight gain or diffi-

continued

culty maintaining your weight, meaning you may have to adjust your ACE.

- **Age.** If you're like most overweight people, you've lost and then regained weight on different diets over the years. You may have noticed that each time it was a little harder to shed the pounds. As you get older, your body just isn't as responsive. Maintaining your slim figure is possible, but it might take a little more effort than it did twenty years ago.

- **Carb creep.** You may simply be unaware that you're eating too many carbs—or maybe you're eating foods that have hidden carbohydrates in them. (See chapter 3, the section beginning on page 40, for more on finding hidden carbs.)

you're an active young man), you can probably achieve your goal weight by starting at 60 grams of Net Carbs a day. If you start losing, gradually increase your carb intake until you stop losing, then back off. If you don't lose (or if you gain) at 60 grams of Net Carbs, scale back in 5-gram increments until you do start to drop pounds. However, if you have a significant amount to lose or experience difficulty losing, you should probably start with the first phase of Atkins, known as Induction.

Pregnant and nursing women should *not* follow any of the weight loss phases of Atkins but can safely follow the Lifetime Maintenance phase, which is the subject of this book, under the guidance of their doctor. Anyone who is losing weight should do so under the supervision of a doctor. This is especially true for anyone aged eighteen or younger as well as the elderly. Exercise is an important element of the Atkins approach, and here too the plan can easily be modified to accommodate your level of physical fitness, even if it's very low or limited by a health problem. Likewise, you should discuss any significant increase in activity level with your physician.

A Permanent Lifestyle

The true test of a successful dietary approach isn't just how quickly and easily you lose weight, it's whether you can keep it off once you've reached your goal weight. Here's where the controlled carbohydrate approach really pays off. Once you know exactly how many grams of Net Carbs you can eat each day, you have the tool that allows your weight to remain constant. Based upon your age, gender, metabolism, and level of physical activity, you will have established your personal ACE.

Moreover, when doing Atkins, you concentrate on whole foods that still have all their nutritional content. On the American diet, you get junk food that's been stripped of its nutritional value. On Atkins you get foods that satisfy your hunger and nourish your body. The foods the typical American diet includes feed your sugar addiction, raise your insulin level, and make you gain weight even as they leave you hungry and malnourished. With the deck stacked so clearly in favor of Atkins, is there any reason not to give it a try? In the next chapter, you'll learn how cutting down on carbohydrates can improve some common but serious health problems.

> **TIP**
>
> Exercise keeps your head clear, relieves your anxiety, restores your energy, keeps your mind off food, and boosts your metabolism.

The Trip of a Lifetime

A terrible family vacation motivated Roseanne Clampet to say "bon voyage" to her extra pounds.

A few months ago, I went to Orlando, Florida, on vacation. It wasn't until I was in one of the theme parks that it hit me: The last time I was there, in 1990, I'd been miserable! Twelve years ago I weighed 210 pounds and was so tired, uncomfortably

Which Foods for Which Phases

See how well informed you are on the four phases of Atkins by taking this self-test:

Phase One: Induction

1. When starting Atkins, you initiate weight loss by cutting carbs and eating lots of greens. How much salad can you eat each day?
    a. None
    ⓑ. 3 to 4 cups
    c. 4 to 5 cups
    d. As much as you want

2. How many cups of other vegetables can you eat each day?
    a. None
    ⓑ. 1 cup
    c. 3 cups
    d. As much as you want

3. Which vegetables are good low carb choices?
    ⓐ. Asparagus
    ⓑ. Broccoli
    ⓒ. Cauliflower
    ⓓ. Spinach
    e. Potatoes
    ⓕ. String beans
    g. Sweet potatoes
    ⓗ. Zucchini

4. Which foods do you skip completely during Induction?
    a. Chicken
    ⓑ. Legumes
    ⓒ. Bread
    d. Butter
    e. Cheese
    f. Eggs
    ⓖ. Apples
    ⓗ. Bananas
    ⓘ. Rice
    j. Salmon
    k. Avocado
    l. Spaghetti
    m. Shellfish
    ⓝ. Fruit juice
    o. Turkey

    p. Eggplant
    q. Tomatoes

Phase Two: Ongoing Weight Loss (OWL)

1. As you begin to add some carbs back to your program, you increase your daily carb intake by how many Net Carbs each week?

    a. 5 grams
    b. 10 grams
    c. 15 grams
    d. 20 grams
    e. 30 grams

2. Some good low carb, high-nutrition foods to add are:

    a. Apples
    b. Sunflower seeds
    c. Bananas
    d. Orange juice
    e. Blueberries
    f. French fries
    g. Macadamia nuts
    h. Milk
    i. Pasta
    j. Strawberries
    k. Breakfast cereal

3. How long do you stay on OWL?

    a. Two weeks
    b. Until you reach your goal weight
    c. Until you are between 5 and 10 pounds from your goal weight
    d. As long as you continue to lose weight

Phase Three: Pre-Maintenance

1. As you deliberately slow your weight loss, you can increase your daily Net Carb intake by how much each week?

    a. 5 grams
    b. 10 grams
    c. 15 grams
    d. 20 grams
    e. 30 grams

2. You stay on Pre-Maintenance until when?

    a. You reach your goal weight
    b. A week
    c. Two weeks
    d. You have maintained your goal weight for a month or more

Phase Four: Lifetime Maintenance

1. Your ACE means what?
    a. The level of carbohydrate intake that will allow you to jump-start weight loss
    b. The level of carbohydrate intake at which you lose weight
    c. The level of carbohydrate intake at which you gain weight
    d. The level of carbohydrate intake at which you neither gain nor lose weight

2. Even after you've attained your goal weight, you should avoid which of the following?
    a. White bread
    b. Low-fat cookies
    c. Doughnuts
    d. White bagels
    e. Regular pasta
    f. Low-fat ice cream
    g. Candy
    h. Sugary sports drinks

Answers:

Phase One: Induction
1. b 2. b 3. a, b, c, d, f, and h 4. b, c, g, h, i, l, and n (Note: You can introduce nuts if you continue with Induction beyond the initial 2 weeks.)

Phase Two: Ongoing Weight Loss (OWL)
1. a 2. b, e, g, and j 3. c

Phase Three: Pre-Maintenance
1. b 2. d

Phase Four: Lifetime Maintenance
1. d 2. a, b, c, d, e, f, g, and h. All of these foods are highly processed, contain bleached white flour and/or sugar, and should be avoided or eaten rarely.

hot, and physically weak from carrying all that weight on my 5-foot 3-inch frame that I couldn't keep up with my kids. I just wanted to get back on a plane and go home to New York.

During that vacation, I never told anyone how miserable I was. I didn't want to ruin the family's trip, so I just carried on for their sakes. But when I finally got home, I broke down in tears. I couldn't take being that heavy any longer.

It seems strange to say, but I had never had a weight problem before. I never worried about what I ate because I was just naturally thin. But after the birth of my first child, I had surgery to correct an intestinal obstruction. I'm convinced that something about that surgery changed my metabolism, because even though my eating habits didn't change, I started to gradually gain weight until I had a

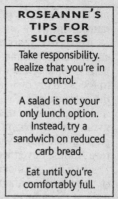

ROSEANNE'S TIPS FOR SUCCESS

Take responsibility. Realize that you're in control.

A salad is not your only lunch option. Instead, try a sandwich on reduced carb bread.

Eat until you're comfortably full.

serious problem. Fortunately, I didn't have any other health issues and my cholesterol and blood pressure were normal.

I started doing Atkins in June of 1990. By November, I was down 50 pounds! I stayed on Induction the whole time because I was comfortable with it and I wanted to continue to lose weight rapidly, which was what kept me motivated.

I did cheat a few times. Even though I didn't keep potato chips and cola in the house, I craved them so much that I actually went out and bought them! I managed to get back on track each time by remembering Dr. Atkins' advice not to beat myself up over the mistakes. I'd feel bad but not guilty. And the weight kept coming off. If you cheat, you're only cheating yourself. I know lots of people who say, "I *had* to eat the cake because it was a birthday party." That's ridiculous! No one ties you down and forces you to eat.

Two years ago, I took up power walking. I had always hated exercise and just didn't have the energy. When I got home from work, I'd collapse. Now, I go for an hour-long walk about four times a week. I think it's really helped me stay healthy and maintain my weight loss.

I've also made some lasting changes in my eating habits. I no longer eat sugar of any kind, but I do sometimes have pasta or bread. The many new controlled carb and sugar-free products out there make it really easy to eat well and keep

off the weight. I can't believe I can have (low carb) chocolate bars now!

About five years ago, when my mother died, I started to
eat for comfort and to soothe my stress. Of course, I regained some of the weight I had lost. When I finally was able
to focus on my own health, I went back on Induction and lost
the extra weight. I've been doing fine ever since.

In fact, I'm more than fine. I have lots of energy and feel
great. On my recent trip to Florida, I visited three theme
parks in one day. I would never have been able to do that before Atkins. I even wore a bathing suit without a T-shirt!

My daily routines are more effortless, too. I bound up the
steps to work without huffing and puffing. When I see the
train at the subway platform, I run for it. I used to just let it
pull away.

ACE: 80	WEIGHT BEFORE: 210 pounds	STARTED DOING ATKINS: June 1990
AGE: 50		
HEIGHT: 5 feet 3 inches	WEIGHT AFTER: 143 pounds	
	WEIGHT LOST: 67 pounds	

2 | A Lifetime of Health

If you're already doing Atkins, or purchased this book because you're pretty much convinced that controlling your carbs is effective for weight control, right on! But if that's your only reason for doing Atkins, you're not seeing the forest for the trees. Losing weight makes you look better and feel better about yourself, but even more important than these compelling motivators is attaining—and then maintaining—health. That's what Atkins for life is really all about. Weight and health are two sides of the same coin.

Many people start doing Atkins for weight loss but wind up staying with the program because they experience a life-altering bonus: better health and a sense of well-being. Now, with increasing research supporting the benefits of controlled carbohydrate nutrition, more and more people are coming to Atkins for health reasons. To turn that around, even if you're not overweight, if you're consuming the American diet jam-packed with bleached white flour, added sugars, and other junk foods, you may have some serious health problems—of which you may or may not be aware. And if you do have a tendency to gain weight, you have a double reason to control your carbohydrate intake. Carrying around extra pounds and putting your glucose and insulin supplies into overdrive are both serious health risks, which is why Atkins is not merely a weight-loss program. In fact, you might go so far as to say that using Atkins only to lose weight, and then going back to your old eating habits—which will cause you to gain weight again—is a waste of time and potentially harmful, to boot. On the other hand, doing Atkins for a

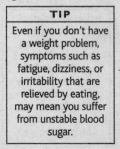

TIP

Even if you don't have a weight problem, symptoms such as fatigue, dizziness, or irritability that are relieved by eating, may mean you suffer from unstable blood sugar.

lifetime will enhance your chances of living longer and enjoying good health.

Enhanced Health

Let's take a closer look at how cutting down on carbs can improve some common health problems.

Blood Lipids

Because Atkins allows you to consume dietary fat, many people worry that it will raise their cholesterol levels. While doing Atkins will almost certainly raise your HDL ("good") cholesterol; at the same time, your triglyceride (TG) level will almost certainly drop sharply. This is an excellent outcome because high TGs and low HDL are considered a very dangerous combination, one that means a heart attack or stroke may well be in your not-too-distant future. Many people also experience a drop in LDL (low-density lipoprotein) cholesterol.[1] It is possible that a small percentage of you will see your LDL level rise slightly.

Recent research points to the possibility that the type of LDL that increases on Atkins is the low-risk variety of LDL (large, fluffy LDL particles). This slight increase in LDL is more than offset by the improvement in other numbers, but it may raise your total cholesterol number, which can be slightly misleading,

> **TIP**
>
> Before automatically accepting a prescription for a pharmaceutical, ask your physician whether there is a natural alternative in the form of a supplement or lifestyle change.

For a large percentage of adults in the United States, low-fat dieting may be a serious risk to cardiovascular health. That's because it has recently been found that a certain subset of the population has a genetic predisposition to a type of LDL cholesterol that means low-fat dieting could greatly increase cardiovascular risk. What happens is that when this subset of individuals eats a low-fat diet, their bodies convert the large, fluffy kind of LDL cholesterol, which is not dangerous, into the small, dense kind of LDL that is dangerous.[2] (Moreover, a related study showed that saturated fat intake *increased* large, fluffy LDLs and lowered small, dense ones in healthy men.[3]) Since there is no easy way to know which subset you fall into, why would you take such a chance?

Glucose Intolerance and Diabetes

If you're overweight or have struggled with your weight in the past, chances are you're extremely sensitive to carbohydrates. If this is true, then even small amounts of carbs can stimulate your pancreas to produce large amounts of insulin. That's probably what originally helped make you gain weight—and that's why controlling carb intake helps you drop pounds so easily. But carbohydrate sensitivity has a darker side than mere weight gain. As explained in chapter 1, for you, eating excess carbs puts you on a blood-sugar roller coaster. When you're on the down side of the ride, you feel tired, shaky, depressed, and unable to think clearly, and crave your next carb fix. But when you control your carb intake, your fluctuating or unstable blood sugar stabilizes and you avoid abnormally low blood glucose levels—a condition called hypoglycemia. Why? Because when you don't feed your body heavy doses of sugars and starches, you don't produce big swings in your blood sugar. Your energy level stays constant, your blood sugar stops its wild ride, and it doesn't interfere with maintaining your weight. What's more, you may have put the brakes on the almost inevitable descent into diabetes that comes after years of unstable blood sugar.

Obesity and diabetes are clearly related. If you've come to Atkins because you've already developed Type 2 diabetes, you'll find that controlling

TIP

Stay motivated by having annual blood tests to affirm that your risk factors remain low on this lifestyle.

your carbs will put you in control of your diabetes as well. You're probably diabetic because you're overweight or you are overweight because you're insulin resistant. (If you're addicted to sugar, you are tempting fate in terms of developing diabetes.) The insulin resistance that causes diabetes (along with many of the medications usually prescribed to treat diabetes) makes it very difficult to lose weight. Insulin resistance occurs when the body becomes desensitized to insulin, meaning that the transport of glucose to the cells for storage is disturbed. The pancreas then releases additional insulin, which becomes increasingly ineffective over time.

By trimming carbs from your diet, you can break out of the insulin/weight trap, because processing fewer carbs means less insulin in your blood and less fat storage. As you slim down, the insulin resistance of diabetes usually lessens and your blood sugar levels improve, often to the point where your doctor may determine that you no longer need glucose-lowering drugs—or at the very least, you can reduce your dosage. You'll feel better and have more energy—and the many health problems related to diabetes, such as high cholesterol and high blood pressure, improve.

High Blood Pressure
Hypertension, or high blood pressure (meaning more than 140/90), is the flip side of the blood-sugar coin. If you have high blood pressure, the chances are excellent that you will soon also have high blood sugar—if you don't have it already. The reverse is also true: If you have high blood sugar from insulin resistance, you very likely will also have, or will soon develop, high blood pressure. Doing Atkins helps bring your blood pressure down in two ways. First, simply losing weight can lower blood pressure. Even better, cutting down on carbohydrates helps the underlying insulin resistance and high blood sugar that are a big part of why you have high blood pressure.

There's an additional benefit if you're among the people with high blood pressure who are also sensitive to sodium (salt): Chances are you are probably eating less salt when you do Atkins. That's because about 75 percent of the salt most people eat comes from processed foods and salty snacks—

and on Atkins you won't be eating those foods. (Salt-sensitive people may need to stay away from even low carb foods with high salt contents.) Moreover, reducing your insulin level contributes to reduction in water retention, which results in a lower sodium level.

Digestive Difficulties

Many digestive problems, such as gastroesophageal reflux disease (GERD, better known as severe heartburn), gallstones, diverticulitis (a painful colon problem), gas, and bloating improve significantly when you start controlling carbohydrates. If you have reflux problems or gallstones, for instance, your doctor may have recommended a low-fat diet. In fact, there's no evidence that a high-fat diet causes GERD or gallstones and no evidence has been found to link fat intake with gallbladder disease.[4] Likewise, cutting fat in the diet doesn't reduce GERD symptoms or help prevent gallstone attacks. Cutting carbs, however, does seem to help reduce symptoms.

Food Allergies

Headaches, abdominal pains, asthma, eczema and other rashes, and other reactions can signal sensitivities to certain foods. Many of the foods that most commonly provoke an allergic reaction are high carbohydrate foods such as corn, wheat, rye, oats, milk, and white potatoes, all of which are eliminated during the Induction phase of Atkins. If symptoms disappear until a specific food is reintroduced, it is pretty clear that this food is an allergen. Other foods, to which people are often sensitive but that can be eaten while doing Atkins from the start, include shellfish, mushrooms, cheese, soy, and members of the nightshade family (as is the potato), specifically tomatoes, eggplant, bell peppers, and other peppers. If you were not aware of being sensitive to one of these foods, doing Atkins will have allowed you to become aware of the sensitivity when you reintroduce it to your diet. This process is referred to as "elimination and challenge" by health care professionals, and unlike costly allergy tests, costs nothing. Although the above foods are allowed in Lifetime Maintenance, if you are highly sensitive to any of them, eliminate them altogether.

Colon problems often improve markedly on a controlled carbohydrate regimen. That's, in part, because Atkins replaces highly refined, low-fiber carbohydrates with salad greens, fresh vegetables, fresh fruit, and whole grains. These foods are high in fiber—and a high-fiber diet is a natural and very effective treatment for diverticulitis and constipation. New dietary guidelines from the Institute of Medicine recommend that women should get 21 to 25 grams of fiber daily and men 30 to 38 grams daily. You should eat at least five standard servings of fresh vegetables and salad greens every day and take a fiber supplement.[5] Numerous scientific studies have shown that overall, people who eat a high-fiber diet have lower cholesterol levels and less incidence of heart disease than those who eat a low-fiber diet. They may also be less likely to get colon cancer, although the evidence is less clear.

Women's Health

Somewhere between 6 and 10 percent of all women between the ages of twenty to forty have polycystic ovary syndrome (PCOS), a hormonal imbalance that causes painful, irregular menstruation, infertility, weight gain, excess body hair, and even symptoms of diabetes. PCOS can be hard to diagnose. Even though there is no cure for it, it is probable that abnormal insulin production and/or insulin resistance play an important role in causing PCOS—researchers don't know for sure. What we do know is that a controlled carbohydrate program can help keep PCOS symptoms under control and help its sufferers avoid long-term complications.

Osteoporosis

As women (and some men) age, they need to take steps to avoid osteoporosis, the condition in which bones become thin, brittle, and prone to breakage. There have been charges that the amount of protein in the Atkins program causes bone-thinning calcium loss. In fact, numerous solid studies show the opposite is true: The more protein you have in your diet, the less likely you are to experience a bone fracture as you age.[6–10]

Controlled Carb Satisfaction Instead of Low-Fat Hunger

Despite these impressive health benefits of moderating carbohydrate intake, chances are that at least one of the low-fat worshipers has told you that the only way to trim down is by cutting out most fat and counting calories. These same people also worship at the base of the Food Guide Pyramid, where they blithely devour bleached white flour and other high carbohydrate foods. Don't let them influence you. Reading this book will soon help you understand why controlling your carb intake is more effective for most than obsessing about calories and fat. To add some ammunition to your arsenal for a friendly dialogue with your calorie-conscious cohorts, let's review the facts on low-fat versus controlled carb approaches to weight control. We prefer to use the term *controlled* rather than *low* because the right amount of carbs varies widely from person to person; for some fortunate individuals, it doesn't even need to be all that low.

TIP

If you are feeling out of control for a few days in a row, drop below your ACE for a few days until your cravings subside.

The most noticeable difference between a program that limits fat and one that limits carbs is a no-brainer: hunger. Low-fat diets typically leave you feeling some degree of deprivation. Let's face it: Salads (dressing on the side, please) and bagels (minus the butter or a schmear of cream cheese) don't make for highly satiating meals. Plus, these high carb foods are digested relatively quickly, so your stomach empties much sooner than when you eat foods containing fat, which digests more slowly. You already know about the second issue: blood-sugar spikes, and nosedives, resulting in more hunger. So while you may lose weight initially on a low-fat diet while you restrict your calories, over the long run you're almost bound to gain it back because we humans just don't like to go hungry. On the other hand, on a controlled carbohydrate eating plan, which allows you to fill up on satiating proteins and fats and select the carbohydrates that don't send your blood sugar soaring, hunger need not be a problem.

Weight Loss Plus Well-Being: A Great Combo

Another reason that controlling carbs works better is that most people see results right away. On a low-fat diet, the pounds come off slowly, so it's hard to stay motivated. When you strictly limit carbs while enjoying sufficient protein and fat, as you do in Induction, your body goes into fat-burning mode (called lipolysis/ketosis). What better motivator is there than stepping on the scale after a week and finding yourself several pounds lighter? Or zipping into a pair of pants a whole size smaller? Such visible results help people stick with the program and reach their goals. So instead of feeling deprived, you feel proud of your accomplishment, which, in turn, strengthens your commitment.

Only seven years out of high school, Ralph Drake, 6 feet 1 inch tall, weighed close to 300 pounds and looked as if he were traveling the same road as his father, who had died at the age of forty-nine of a heart attack. After being unable to adhere to a calorie-restricted diet, Ralph turned to Atkins, quickly dropping the weight, as well as finding that after being asthmatic all his life, he was now breathing normally.

Years later, after a divorce, Ralph's weight seesawed back and forth, and he suffered a severe asthma attack that put him in intensive care. "The only way to control my breathing was through massive amounts of steroids," recalls Ralph. "One of the side effects was that I started eating everything in sight." His weight climbed to 280 pounds again and he was waking up in the night short of breath and with heart palpitations.

A deejay, on April 1, 2000, Ralph announced to his listeners that he was going back to doing Atkins, he says,

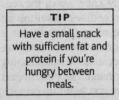

TIP

Have a small snack with sufficient fat and protein if you're hungry between meals.

"because I didn't want to die. As the weight fell off, I felt like a jerk for ever letting myself slide." Now a trim 175 pounds, forty-nine-year-old Ralph is in Lifetime Maintenance, consuming less than 100 grams of carbs a day. He has no problems with asthma. His blood pressure has gone from 110/70 to 92/56, which his doctor says is fine. His LDL cholesterol has dropped from 170 to 118, his total cholesterol from 230 to 172, and his triglycerides from 232 to 69. Newly married and with twin babies, Ralph has everything to live for.

Ralph is only one of countless Atkins followers who enjoyed the two sides of the weight-loss/health improvement coin. Thirty-eight-year-old Luann Lockhart is another success story. After a hysterectomy at thirty-two, her struggle with her weight began—compounded by her decision to quit smoking. Despite walking three miles a day and following a low-fat diet, she reached 211 pounds—she is 5 feet 4 inches tall—and her total cholesterol was hovering at 250. She also suffered from esophageal reflux and colon problems for which she was taking medication. After reading *Dr. Atkins' New Diet Revolution,* Luann realized that she was addicted to carbohydrates. Although her doctor was not familiar with the program, he was concerned enough about her health that he was willing to give Luann his blessing, so long as she returned every three months for a checkup. After two weeks on Induction, Luann had shed 12 pounds; at the one-month point, she was able to eliminate her pills for her gastric problems. Over nine months Luann lost 75 pounds to reach her goal weight of 136. "Now that the weight is off, I feel absolutely wonderful," says Luann. "I have tons of energy and my health problems have disappeared. My cholesterol is down to 175, my blood pressure is 92 over 50, and I have enough energy to referee volleyball and keep up with my seventeen-year-old daughter." But the benefits don't stop there. "People look at me differently," she adds. "Even though my daughter never said anything about it, I could tell that having a heavy mother embarrassed her. Now she's proud of me. In fact, when we go out together, people think we're sisters!"

The Faulty Food Guide Pyramid

Frequently you may find that outside forces—whether friends, nutrition "experts," or media reports—challenge your way of eating. Don't let commonly accepted misconceptions about nutrition mess with your new mindset. The all-powerful and omnipresent Food Guide Pyramid, created by the United States Department of Agriculture in 1992, represents one of the worst nutritional blunders in our nation's history. It promotes a high carbohydrate diet, which an increasing number of mainstream medical experts acknowledge may contribute to an increased risk of health problems and certain chronic diseases. Furthermore, the pyramid advises us to eat liberally—six to eleven servings a day—of "bread, cereal, rice, and pasta," without making any distinction, for example, between wild rice and a slice of Wonder bread or whole oats and Cocoa Puffs! The other major problem with the pyramid is that it lumps fats together at the top (with sweets), in the "use sparingly" area, making no distinction between good fats such as olive oil, and bad fats such as the hydrogenated vegetable oil found in most commercially prepared foods.

We give the pyramid a unanimous thumbs-down and encourage you to look for nutrition guidance elsewhere—starting right here, of course. The pyramid is currently scheduled for revision and one can only hope that the increasing dialogue about excessive carbohydrate intake and awareness of the benefits of many fats will be reflected in a new pyramid (or whatever other shape) that more clearly reflects good nutritional principles. If motivation is lacking, our government "experts" need only look at the outrageous twin epidemics of obesity and diabetes, what we've dubbed diabesity, facing this country today.

We are not alone in calling for a revised food pyramid. According to the Alternative Healthy Eating Index (A.H.E.I.), guidelines developed by a team at the Harvard University School of Public Health, a few simple changes to the federal government's "Dietary Guidelines for Americans" could further reduce the risk of major chronic diseases.[11] Its recommendations are based on studies on 150,000 men and women enrolled in the "Health Professionals' Follow-Up Study" and the "Nurses' Health Study," who filled out detailed lists of their food choices. Researchers then looked at the diseases these individuals got over a fifteen-year period. For example, instead of reducing all fats, the A.H.E.I. guidelines recommend a lower intake of trans fats, which come primarily from margarine and vegetable shortening. They also note that too much emphasis has been placed on carbohydrates. Moreover, nutrient-dense carbohydrates such as broccoli should be stressed and potatoes, which are generally consumed in the form of french fries, should be de-emphasized. Also recommended are one serving a day of nuts and soy protein, moderate alcohol consumption, and multivitamin supplements.

(Almost) Anything Goes

As we said previously, one of the reasons people stick with Atkins is that they are not ravenous all the time—a common complaint on low-fat, calorie-restricted diets. Moreover, when you are in the Lifetime Maintenance phase of Atkins, there are few truly forbidden foods. Nutritionally worthless junk foods such as candy and sugary soft drinks are banished forever, of course, but just about everything else is permitted. You can even eat some bread and pasta—but only if they are made from 100-percent unrefined whole grains—if you limit the portions to the amounts that keep you from gaining weight. That won't be hard to do. In fact, once you've been doing Atkins for a few months, your taste for high carb foods may diminish considerably. Cookies and other sugary foods may be far too sweet for your taste and small portions of carbohydrates such as unrefined whole-grain bread or breakfast cereals, brown rice, and sweet potatoes should quickly satisfy you. It all boils down to one essential fact: Virtually the only way you will maintain a way of eating— and by extension, also maintain your goal weight—is if the food you can eat is enjoyable and the quantities are ample enough to keep you from being hungry. As you increase the amount of carbohydrate foods in your diet, you will also learn to distinguish between those that do and don't cause swings in blood sugar that can lead to hunger. By doing Atkins correctly, you will experience satisfying food in sufficient quantities to make overwhelming cravings a thing of the past.

Exercise: The Not-So-Secret Ingredient

Some people will tell you that you don't have to exercise to
be successful doing Atkins for life. They couldn't be more
wrong. Exercise is a vital component of any healthy lifestyle
and is extremely valuable for permanent weight control.
First, as you should know, whether or not you exercise has a
dramatic impact on your health. Reg-

TIP
Carrying body fat around your abdominal area is associated with an increased risk for cardiovascular disease.

ular physical activity—meaning an
hour a day—reduces your risk factors
for virtually all of the most common
killer diseases. Second, it does amaz-
ing things for people trying to lose or
maintain their weight. Burning calories is the obvious one, but exercise
also does something much less obvious: It increases your
body's ratio of lean muscle to fat. And the more muscle mass
you have, the more calories you burn at *rest*. So not only does
exercise burn away fat while you're pumping or peddling, it
also cranks up the speed at which your metabolism idles.

James Guilbeaux, who lost 100 pounds doing Atkins,
explains that his weight loss really speeded up when he began the simple routine of walking on his lunch hour. "It
helped relieve my stress and burn off the fat," he says.
Later, he discovered that he could blast off a weight-loss
plateau by changing the type of exercise he was doing. If
he was walking every day when his weight loss stalled,
he'd switch to biking, and the fat burning would kick back
into gear. Today, he keeps his weight under control by not
going above 70 grams of carbs each day. That's right: As
Guilbeaux has learned, the other great benefit of stepping
up your exercise program is that it will likely raise your
ACE. In other words, you can eat more carbs every day
without gaining weight!

Make sure you include at least two kinds of exercise in
your regimen. One should be the aerobic kind, which works
your heart and lungs and increases endurance. The other

should be anaerobic, or resistance exercise, which strengthens your muscles. Aerobic exercise includes brisk walking, jogging, swimming, and biking. Anaerobic is weight-bearing exercise, which could be anything from weight lifting in a gym to doing arm lifts with soup cans at home. Both aerobic and anaerobic forms of exercise have been found to be extremely important for your health as well as for maintaining a healthy weight. It is also wonderful to be "addicted" to an activity such as dancing or tennis.

Filling in the Gaps in Our Food Supply

The produce we eat today contains lower levels of many nutrients than it did fifty years ago. Our soil is depleted from overharvesting, and fruits and vegetables shipped from hundreds or even thousands of miles away have lost a significant amount of nutrient value by the time they reach your grocery cart. Finally, some nutrients are lost when food is cooked. So no matter what dietary approach you follow, it is almost certain that your food is deficient in some of the nutrients you assume it contains. Also, there's the issue of our current diet: We Americans eat a lot of junk.

The Atkins Nutritional Approach™ includes the use of supplements for several reasons. During the Induction phase of Atkins, supplements are extremely important to restore those nutrients lost during your previous way of eating. On the American diet it is easy to fall short of your nutritional requirements, especially fiber. Environmental toxins, depleted soil, and the everyday stresses of contemporary life also argue for taking supplements as an insurance policy, no matter how conscientious you are about eating well. But even in the more liberal phases that follow Induction, everyone is strongly encouraged to take a daily multivitamin and mineral supplement—at the very least.

To Your Health

1. How do you feel most of the time? Check all that apply.
   a. Are you low in energy or does your energy level fluctuate widely throughout the day?
   b. Do you have trouble getting a good night's sleep?
   c. Are you hungry again a few hours after eating a meal?
   d. Does even mild exertion leave you short of breath?
   e. Do you suffer from mood swings?
   f. Do you get irritable, tired, or light-headed when hungry?
   g. Do you sometimes have trouble concentrating?
   h. Are you tired even after 8 hours of sleep?
   i. Are you depressed?
   j. Do your joints ache?
   k. Do you catch colds and other bugs easily?

2. Do you have any of these conditions?
   a. High cholesterol
   b. High triglycerides
   c. High blood pressure
   d. High blood sugar
   e. High insulin levels
   f. Unstable or low blood sugar (hypoglycemia)
   g. Prediabetes
   h. Type 2 diabetes
   i. Gastric disturbances, acid reflux, bloating, flatulence, constipation, or diarrhea
   j. Food allergies/sensitivities

Answers:
1. If you answered yes to more than a few of these questions, it is likely that you will see improvements or disappearance of these symptoms after following the Atkins program for several months.
2. If you answered yes to any of these questions, you should see improvements in the clinical parameters reflecting these conditions after several months. Seeing a doctor who understands complementary medicine will help you track your progress.

Call It a Lifestyle

With the book you hold in your hands, you're on your way to adapting Atkins to your own life—for the rest of your life. Pretty soon when you hear people call it the Atkins "diet," you'll hear yourself responding, "It's really not a diet; it's a way of life." Atkins can help you lose weight if you're overweight, improve your lipid profile and blood pressure, increase your energy, and reduce your risk of heart disease, diabetes, and many other life-threatening conditions. It can put an end to the myriad of symptoms caused by unstable blood sugar (hypoglycemia). It can also help you kick a food addiction or uncover a food allergy. Atkins is a healthier, more balanced way of eating and living. Let us be the first to congratulate you on your new lifestyle!

In the next chapter, we'll explore the intricacies of carbohydrates and learn how to tell the difference between those full of nutrients and therefore less apt to impact your blood sugar and those that you should avoid.

I Know I Saved My Life

At the age of thirty-two, April Greer was diagnosed with Type 2 diabetes. But after only three months doing Atkins, her blood sugar level returned to normal. And after six months, she had dropped 99 pounds.

There are three things I do every morning. First, I weigh myself. Next, I measure my waist, hips, and thighs. Last, I do my "fitting." I try on clothes one size smaller than my current size, checking to see how far I've got to go to button that waist or fit sleekly into that skirt.

Not too long ago, I would have added "check blood sugar" to that list. But no more. Not since I started doing Atkins. Controlling my carb intake has helped bring my blood sugar level into a normal range. A year ago it had been so high that I had hurtled headfirst into Type 2 diabetes. I was able to lower my blood sugar without medication, to the astonishment of my doctor, coworkers, and family. As a wonderful side effect, I lost weight faster than I could keep track of it! I've now lost a total of 99 pounds, weighing in at 138 pounds.

My *weight-loss* goal is still to lose another 8 pounds. I've already reached my goal of optimum health, of enhancing the likelihood of long life filled with activity and the joys of family life. I've been released from living under a cloud of worry that I would someday lose my limbs, and ultimately my life, to diabetes. I know that I will be here for my two young sons for many, many years to come.

My wake-up call came in October 2001, when I went to the doctor for the umpteenth time. For two months, I had been back and forth to his office with either a yeast infection or a bladder infection. A blood test revealed an additional problem: "April, you're a full-blown diabetic," my doctor said.

Me a full-blown diabetic? I was thirty-two years old! But, after weighing about 120 pounds throughout my twenties, I then tipped the scale at 237 pounds. I was consuming all the junk food I could get my hands on: doughnuts (homemade, no less), cookies, candy bars, and soda pop. I'd go through a half-gallon of ice cream every other day! Two heaping plates of spaghetti, along with a couple of pieces of bread on the side, were a typical meal for me. I had tried many diets and couldn't stick with a single one. I couldn't walk up a flight of stairs without huffing and puffing. But this—diabetes—was more than I could take.

On November 1, 2001, I started the Induction phase of Atkins. The first week was hard; then, suddenly, my cravings for sweets vanished. I also started to feel a little more ener-

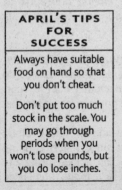

APRIL'S TIPS FOR SUCCESS

Always have suitable food on hand so that you don't cheat.

Don't put too much stock in the scale. You may go through periods when you won't lose pounds, but you do lose inches.

getic. By February, I was down to 170 pounds. My bladder and yeast infections had disappeared and my blood sugar was in the normal range. I had improved completely without medication, and my doctor encouraged me to keep up the good work. "Get down to 140 pounds," he said, "and don't come back." So I did.

Now, instead of sitting on the couch watching television, I play football with my sons, who are nine and six. I sprint up the stairs to my office every workday, instead of laboriously trekking up each step, holding my breath at the top so that my coworkers won't notice that I can't breathe. I swim, lift weights, and walk on a treadmill. I prefer to have several small meals instead of a real lunch, so I'll snack on nuts and string cheese and later have a protein bar. A typical dinner is chicken and vegetables. I don't prepare anything different for my family, so they are also reaping the benefits of eating healthy whole foods. Every night, I have a cup of decaf coffee with sweetener and delicious whole cream. It's my little cup of heaven, my treat that helps get me through the evening without craving an after-dinner snack.

My family and many of my friends have followed in my footsteps. I ran into a former coworker recently. She was blown away by the new me. Plagued with weight problems herself, she was eager to learn how I had done it. Now, I'm coaching her, and it's so exciting to watch somebody change her life for the better!

It's especially wonderful when that somebody is right there in my mirror!

ACE: 60	WEIGHT BEFORE: 237 pounds	BLOOD SUGAR BEFORE: 208
AGE: 33		
HEIGHT: 5 feet 3 inches	WEIGHT AFTER: 138 pounds	BLOOD SUGAR AFTER: 72
	WEIGHT LOST: 99 pounds	STARTED DOING ATKINS: November 2001

A Close Call

After a near-fatal heart attack at age thirty, police officer Matthew Holloway tried every diet in the book and failed to slim down. Now he is 78 pounds lighter and in the best shape of his life.

One day four years ago I was having chest pains, which, I knew from my training as a police officer, could signal cardiac problems. I was able to drive myself to the local hospital and then had a heart attack right there in the emergency room. Two days later, my doctors placed two stents in a blocked artery in my heart. It took ninety minutes just to get the artery open. After the surgery, according to the electrocardiogram, I "died." Fortunately, the doctors were able to resuscitate me, so I'm here to tell my story. When I returned to work in the police department's Gang and Violent Crime Unit, I had a new nickname, "Flatline," for my EKG reading.

MATTHEW'S TIPS FOR SUCCESS

Exercise on a regular basis. Once you get used to moving, you'll feel better physically and emotionally. Establish a time of day and a routine you can stick to.

Check out controlled carb options at health food stores.

As a reward, treat yourself to new clothes in styles you thought you could never wear.

I had known there was a significant history of heart disease in my family, but I had ignored it until then. But after the heart attack, I was on doctor's orders to lose weight and reduce my cholesterol level. I tried a low-sodium diet, a low-fat diet, and a low-calorie diet. Instead of losing weight, I ballooned from my pre-heart-attack weight of 275 to 290. Because I was so out of shape, I had to leave my unit for a desk job at the courthouse, which really depressed me. Not long after my transfer, I noticed a state trooper who had lost a significant amount of weight. "How?" I asked him, and he said he'd done Atkins. "Go buy Dr. Atkins' book and read it!" he told me, so I followed his advice. It made sense to me to cut out sugar and processed food. I had my last high carb meal that Thanksgiving, a little more than a year after my heart attack. It took about three and a half weeks for me to start losing weight, but within two and a half months I had shed 60 pounds. Once the weight started to come off, I felt like I could exercise again. (I had been athletic and even played college football, but had stopped working out when I gained weight.) Now I run two to four miles and lift weights for forty-five minutes, five days a week, on my lunch break. I can't believe I now have a 36-inch waist. That's pretty good for a 6-foot 2-inch guy!

A typical breakfast for me is sausage and eggs. For lunch I might eat a chef's salad with ranch dressing. Dinner is usually chicken or steak with green beans. My favorite snack is sharp cheddar cheese. The key to my success is giving up side dishes like biscuits, french fries, and corn. I also take a multivitamin religiously every day. My LDL is down quite a bit. I still take heart medication, but I eventually want to be able to lower the dose. I also take Zocor for my cholesterol. High cholesterol runs in my family.

I have even converted my mother to the Atkins lifestyle. She lost 30 pounds in three months. People say that I'm like a kid because I'm so full of energy and that I look ten years

ACE: 50	WEIGHT LOST: 78 pounds	LDL BEFORE: 190
AGE: 34		LDL AFTER: 120
HEIGHT: 6 feet 2 inches	TOTAL CHOLESTEROL BEFORE: 284	TRIGLYCERIDES BEFORE: 150
WEIGHT BEFORE: 290 pounds	TOTAL CHOLESTEROL AFTER: 217	TRIGLYCERIDES AFTER: 61
WEIGHT AFTER: 212 pounds	HDL BEFORE: 37	STARTED DOING ATKINS: November 1999
	HDL AFTER: 67	

younger. I went swimming recently and took off my shirt in public for the first time in thirteen years. My social life is better than I ever dreamed. And at work, I'm now on the SWAT team, doing the dangerous stuff I love. Doing Atkins saved my life and changed me completely. My outlook and self-esteem have never been better.

3 | Yes, You Can Eat Carbs!

One of the joys of the Atkins lifestyle is that there are few truly forbidden food categories. And that most certainly includes carbohydrates, which play an important role in any balanced diet. Once you've achieved your goal weight and are doing Atkins for life, even the occasional serving of whole-wheat pasta or a baked potato can turn up on your plate. The Atkins difference is that the carbs you eat must be high-quality carbs—the kind that satisfy your appetite and supply you with vitamins, minerals, and other phytonutrients.

Cracking the Carbohydrate Code

Understanding what carbohydrates are and knowing how they affect your health and well-being are the two keys to success while doing Atkins. As explained in chapter 1, most foods have some mixture of fat, protein, and carbohydrates. Take away the fat, protein, water, and ash (the mineral content) in a food and what you have left are the carbohydrates. In general, that means the starchy or sugary part of the food, along with any dietary fiber. Not all carbohydrates are created equal, however—some are definitely better than others. Nutritionists have traditionally divided carbs into two categories: simple carbohydrates such as sugars and complex carbs such as whole grains. Unfortunately, life—and nutritional science—isn't that simple, and the two categories are confusing because there is some overlap between them. In fact, by traditional standards, sugary breakfast

TIP
Whole vegetables and fruits are less likely than vegetable or fruit juice to have a dramatic impact on your blood sugar.

cereals contain complex carbs as well as simple sugars; the same can be said for raspberries. Today many nutritionists believe that the glycemic index is a much more useful method for evaluating the impact of carbohydrate-containing foods on your blood sugar and insulin production than the categories of simple and complex carbohydrates. It's also a bit more complicated.

Grasping the Glycemic Index

The glycemic index (GI) is a quick way to understand the relative impact that carbohydrates from a particular food have on your blood sugar compared to the effect after eating a similar amount of pure glucose, which enters your bloodstream almost immediately. In general, the lower a food is on the GI, the less glucose it will deliver to your bloodstream and therefore the less insulin your pancreas must produce to transport the glucose to your cells. And the less insulin you produce the less likely it is that your body is going to store fat.

Here's why: When you eat a highly refined carbohydrate food like a sugary cereal or white bread, it is quickly converted to glucose so it rushes into your bloodstream almost at once. The result is a glucose spike, followed by a glucose drop—it's called unstable blood sugar. Eat an unprocessed carbohydrate food that is lower in sugar and also contains a lot of fiber, like berries, and what happens? The amount of glucose from the food enters your bloodstream slowly and steadily. No glucose spike, and no sudden glucose drop—your energy stays on an even keel. That's because the sugar in the berries is in the form of fructose, which must first be converted to glucose in your liver. That takes some time, and the process is slowed down even more by the fiber in the berries. And when your glucose level stays constant, there is no need to send in the heavy artillery in the form of additional insulin to deal with transporting excess glucose to your cells.

TIP

Keep a carbohydrate-gram counter near your refrigerator.

But the GI is not very useful for making day-to-day food choices because it does not take into account the average size of a portion. Instead, you are basically comparing 50 grams of digestible carbohydrate no matter how much food that represents. In the case of carrots, for example, a 50-gram portion is equivalent to six or seven carrots, which is actually about as many half-cup servings, far more than anyone would eat at one time. That leads to the peculiar result that carrots have a slightly higher GI than the quarter cup of sugar that also constitutes 50 grams of digestible carbs. (It actually takes a pound and a half of carrots to have a significant impact on your blood sugar.)

Enter the Glycemic Load

Another measurement, called the glycemic load (GL), *does* take portion size into consideration and compares equal portions. But in real life many other factors, such as the amount of fat and fiber from other foods you eat at the same time, can affect how quickly you absorb the carbohydrate from a single food into your bloodstream. That's why we advise you that when doing Atkins, you eat appropriate carbohydrate foods with protein and fat.

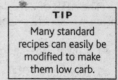

TIP

Many standard recipes can easily be modified to make them low carb.

Although foods *can* be given exact GI and GL numbers, that information doesn't really help you all that much on a practical basis in part because the GL and GI numbers may or may not match up. For example, watermelon has a high GI, meaning that the glucose from watermelon enters your bloodstream quickly; but it has a low GL because watermelon is mostly water.

A Simpler Way

Don't throw up your hands in frustration. Rather than expect you to worry about exact numbers, or having to look at two lists, we've come up with a way to make this data much easier to use. On the basis of both GI and the GL numbers,

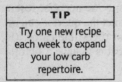

TIP

Try one new recipe each week to expand your low carb repertoire.

we've created the three-tier Atkins Glycemic Ranking™ (AGR™), which compares carbohydrate foods in terms of their impact on blood sugar. In general, the lower a food is on the AGR, the less processed it is and the more fiber it contains. They are also the carbohydrate foods that Atkins followers will eat most frequently. However, not all foods with lower rankings are low in carbs. For example, all legumes are high in carbohydrate content, but rank low on the AGR because of their high fiber content. You must continue to count carbs as you always have. (See Two Complementary Tools, page 43.)

The AGR of a food gives you a quick way to identify how often you should select it, based on three categories:

#1: Low AGR—eat regularly.

#2: Medium AGR—eat in moderation.

#3: High AGR—eat sparingly.

The charts begin on page 49.

Some foods may seem odd in the various groups. A baked potato, for example, is not processed and is high in fiber, but it has a higher GI than table sugar, so we have placed it in the #3 category, meaning it is a food that you should eat sparingly. The carrot has been in ill repute because it places high on the GI; however, it turns out to be low in GL, meaning moderate portions are fine. It's important to remember here that standard portions are used when the tests are performed in the laboratory to measure these values. These portions are small—meaning that they frequently don't represent what has become a typical serving size in today's supersize society. If your portion of, say, brown rice is considerably larger—the effect on your blood sugar will be substantially more as well.

Looking at the effect of foods on your bloodstream is a fairly new concept, and many foods have not yet been analyzed in the lab. If you don't see a favorite food in one of the categories, chances are it's because the information isn't yet available. One way to check whether a new food is increasing your blood sugar level or your insulin production is to take note of how you feel a few hours after eating it. Are your hunger and appetite levels any different than they usually are before the next meal? After eating this food, if you feel really ravenous or experience cravings, you might need to omit that choice or eat it in a much smaller portion than you did at that previous meal. These lists are not a guarantee that you won't experience some carb response to a given item. Always pay attention to your own hunger and appetite cues while introducing new foods.

Two Complementary Tools

When you combine the Atkins Glycemic Ranking™ (AGR™) with a carb-gram counter, you have a powerful method for choosing the best carbohydrates to eat. Some of the foods that rank lower in the AGR may still contain a lot of grams of carbs. Let's take an example. A half-cup of cooked oatmeal contains 10.7 grams of Net Carbs and is in Category #1 of the AGR. So while oatmeal (the old-fashioned kind, not instant or flavored versions) can be eaten regularly, you'll want to have it in small portions. A half-cup of cooked sweet corn has 12.6 grams Net Carbs—only 2 more than the oatmeal—but we've placed it in Category #3 because it has a much more profound effect on blood sugar. The oatmeal is much gentler in its impact on your glucose/insulin levels. Even with Category #1 foods, you must always consider the Net Carb gram count of a food so that you don't exceed your ACE.

What Are Net Carbs?

When you do Atkins, you actually count Net Carbs, which means the total carbohydrate content of the food minus the fiber content (along with glycerine and sugar alcohols found in some reduced carb foods). The Net Carbs number reflects the grams of carbohydrate that significantly impact your blood sugar level and are the only carbs you need to count when you do Atkins. The Net Carb number is almost always lower than the total carbohydrate number. The exception is foods such as cream with virtually no fiber content: The total carbs and Net Carbs are the same.

If you don't have a carb-gram counter handy, you can guesstimate the Net Carb count for a particular food by information provided on the food label. (This obviously won't help you with fresh vegetables or other nonpackaged foods.) Subtract the grams of fiber from the amount of total carb grams per serving and you've got a pretty good sense of the Net Carb number. Sugar alcohols, glycerine, and some other carbs that have minimal impact on blood sugar are also netted out of total carbs, but these may not be listed on labels. (You can also refer to Dr. Atkins' New Carbohydrate Gram Counter or go to www.atkins.com.)

The Impact of Fiber and Fat

Carbohydrate foods that are low on the Atkins Glycemic Ranking contain plenty of dietary fiber. Fiber slows down digestion, which in turn slows the movement of carbs (in the form of glucose) into your bloodstream. Fiber is also valuable in helping you fend off hunger pangs. That's because fiber—and the water content—fills you up quickly and stays with you. Imagine eating six chocolate chip cookies in a row, for example. All too easy, right? Now imagine eating six apples in a row. Impossible—you'd be full long before you got to the sixth apple. What's more, after eating those cookies you'd be hungry again soon. However, after eating a Granny Smith apple—preferably with a slice of cheddar cheese—it would be much longer before you'd feel hungry again.

Combine dietary fiber with dietary fat and you can slow down the onset of hunger even more. Like fiber, fat also slows down the rate at which food leaves your stomach and thus the rate at which glucose from a food enters your bloodstream. So, for example, the fat in premium ice cream slows down the entry of the sugar into your bloodstream. That doesn't mean, of course, that you can eat a big bowl of chocolate-fudge ripple every day, but it does mean that when you've reached the Lifetime Maintenance phase of Atkins you can occasionally treat yourself to a good quality low-carb ice cream.

Fat also plays an important role in adding flavor to food and helping you feel full. That's why a serving of plain steamed broccoli may leave you wanting something more, while a serving of broccoli lightly sautéed in olive oil is more filling—and tastes a lot better, too! Recent research shows that fat actually stimulates a hormone that elicits the feeling of satiety.[1] Fiber works in concert with the fat, prolonging the elevation of the hormone during digestion, which helps keep you satisfied longer. That's also why we recommend you have that apple with a small wedge of cheddar cheese or some peanut butter or eat blueberries with a tablespoon of chopped nuts or mascarpone cheese.

Does Fiber Count?

When you do Atkins, fiber offers another bonus: It allows you to enjoy some extra carbs—without exceeding your ACE, your threshold for carb intake without gaining weight. What's the secret? Net Carbs. Here's how they work: In the most simple terms, dietary fiber is nothing more than carbohydrates that the body cannot break down and convert to blood sugar.

At this time, government regulations generally do distinguish between carbohydrates that you can digest and carbohydrates that get a free ride and pass right through you.

However, the government does *not* distinguish those that impact blood sugar from those that do not. On a food label, they're all lumped together as just carbohydrates. That's very misleading, because it suggests that all carbs behave the same way in your body. Take a look at two crunchy snack foods with similar carb counts but vastly different nutrition. Just one Famous Amos oatmeal raisin cookie (and who can eat just one?) contains 5 grams of carbs with less than half a gram of fiber. About fourteen macadamia nuts also contain 5 grams of carbs—but about 3 of those grams are fiber. Full of sugar and white flour, the cookie won't satisfy you for long, even as it eats up 5 precious grams of carbs in your daily count. In contrast, the filling, satisfying high-fiber nuts are rich in potassium and calcium, among other nutrients. And because the nuts have only 2 grams of digestible carbs—the other 3 grams are nondigestible fiber—you only have to add 2 grams to your daily carb tally.

Sorting Out the Carbs

Interestingly, while protein, fat, water, and ash (minerals) can be assayed (quantitatively and/or qualitatively measured) by a variety of lab tests, carbohydrates are *not* assayed. Instead, the amount of carbohydrate in a food is determined by subtracting all these other components from the total weight in grams. Whatever isn't one of the other components is considered carbohydrate. This "everything but the kitchen sink" approach means that a whole plethora of compounds are lumped together, some of which are similar to each other—and some of which are completely different from each other—in terms of both chemical structure and how they behave in our bodies.

So although we said at the beginning of this chapter that carbs basically can be divided into simple or complex categories, what is actually listed on a food label could include unfamiliar ingredients such as lignins, organic acids, sugar alcohols, glycerols, flavonoids, pectins, and gums. Although included in the carb count on the label, many of these compounds actually have minimal impact on blood sugar.

Climbing the Carbohydrate Ladder

If you did the weight-loss phases of Atkins, you gradually added back different types of carbohydrate foods to your diet. We refer to the progressive addition as climbing the carb ladder. The carb ladder is an equally valuable tool now that you're doing Atkins for a lifetime. The carb ladder encourages you to eat a variety of carbohydrate foods, which in turn means that you get a balance of nutrients and are less likely to get bored with your food choices. The ladder also helps you choose the relative amounts of different sources of carbs to eat.

At the most basic level, the carb ladder indicates that you should be eating more vegetables, for example, than whole grains. The ladder allows you to achieve variety, but reminds you that amounts of foods higher on the ladder should be eaten less often. As always, the higher your ACE, the more variety you can enjoy and the more you can sample the buffet table of foods high on the carb ladder. The carb ladder also helps you to balance your occasional intake of high carb foods with lower ones, and to identify which foods are fine to have in moderation and which are the real basis of your lifetime regimen. In general, the higher up the carb ladder a food is, the less frequently you will consume it and the smaller your portions will be. Within each rung of the ladder, the AGR helps you further prioritize your food choices.

When adding carb-containing foods to your menus, select most often from Category #1, adding some items from Category #2 for variety. Occasionally, select an item from

What Are Sugar Alcohols?

As the name implies, sugar alcohols are compounds that are derived from sugars but have an alcohol chemical structure. Like other carbohydrates, sugar alcohols have bulking and sweetening properties, but they provide fewer calories and don't impact blood sugar the same way. This makes them a useful ingredient in the manufacture of reduced carb chocolate bars and other products.

Category #3. You'll find the three groups listed after each type of food in the carbohydrate ladder, below.

STEP 1 : The Vegetable Rung. When you moved past the Induction phase of Atkins in your weight-loss journey, your first additions were more vegetables. In Lifetime Maintenance, veggies such as salad greens, spinach, tomatoes (technically a fruit), broccoli, and a host of other foods remain your most valuable source of carbohydrates. What else do these foods contain? Let's look at the vitamins and minerals in one cup of cooked broccoli. You get 116 milligrams of vitamin C, 76 micrograms of folate, 456 milligrams of potassium, and 72 milligrams of calcium. Each one of those amounts is a goodly proportion of your daily needs—all for just under 5 grams Net Carbs. Similarly, cruciferous veggies such as broccoli, Brussels sprouts, cauliflower, kale, and cabbage provide isothiocyanates and indoles, phytochemicals that, according to numerous studies, appear to be powerful cancer fighters.[2-4]

> **TIP**
>
> When eating in a restaurant, ask the server to replace your rice or potato with an extra serving of vegetables.

The phytochemicals zeaxanthin and lutein are found in dark yellow and orange vegetables—such as yellow summer squash and carrots. These nutrients play an important role in keeping your eyes healthy. Kale, garlic, onions, salad greens, broccoli, Brussels sprouts, spinach, and red bell peppers are also all particularly high in antioxidants. By fighting the oxidation damage that highly reactive free radical molecules can do to your cells, antioxidants may help protect you against cancer, heart disease, and many other age-related health problems such as vision loss from macular degeneration. The more variety in the vegetables you eat, the better. And most vegetables are low on the AGR, so eating your fill has very little impact on your blood sugar.

#1 EAT REGULARLY	#2 EAT IN MODERATION	#3 EAT SPARINGLY
Artichokes	Beets	Corn, sweet
Asparagus	Carrots	Parsnips
Bamboo shoots	Peas, green	Pea soup
Beans, string or green	Squash, acorn	Potato
Bok choy	Squash, butternut	
Broccoli	Taro	
Broccoli rabe	Tomato juice	
Brussels sprouts	Tomato soup	
Butter beans	Sweet potato	
Cabbage, all varieties	Yuca	
Cauliflower		
Celeriac		
Celery		
Chard		
Chayote		
Collards		
Cucumber		
Dandelion greens		
Eggplant		
Endive		
Fennel		

continued

#1 EAT REGULARLY	#2 EAT IN MODERATION	#3 EAT SPARINGLY
Jicama		
Kale		
Kohlrabi		
Lettuce, all varieties		
Lima beans, baby		
Mushrooms, all varieties		
Mustard greens		
Okra		
Onion		
Pea pods/snow peas		
Peppers, all varieties		
Pumpkin		
Radishes		
Rutabaga		
Sauerkraut		
Spinach		
Sprouts		
Squash, zucchini		
Tomato		
Turnip greens		
Water chestnuts		

STEP 2: The Dairy Rung. The next rung on the ladder is dairy foods. Most aged cheeses are wonderfully low in carbs. An ounce of cheddar, for example, has less than half a gram of Net Carbs. The trick with cheese is to be aware of how little an

TIP

If you aren't sure what to order in a restaurant, stick with basics such as fish, lamb chops, or roasted chicken.

ounce really is. You should be eating no more than 4 ounces a day. Now that you're maintaining your weight, you can even have full-fat yogurt or some whole milk with your cereal or your tea. (Unsweetened soy milk is another option, although not true dairy, but make sure it is fortified with calcium.) Remember that skim milk is higher in carbs. Cheese is an excellent source of dietary calcium. Five ounces of farmer's cheese, for instance, gives you 1,000 milligrams of calcium—or much more than half of most people's daily requirement.

#1 EAT REGULARLY	#2 EAT IN MODERATION	#3 EAT SPARINGLY
Cheese, all nonprocessed hard varieties*	Buttermilk	No-sugar added ice cream
Cottage cheese	Milk, whole	Other milk (skim, 2%, etc.)
Cream, heavy and light*	Low carb ice cream	
Farmer's cheese	Yogurt, full fat, plain	
Half-and-half*		
Low carb dairy beverages		
Low carb yogurt		

continued

#1 EAT REGULARLY	#2 EAT IN MODERATION	#3 EAT SPARINGLY
Pot cheese		
Ricotta cheese		
Sour cream*		

*Keep portions small.

STEP 3: The Nuts and Seeds Rung. Keep climbing the carb ladder and you get to the crunchy pleasures of almonds, pecans, macadamias, sunflower seeds, and the rest of the nuts and seeds. Both nuts and seeds are excellent sources of fiber, minerals, vitamin E, and good dietary fats. To avoid processed oils, choose dry-roasted nuts whenever possible.

#1 EAT REGULARLY	#2 EAT IN MODERATION	#3 EAT SPARINGLY
Almonds	Cashews	Chestnuts
Brazil nuts	Peanuts	
Coconut	Soybeans, roasted	
Hazelnuts/ filberts		
Macadamias		
Pecans		
Pine nuts/ pignolis		
Pistachios		
Pumpkin seeds		

#1 EAT REGULARLY	#2 EAT IN MODERATION	#3 EAT SPARINGLY
Sesame seeds		
Sunflower seeds		
Walnuts		

STEP 4: Berries. Berries are lower in carbs and have a lower GI than many other fruits, which is why you were able to reincorporate them into your meals before other fruits. They also make great snacks. Blueberries, raspberries, strawberries, and other berries are sweet little powerhouses full of valuable nutrients. The deep, vivid colors of berries come from their phytonutrients—natural chemicals such as vitamin C, polyphenols, and anthocyanins (which are helpful for preserving your vision) that are powerful antioxidants.[5,6] When it comes to antioxidants per gram, berries are at the top of the list, which is why the Atkins Ratio™, which compares antioxidant capacity to grams of carbs, ranks berries high. (The lower the carb count and the higher the antioxidant capacity, the more antioxidant power you get for your carb buck.) Half a cup of fresh strawberries has fewer than 3.4 grams of Net Carbs and gives you 40 milligrams of vitamin C along with 125 milligrams of potassium. Frozen berries are fine—they're convenient, available year-round, and they're just as rich in nutrients as fresh ones. Read the ingredient list carefully, however, and choose brands that are just frozen fruit without any added sugar.

STEP 5: Beans and Legumes. Don't skip lentils, kidney beans, pinto beans, black beans, and some fifty other varieties of legumes. Their relatively high carb content is offset quite a bit by their high fiber content, which slows their impact on blood sugar. Nonetheless, you still need to keep the portions

> **TIP**
> If you have not been regularly eating high-fiber foods, especially raw vegetables, add them gradually and in small quantities to allow your system to adjust.

small. You'll get about 12 grams of Net Carbs from just a quarter-cup of cooked beans. By themselves or added to soups, stews, and sauces, beans are very satisfying. Even a small portion contributes protein and B vitamins and is an outstanding way to add important minerals, such as calcium, magnesium, iron, and potassium to your diet. Watch out for baked beans (unless they're homemade; see our low carb recipe on page 387), however. Commercial versions are prepared with brown sugar or molasses, which bumps up their carb count. It's worth noting that tofu, also known as bean curd, is very low in carbohydrates and is an excellent source of protein. Half a cup of regular tofu contains just 2 grams of Net Carbs. Firm, soft, and silken versions are just slightly higher. Bean sprouts, which add interest to salads and stir-fries, are also low in carbs and can be eaten even in Induction.

#1 EAT REGULARLY	#2 EAT IN MODERATION	#3 EAT SPARINGLY
Hummus	Chick peas	Black-eyed peas
Lentil soup	Kidney beans	Lima beans (dried)
Minestrone soup	Lentils	Navy beans
Soybeans	Peas, dried	Pinto beans
Soy milk, no sugar added		
Tofu/bean curd		

STEP 6: Other Fruits. Plums and other relatively low carb fruits such as grapefruit, kiwis, peaches, and apples are a great low carb way to satisfy your sweet tooth while also getting a good dose of fiber and a healthy amount of vitamin C, potassium, and other important nutrients. The rule here is the more colorful the fruit, the better. Only fresh fruit gives you the magic combination of low Net Carbs and nutrition;

canned fruit usually has added sugar, as do many frozen fruits. Read labels carefully and purchase only products free of added sugar or corn syrup. When it comes to dried fruit, proceed cautiously. Drying tends to concentrate the fruit's natural sugars so a small piece may be as high in carbs as a whole fresh fruit. Take papaya, for example. A half of a small fresh papaya contains about 6 grams Net Carbs; a single piece of dried papaya contains twice that. Also, some dried fruit, such as cranberries or cherries, contain added sugar.

#1 EAT REGULARLY	#2 EAT IN MODERATION	#3 EAT SPARINGLY
Apple	Apricots, canned in juice	Banana
Blackberries	Apricots, dried	Cranberry cocktail, no added sugar
Blueberries	Apricots, fresh	Cranberry juice, no added sugar
Cherries	Grapes, green and red	Fruit cocktail, canned in juice
Cranberries	Grapefruit juice, no added sugar	Grape juice
Grapefruit	Kiwifruit	Orange juice
Orange	Mango	Prunes
Peach	Melon, cantaloupe	Raisins
Pear	Melon, Crenshaw	
Plum	Melon, honeydew	
Pomegranate	Papaya	
Raspberries	Pineapple, fresh	
Strawberries	Watermelon	
Tangerine		

TIP

Get into the habit of adding lentils, chickpeas, and other legumes to your luncheon salads for a filling, fiber-rich meal.

STEP 7: Higher Carb Vegetables. Certain veggies were restricted in the earlier weight-loss phases of Atkins, but they deserve a place at the table when you are doing Atkins for life. This category includes vegetables such as acorn and other winter squash, carrots, peas, and sweet corn (which is properly a grain). This grouping also includes many of the root vegetables such as beets and parsnips, and tubers such as white potatoes and sweet potatoes, which are loaded with minerals such as potassium. Most of these vegetables are also good sources of vitamin C. Color is a good indicator of nutrient content so, for example, yellow squash and pumpkin are great sources of beta-carotene. Your portions of these high carb foods have to stay small, but even a small serving adds interest and variety to meals. (Note: We used to call this category starchy vegetables, but we now prefer to use the more inclusive term higher carb vegetables.) For a full list of these vegetables and their AGRs refer back to the ladder for Step 1.

STEP 8: Whole Grains. There's a whole world of nutrient-rich whole grains waiting for you. Again, these foods have a place in your lifetime regimen; just keep portions small and focus on the whole, unprocessed grains. The rich, nutty flavor of whole grains such as kasha, (buckwheat), barley, whole-wheat couscous, wheat berries, and wild rice makes them very satisfying even in small amounts. As sources of fiber, B vitamins, vitamin E, and minerals such as magnesium and zinc, whole grains are hard to beat. When it comes to bread, your best choices are unrefined, whole-grain products. Eat cereals with fat or protein to curb their impact on blood sugar. Look for whole-grain bread and breakfast cereal products made with stone-ground flours, which you will more likely find in a health food store than at most supermarkets.

#1 EAT REGULARLY	#2 EAT IN MODERATION	#3 EAT SPARINGLY
Barley	Amaranth	Bagel, 100% whole grain
Low carb (soy) bagels	Bran flakes	Corn flakes, no added sugar
Low carb (soy) bread	Bread, 100% whole grain	Cream of Wheat
Low carb (soy) cereal	Bread, 100% whole wheat	Crackers, 100% whole wheat
Low carb (soy) muffins	Bread, dark rye, 100% whole grain	Grapenuts
Low carb (soy) rolls	Bread, multigrain, unrefined	Grits
Low carb (soy) snack chips	Bread, pumpernickel, 100% whole grain, no molasses	Millet
Low carb (soy) pasta	Bread, rye, 100% whole grain	Pasta, whole wheat
Oat bran	Bread, sour dough, 100% whole grain	Pasta, brown rice
Oatmeal, old-fashioned	Buckwheat (kasha)	Pita, 100% whole wheat

continued

#1 EAT REGULARLY	#2 EAT IN MODERATION	#3 EAT SPARINGLY
Tortilla, low carb (soy)	Bulgur	Pizza, cheese 100% whole wheat crust
Wheat bran	Cornmeal	Pretzels, whole wheat
Wheat germ, no added sugar	Couscous, whole wheat	Puffed brown rice cereal, no added sugar
Wraps, low carb (soy)	Crispbread, 100% whole grain	Rice cake, 100% brown rice
	Flatbread, 100% whole grain	Rice, basmati, unprocessed brown
	Melba toast, 100% rye or whole wheat	Rice, brown
	Muesli without added sugar	Shredded wheat
	Pizza, low carb	Wild rice
	Popcorn, without hydogenated oils	
	Tortilla, corn or 100% whole wheat	
	Wrap, 100% whole wheat	

Now that you have a handle on which carbohydrates you should be eating most often, which you should eat more moderately, and which deserve only an occasional cameo role, it's time to take a similarly close look at dietary fat and protein in the next

TIP

Bring a pocket-size carb-gram counter with you when shopping for food or dining out.

chapter. You will then have the tools necessary to create your own personalized eating plan, along with the recipes, meal plans, and other information you will find in Part 2.

Can You Drink Alcohol?

In *Dr. Atkins' New Diet Revolution*, we included wine and spirits as a rung on the carb ladder, but we have since decided to remove it because alcohol is not a nutritive carbohydrate and shouldn't be consumed in place of food. This is not to say that you can't enjoy alcohol occasionally, assuming that you are not a diabetic or have trouble controlling how much you drink. The good news is that a number of recent studies have shown that drinking alcohol, particularly wine, with a meal diminishes the impact of the carbohydrate on blood sugar. Other studies show a favorable impact from drinking wine in the prevention of cardiovascular disease in patients with diabetes. Most spirits are very low in carbs, especially vodka and gin, but the alcohol is burned before fat for energy, so limit your alcohol intake to no more than one drink per day, at most, once you are beyond induction. The higher the proof, the lower in carbs the spirits will be. Dry wine is lower in carbs than sweet wines such as sherry and port, which can be quite high (no pun intended). Liqueurs also tend to have a high sugar content. Use low carb mixers such as seltzer or sugar-free tonic water. Also avoid the use of fruit juices, which are high in carbs, as mixers. Beer is too high in carbs to drink more than occasionally and in moderation, even when you're at the Lifetime Maintenance level. Light beer or the newly introduced low carb beer, however,

Making the Right Choices

In the match-ups below, assuming comparable portions, which of these carbohydrate-containing foods is the better selection in terms of its impact on your blood sugar?

1. Breakfast:

    a. Prunes or plums?

    b. Yogurt or cottage cheese?

    c. Whole-wheat toast or corn flakes?

    d. An orange or orange juice?

    e. Oatmeal or Cream of Wheat?

    f. Skim milk or whole milk?

2. Lunch:

    a. Pea soup or tomato soup?

    b. Pumpernickel bread or stoned-wheat crackers?

    c. Sauerkraut or deli cole slaw?

    d. Fruit cocktail or a tangerine?

    e. Navy beans or lentils?

    f. Cheddar cheese or yogurt?

3. Dinner

    a. Green beans with chestnuts or green beans with water chestnuts?

    b. Eggplant or carrots?

    c. Snow peas or green peas?

    d. Sweet potato or pumpkin?

    e. Wine or beer?

4. Snack:

    a. Peanuts or walnuts?

b. Roasted pumpkin seeds or roasted soybeans?

c. Dried apricots or raisins?

d. Whole-wheat pretzels or popcorn?

Answers:

1. Breakfast a. Plums b. Cottage cheese c. Whole-wheat toast
d. An orange e. Oatmeal f. Whole milk

2. Lunch a. Tomato soup b. Pumpernickel bread c. Sauerkraut
d. Tangerine e. Lentils f. Cheddar cheese

3. Dinner a. With water chestnuts b. Eggplant c. Snow peas
d. Pumpkin e. Wine (preferably dry)

4. Snack a. Walnuts b. Roasted pumpkin seeds c. Dried apricots
d. Popcorn

is lower in carbs and can be used in place of other alcoholic beverage selections.

Seeing the Light

Vegetarian John Troy was worried that eating the Atkins way would deprive him of his spiritual awareness. Instead, he regained his health and something equally important: inner peace.

I was a vegetarian for about twenty years. I cycled in and out of various phases of that lifestyle—lacto-ovo, vegan—and sometimes, I would add a little fish. I run a natural foods company, and like many people in my field, I was part of a New Age food culture that linked spirituality with diet. I also thought that eating meat would put me at risk for health problems as I grew older.

Vegetarianism worked for me for some time, but as I aged, I gradually gained weight. I was eating a lot of pasta, rice, and other grains, as well as honey and soy, but my diet didn't tell on me until I was about fifty and my metabolism changed.

JOHN'S TIPS FOR SUCCESS

Master the science: If you understand why and how Atkins works, you can win over people who challenge your lifestyle.

Focus on all the neat things you can eat now, not the things you have given up.

Suddenly, my health started to decline. I developed osteoarthritis, elevated blood pressure, and started having chest pains. I suffered from sleep apnea and nocturnal seizures—sometimes as many as eight a night. Every time I lay down, I'd have an episode. Perhaps not surprisingly, I also suffered from clinical depression.

I took medications for all these conditions and there seemed to be no hope in sight. My doctors told me there was no cure for my arthritis and that it would get progressively more serious. To make matters worse, the drugs I took to control it gave me ulcers. Meanwhile, the doctors who treated my sleep apnea wanted to put me on a monitor while I slept. At about this time, I was building a house, so I made certain that all the rooms were accessible by wheelchair—I fully expected to be using one soon. Truthfully, I thought I'd be dead by now or in such poor health that I wouldn't enjoy life.

My initial dietary response to my health crisis was to cut out all fat. Unfortunately, that didn't do me any good and seemed to compound my weight problem. I kept gaining weight because I was hungry all the time. I couldn't get through the night without going to the refrigerator. I forced myself to start walking regularly but even that didn't seem to make a difference.

About five years ago, I realized that I was addicted to carbohydrates and gradually let go of my exclusively vegetarian diet. My peers in the natural products industry had suggested that I look into Atkins, but I had resisted because I love animals and I'm not a violent person. I enjoy peace of mind and didn't want to relinquish any of that. On my own, I had reduced the number of carbohydrates in my diet. Then, about three years ago, I read *Dr. Atkins' New Diet Revolution* and experienced a paradigm shift. I got it!

Atkins was difficult at first, but the Induction Phase worked really well for me. My cravings went away. I used to have restless leg syndrome—I called it the screaming willies. When I lay down at night, I'd get nervous energy in my legs and all over my body. When I started Atkins, that nervousness was replaced a feeling of peace. That sealed the case for me. Inner peace is the goal of all spiritual practice and meditation. My motive for being a vegetarian was to enjoy a peaceful mind and body, but instead, I found that was achieved by doing Atkins.

In the first few months of doing Atkins, my health problems gradually disappeared. Under my doctor's supervision, I did away with the pharmaceuticals and now take nutrients instead. It took me two and a half years to lose the weight. Even now, I keep my carb intake very low. I can feel the difference when I eat more than 50 grams of carbs a day.

A year and a half ago, my doctors gave me an MRI and found no arthritis. I bought a gym set about a year ago and I use it regularly. I still go to my doctor, and "Are you still on that weird diet?" has changed to "Whatever you're doing, keep it up because it's working." My blood pressure is fine, I sleep peacefully, and I look and feel ten years younger than I did ten years ago!

I've been rejuvenated as an entrepreneur, too. I have more energy to put into business and I have the energy it takes to travel. I develop products for different natural food companies. My company makes low carb condiments and dressings.

It's very satisfying to combine my love of great food with my enjoyment of this new way of living. It is a privilege to be able to share this story with others who struggle with carbohydrate addiction and who seek a path to a more healthful and peaceful existence.

ACE: 50	**WEIGHT BEFORE:** 280 pounds	**WEIGHT LOST:** 93 pounds
AGE: 63		
HEIGHT: 6 feet 3 inches	**WEIGHT AFTER:** 187 pounds	**STARTED DOING ATKINS:** November 1999

4 | The Skinny on Fat and Protein

If you have being doing Atkins, you were probably initially surprised to discover that you could comfortably eat fat. It might also have been hard to accept, because it goes so against the relentless low-fat message you've been hearing for years. In this chapter, you will learn that concerns about eating fat (and protein) when you are controlling your carbs are unfounded. You'll also find out that natural fats are actually important both for good health and weight control. We'll look at the differences among fats and why it is important to eat a variety of types, with one notable exception. We'll also discuss the important role that protein plays in sustaining life. So let's set the record straight, starting with fat.

In fact, a watershed article published in *The New York Times Magazine* in July of 2002 did just that. Building upon an earlier article published in *Science* magazine, investigative science journalist Gary Taubes exposed the biases and lack of definitive research that has led to the federal government's present antifat, anticholesterol guidelines and dietary goals. Moreover, the very government policy that has prevailed for the last couple of decades may have played a role in the twin epidemics of obesity and diabetes.[1] Many of his reported findings are still controversial, but Taubes has challenged the accepted wisdom on dietary fat and displayed the chinks in its armor, making it clear that what has been taken as scientific fact is merely opinion.

> **TIP**
>
> If you find yourself plagued with food cravings, increase your intake of fat and protein and cut back on carbohydrates.

It was rewarding to see this article in print, but we at Atkins have known for a long time that fat has been unfairly maligned. And if you've been doing Atkins for a while, you know it, too—from personal experience. You've not only lost weight and kept it off, you've probably also improved your cholesterol levels and other aspects of your health. Once you know more about dietary fat and look carefully at the low-fat claims, you'll understand that controlling carbs works so well precisely because it *doesn't* limit your intake of fat calories to the extent that low-fat diets do.

Dispelling the Fear of Fat

Despite the fat phobia out there, it's important to remember that to maintain normal good health, your body *requires* adequate amounts of essential fatty acids. Essential means you have to get them from your food or supplements—your body can't produce them on its own—and they're just as important to your health as vitamins and minerals. (We'll talk more about essential fatty acids later in this chapter.) Overall, you also need an adequate amount of dietary fat to absorb important fat-soluble nutrients such as vitamins A, D, E, and K as well as beta-carotene from your food. Dietary fat gives you steady energy—not the peaks and valleys that can be caused by excess carbs. And fat acts as a flavor carrier, making your food taste good. It also helps satisfy your appetite and keeps you from getting hungry again too soon.

The Perils of a Low-Fat Diet

Assuming that many of you have already followed the weight-loss phases of Atkins, you know that you didn't have to limit your intake of natural fats to lose weight and keep it off. If you have not done Atkins before or need a reminder, an explanation is in order. After all, a gram of fat has 9 calories, while a gram of carbohydrate or protein has only 4, so in theory you should lose more weight if you follow a low-fat diet. But, when you cut back on your carbohydrate consumption, your body primarily burns its backup fuel, fat, so you lose weight.

TIP
Plan ahead. Carry nuts, individually wrapped cheese packets, or low carb protein bars in case you get the nibbles.

In contrast, if you've ever suffered through weight loss on a low-fat diet, you know that the fewer calories theory is not all it's cracked up to be. You may have slowly lost weight, but it was probably a constant struggle and you probably gained the weight back quickly as soon as you stopped dieting. Why? Because by substituting carbohydrates for fat, you were making your body produce more insulin to handle all that excess blood sugar—and more insulin translates into slow or no weight loss because it interferes with fat burning. And because the low-fat diet left you feeling constantly hungry and unsatisfied, you likely couldn't stick with it.

Even worse, while you were restricting fats you may have been harming your health. You most likely cut back on fat-rich foods such as nuts, seeds, and vegetable oils that are good sources of vitamin E. Low-fat diets also often recommend substituting lower-calorie, lower-fat margarine for butter—but most margarine is very high in hydrogenated oils, which you'll soon learn are dangerous. On a low-fat, low-calorie regimen, it's very difficult to get all your nutrients unless you're extremely conscientious about every bite you eat. And, of course, when you cut out something, you have to make up for it by increasing intake of something else—in this case, more insulin-stimulating carbs.

There is another reason to not go low-fat. Some individuals have a genetic predisposition that increases their risk of cardiovascular disease when they follow a diet with less than 30 percent fat. For them, such a diet makes the particles of a specific type of cholesterol in the blood get even smaller and denser, meaning there are more of them—which can translate into a higher risk of heart disease.[2-7] Very low-fat diets also raise triglycerides and lower HDL, a deadly combination.[8, 9]

Finally, if you don't eat enough fat, your liver will manufacture fat—mostly saturated fat—which it can make from carbohydrates. Consider a well-marbled steak. The cow

---

The Low-Fat Lie

Fat phobia is so widespread in our society that food manufacturers can sell just about anything, as long as it claims to be low in fat. From low-fat cheese and skim milk to low-fat cookies and low-fat salad dressing, there are reduced-fat versions of most popular foods. There's even low-fat peanut butter—although the calories per tablespoon are almost identical to those in the full-fat version. These low-fat foods aren't any healthier—in fact, they're just the opposite. To make up for the missing flavor fat provides, manufacturers simply add more sugar, with the result that these foods contain more carbs, not less, than their full-fat counterparts. Our advice: Give them a wide berth.

---

from which it came was likely fed a very low-fat, high carbohydrate diet, so where did all the fat come from? Not from dietary fat but from the excess carbohydrate that was stored as fat. The same thing occurs in humans.

The Truth About Cholesterol

So let's deal with your inevitable question: Does eating a high-fat diet raise my blood cholesterol level and contribute to an increased risk of heart disease? In most cases, the answer is no, *except in the presence of excess carbs and excess calories*—the very way of eating that typifies the American diet. A perfect example is a Big Mac on a bun with fries washed down with a supersize cola. Studies following individuals for up to one year actually show that when fat is consumed in a controlled-carb setting, it actually lowers the risk of coronary/vascular disease.[10–16]

Cholesterol, a waxy, fatlike compound, is manufactured by your body—and by all other animals—and is not technically a fat. It has no calories so your body doesn't burn it for fuel. You need cholesterol to make the membranes of your cells, for normal cell function, and to produce hormones such as estrogen, testosterone, and adrenal hormones. You absorb some cholesterol from eating animal products, but most of your cholesterol is manufactured by your own body, primarily in your liver. In fact, when you try to restrict cholesterol, you may simply make more. Important as cholesterol is to your health, however, high levels of it in your bloodstream can be associated with heart disease. That's why it is important to understand your cholesterol numbers.

To help waxy cholesterol travel through your watery bloodstream to where it's needed, your body wraps each tiny particle of cholesterol in a thin coat of protein. The particles fall into two major categories: low-density lipoprotein (LDL) and high-density lipoprotein (HDL). The latter is often called the "good" cholesterol because it carries the LDL cholesterol away from cells and arteries and back to your liver, removing it from your bloodstream.

TIP

Store nuts as well as nut and seed oils in the refrigerator, rather than the pantry, where they are more likely to spoil.

In addition to the cholesterol in your blood, another form of lipid, called triglyceride (TG) may be just as important. High TGs are associated with a high-carbohydrate, low-fat diet. High TGs can also lead to smaller, denser, and more harmful LDL particles. Many studies indicate that high TGs are as dangerous as high cholesterol, so now doctors should check your blood for all four lipids: total cholesterol, HDL, LDL, and TG.

What do the numbers mean? Here's what the ideal blood lipid levels would be, according to the guidelines set by the National Cholesterol Education Program (NCEP)[17]:

- Total cholesterol (HDL and LDL combined) less than 200 mg/dL

- LDL cholesterol is optimal

- HDL cholesterol of 40 mg/dL or more; 60 mg/dL is even better

The NCEP doesn't specify an upper limit for TGs, but in general, TGs of over 150 mg/dL is considered high. In our opinion, your TG should be less than 100 mg/dL.

A good indicator of heart health is the combination of high HDL cholesterol and low triglycerides. When you do Atkins, you'll almost certainly see your HDL climb and your TG level drop sharply. Even with increased carb intake in Lifetime Maintenance, you continue to burn fat (along with carbs) for energy. So long as you're not gaining weight, you're *not* eating too much fat, meaning you *are* eating a good balance of fat, protein, and carbs. And if you do gain, cut back on carbs, instead of fat.

Although we have all been conditioned to focus on our cholesterol level as the main predictor of cardiovascular health, more than 50 percent of people who have heart attacks have normal cholesterol.[18] Moreover, although LDL has traditionally been labeled the "bad" cholesterol, simply having an elevated LDL level is not enough to know whether you are at risk because it does not take into consideration whether the kind of LDL is the small, dense, high-risk type or the large, fluffy, low-risk type that we told you about in chapter 2.

TIP

Taste nuts before chopping or grinding: Because of their high fat content they can become rancid quickly.

Good Fats

Depending upon chemical structure, there are three different kinds of dietary fat: saturated, monounsaturated, and polyunsaturated. Monounsaturated and polyunsaturated fats are liquid at room temperature. In general, saturated fats are hard at room temperature. Almost all fats, despite their nominal type and whether of vegetable or animal origin, are actually *mixtures* of the three different kinds. Butter, for instance, is called a saturated fat, but actually only about two-thirds of the fat is saturated—the rest is mostly monounsaturated.

MONOUNSATURATED FATS. When you eat vegetables sautéed in or salads dressed with olive oil and handfuls of satisfying nuts, you're getting a healthy dose of monounsaturated fat. Many scientific studies have shown that both olive oil and nuts have positive health benefits. Recent studies that looked at people in Mediterranean areas such as Italy and Crete, where olive oil is a food staple, have shown that this monounsaturated fat can help protect against heart disease, stroke, and possibly some kinds of cancer.[19-28] In fact, most of the people in these studies got 40 percent or more of their daily calories from dietary fat, mostly in the form of olive oil (and about 40 percent from carbs). That's considerably more than the 30 percent or less of calories from fat that's recommended by our fat-phobic authorities, yet these Mediterranean people tend to be mostly of normal weight and to live long and healthy lives. In the United States, results from Harvard's long-running Nurses' Health Study have shown that the women who ate the most nuts had the least incidence of heart disease. The amount needed to provide the protection wasn't much—just a couple of ounces each day.[29-32]

POLYUNSATURATED FATS. Found in vegetable oils such as canola, safflower, grapeseed, and flaxseed oils, as well as in fish, polys can be just as beneficial as monounsaturated fats. But use vegetable oils sparingly and carefully. They're not as helpful to your health as olive oil, and when they're heated to the high temperatures used for frying, they can break down into harmful byproducts.[33] We discourage frying foods; instead, whenever possible, stir-fry with canola, peanut, or grapeseed oil. (See Smoke and Fire on page 192 in the Getting Your Kitchen in Order section for guidelines on safe cooking temperatures.)

SATURATED FATS. Butter, lard, and tallow (beef fat) are all rich sources of saturated fat; however, not all saturated fats are animal fats; coconut and palm oils are also saturated. Interestingly, beef fat usually contains slightly more mono- and polyunsaturated than saturated fat and lard usually contains more monounsaturated fat than saturated. Yet coconut oil is more than 90 percent saturated. In addition to the fat in meat and poultry, saturated fat is found in butter, cream, and other dairy products.

Although they have been demo-nized in recent decades, there is ab-solutely no need to avoid foods that contain saturated fats, which is not to say that we recommend you overcon-sume them. First let's look at the pos-itive effects of eating saturated fats,

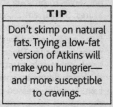

TIP

Don't skimp on natural fats. Trying a low-fat version of Atkins will make you hungrier— and more susceptible to cravings.

which have been associated with a rise in HDL and a lower-ing of another lipoprotein, called lipoprotein (a), that could accelerate blood clot and plaque formation—a major risk factor for heart disease.[34] As with other fats, saturated fat is important for normal cell membrane function. Saturated fats are also highly stable, meaning that they do not form free radicals or become rancid. That's why palm and coconut oils are added to foods to increase shelf stability. In the past three decades, there has been a lot of media attention given to the connection between a diet high in saturated fat and heart dis-ease. In a low carb environment, just the opposite is true. Also, remember that all fats are mixtures. There are about 22 grams of fat in a 3.5-ounce pork chop, for instance, of which only 8 grams are saturated fat; 10 grams are monounsatu-rated fat and the rest are polyunsaturated fat. You should al-ways eat a balance of different types of natural fats.

Getting Down to Essentials

Polyunsaturated fats include the essential fatty acids (EFAs) known as omega-3, omega-6, and omega-9. Essen-tial fatty acids come from a variety of foods, including fish, eggs, nuts, seeds, and vegetable oils as major sources; green leafy vegetables and whole grains also contain them. Now that you're doing Atkins, you're eating a lot more of

Processed Versus Unrefined

Most of the oils found on supermarket shelves have been heavily processed into pale, tasteless, low-nutrient versions of their original selves to prolong shelf life and allow heating to higher temperatures. Skip them all, especially processed corn oil. Instead, check your natural foods store or gourmet market for high-quality, unrefined cold-pressed fresh vegetable and nut oils, which tend to be more expensive. These oils haven't been heated and treated with harsh chemicals to strip away their nutrients, so they still have their rich flavor, essential fatty acids (EFAs), and high vitamin content. Expeller-pressed oils are exposed to heat but retain more of the natural flavor and aroma of the seeds from which they were mechanically pressed than do refined oils.

To keep unrefined oils fresh, buy in small quantities, select those with opaque containers to protect them from light, and store in the refrigerator. Unrefined vegetable and nut oils will go rancid faster than processed oils. Fats become rancid when they are exposed to too much heat or light or simply with the passage of time. Rancid fats don't just taste bad; eating them also enhances the risk of heart disease. Also avoid reusing oil. Doing so may make it rancid, plus trans fats that were in the foods previously cooked in the oil can be transferred to the oil.

these very foods, which means that you're naturally getting a lot more of the nutrients your body needs. That may have a lot to do with why you're feeling better in general. The EFAs play an important role in the production of hormone-like substances that help control a lot of important bodily functions. The benefits of omega-3 fatty acids for your heart and other health factors have been shown time and again in many scientific studies. If you don't have enough of the EFAs needed to make these substances, your health may suffer. Give your body the raw materials it needs to make them, however, and you might see a real improvement in how you feel.

Ideally, you want to have a good balance of omega-3 and omega-6 fatty acids. In the American diet, however, omega-6 levels tend to predominate. That's because the diet includes a

lot of heavily processed vegetable
oils, which are high in omega-6s but
low in omega-3s. Corn oil is particularly high in omega-6s and low in
omega-3s. Canola oil, on the other
hand, has a much better ratio, which is
why we recommend canola over corn
oil. When you eat fish and/or fish oil
supplements, flaxseed oil, and walnuts

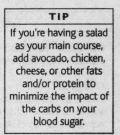

TIP

If you're having a salad
as your main course,
add avocado, chicken,
cheese, or other fats
and/or protein to
minimize the impact of
the carbs on your
blood sugar.

as is recommended on Atkins—along with lots of other whole
foods—you're likely to get more omega-3s and a much better
balance of fats. Flaxseed oil has a pleasant buttery flavor
when used in salad dressings, on cooked veggies, or in a
smoothie, but heat destroys its nutrients. You can also add flax
meal to shakes or salads. For more on sources of EFA, see Get
Your Omegas Here.

There are two situations in which you should be mindful
of your fish intake. The Food and Drug Administration recommends that pregnant women limit their consumption of
ocean fish to 12 ounces per week because of the possibility
of mercury contamination. The FDA also recommends that
pregnant women avoid eating shark, swordfish, king, mackerel, and tilefish. We can't disagree with the FDA here; because these large fish are higher on the food chain, levels of
mercury may be compounded. If you're taking a blood-
thinning medication, be aware that fish oil capsules (but not
eating fish itself) may thin the blood—so ask your doctor
whether it is safe to also take fish oil capsules.

The Killer Fat

There is one kind of dietary fat that really is dangerous to
your health. Hydrogenated or partially hydrogenated vegetable oils are trans fats made from inexpensive vegetable
oils that have been heavily processed to make them thicker
and more stable. During hydrogenation, the chemical struc-

Get Your Omegas Here

No matter how good the balance of dietary fats in your diet, adding these mainstays ensures you get what you need.

Omega-3s
Good sources: flaxseed oil, meal or capsules; fatty cold-water fish such as salmon, cod, trout, mackerel, sardines, tuna, and eel; fish oil supplements; unrefined canola oil; wheat germ oil or capsules; walnuts or walnut oil; raw pumpkin seeds; hempseed oil.
Daily requirement:
1,000 milligrams

Omega-6s
Good sources: supplements that contain borage, evening primrose, black currant seeds, and gooseberry oils.
Be wary of refined corn, safflower, sunflower, soybean, and cotton-seed oil—the processing removes the omega-6s.
Daily requirement:
250 milligrams

Omega-9s
Good sources: extra-virgin or virgin (not just "pure") olive oil, sesame oil, avocado, peanuts, all tree nuts, seeds, poultry, and pork.
Daily requirement:
250 milligrams

---

ture of the fat is reconfigured, producing an abnormal form that disrupts cell membranes and their function. (Trans fats occur naturally in our own intestines and those of other animals in trace amounts.)

These manufactured trans fats are everywhere. They're used as the shortening in commercial baked goods such as cookies, cakes, and bread products. Check the label of almost any package of cookies, for instance, and you'll see that partially hydrogenated vegetable oil is one of the top ingredients. It usually comes right after the enriched white flour and the sugar. Hydrogenated oils are also used in snack foods such as most potato chips and pretzels. They lurk in just about all prepared convenience foods, but especially in baked goods and foods such as breaded fish fillets and french fries. Many fast-food restaurants cook their french fries, chicken nuggets, fried chicken, mozzarella sticks, and other fried foods in partially hydrogenated oils. Most margarines and peanut butters (in both cases, with the exception of nonhydrogenated versions usually found in natural foods stores) contain manufactured trans fats—as does Crisco—it's what makes vegetable oil become solid or creamy.

What's so dangerous about them? Everything! Hydrogenated oils accumulate in your body and have adverse effects on your health. These unnatural fats have been shown to raise LDL cholesterol and lower HDL cholesterol. In each case, this is exactly the opposite of what is desirable. Even worse, they raise the level of triglycerides in your blood. In fact, when it comes to impact on blood lipids, hydrogenated oils, rather than saturated fats or dietary cholesterol, are the real demons. Long-term studies at the Harvard School of Public Health have shown that overall, people who eat the most manufactured trans fats are also the most likely to develop heart disease.[35] Similar studies have shown that people who eat the most of these trans fats are also the most likely to develop diabetes.[36] And manufactured trans fats are implicated in a host of other serious health problems, including breast cancer and asthma.[37-41]

TIP

Often called the perfect food, eggs are rich in protein and healthy fat, contain thirteen vitamins and minerals, and are low in sodium.

Here's where doing Atkins for life may have the biggest payoff of all: When you stop eating packaged cookies, snack cakes, doughnuts, chips, most convenience foods, and high carb fast food, you've cut down not only on carbohydrates but also on hydrogenated oils. Even better, you've replaced the dangerous trans fats with health-giving natural fats. One piece of advice: Even some low carb products contain hydrogenated or partially hydrogenated oils, so check the ingredient list carefully.

A Matter of Balance

The whole issue of fats is a complex one, but in terms of daily life, it comes down to the following basics:

- Choose your fats with care, in terms of both source and method of extraction.

- Avoid hydrogenated and partially hydrogenated as well as large amounts of corn and other oils that have a high ratio of omega-6 to omega-3 fatty acids.

- Use extra-virgin (meaning the first pressing) olive oil and unrefined flaxseed oil whenever possible.

- Use oils such as grapeseed and canola for cooking at higher temperatures.

- Use butter (preferably organic) for baking.

- Explore the use of oils such as walnut and hazelnut for dressing vegetables.

If you come away with only one lesson from this chapter, let it be that it is crucially important to eat a variety of healthy fats for health reasons. For example, for breakfast you might have a vegetable omelet cooked in butter, supplying saturated, mono-, and polyunsaturated fats. At lunch, if you have a spinach, avocado, and chicken salad topped with chopped walnuts and olive oil vinaigrette, you would be getting mononounsaturated oil in the dressing and avocado, saturated in the chicken, omega-3 in the walnuts, and omega-9 in the dressing. For dinner, if you have baked salmon and kale sautéed with garlic in safflower oil, you are getting omega-3 from the salmon, saturated and monounsaturated fat from the butter, and omega-6 from the safflower oil.

The Meat of the Matter

Along with protein, meat and eggs contain saturated fat and cholesterol, but quality and cooking techniques are far more important than the fat content in these foods. Eggs are a good and relatively inexpensive source of protein and other nutrients. We strongly recommend selecting organically raised, free-range meat, poultry, and eggs whenever possible. Not only are they more flavorful, they're also more healthful, because they don't contain harmful hormones, including growth hormone, and antibiotics. Follow these additional guidelines when purchasing:

Eggs: Domesticated chickens fed animal feed high in n-3 fatty acids produce eggs higher in omega-3 fatty acids. Wild chickens also produce eggs containing higher amounts of n-3 fatty acids compared to domesticated chickens.

Cold cuts and hot dogs: Less expensive brands may be full of added sugars and other hidden carbohydrates. Processed meats such as hot dogs, bologna, salami, olive loaf, and the like usually contain nitrates and nitrites. These preservatives are major sources of nitrosamines, which may contribute to insulin resistance and Type 2 diabetes.[40] They have been linked to stomach and colon cancer. Whenever possible, choose nitrite- and nitrate-free deli meats or plain sliced roast beef, turkey, and the like.

Bacon and such: Most sausages, bacon, and aged hams also contain nitrates and nitrites. It is a common misconception that doing Atkins means eating large amounts of bacon and sausage. Both should be eaten occasionally and in moderation. Seek out preservative-free brands sold primarily in natural foods stores.

How you cook your meat also makes a difference. High-temperature frying, broiling, charring, and grilling can create substances that may increase your risk of cancer. In general, the more well done or charred your meat is, the more of these substances it will contain. To minimize your exposure when cooking at home, we offer the following tips for grilling:

• Lightly grill meats and fish; do not let them get black.

continued

> • Parboil or bake chicken before grilling so that you minimize time on the grill.
>
> • Bake spareribs or pork before finishing off on the grill.
>
> • Brush barbecue sauce on meat after you remove it from the grill, instead of before.
>
> • Use marinades with little or no oil. Oil can drip into the fire, causing flare-ups that burn food.
>
> • For the same reason, remove excess fat from meat before grilling.

The Building Blocks of Life

Many foods that contain fat are also protein foods, and the two macro-nutrients work in concert to moderate the impact of carbohydrates on your blood sugar. Protein, which is made up of amino acids, is essential for our bodies to form nerves, muscles, and flesh. There are twenty-two amino acids, of which only nine are considered essential nutrients for adults. When all nine nutrients are present in your diet, your body can usually use them to build the other, nonessential amino acids. But if just one essential amino acid is missing your body cannot synthesize any of the other aminos.

TIP

To retard spoilage of unrefined vegetable, nut, and seed oils, prick a vitamin E capsule with a pin and place it in the container.

Animal protein is the only complete source of all essential acids, which is why people who eat no animal foods can find it difficult to meet nutritional requirements. Protein is also necessary for bodily functions such as the clotting of blood, hormonal regulation (in concert with fat), formation of milk when a woman is nursing an infant, and for the acid/alkaline balance in blood. When protein is insufficient, the blood and tissues can become too acid or too alkaline. Sulfur-containing amino acids, which are found primarily in meat and eggs, are of particular importance to the health of the brain.

As with fat, there are a number of myths about the dangers of eating too much protein, particularly animal protein. The first myth to put to rest is that Atkins is all about eating beef and bacon. In fact, we recommend a balance of protein sources, including poultry, fish and shellfish, eggs, and cheese as well as pork, lamb, veal, venison, and other game meat in addition to beef. Moreover, if you choose not to eat red meat, you can do Atkins perfectly well eating only fish and fowl. You could probably even maintain your weight deriving your protein only from eggs, cheese, nuts, seeds, and legumes, including soybean products such as bean curd. Soy is the most complete vegetable source of protein. A vegetarian would have to be careful to consume enough complementary proteins to ensure adequate intake of all the essential amino acids. Vegetarians should also supplement with vitamin B_{12} because non-animal sources of protein are low in this key nutrient.

TIP

Whenever possible, stir-fry instead of frying foods.

You may have heard that eating animal protein causes cancer, particularly cancer of the colon. In fact, studies of societies in which people do not eat highly processed foods, sugar, and trans fat show there is no correlation between meat consumption and cancer. [41–45]

When you are controlling your intake of carbohydrates, as you do on Atkins, there is no need to cut back on red meat and dark poultry. Nor need you take the skin off chicken or trim the fat off meat. In fact, protein should always be served with fat to ensure absorption of vitamins and minerals. So, if you prefer to remove the skin on chicken, be sure to have some olive oil at the same meal. Processing can devitalize protein, just as it does fats and carbohydrates. You will get more nutritional bang for your buck with fresh meat, poultry, or fish.

TIP

Sprinkle flaxseed meal on yogurt, cottage cheese, a salad, or soup for added fiber and an omega-3 boost.

How much protein, or more specifically animal protein,

How Much Do You Know About Fat and Protein?

1. Which of the following contain a majority of saturated fats?
   - a. butter
   - b. olive oil
   - c. corn oil
   - d. flaxseed oil
   - e. coconut oil
   - f. peanut oil
   - g. canola oil
   - h. palm oil

2. Which of these foods contain the most omega-3 fatty acids?
   - a. corn oil
   - b. striped bass
   - c. flaxseed oil
   - d. tuna
   - e. salmon
   - f. shrimp
   - g. peanut oil
   - h. walnuts
   - i. catfish
   - j. flounder

3. Where are you likely to find hydrogenated or partially hydrogenated oils?
   - a. packaged bread
   - b. cookies
   - c. pork chops
   - d. sesame oil
   - e. margarine
   - f. crackers
   - g. potato chips
   - h. butter

4. The following are complete sources of essential amino acids:
   - a. turkey
   - b. bean curd
   - c. crab cakes
   - d. almonds
   - e. soybeans
   - f. chicken kabobs
   - g. veal chops
   - h. stuffed trout

---

    i. feta cheese
    j. spinach omelet
    k. peanut butter
    l. filet mignon
    m. baked beans

Answers:
    1. a, e, and h
    2. b, c, d, e, and h
    3. a, b, e, f, and g
    4. a, c, f, g, h, i, j, and l

---

should you be eating? To a large extent, this is a personal decision. Depending upon your genetic makeup and hormonal status, your individual requirements for amino acids can vary enormously. While you may feel perfectly well eating a fairly large amount of meat, another person may prefer smaller portions or to concentrate on fish and fowl. So long as you are getting a minimum of six ounces a day of complete protein, you should be meeting your nutritional requirements. Of course, if you are eating too much protein, some of the excess may convert to glucose and behave the way carbs do in your body. Rather than have all your protein at one meal, spread it out across the day. If a meal contains no protein, make sure that it has enough fat to moderate the impact of the carbohydrates on your blood sugar level.

Now that you are doing Atkins for life you should also balance your increased intake of carbohydrates by eating less meat, poultry, cheese, fish, salad dressings, butter, and other fat, and protein foods than you did in Induction and Ongoing Weight Loss. It is crucial to understand that at this point, your increased carb intake should not be cumulative; instead, it is a matter of offsetting some of your protein and fat choices with additional carb selections. As you add back carbs, you must cut down on your servings or serving sizes of proteins and fats. You will see this redistribution of foods in the menu plans that start on page 200. Meanwhile, we'll help you put into practice all you've learned about carbs, fat, and protein in the next chapter.

There's Nothing She Can't Do

Christianne Bishop went to medical school at a time in her life when most doctors are in mid-career, then made another dream come true by losing weight.

I started medical school when I was forty-four. It was one of the final hurdles in my lifelong dream of becoming a doctor. Most of my classmates were in their early twenties and had just finished their undergraduate studies. I had already lived a fairly full life: I had worked as a court reporter, raised a child, and gone to college part-time for years to earn an undergraduate degree in physical therapy. That wasn't enough for me, though, and in 1998 I became the oldest graduate of the Creighton University School of Medicine in Omaha, Nebraska. I recently completed my residency in physical medicine and rehabilitation, a field I adore because every day it lets me see miracles.

I have experienced a miracle, too. I consider it a small one compared with what I witness when, for instance, patients arrive wheelchair-bound and weeks later walk out of the hospital on their own two feet. But after realizing my dream of becoming a doctor, I took it upon myself to realize another dream: to be thin. Fed up with being chubby all my life and worried about my high cholesterol and family history of heart disease, I did Atkins to drop 50 pounds.

I had followed low-fat diets and only gained weight. I had tried doing Atkins when Dr. Atkins' very first book came out in the 1970s and had

> **CHRISTIANNE'S TIPS FOR SUCCESS**
>
> Discuss your weight-control plan with your physician.
>
> Buy convenience foods such as prewashed, bagged salad and precooked chicken—to ensure that you always have plenty of such foods on hand.

lost 40 pounds at the time. I decided I would try it again and keep a close eye on my cholesterol; if my numbers rose, I'd quit.

My breaking point came around November 2000. Three months earlier I had turned fifty. I had long, brown hair and "Coke-bottle" glasses. And after several years of the grueling, high-stress schedule of residency, when even finding the time to take a shower was a luxury, my weight had gradually crept up to 160. I felt like a fat blob. Finally my schedule let up a little and I was ready.

I had my blood work done, set up a daily chart to track my success, and plunged in a few days before Thanksgiving 2000. While doing Induction, I never really strayed except for adding some nuts to my daily menu, and I lost 6 pounds in the first week. By January 2001, I was down to 134 pounds. By mid-June, I weighed only 115 pounds and stopped keeping records. I cut my hair and dyed it blond and also had LASIK surgery to correct my eyesight. My fatigue vanished. I then dropped down to 108 pounds, but people said I was too thin, so I gained a couple of pounds back. I did this without being obsessive, but also without cheating. I was never hungry.

I did not start an exercise program until after I had shed the pounds for fear I would injure myself carrying all that extra weight. (Today I power-walk four miles four or five days a week.) I eat hard-boiled eggs, steaks, bacon-cheeseburgers without the bun, lots of salads topped with grilled chicken or tuna salad, as well as peanuts and macadamia nuts. My new favorite restaurant? Outback Steakhouse, where I can get my perfect meal: a filet mignon, salad, and steamed broccoli and cauliflower. Now that I'm maintaining my weight, I occasionally reward myself with, perhaps, popcorn at the movies or one of my old favorites like a café mocha or a bagel. I even drink diet soda now and then. But I never, ever touch the chocolate kisses, croissants, and ice cream in the refrigerator. Really! I find them comforting in an odd way, but I know that if I cheat, I will not maintain my weight. So they stay put.

Several of my colleagues have adopted the controlled carbohydrate lifestyle after seeing my success. My husband, John, who is also a physician, has joined me, and has lost 50 pounds on the Atkins program. At 6 feet tall and 210 pounds, he still has about 30 pounds to go, and we know he'll get there in no time.

I am so grateful every day for the life I am leading. We are here on this planet for such a short time. We owe it to ourselves to take care of our bodies, to be healthy and fit. Our strength comes from within, and there is truly no limit to what we can do.

ACE: 45	WEIGHT LOST: 50 pounds	LDL BEFORE: 84
AGE: 52		LDL AFTER: 60
HEIGHT: 5 feet 6 inches	TOTAL CHOLESTEROL BEFORE: 147	TRIGLYCERIDES BEFORE: 52
WEIGHT BEFORE: 160 pounds	TOTAL CHOLESTEROL AFTER: 125	TRIGLYCERIDES AFTER: 47
WEIGHT AFTER: 110 pounds	HDL BEFORE: 53	STARTED DOING ATKINS: November 2000
	HDL AFTER: 56	

5 | Putting It All into Practice

Now that you have a basic understanding of how the proper balance of carbohydrates, fats, and protein impacts your weight, blood sugar, and overall health, you probably don't want to wait another minute to begin to put this knowledge into practice at the dining table. Will eating this way for the rest of your life be hard? Not really. Does it require a different mindset than the one under which you have been operating until now? Absolutely. We won't lie to you. In addition to knowledge, in order to permanently maintain a healthy weight you also definitely need a dose of determination. You will probably be able to eat many foods you may have thought were off-limits, but it is crucial to understand that you still need to control your carbohydrate intake, especially of high glycemic foods that could play havoc with your blood sugar. By moderating your intake of high glycemic foods, you keep cravings that could undermine your determination under control. If you've experienced the weight-loss phases of Atkins, your cravings for sweets and starchy foods should have diminished somewhat, but adding new foods can provoke them anew. However, if you proceed carefully and mindfully, you can remain comfortably in the driver's seat. With time and practice, it does get easier.

If you're an old hand at doing Atkins, you already know that the Pre-Maintenance phase is designed to serve as a dress rehearsal for your new way of eating. When you've reached your goal weight and found your ACE (Atkins Carbohydrate Equilibrium), you've arrived officially at Lifetime Maintenance. Far from a lifetime

> **TIP**
>
> Don't include coffee or tea (both of which act as diuretics) or other beverages as part of your daily water intake. They are fine only above and beyond your eight glasses of water.

sentence of limited food choices and preoccupation with the
scale, this phase can be a life-expanding opportunity, one in
which you get to savor delicious foods, all the while keeping
your weight under control and optimizing your health. And
that kind of control over your diet and your weight gives you
a confidence and pride that spills over into other aspects of
your life. That's why Atkins is also about opening your mind
to the world of possibilities that life offers and to embracing
a healthy, vital lifestyle in ways that complement your new
way of eating.

Over and over again, we hear from Atkins followers who
have dramatically changed or even saved their lives by losing weight the controlled carb way. Not only do they feel
better about themselves in general and their bodies in particular, they often embark on new careers, enter new relationships, find new athletic pursuits, and experience myriad
other life changes. Our files are full of such inspiring stories.

Take Barton Landfair, for example. Once a size 5 body
builder, more recently Barton had abused alcohol and drugs.
Although she had been able to kick drugs, in 1999 she was
still drinking a bottle of tequila a day. She had also abandoned her weight-lifting regimen. All had taken their toll. At
thirty-six, Barton weighed more than 200 pounds and wore a
size 18. "I had no energy to pursue my work as an artist or

even to take care of myself," she recalls. "All I wanted to do was watch
TV." She began to turn her life
around in April of that year when she
started doing Atkins. "I stopped
drinking that day," she says. "Limit-
ing my carbohydrates seemed to take
away my craving for alcohol. And before, I would get depressed before my
period and close all the windows in
my room and lie in bed. Six months

TIP

Bring a 32-ounce
water bottle to work
with you. If you
consume it before
lunch, refill it, and
finish it by the end of
the day, you will
effortlessly reach your
64-ounce minimum
for the day.

into the program, all that had changed. I finally felt healthy
and in balance." It took Barton about a year and a half to
reach her goal weight of 135 (she is 5 feet 7 inches). "When

I started doing Atkins, I also rediscovered exercise," she says. She became interested in the body-shaping benefits of yoga, which she now practices daily, in addition to light weight training and working out on a step machine. "As I've gotten leaner, my whole outlook has improved and I'm more successful," she says. "I plan to have a solo show of my art in about a year. I've been absolutely sober and, other than vitamins, I don't take any pills. I've surprised a lot of people who didn't think I had it in me to change. But I was determined to succeed right from the start, and today I can say with confidence that I've turned my life around."

You will meet even more people in this book who've had life-changing experiences. While every one is an inspiration, they are just the tip of the iceberg. These individuals will probably never meet but if they did, all would undoubtedly agree that losing weight was only part of their personal success story. They have also regained their self-respect and their passion for life. Atkins is not just about being able to eat eggs for breakfast without gaining weight or feeling guilty, it's about taking control of your life—and making a host of healthy choices.

How to Design Your Own Personal Program

One of the beauties of doing Atkins is that you can individualize it to fit your food preferences and lifestyle. Do you like to eat six small meals each day? No problem. Do you travel a lot and find yourself often eating in restaurants? You can easily navigate menus without increasing your waistline. Do you make meals for a horde of hungry teens who aren't interested in sharing your way of eating? The Lifetime Maintenance phase is so flexible that most people won't even notice you are on a special program. Do you prefer to have your main meal at lunch? Go ahead; just be sure to have a light meal later in the day. Whatever your lifestyle, you can adapt Atkins to your needs.

If you've lost weight with Atkins and followed the four

phases to the letter, you have gradually added back different carbohydrate foods. That means that you already have an idea of how much variety awaits you at the dining table. On

the other hand, if you basically stayed on Induction most of the way through the weight-loss process (don't be embarrassed—you're not alone in having bent the rules in your desire to speed up weight loss), now is the time to gradually reintroduce a greater array of carbohydrate foods.

It's always a good idea to introduce new foods one at a time. That way, if one food once again provokes cravings or other symptoms, you can identify which is producing such results and discontinue it.

ACE Is the Place

Your ACE may be 60 grams of Net Carbs and your spouse's or a friend's might be 100. The magic number can vary quite a bit from person to person, but it usually ranges between these two extremes. Some lucky—or more likely—young, active (and usually male) people can go as high as 150 or even higher. On the other hand, if you have a history of obesity and yo-yo dieting, it is unlikely that you will ever be able to get your ACE much above 60. Remember that the more you exercise, the higher your ACE, so if you are determined to get it up a notch or two, get moving! Literally. Be aware that other factors over which you have no control—namely genetics, basic metabolism, age, and hormonal status—also play a large role in how much carbohydrate you can consume while maintaining your goal weight. Among the many indignities of age is that our metabolisms tend to slow down with the passage of years. Menopause also can play havoc with a woman's metabolism, which is why so many women who have never had a weight problem suddenly develop one in their early fifties. That's also why some older women, particularly those who are not that active, may have to settle for an ACE of less than 60.

Our meal plans, which begin on page 200, reflect the span that most individuals fall within; the suggested menus are comprised of 45, 60, 80, and 100 daily grams of Net Carbs.

Now that you are at your goal weight, you can take a more flexible approach to your carb grams than you did while you were losing weight—*so long as you don't start to regain pounds*. If your ACE is 60, for example, you can eat 40 grams of Net Carbs one day and 80 grams the next—as long as you average out to 60 grams a day over the course of the week. Of course, you can't save *all* your carb grams for a week and then gobble them up in one sitting, but holding back a little one day and indulging a little the next is fine. This is particularly useful when you know a special occasion—a holiday dinner, say—is coming up. You can splurge a little because you've "banked" some carbs earlier in the week. Don't go overboard with this approach, though. It's easy to lose track and end up eating more carbs than you planned. And if this approach reactivates any cravings, discontinue it. As always, spread your carb intake across the day instead of blowing it all in one sitting.

> **TIP**
>
> Shop the perimeter of the grocery store where the unprocessed foods such as meat, cheese, and vegetables are usually placed. Snacks and other junk foods tend to occupy the center aisles.

Go for Quality, Not Quantity

One of the best things about doing Atkins is that it is the quality of the foods you eat, not just their quantity, that helps you manage your weight. Moreover, you can select from so many different delicious foods that you need never get bored. The best way to stay motivated on any dietary regimen is variety. So the best road to permanent success with Atkins is to become adventurous! Today's supermarkets are

How to Find Your ACE

If you're new to Atkins, you probably haven't the foggiest idea of what your ACE is. Relax; it isn't that hard to figure out, although it may take you a few weeks to zero in on your individual threshold for carb consumption. If you do need to trim some pounds, it will take longer to find your ACE because you first have to establish how many carbs you can eat while you lose your excess weight. In either case, we suggest you start at 60 grams of Net Carbs a day. (Remember, if you have more than a few pounds to lose, however, you should begin with the Induction phase of Atkins.)

To lose weight: Start with 60 grams of Net Carbs a day. If you start to trim down at this level, gradually increase your intake in 5-gram increments so long as weight loss continues. Remember that the more slowly you lose, the more your new eating habits become ingrained and the more likely you are to keep the weight off. When you reach your goal weight and maintain it for at least a month at a consistent level of carb intake, you are at your ACE. However, if you don't start losing after a week at 60 grams a day, drop down to 50 grams and see if that gets your fat-burning engine in gear.

To maintain weight: If you maintain your weight after eating 60 grams of Net Carbs a day for several days, try going to 70 grams. Keep inching up slowly so long as you do not gain weight. If you do put on a few pounds, back off 5 or 10 grams and you should have found your ACE. On the other hand, if you initially gain weight after a few days at 60 grams a day, cut back to 50 and see if you can maintain at that level. Continue to play with the number of carb grams until you are neither losing nor gaining. At that point you have found your ACE!

full of interesting, great-tasting vegetables from all over the world—try them. Add some excitement and crunch to your salads with flavorful fresh greens such as arugula, radicchio, and fennel. In addition to cabbage, try kale, Swiss chard, collards, or spicy mustard greens—they're all flavorful, low in carbs, and packed with high-quality nutrients. An exciting world of Asian vegetables—now available in most well-stocked supermarkets—await you in the form of bok choy, napa cabbage, pea pods, mung bean sprouts, and daikon.

They're great in stir-fries and in salads. Also explore vegetables popular
in Hispanic cuisines, such as chayote
and jicama.

TIP

To keep fresh herbs
fresh longer, rinse
them and lightly wrap
in paper towels. Place
wrapped herbs in
plastic bags and
refrigerate.

When it comes to grains, even if
your ACE is high enough to have
them fairly regularly, you should stay
away from conventional (semolina)
pasta and white rice. Brown rice is lower in Net Carbs, has
a lower AGR, and is a more nutritious replacement for
white rice. Your best bets in the grain department are the
whole, unrefined grains such as rolled oats and barley. And
although beans and legumes are fairly high in carbs,
they're also high in fiber, which makes them a good choice
overall. Small portions of both legumes and whole, unrefined grains will provide you with needed nutrients without
blowing your carb budget. These are foods that you may
not eat every day, but are usually fine to have a few times a
week.

General Guidelines

To help you select foods that will provide a wide array of nutrients, including fiber, without compromising your weight,
we suggest you adhere to the following guidelines. First, at the
risk of stating the obvious, continue to count your grams of
Net Carbs. Secondly, keep an eye on your intake by becoming
familiar with the seven rungs of the carb ladder described in
chapter 3 starting on page 47. Ideally, each meal should include adequate protein and healthy fats, plus some carbs.
Over the course of the day, your carb intake should include:

- 4 to 5 servings of vegetables (Remember that a serving is
  typically a half-cup of cooked vegetables or a cup of raw
  ones. So a big salad at lunch could comprise 3 servings of
  veggies and constitute more than half your intake for the
  day.)

- 1 to 2 servings of fruit (Remember that a whole fruit is not necessarily a serving. For example, half a medium apple or half a grapefruit is 1 serving as are 2 fresh apricots.)

- 3 servings of dairy (Examples include 1 ounce of cheese, 1 cup of yogurt or whole milk, ½ cup cottage cheese.)

- 2 to 4 ounces of nuts and/or seeds

Depending upon your ACE, you may well be able to eat whole grains and/or legumes at least once a day. Following the Atkins Glycemic Ranking (AGR), select first from the foods in the #1 (eat regularly) category, less frequently from the #2 (eat in moderation) category and least frequently from #3 (eat sparingly) foods. Individuals with higher ACEs may also choose to eat more fruit, if they can do so without finding that it elevates their blood sugar. As long as you add new carbohydrate foods one at a time, you will find how varied your diet can be.

Remember, too, that you can mix and match foods, as long as you keep track of your total carb intake. Our meal plans offer lots of ways to trade out one food for another, all the while adhering to your ACE. Also refer to Carb Counting Made Easy on pages 276–280 for items you can substitute for those in the meal plans. Try some interesting new combinations—sprinkle your broccoli with sunflower seeds or chopped walnuts, for instance, or toss your blueberries with creamy fresh ricotta cheese. Your goal is to always eat as wide a variety of foods as possible. Don't be saddled with conventional expectations about what to eat when. If you want to emulate the Japanese and have miso soup with tofu and scallions for breakfast, go ahead. Or if you want to add some interest to your breakfast of scrambled eggs by tossing in last night's leftover asparagus, feel free.

A Typical Day

Let's look at the meal plan on page 220 as a way to get a handle on what you might eat in a typical day. For comparison purposes, let's assume you are a woman with an ACE of 45. Let's also assume that you have a spouse who has an ACE of 100. For breakfast, you can each enjoy Zucchini Frittata and a sliced tomato. He could add a slice of rye bread toast, a half-cup of grapefruit or honeydew melon, and a decaf latte. Come lunch, you can each have a Chicken and Sun-Dried Tomato Quesadilla. You'll have your quesadilla with a cucumber and radish salad. He can have his with Mexican Chopped Salad and some chickpeas. For dinner, serve Baihian Halibut accompanied by sautéed spinach and a large green salad. He also gets some whole-wheat pasta. For dessert, enjoy some strawberries and cream. If either of you prefers, you could have a couple of apricots, some cherries, or Lime Granita instead. (Recipes begin on page 288.)

Okay, you now know how many grams of Net Carbs you should be eating each day. You also are getting a grasp on why some carbohydrates put a greater burden on your system than others. You're all set to do Atkins for life, right? Maybe. But before you get too cocky, let's look at some of the pitfalls ahead, along with strategies for staying on top of them. (We'll look at one of them, the role of exercise, in designing your healthy lifestyle in the next chapter.)

Identifying Real Hunger

You never need to go hungry on Atkins, but nor should you ever go beyond the point of satisfying your hunger. This is a polite way of saying don't stuff yourself. Of course, it's pretty hard to gorge on a controlled carb regimen, because all those salad greens, vegetables, and protein dishes fill you up fast and sate your appetite. Even so, if your past eating patterns included lots of overeating and binges, you may carry

TIP

In general, the smaller the vegetable, the better the flavor. If a recipe calls for one pound of zucchini, it's better to buy two small ones instead of one large one.

this pattern over when you're doing Atkins—just with different foods. How can you break the pattern? You must nip overeating in the bud to remain in fighting trim—permanently.

The first step is learning to distinguish real hunger from the simple desire to eat. This isn't always easy, because we all use food to satisfy an array of emotional needs. You may eat to cheer yourself up, reward yourself, calm yourself, because you're tired, or just to cope with boredom or dissatisfaction. Whether you're having a lousy day or a great one, be mindful of how your mood affects your food choices. Once you become aware of the mood-food connection, you can cut back on emotional eating. You'll probably find that with greater awareness, you'll eat less or even eliminate this nonproductive behavior altogether and do something else you enjoy—like taking a walk, reading a magazine, or phoning a friend. And if you must eat, make a it good, low carb choice.

After all, your goal isn't just to manage your weight but to learn a more rational and realistic way of eating—and that means eating until you feel comfortably satisfied, not stuffed. Sometimes it's hard to tell when you've reached satiety—you might still feel hungry even though you've eaten a hearty meal. The problem here is that your brain hasn't yet caught up with your stomach. If you find that once you start eating you have a hard time stopping, you may be waiting too long between meals and allowing your hunger to shift into overdrive. If you have not gone too long between meals but are still hungry after eating dinner, try this tactic: Once you've finished your basic meal, wait about twenty minutes to see if you still feel hungry. If you are, have another portion of the protein part of your meal or an Atkins-friendly dessert such as berries with whipped cream. But more likely, in that short time your blood sugar will rise slowly as you digest your food; the fat and protein send satiating signals to your brain and your hunger will diminish.

When you wait, the desire for a second helping or dessert simply passes.

If hunger comes upon you between meals, remember that snacking is perfectly permissible on Atkins. In fact, it's a great way to keep hunger from getting the upper hand and putting you in a position where you might make bad choices. In addition to all the delicious snack recipes in this book and on www.atkins.com, you can always resort to a handful of nuts, some olives, a piece of cheese, or a slice of ham wrapped around a stalk of celery or a cucumber spear. This approach can also be helpful if you get the after-dinner munchies. However, eating *right* before bed could interfere with getting a good night's sleep, so a cup of hot herb tea to soothe and fill you up might be a better choice.

Suitable-Size Portions

The next important step to avoid overeating is to get a firm grasp on portion size. In order to keep track of your carbs, you need to have a sense of a standard (meaning not supersized) serving of each food. It's all too easy to underestimate the size of the portion in front of you, which means you end up eating more carbs than you realize. Many people who have had a weight problem over the years have simply been eating too much food for so long that they assume gargantuan portions are the norm. If "I can't believe I ate the whole thing!" is a familiar echo in your ears, you may be an overeater. And you are not alone. In this land of plenty, restaurants—

TIP

Some airlines have a controlled carb meal option. Otherwise, consider ordering the kosher meal or simply order a salad plate and bring along a source of protein.

particularly fast-food places—tend to serve supersize portions. Your mother probably told you to eat all the food on your plate because she was worried about your health, but the reality is that as a society we need to learn to push back before we do eat the whole thing to be healthy.

A few statistics are instructive: The U.S. Department of Agriculture's Economic Research Service estimates that the average daily caloric intake in 1994 increased by 14.7 percent, or about 340 calories, from 1984. It remained stable between 1994 and 1997, the latest year for which there is data.[1] According to this same source, in 1957, the size of a hamburger at a typical fast-food restaurant was 1 ounce. By 1997, the typical patty size had jumped to 6 ounces! A typical serving of soda was 8 ounces in 1957; by 1997 it had moved up to 32 ounces. When your parents went to the movies in 1957 they may have shared a 3-cup bag of popcorn; today, when you order a medium bag of that classic snack, you get 16 cups. Just one more example: That 1950s muffin weighed in at less than 1½ ounces; the 1990s muffin had bulged to 5 to 8 ounces.

To buck the trend, take a good look at your serving sizes. Just as in the past your body got used to eating overlarge portions and came to expect that, with every meal, you can get used to eating smaller portions, particularly when it is full of satiating foods high in protein and healthy fats. Conversely, if you find you're putting weight on again after achieving your goal weight, your problem might be that your portion sizes have crept up. Listen to your body. It is sometimes wiser than your hunger-driven brain. When you eat moderately, you feel good after a meal, not bloated and sluggish.

A good way to get a handle on portion sizes is to spend a little time in the lab—meaning your kitchen. Using a measuring cup and a kitchen scale (or even a postage scale), measure out the standard portions of some of the foods you eat most often. Take each portion and put it on an empty dinner plate to get an idea of how it looks. Now that you know what a cup of cooked cauliflower, for example, really looks like, you'll be able to estimate your carb intake much more accurately in the future. Do the same with protein foods such as meat, poultry, and fish to ensure that you are not eating excessively large portions.

Portion Size Guidelines

Even on Lifetime Maintenance, it's important to be able to judge portion size, especially for higher carb foods. How much is ½ cup? What does a 3-inch slice look like? These charts should help you estimate portions at a glance.

Bread, Grains, and Pasta	**Think of**
1 one-ounce slice of bread	An index card
1 two-ounce piece of Italian bread	A bar of soap
1 three-ounce bagel	A can of tuna
½ cup rice, cereal, or pasta	½ baseball
1 two-ounce muffin	A cupcake wrapper

Fruits and Veggies	**Think of**
1 medium fruit or ¾ cup cut-up fruit	A tennis ball
1 cup green salad	A fist
½ cup cooked vegetables	A scoop of ice cream

Protein and Cheese	**Think of**
2 tablespoons peanut butter	Two tea bags
3 ounces beef, chicken, or pork	A small pack of tissues or cigarettes
1 ounce of cheese	A pair of dice
1 ounce of nuts	One Ping-Pong ball or a small child's handful

Snacks and Desserts	**Think of**
1 ounce of chips	A medium-size handful
1 three-inch piece of cake	A small stack of business cards
1 cup of ice cream	A baseball

Measurements	**Think of**
1 tablespoon	A tea bag
1 teaspoon	A thimble
1 cup	A fist or a baseball
¼ cup	A large egg

Breaking the Junk Food Addiction

There's another important step for breaking out of past eating patterns: no more junk food. That means no more conventional cookies, snack cakes, doughnuts, sodas, or candy bars. These foods are incredibly high in carbohydrates and are generally full of dangerous trans fats and chemical additives—and incredibly low in anything resembling nutrition. The problem is that they surround you. Just think of the array of sugar- and white-flour-filled choices beckoning you at the supermarket checkout line. Without question, they are seductive. Nobody ever lusts for asparagus or cabbage, but cravings for a candy bar or pretzels are legion.

It's not easy to break the junk food habit, but you can do it. If you have lost weight doing Atkins, you probably followed our advice to get rid of whatever junk food was in your home. If you are new to Atkins, it is quite simple, get rid of anything that has sugar or bleached white flour. Quite simply, if it's not there, you can't eat it. Now that you're doing Atkins for life, there is less reason than ever to have junk foods around. In Lifetime Maintenance, the different mindset now is that you have to accept that you're giving these foods up forever, not just until you achieve your goal weight. That's because as surely as night follows day, if you resume your habit of eating junk food, you will once again become addicted and your weight problem will be déjà vu all over again, to paraphrase Yogi Berra. And that's not even mentioning all the ingredients in junk foods, starting with trans fats, that can imperil your health. If your kids complain, use the opportunity to teach them better eating habits by giving them a good snack such as nuts, a chunk of cheese, or a piece of fresh fruit instead. Junk food isn't any better for them than it is for you. Some parents find that a

> **TIP**
>
> Variety is not just the spice of life. It ensures more nutrients. Strive to eat at least ten different kinds of food a day.

Finding the Hidden Sugars

Simple sugar lurks in many foods, disguised by the manufacturers under misleading names. When you're deciding if a food is a good controlled carb choice, look for the hidden sugars on the food label. No matter what it's called, sugar is sugar and has at least 4 carb grams per teaspoon. Even when a food seems low in sugar or other carbs, check the portion size on the food label carefully. The amount of carbs is given by the serving size, and that serving is often much smaller than you realize. You could end up getting a lot more carbs than you want. Here are the various aliases for sweet carbs:

- Brown sugar
- Corn sweetener
- Corn syrup
- Corn syrup solids
- Dextrose
- Fructose
- Fruit juice concentrate
- Glucose
- High-fructose corn syrup

- Honey
- Invert sugar
- Lactose
- Maltose
- Malt
- Malt syrup
- Molasses
- Raw sugar
- Sucrose (table sugar)

workable compromise is to allow their children to eat such foods only when they are out.

Some people are able to have a taste of cake, regular pasta, or a few french fries and stop there. If you don't have that degree of self-control, it's probably better for you to stay away from the very foods that once did you in. Realistically, does this mean you will never again have a piece of birthday cake or dip a conventional crispy cracker into a dip at a party? Of course not, but you do have to know where you stand in terms of such deviations. Some people have the metabolic and psychological ability to have, say, a tiny piece of cake or a couple of crackers and stop there. Then there are those who know that if they have even a taste of such foods, they may veer out of control. Most of us land somewhere in the middle. Fortunately, the ever-growing array of controlled carb foods means that doing Atkins needn't mean a lifetime sentence of never enjoying a sweet treat, like mom's pumpkin pie, or the satisfying crunch of a savory chip.

The Best Beverages

Some beverages can be your friends in the health and weight control game. Others are just the opposite. The next time you feel hungry between meals, stop and think about when you last had something to drink. If it's been more than a couple of hours, your hunger might actually be thirst. Instead of eating, drink some filtered or bottled water—always the best choice because it has no carbs. If you want something fizzy, try seltzer or sparkling water with a slice of lemon or lime, unsweetened essence-flavored club soda, or a diet soda sweetened with sucralose (Splenda). Or make your own sodas using sugar-free flavored syrups. Try not to overdo the fizzy drinks, though. The bubbles fill you up quickly and could keep you from getting your daily tally of eight 8-ounce glasses (64 ounces total) of high-quality fluids.

Sugar-free iced tea and lemonade are also good choices. Avoid beverages sweetened with sugar, corn syrup, or other caloric sweeteners; instead opt for those with sucralose. (See Sugar-Free Sweeteners.) Orange juice, grape juice, apple cider, and other fruit juices are relatively high in natural sugar, and they don't have any fiber to slow their absorption. Drink them rarely, in small portions, and with food to slow absorption. It's also a good idea to add pure water or sparkling water to just a couple of ounces of fresh fruit juice.

If you prefer a hot drink, go for decaffeinated coffee or tea or herbal tea—or for a change of pace, have some clear chicken or beef bouillon. Lighten your coffee or tea with cream, and sweeten it with your favorite sugar substitute. Hot drinks are very satisfying—meaning they can take the

---

Sugar-Free Sweeteners

By replacing sugar and other sweeteners such as syrup with a sugar-free version, you get the sweetness without the carbs. Sugar-free sweeteners are very intense, so a tiny amount goes a long way. Our preference is sucralose (Splenda), but acesulfame K (Sweet One, Swiss Sweet) and saccharin (Sweet 'N Low, Sweet Twin, and generic brands) are other options. Which sweetener you prefer is a matter of personal taste. The Food and Drug Administration does not recognize the use of the herb stevia as a sweetener, although it can be sold as a dietary supplement in health food stores.

---

edge off your appetite. If you have a tendency to overeat, try having some broth or a cup of herbal tea about half an hour before a meal—it may help you feel satiated sooner. If you feel the need for something sweet after a meal, try a cup of hot decaffeinated tea or herbal tea instead of dessert.

The high level of caffeine in many popular beverages can be a problem for some people. Excess caffeine can increase hunger, which could result in cravings for sweets. Caffeine is found not just in coffee and tea but also in cola and even some herbal teas. Many people enjoy the taste and health benefits of green (and black) tea without such side effects. If you find that caffeinated beverages deplete you of energy, make you feel shaky or jittery, or send you on a search-and-devour mission for doughnuts, switch over to decaffeinated versions. If you are caffeine sensitive, limit caffeine intake to 1 to 2 servings a day.

Meeting All Nutritional Needs

When you have reached the Lifetime Maintenance phase and are eating more carbs, you will be eating less fat than you did in the weight-loss phases of Atkins. Protein will still provide from 30 to 35 percent of your energy needs. It is important not to cut back too much. The amino acids in protein are

Understanding Where Carbs Hide and What Influences ACE

1. Which of these products might contain hidden sugars?
   a. Bacon
   b. Breakfast cereal
   c. Bottled iced tea
   d. Barbecue sauce
   e. Ketchup
   f. Salad dressings
   g. Fruit juice
   h. Cough syrups
   i. Chocolate milk

2. All other things being equal, who is likelier to have a higher ACE?
   a. A 29-year-old man or a 49-year-old man?
   b. A 49-year-old woman or a 49-year-old man?
   c. A dog walker or a truck driver?
   d. A woman taking birth control pills or a woman who is not?
   e. A man taking antidepressants or a man who is not?
   f. A person taking insulin or a person taking Metformin?
   g. Someone whose parents are obese or someone whose parents are slim?
   h. A person with a broken ankle or a person with a broken hand?

Answers:
1. All of these foods could contain sugar in one form or another.
2. The people who are most apt to have a higher ACE are:
   a. The 29-year-old. Younger people usually can consume more carbohydrates without gaining weight. b. The man. Men typically have a metabolic advantage because they don't have as much estrogen and their bodies have more muscle mass. c. The dog walker. He is probably getting more exercise than the truck driver. d. The woman who is not taking hormones. Estrogen can increase insulin resistance, which in turn can contribute to weight gain. e. The man not taking antidepressants. Many antidepressant drugs can interfere with weight control. f. The person taking Metformin. Unlike insulin, this medication does not seem to interfere with weight control. g. The person with slim parents. A person with a genetic predisposition to put on weight will likely have to eat fewer grams of carbs. h. The person with a broken hand. He or she can presumably still walk or engage in some form of exercise that the person with a broken ankle cannot.

the building blocks for muscle, so be sure to consume an adequate amount, as the meal plans that start on page 200 indicate. In addition to a healthy diet, supplemental vitamins, minerals, and other nutrients ensure that you meet your nutritional needs. Each person has different nutritional needs, which can best be ascertained by consulting with a nutritionist, but at the most basic, you should be taking a daily multivitamin/mineral as well as eating food with omega-3, omega-6, and omega-9 essential fatty acids and supplementing as needed. Adequate mineral intake is especially important if you find yourself perspiring profusely while working out, which could deplete your body's store of calcium, magnesium, potassium, and other minerals—also known as electrolytes. A personal fitness program—the subject of the following chapter—is the final essential ingredient for optimal health.

TIP

Swap recipes with other people who are controlling their carb intake. You'll increase your enjoyment and compliance when there's variety in your meals.

A Successful Wager

Terry Free bet a friend that he could lose weight in just two weeks by doing Atkins. He did, and then some. A year later and almost 80 pounds lighter, he's the big winner.

Being overweight had been a problem for me since I was nine or ten years old. I had fallen into a pattern of eating to excess, especially when I was bored or unhappy. By the time I was in junior high, the kids had begun to call me "Fat Albert" because I looked like the Bill Cosby TV character.

I'm thirty years old now, and over the years I've tried several diets. I lost 60 pounds on one program, but was hungry all the time. I just couldn't stick to it, and eventually gained all the weight back, and more. It didn't help that I live in a college town, where junk food is always readily available— and sometimes, the temptation was overwhelming. Before I learned about Atkins, I'd eat whatever I wanted whenever I wanted, just like a kid. It wasn't uncommon for me to eat a large pizza with two cans of soda, followed by a pint of ice cream for dinner. I could even down an entire gallon of milk in a day. I ate out a lot, and buffets were really big with me.

In February of 2002, two friends told me they had started doing Atkins. I had never heard of it, but they were losing weight so I thought I'd give it a try. I asked another friend, who only needed to lose 10 pounds, to try Atkins with me, if only for two weeks. "Let's show these other two guys up," I said. He agreed, so I went to the Atkins Web site and bought a copy of *Dr. Atkins' New Diet Revolution.*

At the end of the two-week Induction phase, I had lost 12 pounds and my friend had reached his 10-pound weight loss goal. "Hey, giving up bread is a little hard, but not as bad as I thought," I said to myself. So I decided to keep going and began to set reasonable, short-term goals for myself. The next step for me I called "30 by 30"—to lose a total of 30 pounds by my thirtieth birthday, or about 18 pounds in the next six weeks. I was ecstatic when I made my goal on the exact day, April 7. Then I decided to set my next goal. I knew I would be seeing my entire family at my cousin's graduation, approximately one month after my birthday. I decided to try to lose 12 more pounds, again about 3 pounds per week. When the graduation day arrived, my relatives came to pick me up at my apartment. When I opened the door, my mother's mouth fell open and she almost started to cry. By then, I had lost 45 pounds, 3 more than I had even intended. "Are you starving yourself?" she asked. So I explained the Atkins program and all its health benefits.

By this time, a day didn't go by that someone didn't ask

> **TERRY'S TIPS FOR SUCCESS**
>
> Don't weigh in more than twice weekly.
>
> Be sure to drink the recommended eight glasses of water per day.
>
> Talk about your success. You'll not only continue to pump yourself up, but will feel good about sharing what you've learned.

me how I'd lost the weight. I had become a phenomenon. It was such a hoot and a holler when people didn't even recognize me. I work as a phone sales rep for a mail order medical and dental supply company, and people in the office began to bring me clothes that no longer fit them or their family members. I didn't want to buy any new clothes until I reached my final goal weight of less than 200 pounds. I had to lose 25 more pounds and thought it would take me about eight more weeks, by about the Fourth of July. On July 1, I hit 199 pounds. I made a banner, brought it to work, and hung it over my desk. All it read was "199." People kept asking me what it meant, and when I told them, they just couldn't believe my accomplishment. Now, several coworkers are doing Atkins, too, and I'm sort of a coach for them. I've lost another 7 pounds for a total of 77 pounds lost. I'm 5 feet 10 inches and weigh 193 pounds, a weight I can really live with.

The whole time I was on the weight loss phases of Atkins I exercised, though not strenuously. I walked two miles to work five days a week, and at least two days a week I also walked home. Once a week I went roller-blading. I also recently bought an abdominal exercise machine to help me tone up my middle. Before I took off the weight, I'd sometimes take a nap after work and sleep ten or eleven hours per night on the weekends. Now I'm never tired, and six hours of sleep is plenty. Luckily, before Atkins I had no major health problems other than slightly elevated cholesterol and blood sugar levels. Now those numbers are just fine.

As I maintain my weight, I don't even think about being on a diet anymore. I'm cooking for one, so grocery shopping is easy. I know which aisles to go down and which to avoid. I grab hard-boiled eggs or string cheese for breakfast. At work during lunch, I might have a turkey wrap with mozzarella cheese or a taco salad with all the seasoning but no chips. For dinner I might fix controlled carb pasta with packaged Alfredo sauce and bacon bits, skillet-browned chicken, and sugar-free gelatin for dessert. I try to have a salad once a day for lunch or dinner.

Being able to wear regular-size clothes is the best part of shedding pounds, so when I reached my goal weight I splurged and went shopping. They just don't make cool clothes in those big sizes! My waist measurement has dropped from 44 or 46 inches to 32 or 33 inches. I went from XXXL shirts to just a large. I've always been a pretty happy-go-lucky guy, but now I am more genuinely so. I don't get depressed by wondering if people are thinking, "Gee, that guy is fat!" I just can't count all the benefits. I feel two million percent better in every way.

ACE: 45	WEIGHT AFTER: 193 pounds	TOTAL CHOLESTEROL AFTER: 175
AGE: 30		
HEIGHT: 5 feet 10 inches	WEIGHT LOST: 77 pounds	STARTED DOING ATKINS: February 2002
WEIGHT BEFORE: 270 pounds	TOTAL CHOLESTEROL BEFORE: 215	

6 | Get Moving!

Exercise is a powerful ally in the battle for weight control. If you're not exercising regularly in addition to controlling your carbs, you're shortchanging yourself in several important ways. Just as you will need to deal with the way you eat every day for the rest of your life, regular, ongoing exercise is like adopting the controlled carbohydrate approach to eating: It can significantly improve your cardiovascular risks, your energy level, and your productivity.

A frequent result of losing weight is an increased interest in exercise; in fact, many Atkins followers who were once classic couch potatoes morph into exercise nuts. Others, like George Osmond, resume routines they had abandoned when they piled on the pounds. A Canadian, George had always worked out regularly and once was in perfect shape, allowing him to carry 178 pounds well on his 5-foot 10-inch frame. But after he and his wife separated in 1996 and later divorced, he says, "I went into a frenzy of partying. I was always eating and drinking and I stopped working out." George's hobby had been professional motorcycle racing—he had even won a Canadian championship in 1993. "It's a sport in which the rider needs to be almost as weight-conscious as a jockey," he explains. "That is, the smaller guy has the advantage." By 2000, George had ballooned up to 275 pounds. One day when he revisited the track—he was no longer able to race—he met an old friend he hadn't seen in two years, who had lost 130 pounds doing Atkins. "I, on the other hand, couldn't even get the pants of my old leather motorcycle suit over my legs!" he jokes. George proceeded to lose 84 pounds doing Atkins and is now working out again to

TIP

Wait at least two hours after eating before strenuous exercise and you'll find you have greater stamina and endurance.

help build the stamina he needs for motorcycle racing. "Now that I'm back in full gear, I run and bicycle up to five kilometers a day at the gym," he says.

The beautiful thing about exercise is that not only does it help build muscles—meaning it banishes flab—and enhances your cardiovascular fitness, it works for you in three additional ways.

- The more physically active you are, the more carbohydrates you can consume without gaining weight.

- The more muscle you have relative to fat, the more calories your body burns naturally.

- Even after you've completed your exercise regimen, your metabolism remains at an increased level and continues to burn calories.

- Your body is less likely to store carbs as fat through the action of aerobic exercise, meaning that you may be able to tolerate a greater amount of carbohydrate intake in the sixty to ninety minutes following an exercise session. During this period, the body refills the muscles with glycogen (stored carbs), rather than storing excess calories as fat. So you may find that exercising and then eating a bit more grams of carbs than you usually do may allow you to raise your ACE somewhat. This window of opportunity is not an occasion to splurge; instead, regard it as an opportunity to gain even more from exercise.

Exercise also has a multitude of intrinsic health benefits that could save your life. Let us share with you some research findings that illustrate the value of exercise. One study, published in *The New England Journal of Medicine*, tracked 73,000 postmenopausal women for an average of three years. The researchers found that women who either walked briskly or exercised vigorously at least two and a half hours per week had a 30 percent lower risk of cardiovascular problems than the least active women.[1] Another study, which came out of the well-known Honolulu Heart Program, looked at 2,600 men over the age of 70 and found that the risk of heart disease decreased by 15 percent for every half mile walked each day. These are powerful reasons to get out there and move.[2]

> **TIP**
>
> Make exercise part of your regular routine so that being physically active becomes a habit, not something that can be pushed off when other activities intrude.

How Much Exercise Is Enough?

Until recently, the generally accepted prescription was 30 minutes of at least moderate activity, such as brisk walking, on all or most days of the week. However, the National Academy of Sciences, in their 2002 recommendations on physical activity, advised at least one hour a day of moderately intense exercise. That's a tall order, of course. The good news is that every little bit counts and something is better than nothing. Let's look at those recommendations and the claims associated with each of the two studies cited above. In the first, two and a half hours of exercise each week lowered the risk of heart-related problems.[1] In the second, every half-mile walked daily made a deeper dent in heart disease risk.[2] No matter who you are or what your life is like, there are ways to fit in some exercise. Even someone with severe mobility problems can do chair exercises or water aerobics. If you have been overweight in the past, you may have found exercise taxing on both your cardiovascular system and your bones and joints. You will likely find it much more enjoyable now that you are at or close to your goal weight. Slimming down is also a great cure for aching joints and sore feet.

Not only do Americans eat too much, they also exercise too little. With every technological advance, it seems we become more physically inactive. The current epidemic of inactivity is credited with causing upward of 250,000 deaths per year, or 12 percent of the total deaths in the United States.[3] Need more reasons to be motivated? Sedentary lifestyles have been blamed for increasing the incidence of heart disease, obesity, diabetes, osteoporosis, and certain forms of cancer. A recent study published in *The New England Journal of Medicine* has shown exercise capacity (as measured on a treadmill stress test) to be a more powerful predictor of mortality among men than other established risk factors for cardiovascular disease.[4] Lastly, work by leading sports psychologists has demonstrated that adopting a routine of cardiovascular training results in improved productivity in business.[5] So taking the time to increase your fitness level may actually pay off in the workplace. So much for the excuse that you're too busy to get in shape!

Your Personal Fitness Program

It is important to engage in both aerobic and anaerobic exercise. Aerobic forms of exercise increase your heart rate and your consumption of oxygen and include activities such as racewalking, running, playing singles tennis, swimming, roller-blading, and the like. Anaerobic, or resistance, exercise is any activity that is not significantly aerobic and helps to build muscle. Among the most effective methods are weight training and resistance training with rubber bands. In addition to reducing body fat, both aerobic and anaerobic exercise improve insulin sensitivity and high blood sugar (hyperglycemia), decrease blood pressure, and raise HDL. We'll come back to weight training after looking at the benefits of exercise that strengthens your cardiovascular system.

Strengthening Your Heart

No matter what your fitness level, you can maximize the
benefit of exercise, and minimize the time required, by
working out at the proper intensity. Taking your pulse will
help you gauge your heart rate (HR). Some people find a
heart monitor—an electronic device you wear on your chest
that displays your HR in real time—easier to use and more
motivational. Regardless of which method you use, your first
objective is to ascertain your maxi-
mum heart rate and the various markers to aim for.

To determine how much energy
you expend when exercising, you
need to calculate how hard you're ex-
erting yourself and multiply it by the
length of time involved. The science
behind HR training is based on working the heart in zones that represent
percentages of maximum heart rate.
This allows the intensity of effort to
be objectively monitored to assure that you achieve the appropriate training benefit (including total calories burned) in
any given workout session. Maximum HR is a number that
can be roughly predicted and is related to age but not to fitness level. It is often roughly calculated by taking into account one's age but not actual fitness level. Since each of us
has a different level of fitness, we each have our own maximum HR. Therefore, you and a friend of the same age could
work out and achieve the same HR but you might be working
significantly harder than your friend.

TIP

Find an exercise buddy
to keep you on the
straight and narrow
and make the process
more enjoyable. He or
she should be
someone whose
fitness level is similar
to yours so that the
two of you can handle
the same activities.

Calculating Your Predicted Maximum Heart Rate

Maximum heart rate (MaxHR) involves a rather complicated
set of computations, which are available on many Web sites,
including www.atkins.com. The point is that once you've calculated your predicted MaxHR, you can determine how hard

you should be working your heart when you exercise. The key here is that more isn't always better. In fact, frequently more is *not* better if you're working so hard that you either can't exercise long enough to get much benefit or you can't recover enough to do it again within a day or two. Herein lies the biggest benefit of heart rate training: You work out only hard enough to get the benefit you need in terms of cardiovascular conditioning and calories burned without overdoing it—or underdoing it and wasting your time. There is a bell curve to exercise, meaning on the upside at the height of the curve, your routine is providing health benefits and energizing you. On the downside of the curve, you're either just going through the motions without benefit or are depleting the body by overexercising, making it counterproductive. This is why establishing your MaxHR is so important.

There are basically four different zones, or percentages of the MaxHR:

- Baseline or daily activity

- Light exercise: warming up and exercising for general health

- Cardiovascular training for fitness

- High-intensity intervals for performance training

Unless you are an elite athlete, working at the second and third levels of intensity allows you to exercise long enough to produce the desired results of overall fitness and improved body composition. People who follow a controlled carbohydrate lifestyle frequently do so because they are more sensitive to the effects of insulin. Your energy may fluctuate significantly if you eat carbohydrates immediately prior to exercise, so you are better off exercising on an empty stomach than eating a quick snack before working out. Even more important than not eating an hour before exercise is rehydrating yourself as you work out. Drink up even if you're not thirsty or sweating. Aside from its other detrimental effects on the body, dehydration causes more lactic acid buildup and more soreness in the muscles. Also, be sure to get enough calcium, magnesium, and potassium so that sweating does

not deplete you of electrolytes. *Remember that it is a good idea to consult with your physician before beginning any exercise program; if you have any preexisting cardiovascular disease or have been leading a very sedentary lifestyle, a thorough consultation with a cardiologist is imperative.*

Beyond Walking

Walking is an excellent activity, but it has its limitations. Consider whether it's time to complement your walks with another form of exercise. But if you haven't exercised in a while or have experienced injuries or knee problems, you'll likely hear one common piece of exercise advice: Start walking. What's so wonderful about walking? Well, to start with, it's natural, functional movement that puts minimal stress on your joints. You can do it just about anywhere, and no gym membership, special equipment, or instruction is required. And although it's no substitute for weight training, walking is also a load-bearing exercise in that it requires you to carry your body weight. The gentle stress this puts on your skeletal system is good for your bones. Certain types of exercise equipment rob you of this particular advantage. A recumbent exercise bike, for example, supports your body weight by giving you a comfy seat and backrest.

If walking has so much to offer, you might ask, why do anything else? Because no one exercise, not even walking, is sufficient. Doing just one thing over and over again has built-in limitations and potential pitfalls. Here are three reasons to make walking part of your fitness program, but not the only component:

- **Diminishing Returns.** If you exercise by walking, your body gets very efficient at it. Your muscles become accustomed to being used in the same way and they get very good at responding to the challenge. In practical terms, this means that even if you increase your distance, speed, or both, you aren't going to be getting as much bang for your exercise buck as you did when you started your walking regimen.

- **Low Intensity.** While it's certainly possible to get your heart rate up by walking, many people just stroll, figuring that a slow forty-five-minute walk is the equivalent of a vigorous twenty-five-minute jog. Wrong! Your heart, like any other muscle, has to be pushed in order to grow stronger. If you're working in an aerobic training zone, you should be sweating, somewhat short of breath (you should be able to talk in short sentences but not hold forth on last night's TV special), and genuinely feeling as though you're doing a little work. If you're going to walk on a treadmill, you'll have to play around with the elevation and speed controls to make it a real cardiovascular workout. If you're walking outside, you'll need to push yourself to go faster and find a few hills.

- **Boredom.** If you've tried walking with friends, walking in malls, walking your dog, walking with headphones, walking while watching TV, and walking backward, it's time to try something new. With boredom can come lack of motivation. Even if you're still enjoying walking, it's time to broaden your repertoire. If you're enjoying your current walking program, mix in a few other modes of exercise to keep your walking from getting stale. Add a little variety and you'll get more results for your effort.

Instead of Walking

As you become more physically fit and look for challenges beyond walking, a whole world of alternatives unfolds. Try several of these activities to see which you enjoy most and which pleasantly challenge you to new levels of fitness.

- **Bicycling.** You can easily get your heart rate up on a bike without pounding your joints. The recumbent bike is easier on your back and bottom than a standard model.

- **Running.** This is not for everyone, and if you have knee problems or other skeletal injuries, it's definitely not for you. Still, running is more challenging than walking, and for many people it's a logical and thrilling progression from walking. How to tell if you're ready to run? If you can walk forty-five minutes quickly, without rest, you're probably ready to pick up the pace. Start by finding a treadmill or a local high school or college track—they're generally about a quarter-mile long, closed to traffic, and have an ideal surface. Walk a few laps (or about fifteen minutes on a treadmill) to warm up, then try one lap (two to three minutes) of jogging at an easy pace. Alternatively, jog the straightaway and walk the curves at the end of the track.

- **Swimming.** If you have arthritis, knee pain, or still have a lot of weight to lose, swimming is ideal. The water supports your body, giving you the freedom to move in an impact-free environment. Try water aerobics classes (check your local Y or health club) for even more variety. Because swimming uses so many muscle groups at the same time it is an efficient way to exercise.

- **Elliptical Trainers.** These machines, which have two footpads connected to a flywheel, move each leg in an oval-shaped motion. Some models have handlebars that you push and pull in sequence with the footpads for an additional upper body workout. The very low-impact motion is smooth and comfortable, an appropriate choice for someone with knee injuries. Gym models and some home machines typically can be programmed for varied resistance and offer an alternative for those who enjoy running but find it too painful.

- **Group Aerobics or Dance Classes.** Jazz Dance, World Beat, kick boxing, you name it. Take whatever appeals to you, but remember: Just because you're in a group doesn't mean you have to keep pace. Do what's right for you. If you need to slow down or modify a move, do it. If the class isn't challenging enough for you to get your heart rate up, pick up your pace.

- **Steppers and Stair Climbers.** These are definitely not for everyone. Stepping machines can aggravate knee problems and they're easy to misuse. If you make any of the common mistakes of leaning on the console, letting the pedals touch the ground or hopping like a bunny from one pedal to the other, you aren't getting much benefit. Such mistakes may actually increase your risk for carpal tunnel syndrome. Still, when used correctly, they offer a simple, effective workout. These machines can provide quite an aerobic challenge and should be approached with care by individuals who are not very fit or accustomed to the demands of stair climbing.

- **Rowing Machines.** If you have access to a rower, try it! These machines work your trunk muscles and arms—a rarity in the leg-centric cardio room. They're great to throw into your cardio mix.

What Is Weight Training?

Most people are familiar with walking, running, and other aerobic activities, but weight training may seem intimidating if you have not done it before. (By the way, women need not worry that weight training will make their muscles bulge. It will instead give attractive definition to their arms, legs, and the rest of the body.) Like initiating any new exercise program, begin weight training slowly and move up gradually or you may become discouraged, sore, or even hurt yourself—three sure ways to fall off the exercise bandwagon. Begin by lifting weights twice a week for the first two weeks; then advance to three times a week. Try to space the days so that your body has a chance to recover before enduring more weight training. Feel free to do aerobic exercises on both weight-training and recovery

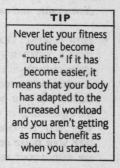

TIP

Never let your fitness routine become "routine." If it has become easier, it means that your body has adapted to the increased workload and you aren't getting as much benefit as when you started.

days. To make weight training more challenging, you can add weight *or* increase the number of repetitions and/or shorten the rest intervals between sets. Each variable provides a different kind of challenge: More weight heightens muscle strength and size; increased repetitions improve muscular endurance; and shorter rest intervals also improve endurance as well as enhance calorie burning. You can combine and rotate these different variables to work toward specific fitness goals.

How Often, How Long, How Intense?

Weight training will help you maintain your weight and will help build muscle. (Because muscle weighs more than fat, this could mean that you actually put on a few pounds with weight training, but your clothes will fit better. You also should be able to increase your ACE if your workout regimen is intense. To enhance your level of fitness follow these guidelines.

- **How Often:** You will probably need to do four to six aerobic workouts per week.

- **How Long:** This depends on your current level of fitness. Beginners should start with twenty to thirty minutes of exercise and build up to as much as sixty minutes as they become increasingly fit. Experts disagree about the ideal length of a workout session, but most seem to concur that forty-five minutes is long enough to get significant cardiovascular and calorie-burning benefits.

- **How Intense:** Don't make the common mistake of confusing output with effort. The fact that you ran three miles in forty-five minutes says nothing about whether or not that was a tough workout. So what does? The gold standard is your heart rate. To know if you're working at the right level of intensity, you need to know how hard your heart is working while you exercise. You can either take your pulse or use a heart rate monitor to see if you are within your aerobic training zone. If you're just starting to exercise, start by working out at 65 percent of your maximum heart rate. Once you are comfortable exercising at that intensity for twenty minutes a day, four days a week, for two consecutive weeks, you'll be able to progress to the next level—true aerobic training.

For most nonathletes, 70 to 80 percent maximum heart rate is an appropriate aerobic training zone. The simplest way to calculate this heart rate target is by using this formula: $220 - \text{(your age)} \times 0.85$. According to this formula, a forty-year-old's 85 percent maximum heart rate is 153. However, individual heart rates vary and your own maximum heart rate may be as much as fifteen points higher or lower. In addition to the other reasons for taking an exercise stress test, this type of examination allows even greater personalization of heart rate training zones.

To fine-tune your efforts (or monitor your exertion without checking your pulse), pay attention to how your body feels. Are you feeling a little out of breath? You should be huffing a little but not gasping for air. Can you talk? You should be able to speak in short sentences but not hold long conversations. Are you working hard? You should feel as though you're pushing yourself but not as though you're about to keel over.

Finding the Time

Unless you're one of the lucky people who become addicted to exercise, you must make yourself—sometimes even force yourself—to work out. Remember that exercise isn't just about jogging or going to a gym. It's also about being active and mobile all the time, whether playing baseball with your kids or running up and down the cellar stairs to do the laundry. Here are ten tricks for working in workouts:

1. Walk to work if you live close enough to your job. If you have a shower at work, you might even be able to run or ride your bike. This is a great way to start the day and make the most of your time.
2. Work out at lunchtime. A midday exercise break helps boost energy and can make you more productive in the afternoon.
3. Exercise in front of the television. The boredom of using a stationary bicycle, rowing machine, or treadmill can be mitigated by watching your favorite sitcom. Weight-lifting or stretching exercises are particularly suited to such multitasking. Watching the tube can become a reason to work out, rather than a deterrent.
4. Exercise with friends or coworkers. Group workouts are also a great way to meet new people with a shared interest, so check out local running clubs, spinning classes, or aerobic studios.
5. Get up early. With practice, early morning exercise sessions can become found hours. Also, you're less likely to skip workouts because distractions are unlikely to come up at this time of day.
6. Little things add up. Take the stairs instead of the elevator or escalator. Get off the bus or subway a stop or two before your regular stop and walk the rest of the way.
7. Make a plan. Following a schedule is a powerful tool in the battle to stay on target. Schedule exercise time just as you would a haircut, dentist appointment, or lunch with a friend.

continued

8. Make a date. If you commit to meeting someone for a workout, you have to show up!
9. Vary the program with cross training. To avoid boredom switch off with different fitness programs. You might jog twice a week, take an aerobics class one evening, or go to yoga twice a week and do weight training the other two days.
10. Engage in family activities like bike rides, canoe trips, and hikes. Introducing your children to the pleasures of being active is a lifelong gift.

Partners for Life

Exercise can not only help you take your health up a notch and your belt in several notches, it can help bond relationships. Debra and Jesus Ramirez had both let themselves put on weight. "Although I've practiced martial arts for years, I haven't always been in shape," recalls Jesus. "I watched my weight gradually climb from 220 to 270 pounds over a nine-year period. With no stamina, if I didn't win a bout in the first twenty seconds, I had nothing left. I had to stop jujitsu because I was just too big to fight." Meanwhile, Debra had her own moment of reckoning. "After a car accident forced me to take time off from my job, my weight ballooned to 210 pounds and my cholesterol was dangerously high."

The two went to The Atkins Center in October of 1999 where they worked with the director of medical education, Jacqueline Eberstein, R.N., to lose weight and reduce their cardiovascular risk factors. The couple supported each other to adhere to the program. "When I was tempted to cheat, Debra helped me stay strong," says Jesus. "And when she was tempted, I'd help her." Jesus suggested that they start martial-arts classes, which brought them even closer. By combining this rigorous fitness program with a low carbohydrate regimen, Jesus lost 76 pounds and Debra 63 pounds. "We practice Tae Bo, a very aggressive form of jujitsu created by a woman," adds Debra. "Tae Bo gives me a

Warm Up Before You Exercise

Test your fitness savvy by answering these three questions.

1. Which of the following are benefits you might expect to see as a result of sustained and challenging exercise?
   a. Reduced flabbiness
   b. A higher ACE
   c. Enhanced metabolism
   d. Reduction of cardiovascular risk factors
   e. Greater muscle mass
   f. Greater energy
   g. A more sculpted physique
   h. Your body will store less fat even when you are not working out.

2. Which statements about weight training are true and which are false?
   a. It will overdevelop a woman's muscles.
   b. You shouldn't engage in aerobic exercise on the same day that you also weight train.
   c. Increasing the weight increases muscles' strength and size.
   d. Doing resistance training twice a week is enough to get results.
   e. The more weight you lift and the longer you do it, the greater the benefits.

3. Which forms of exercise are primarily aerobic?
   a. Playing singles tennis
   b. Swimming
   c. Racewalking
   d. Kick boxing
   e. Power yoga
   f. Jogging
   g. Weight training

Answers:
1. All are possible benefits except h. Your body will burn carbohydrates for energy while you are working out and perhaps for a while afterward, but working out does not mean you can gorge on carbs and expect to maintain your weight.

continued

2. All but one is false. a. False. It will not create bulging muscles, but it will add definition to muscles. b. False. You can do both in one day. c. True. Increasing the weight increases both strength and muscle size. More repetitions improve endurance. d. False. More likely at least four workouts a week are needed to get significant results. e. False. Actually, this can be counterproductive, making you too tired to work out well, increasing the chance of injury, and possibly being a disincentive to continue.

3. a, b, c, d, e, and f. Only weight training is anaerobic.

special sense of achievement and confidence because I have been called a klutz most of my life." This 5-foot 9-inch-tall former klutz now wears a size 8 and weighs 147 pounds. Moreover, she has seen dramatic improvement in her blood lipids: Her total cholesterol has dropped from 259 to 223 and her triglycerides from 262 to 57. Meanwhile, her HDL rose from 58 to 74 and her LDL dropped from 189 to 137. Jesus, who is 5 feet 11 inches tall and now weighs 182, experienced similar dramatic improvements: His total cholesterol went from 221 to 198 and his triglycerides from 202 to 52, while his HDL rose from 42 to 62 and his LDL dropped from 159 to 126. Jesus sums it up: "Get moving. Exercise speeds up a sluggish metabolism."

Once you fully understand the importance of exercise and that it is the natural complement to the controlled carb way of eating and tailor a combination of activities that you enjoy and can be fit into your schedule, you have taken a giant step toward enhanced health and weight control. Taking a proactive approach to other issues is also essential, as you will learn in the next chapter, where we'll defuse landmines such as business socializing, travel, and the opinions of friends and family that could get in the way of your chosen lifestyle.

TIP

Exercise isn't just going to the gym: Every time you use a push lawn mower, carry a heavy backpack, or park at the far end of the parking lot, you're enhancing your fitness level.

She Had to Lose Before She Could Win

Kerry Feather experienced both personal and athletic victories and met her future husband when she changed her lifestyle.

These days, when I go to daylong volleyball tournaments, people are always teasing me about the food I bring. On a good day, you can be there from eight-thirty in the morning until eight at night, and everyone is carb-loading like crazy. The other players all bring bagels and oranges and I'm sitting there with my pieces of grilled chicken, slices of ham, and turkey from the deli—and Atkins bars—lots of Atkins bars! (I also bring salad and strawberries.) But by the end of the day, they're exhausted and I still have the energy I had at eight-thirty A.M.

That energy is the real Atkins advantage, and it's what gave me the strength to get serious about exercise again. I'd always been athletic. I played volleyball in college and continued to play in a local league even when I was at my all-time heaviest weight of 180 pounds. That was a really difficult period in my life. I was at the end of a bad marriage and very depressed, so I was eating up a storm. In 1997 and 1998 alone, I actually put on 60 pounds. I kept steadily getting bigger, buying new clothes when the old ones didn't fit, until one day I realized that I'd gotten up to a size 16! Not only was I miserable, but also my blood pressure was high enough that my doctor put me on medication. I chalked the hypertension up to family history, but my doctor said that my weight was probably to blame.

So I went on a low-fat diet, eating a muffin for breakfast, low-fat yogurt for lunch, and pasta for dinner— every single day. I bought some Tae Bo exercise tapes and worked out until I was sweating like a pig. But I

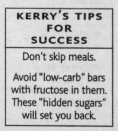

KERRY'S TIPS FOR SUCCESS

Don't skip meals.

Avoid "low-carb" bars with fructose in them. These "hidden sugars" will set you back.

never lost a pound and I was always starving. Although I was skeptical of Atkins, my mother had lost 10 pounds on it so I figured I'd try it, and when it failed to work, I'd join Weight Watchers. I did get my doctor's blessing to try Atkins and I read *Dr. Atkins' New Diet Revolution* before starting Induction in January 2000.

The weight came off so fast that five months later I had taken off 60 pounds and reached my goal weight of 120. My blood pressure had come down and I was able to go off the medication. Now that excess weight wasn't slowing me down, I started to get my volleyball game back. I also began dating the man who became my new husband. He was a fellow teammate and together we started running. We began talking about doing a triathlon together and ran our first one, the Wild Dog Triathlon in North Kingstown, Rhode Island, in July 2001. The race consisted of a quarter-mile swim, a thirteen-mile bike ride, and a five-kilometer run. My husband, his boss, and I raced as a team and came in first. We've done a few more triathlons since, and we're planning to do the Wild Dog again this year.

Atkins isn't a "crash diet," it's a way of life. I'm in the best shape of my life and my blood pressure and cholesterol levels are perfect—and I've been doing Atkins for three years. Anyone who tries to make you feel bad just doesn't understand or is jealous of your success.

ACE: 50	WEIGHT LOST: 60 pounds	HDL AFTER: 89
AGE: 27		LDL AFTER: 87
HEIGHT: 5 feet 4 inches	BLOOD PRESSURE BEFORE: 140/95	TRIGLYCERIDES AFTER: 52
WEIGHT BEFORE: 180 pounds	BLOOD PRESSURE AFTER: 110/70	STARTED DOING ATKINS: January 2000
WEIGHT AFTER: 120 pounds	TOTAL CHOLESTEROL AFTER: 186	

7 | Everyday Challenges

No matter how firmly you believe in the Atkins lifestyle—
and no matter the strength of your resolve—the fact is that
you live in a society that revolves around food, and unhealthy food to boot. At virtually every celebration, you'll
find cake and ice cream. At every dinner party or restaurant,
bread made with bleached white flour and sugar-laden
desserts beckon. Every office meeting is an occasion to
bring in a platter of bagels, Danish, or cookies. And let's not
even talk about the selections you find in every vending machine, convenience store, food court, and fast-food chain.

If you are someone who has already experienced the positive results of doing Atkins—whether for health reasons or to
lose weight—you're already ahead of the game. You've convinced yourself that Atkins works in
the short run. You understand the link
between carbohydrate foods with a
high glycemic content and your blood
sugar levels. (If you are new to Atkins
and either want to lose a small amount
of weight or address a health problem,
after reading chapter 3 you should

> **TIP**
> To avoid blood sugar
> spikes, spread your
> carbohydrate intake
> throughout the day
> rather than having a
> big carb blowout.

have an intellectual understanding of this phenomenon. It
may take longer until you actually experience it.) Now you
need to work on developing tools that will help you hold on to
your commitment permanently. If you get lazy and gradually
chip away at the success you've achieved, renewed weight
gain—with all the health implications and emotional baggage
associated with it—is almost inevitable. In this chapter, we'll
address the day-to-day challenges that life throws in your path
and share ideas for how to deal with them. In the next chapter,
we'll look at normal life changes—as well as some situations
beyond your control—and how to cope with them.

The trick to maintaining your self-control is to keep your eye firmly on the prize. That prize is the energized, healthy, permanently slim you—and that comes from sticking to your program. You will always have to be mindful about your eating habits, not sometimes, not most of the time, but consistently. Unfortunately, as the old saw goes, when it comes to doing what you know is good for you, all too often you are your own worst enemy. So first of all, let's look at some familiar demons.

Residual Hunger and Cravings

Long-term success doing Atkins, or any weight-control program for that matter, depends upon confronting your personal temptations and figuring out how to stand up to them. Think of yourself as a general planning a military campaign. In this case, the enemy is food that you know you shouldn't eat but that still exerts a powerful hold over you. Despite your commitment to your eating plan and to good nutrition, you're only human. Like most people, you probably have a weakness for at least one item that occasionally results in "naughty" behavior. A smart general knows his own strengths and weaknesses and respects his enemy. Learn to change what you can: your response to food; and accept that there are other things you cannot change: the power that food has over you. Temptation will not disappear. Even if you resist those M&M's today, there will be another sugary food beckoning tomorrow.

During the Induction phase of Atkins, the physiological "gift" of lipolysis/ ketosis suppresses hunger. If you've done Induction, you'll probably remember the feeling of freedom, of no longer being a slave to your appetite that's a wonderful side effect of burning body fat for energy. But Induction is just a stepping stone, and when the slimmer and more ener-

> **TIP**
>
> When eating out, ask that your food be prepared without sugar or flour.

getic you graduates from that phase and you begin eating progressively more carbohydrates, you have to give up that ever-present appetite suppressant as your body burns both fat *and* carbs for energy.

Fortunately, even in Lifetime Maintenance, you have a "secret" weapon, which will assist you in staying in control of your hunger. The way to keep such cravings under control is to stay at or below your ACE (Atkins Carbohydrate Equilibrium). This level of carb consumption allows you to burn both carbs *and* fat for energy, meaning that you are less likely to experience the ups and downs of blood sugar fluctuations that can cause carb crav-

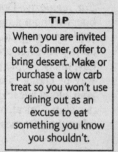

TIP

When you are invited out to dinner, offer to bring dessert. Make or purchase a low carb treat so you won't use dining out as an excuse to eat something you know you shouldn't.

ings. But in addition to this physiological mechanism, you need to add mental fortitude. People who are permanently slim are not any less tempted by food; they simply deal with temptation differently. And once you have made up your mind that you simply will not eat certain things—ever—there is a remarkable sense of relief and pride in your resolve that signals closure.

But quite possibly you will still need to strengthen your relationship with your old familiar friend called self-control. That means developing strategies for dealing with the occasional hunger pangs or cravings that can be brought on by stress, going too long between meals, going above your ACE, or simply eating a high-glycemic food that you haven't had in a while. Here are a few ways to handle those situations:

- *Space out your carbs throughout the day.* If you have a big carb blowout at lunch, you may feel the effects of the resulting blood sugar spike: that is, a dip in energy later in the day that leaves you lusting after something sweet. So, instead of a regular sandwich, opt for an open-face one. Make sure your salad has a good-size protein component and a tasty oil-based dressing. Eat some protein and/or fat with every meal or snack to slow down the release of glucose into your bloodstream.

- *Eat regularly.* Don't go more than four to six waking hours without a meal or a snack. When you're ravenous, you're more apt to lose control of yourself. Although our culture revolves around what we call three square meals a day, many people prefer to eat more, smaller meals. This way of eating is actually healthy because it helps keep your blood sugar on an even keel. It is essential that you not skip a meal, which could make you overly hungry when the next meal rolls around.

- *Snack.* The best way to keep a craving from becoming a monster binge is to give in to it—with a low carb snack. Snacking also keeps your metabolism working most efficiently, burning calories for energy instead of going into starvation mode, when it slows down and hordes energy. Whether you call it a mini-meal or a snack, feel free to enjoy a mid-morning or afternoon treat.

- *Sip.* Drinking water helps fill you up. We sometimes confuse hunger for thirst—especially as we get older. Many people find that they eat less when they have a glass of water before a meal. A cup of broth has the same effect. As always, drink at least eight 8-ounce glasses of water every day.

Treating Favorite Foods with Kid Gloves

One of the misconceptions about Atkins is that it means never eating bread, pasta, or other higher carbohydrate foods again. Once you're doing Atkins for life, this simply isn't true. For people who feel that a meal isn't a meal unless it in-

cludes a bread, pasta, or rice, there are many low carb alternatives. And as detailed in chapter 3, many people *can* eat
whole grains and products made from
them—but always in *moderation*.

For example, if bread has been
your undoing in the past, learn about
the different kinds. You'll soon understand why you want to avoid bread
made with bleached white flour. One
option is carb-reduced bread made
with alternative ingredients such as resistant starch (meaning it is resistant
to being broken down by enzymes in

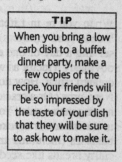

TIP

When you bring a low
carb dish to a buffet
dinner party, make a
few copies of the
recipe. Your friends will
be so impressed by
the taste of your dish
that they will be sure
to ask how to make it.

your digestive tract and impacting your blood sugar). Do note
that some products are labeled low carb, others high protein.
These terms are not synonymous, so check carb counts and
subtract the fiber content to get the grams of Net Carbs, the
only ones you need count when you do Atkins. When you review the menu plans that start on page 200, you'll see that low
carb bread regularly turns up in the lower ACE plans and 100-
percent whole-grain bread on the higher ACE plans.

In addition to learning which are the better breads,
other techniques may help you enjoy bread without overdoing it.

- Have the bread be your only high-glycemic food that day.

- Allow yourself only one piece of bread a day.

- Slice bread extra thin.

- Eat only the crust.

- Eat only low carb bread.

Bread Basics

When you're in Lifetime Maintenance, choosing the right breads (and crackers) can mean the difference between a serving a day or one every two to three days. (Your ACE is obviously a factor as well.) All breads are most definitely not created equal. How do you find bread that's relatively low in Net Carbs? Or a cracker that's low carb and free of partially hydrogenated oils? You're not likely to find healthy choices in the bread (or cracker) aisle of your supermarket. Instead, bakeries (including those in supermarkets) may offer specialty breads like seeded corn rye or seven-grain sourdough; and natural foods stores or sections of grocery stores may stock loaves made with spelt or soy, or sprouted (sometimes called live) grains. Your objective is to find bread with a high unrefined whole-grain, and high fiber content. All these add up to fewer grams of Net Carbs and a lower AGR (Atkins Glycemic Ranking). Low carb breads are also available. Here's how to proceed:

CHECK OUT THE INGREDIENTS. Compare the ingredient lists on a standard loaf from the bread aisle and on specialty bread. Most bread contains a small amount of sugar, some of which occurs naturally in grains, but many also have added sweeteners such as fruit juice, barley malt, honey, or molasses. Sometimes only a teaspoon or so per loaf is added to proof the yeast, but larger amounts are often used to yield a deeper color or crisper crust. Avoid products with added sugars. Some specialty products have no added sweeteners. Others, like cinnamon-raisin, are high in sweeteners—and may contain partially hydrogenated oils, too. Bottom line: Read labels—carefully.

COMPARE THE SERVING SIZE ON THE NUTRITION FACTS PANEL. Bread typically supplies 13 to 17 grams of carbs per ounce. White bread might have less than 1 gram of fiber per serving; 100-percent whole-grain breads often have at least 3, which means fewer Net Carbs. Also pay attention to the weight of each serving. Most Nutrition Facts information is listed by the slice, which is generally about 1 ounce (or 28 grams), but can vary between 24 and 38 grams—a difference of ½ ounce, or half a slice! Unsliced bread provides information based on weight; often a 2-ounce serving is standard.

DEFINING THE TERMS. You may see some of these terms on bread labels. Here's what they mean.

Organic: The grains were produced without either pesticides or chemical fertilizers.

Seeded: Whole seeds or grains (usually rye, but corn and wheat are common) are added.

Stone-ground: Generally, the flour is crushed between rotating stone disks, rather than high-speed rollers that generate high temperatures, meaning more nutrients are preserved.

Unrefined: Flour that is minimally processed and thus still has most (if not all) of the nutrients found in the germ as well as the fiber.

HOW ABOUT CRACKERS? Most crackers are made with vegetable shortening, whose prime ingredient is partially hydrogenated vegetable oil—aka trans fats. In addition, these crackers contain mostly enriched white flour, even the rye or whole grain varieties, and added sweeteners. The result: high carbs, low fiber, and killer fats. Look for crackers made without hydrogenated oils in natural foods stores or the health food sections of supermarkets. The packages may say "No Hydrogenated Oils" or "No Trans Fats" on the front. If you're looking for crunch, flat breads are another alternative. Their high fiber content keeps their Net Carbs under 10 grams per serving and some can be as low as 4. If you don't see them near the crackers, look in the bread aisle.

Deciphering the Labels

Here are some more tips on understanding bread and cracker labels, which generally apply to rolls and bagels as well:

WHAT IT SAYS	WHAT IT MEANS	NET CARBS
White	No whole grains are used. Usually very low in fiber.	high
Enriched wheat flour	White flour with riboflavin, niacin, thiamin, and iron added. (By law, these nutrients must be added to any flour that has the wheat germ removed.)	high
Wheat	It is meaningless. "Wheat" breads typically contain little or no whole-wheat flour. Their darker color comes from caramel or molasses.	high
Whole wheat	Some whole-wheat flour is used. May be slightly higher in fiber and other nutrients than white bread depending on the amount of whole-wheat flour used.	high

WHAT IT SAYS	WHAT IT MEANS	NET CARBS
100% whole wheat	Only whole-wheat flour is used. Whole-wheat flour is higher in fiber, vitamin E, some B vitamins, trace minerals, and protein than is enriched flour.	medium
Whole grain	Made with oats, barley, millet, rice, rye, or triticale (a hybrid of wheat and rye)—but check labels to ensure these grains are added to whole-wheat flour, not enriched white flour.	medium
Rye	May have more wheat than rye flour; bread made only with rye flour would be very dense. Rye is high in fiber— depending on how much rye flour is used, rye bread may be comparatively low in Net Carbs.	medium

continued

WHAT IT SAYS	WHAT IT MEANS	NET CARBS
Sprouted	Grains such as wheat berries or soy are soaked until they sprout. The water is drained, and the sprouts are ground. Sprouted breads can be lower in carbohydrates than other breads.	medium
Sourdough	Bread that is leavened with a "starter" of fermented, or sour, dough. Sourdough breads are typically made with enriched wheat flour; look for those made with rye or whole-wheat flour.	medium
Pumpernickel	A dark rye bread, often made with a higher proportion of rye flour to wheat than most rye loaves. May get its deep coloring from caramel.	medium
Protein	Often made with soy flour or high-protein grains that can have up to	medium to low

WHAT IT SAYS	WHAT IT MEANS	NET CARBS
Protein (continued)	8 grams of protein per slice (most whole-grain breads have 3 grams). Somewhat lower in carbs and significantly higher in fiber than other whole-grain breads. Net Carb content can range from 5 to 9 grams per slice.	
Low carb (or reduced carb)	When made with soy and resistant starches, such bread can contain as few as 3 grams Net Carbs per slice; has a high fiber content.	low

Have a Battle Plan

Whether your favorite foods are mashed potatoes, macaroni and cheese, tortilla chips, pizza, or ice cream, once you're doing Atkins for life, you don't necessarily need to abandon them forever. There are several possible battle plans:

- Have the food rarely and that day go easy on other foods in the #3 (Eat Rarely) categories

- Have only a small portion

- Think of the big picture

- Cut back after a small indulgence

Confronting Comfort Foods

If you're craving pasta, check out pasta made from soy flour, which has only about 5 grams Net Carbs in a half-cup of cooked pasta, compared to about 19 grams for a comparable serving of the regular semolina) type. There are also plenty of lower carb substitutes for other popular foods. High-protein or whole-grain (rolled or steel-cut oats are a good bet) hot or cold breakfast cereals, for instance, are a much better choice than the sugary stuff most people gulp down in the morning. A mix of wild and brown rice makes a great lower carb, more nutritious replacement for white rice. No one has invented a substitute for baked potatoes, but now that you are maintaining your weight you can probably eat a small baked potato now and then, especially if you add a pat of butter or dollop of sour cream to slow down the absorption of glucose into your bloodstream.

Jef Gray, a thirty-seven-year-old information technology executive, employs a variation on the first tactic by keeping a close eye on his carb intake during the week so that on weekends he can eat popcorn or ice cream with his kids. "Fortunately, I don't crave the bread and sugary things like I did before so I still stay close to the plan even in my weekend 'free zone,'" says Gray, who has been able to continue to control his weight for a year with this strategy.

Aerobics instructor Adrienne Chavers, who lost 36 pounds doing Atkins, is a proponent of the second battle plan. She can satisfy her taste buds with small portions of favorite foods. She is famous among her friends and family for her cornbread dressing. "I eat one small serving," she says. "And I might have two spoonfuls of cherry cheesecake for dessert. It is just enough!"

Fearing that he would die as his father had at an early age, thirty-five-year-old James Winterscheid lost a whopping 122 pounds in 1998. His three children were prime motivators for him. Speaking of how the family went out for ice cream to celebrate his older son's birthday, James says, "No, I didn't indulge, and I didn't feel deprived. I felt alive!"

Other people, such as Bob Keown, are able to indulge themselves in something, cut back on carbs for a few subsequent days, and stay on track. Bob has been on Lifetime Maintenance since January 2000. "I'm confident that the weight is off for good," he says. "I monitor my carbohydrate intake a little less rigorously, but I'm still aware of what I'm eating. If I've done something to push my carb limit, I'll back off for a week."

The important thing is to create a decisive and workable plan so that you, and not that appealing food, are controlling the situation. That way you remain in charge of your hunger and cravings—and of your weight and health. With a strategy tucked neatly under your belt, you don't have to go through the internal song and dance each time you are confronted with temptation. You will have learned to get into your battle mode. Otherwise, you'll find yourself having to make a decision every time you are confronted with these favorite foods. Human nature is such that when confronted by such a delicious demon, you will give in to it more often than not.

Understand this: Willpower *alone* won't cut it, as anyone who has ever been unable to stick with any diet will attest. But willpower *in concert* with suppression of certain physiological demands can work. No amount of willpower will overcome the body's need to raise low blood sugar when it gets too low: the result of eating excessive carbs, leading to high blood glucose, which in turn leads to overproduction of insulin to transport the glucose to cells. To reiterate the point: As long as you are not under the influence of fluctuating blood sugar and resultant hunger, you should be much more able to call the shots. And that is where willpower comes in.

Not all of us are as lucky as Jef, Adrienne, James, and Bob, however. Other people simply find it easier to avoid certain foods altogether. A food writer and recipe developer, Karen Rysavy had reached a weight of 271 and had sky-high cholesterol, blood pressure, and triglycerides before she turned to Atkins on the eve of her thirty-fifth birthday. Three years later and 61 pounds lighter and now on Lifetime Maintenance, she says, "No sugar or white flour has passed my lips in all this time. I don't want to mess up this wonderful feeling of wellness."

Jan Baumer, who follows Atkins to keep her cholesterol under control—she did lose 19 pounds and now is a trim 123 pounds—encounters temptation at her office every day. "Someone is always bringing in home-baked treats to share. I have a hard time saying no to something like homemade cranberry nut bread. Instead, I bring Atkins bars to work."

For those of us who need to limit our favorite foods to only very special occasions, substitution is the way to go. By having stand-ins always available, you can fall back on them when food you know you shouldn't eat beckons. See if any of these fit the bill:

INSTEAD OF . . .	CHOOSE . . .
• Ice cream (made with sugar)	berries in heavy cream or in sour cream with Splenda or low carb ice cream
• Salty chips	macadamia or soy nuts, pumpkin seeds, soy chips
• Mashed potatoes	mashed cauliflower or turnips with cream and butter
• Sugary soft drinks	sugar-free beverages or add sugar-free syrups to seltzer water
• A fruit smoothie	blend berries, ice cubes, heavy cream, and a packet of Splenda
• Tortillas	wrap fillings with low carb tortillas or lettuce leaves
• Chocolate	low carb chocolate candies, including peanut butter cups, sweetened with sugar alcohols

The Breakfast Dilemma

Many people who find doing Atkins easy most of the day continue to regard breakfast as a challenge. Some people simply are not going to cook in the morning, not when they have to get children—or themselves—out the door ASAP. Others just aren't hungry for anything substantial first thing in the morning. Still others bemoan the boredom of eating eggs. We'll address each one of these dilemmas individually, but it is important to remember that by the time you're doing Atkins for life there should be a considerable variety in the breakfast foods available to you, as you will see in our meal plans starting on page 200. Here are some ways to tackle the most important meal of the day:

Dilemma: I just can't face eggs every morning.
Solution: There are many other high-protein choices. Consider these for starters:

- A breakfast smoothie made with fruit and tofu or unsweetened soy milk
- Old-fashioned oatmeal (not the instant kind) served with nuts, heavy cream, or butter and sugar-free pancake syrup. Or add protein powder, organic peanut butter, or olive oil
- Cold cereals made from whole, unrefined grains without sugar and served with unsweetened soy milk or whole milk
- Nuts, seeds, and unsweetened coconut flakes sprinkled over whole-milk yogurt, cottage cheese, or ricotta. Or, whole-milk yogurt and fruit
- Sliced turkey or smoked salmon wrapped around cream cheese
- Other smoked fish
- Last night's leftovers

Dilemma: I'm just not hungry first thing in the morning
Solution: Spread it out. Have a low carb snack such as some cheese and fruit along with a cup of tea or decaf early in the morning. Then a couple of hours later have another small breakfast, such as reduced-carb toast or flatbread topped with butter or cream cheese and preserves without added sugar. Do not go for more than two hours after arising without eating.

Dilemma: I just plain miss my old sweet comfort foods like Rice Krispies and cinnamon buns for breakfast.

continued

Solution: From muffins to breakfast cereals, there are numerous products manufactured specifically for people who are following controlled carb regimens.

Dilemma: I don't have time to make and/or eat breakfast before leaving the house.
Solution: Either use the low carb products mentioned above or make breakfast foods over the weekend, freeze them, and then pull out of the freezer when you get up. Pancakes and muffins are two breakfast favorites that freeze well. Pop in the microwave for a few minutes before serving. Or make breakfast the night before. Hard-boiled eggs, slices of cheese, cut-up fruit, nuts, and seeds can all be prepared ahead and placed in plastic bags so you can take them to work with you. You can also make a batch of natural oatmeal that will last in the fridge for a week—just add water and microwave each morning.

Eating in Restaurants: Atkins Cuisine-ology

If you love dining out, adopt a few easy strategies to block temptations before they appear. First, if you live in an area with lots of restaurant choices, head for cuisines with more low carb options than others. For example, Chinese, Japanese, or Thai restaurants can be good choices so long as you skip the rice and noodles or have only small portions of either. You do need to watch for sugar or cornstarch in the sauces. Typical Mexican restaurants, on the other hand, will be more challenging since tortillas, rice, and beans are cornerstones of most dishes. Similarly, Italian restaurants often load your table with bread, pasta, and sugary marinara sauce unless you ask them not to. Whatever cuisine you choose, however, will have something for you as long as you stay focused. See What to Order for help in making choices in several popular cuisines.

For some people, the challenge of eating in restaurants is not pushing

TIP

Natural foods stores usually keep 100-percent whole-grain or sprouted breads in the refrigerator and/or freezer sections because without preservatives, these breads spoil quickly.

away the bread basket as much as it is telling their dining companions or waiter about their food preferences. If you're uncomfortable calling attention to yourself by asking about ingredients ("Is that made with sugar?" "Is the fish breaded?"), we have two suggestions. First, when you can, call the restaurant ahead of time and ask

TIP

Working in an air-conditioned office or traveling by plane dehydrates your body, so be especially diligent about drinking your eight 8-ounce glasses of water a day.

which entrées are appropriate for someone who cannot have any sugar, flour, or starch. Second, remember how important this is to you. Controlling carb consumption is not a fad or a political statement—it's for your health. For tips on talking to intimidating or skeptical dining partners, see How to Turn Friends and Relatives into Allies (page 155).

What to Order

It may take a little reconditioning to eat the low carb way at your favorite restaurants. Here are some good substitutions and tips for seven popular cuisines.

At Italian Restaurants

CHOOSE . . .	INSTEAD OF . . .
insalata frutti di mare (seafood salad)	deep-fried calamari
mixed grilled vegetables or sautéed Portobello mushrooms	deep-fried mozzarella sticks
antipasto (assorted meats and cheeses); marinated peppers and mushrooms; clams	baked stuffed clams
escarole or *stracciatella* soup	fettucine Alfredo

continued

CHOOSE . . .	INSTEAD OF . . .
roasted red snapper or salmon; grilled calamari or shrimp scampi	linguine with clam sauce
grilled chicken paillard (boneless breast, pounded thin) or pork loin	any risotto
veal or chicken piccata or scallopini with lemon and capers	veal, chicken, or eggplant Parmesan

TIPS

- As you're being seated, tell the maître d' or server that you'd like a dish of olives rather than a bread basket.

- Do as the Italians do: Start your meal with a bowl of soup (choose clear broth or *stracciatella*—a sort of Italian egg-drop soup. Note that some versions contain pasta or beans).

At Chinese Restaurants

CHOOSE . . .	INSTEAD OF . . .
egg-drop soup	egg rolls
sizzling shrimp platter	shrimp fried rice
steamed tofu (bean curd) with vegetables	any chow fun (wide noodle) dish
stir-fried pork with garlic sauce	sweet-and-sour pork
beef with Chinese mushrooms	beef lo mein
steamed whole fish	shrimp with black bean sauce
chicken with walnuts	chicken with cashews
sautéed spinach with garlic	moo shu vegetables (with pancakes)

TIPS

• Many Chinese sauces are prepared with sugar or cornstarch; stick to dishes that are stir-fried, steamed, or broiled.

• Instead of white rice, ask for a small serving of brown rice.

At Mexican Restaurants

CHOOSE . . .	INSTEAD OF . . .
grilled chicken wings with ranch dressing	chili peppers or chiles rellenos
sopa de albóndigas (meatball and vegetable soup)	quesadillas
jicama salad	beef nachos
grilled *pescado* special (fresh fish of the day) with grilled vegetables and chilies, or mixed seafood (*marisco*)	any taco platter
pollo asada (grilled marinated chicken) with *pico de gallo* salsa	chicken chimichanga
camarónes al ajillo (shrimp in garlic sauce)	shrimp enchilada
grilled skirt steak with onion and chilies	beef burrito
turkey mole	chicken tortilla

TIPS

• Ask the waiter to skip the standard bowl of tortilla chips that comes with meals. Instead, order guacamole and ask for jicama or cucumber slices for dipping.

• A real margarita made from tequila, lime juice, and triple sec will be lower in carbs than the kind made from a sugary mix.

At Thai Restaurants

CHOOSE . . .	INSTEAD OF . . .
tom yum koong (shrimp and mushrooms simmered in hot-and-sour broth with coriander, lime leaves, and lemongrass)	dumplings or spring rolls
sautéed shrimp or beef with basil, onion, and chilies	*pad thai*
sautéed scallops and shrimp (or beef or pork) with mushrooms, zucchini, and chili paste	any curry dish
sautéed beef, chicken, or pork with shrimp paste and green beans	sautéed beef, chicken, or pork with ginger, black bean sauce, and green onion
sautéed mixed vegetables	Thai fried rice with vegetables and eggs
steamed mussels with Thai herbs and garlic sauce	deep-fried whole fish with sweet-and-sour sauce

TIPS

- Avoid bean thread, a thin noodle that appears in many dishes.

- Anything listed on the menu as *pad* will almost certainly be stir-fried.

- If you order curry, you're better off with one that doesn't contain potatoes.

At French Restaurants

CHOOSE . . .	INSTEAD OF . . .
frisée salad with lardons (thin strips of bacon) and poached egg	Alsatian tart (bacon, onion, and egg pie)
coquilles St. Jacques (scallops in cream sauce with cheese)	*langoustine en croûte* (lobster in puff pastry)
moules marinière (mussels in white wine and herbs) or bouillabaisse (fish stew)	vichyssoise (cream of potato soup)
coq au vin (chicken in wine sauce)	*caneton à l'orange or aux cerises* (duck with oranges or cherries)
entrecôte or tournedos Bordelaise (steak in reduced shallot and red-wine sauce)	croque monsieur (egg-dipped fried ham-and-egg sandwich)
veal marengo (veal stew with tomatoes and mushrooms)	veal Prince Orloff (veal roast stuffed with rice, onions, and mushrooms)
haricots verts *au beurre* (buttered young green beans)	*pommes* Anna (upside-down potato cake)
assorted cheese plate	crêpes Suzette (crêpes with orange butter and orange liqueur, served flambéed)

TIPS

- It is okay to order the butter-and-cream dishes, but simpler dishes, such as fish Provençal with tomatoes and herbs or steak *au poivre* are smarter choices.

- Beware of *pommes frites*, aka french fries. Heaps of them often accompany steak dishes, and they are practically irresistible.

At Middle Eastern Restaurants

CHOOSE ...	INSTEAD OF ...
loubieh (green beans cooked with tomatoes)	tabbouleh (bulgur salad)
eggplant with garlic, tomatoes, and peppers	*fattoush* (bread, cucumber, and tomato salad)
shish kebab (grilled spiced cubed lamb on skewers)	*kibbe* (ground lamb and bulgur patties)
kofta (balls of ground lamb and onions, skewered and grilled)	*falafel* (chickpea patties)
shish taouk (skewered pieces of marinated chicken grilled over charcoal)	*b'steeya* (Moroccan chicken pie with almonds)

TIPS

- Ask to have a glass of delicious Middle Eastern mint tea with your meal. It will help fill you up and aid digestion.

- If you order the thickened *labnee* yogurt flavored with mint or hummus (chick-pea dip) as an appetizer, ask for raw vegetables to dip with instead of pita bread.

At Indian Restaurants

CHOOSE ...	INSTEAD OF ...
shahi paneer (homemade cheese in creamy tomato sauce)	vegetable *samosas* (pastries)
roasted eggplant with onions and spices	any *pakora* (fritter)
chicken shorba soup (made with garlic, ginger, cinnamon, and spices)	lentil or mulligatawny soup

CHOOSE . . .	INSTEAD OF . . .
any *korma* (meat in cream sauce)	any *biryani* (rice dish)
tandoori chicken or shrimp	chicken or shrimp *vindaloo*
lamb or chicken curry	any *dal* (lentil or bean dish)
any lamb, chicken, or shrimp kebab	lamb, chicken, or shrimp *saag* (cooked with spinach and spices)

TIPS

- Call it *nan, chapati, poori,* or *paratha,* it's bread. India boasts a variety of breads. Ask for some spiced cooked vegetables or a cooked cheese dish such as *shahi paneer* (see chart) instead.

- Inquire about all the elements in a specific dish. Because Indian food combines so many different ingredients, menus often do not list them all. Remember that vindaloo usually includes potatoes.

- Stick to kebabs, *tandoori* dishes, and curries, which are pretty straightforward and basically derive their flavor from herbs and spices.

Pointers for Dining Out

Follow these golden rules and you'll become adept at restaurant dining without paying the price in pounds!

- Don't skip a meal before eating out (you should never do this anyway but the temptations in a restaurant could compound the problem) or arrive starving. If you do, you might have trouble resisting the bread or some high carb appetizer. Instead, snack on a hard-boiled egg or a few slices of cheese before you go out. If all else fails, ask for some olives, crudités, or steamed veggies to nibble on before your main course arrives.

- Drink a couple of glasses of water before your meal to help fill you up. Feel free to enjoy a glass of dry wine with your meal, occasionally.

- Many restaurants feature their menus on-line. Try to visit their Web sites to review the offerings and map out your dining plan ahead of time.

- Ask to have your dishes served without the extras of rice, beans, potatoes, or pasta. Most restaurants will accommodate requests for another portion of vegetables in lieu of such high carb foods.

- Ask for sauces on the side so you can decide whether and how much to consume.

- Soup is a great appetite squelcher. Miso soup, many cream soups, and clear broth with meat or vegetables are all satisfying and delicious ways to get your appetite under control before the main dish.

- Decide *before* dinner whether or not you will order dessert. If not, fill up on everything else so that you are pleasantly full by the end of the meal and able to resist temptation, particularly if your dining companions are indulging. If you plan to order dessert, make a point of skipping the bread, rice, or pasta. Even so, your best dessert choice is always berries with whipped cream or melon. Or make a low carb dessert and plan on having it when you get home.

- Don't feel you have to finish something just because it is put in front of you. Restaurant servings are notoriously large. Instead, ask for a "doggie bag" and enjoy the rest for lunch the next day.

- Don't give in to the "I deserve it" mode. What you deserve is to be healthy while still enjoying the foods you already love, not succumbing to unhealthy indulgences.

- Don't torture yourself if you accidentally consume something that's been batter-dipped or breaded. Remember that it's only one meal.

Navigating a Dinner Party

Now that you are doing Atkins for life, dinner parties should be reasonably easy to handle. By the time you are in this phase, there is no need to tell your hosts that you cannot eat certain foods. If the meal is served buffet-style, just load up on protein dishes and vegetables. Select small portions of starches if you can handle them. When you do not have much choice about what is served, you can certainly politely ask for a small serving of rice or potatoes or even none at all. Nor is it a faux pas to pass on dessert. Regardless of whether they are following a low carb or a low-fat regimen, many people do not eat dessert. The real issue when eating at the home of friends or family is whether you can keep your eye on the prize and not use the occasion as an excuse to claim that you are not in control of the situation.

When you are the host or hostess, you're in the catbird seat. Whether or not you serve foods that you are not going to eat is up to you. If you are completely in control and love to feed others, you may want to make some special high carb dishes and pass on them yourself or have just a small bite. But if making those dishes for guests is really just an excuse for you to indulge, you might be wise to confine your menu to dishes you can comfortably eat. The recipes in Part 2 are full of choices that people watching their carbs, and those who wouldn't know a carb if they fell over it, can both enjoy.

On the Move

Even if you like to eat out a lot, it's easier to maintain your eating plan when you're close to home. Your own kitchen, local grocery stores, and restaurants have already been subjected to your carb-o-meter, so you know how to navigate them skillfully. But once you leave your home territory—be it by plane, train, or automobile—you'll find "foreign" landscapes teeming with deep-fried carbs and sugar in every color, shape, and form. Whether you travel for business or simply make the occasional trip to visit the relatives, you'll have to confront the fast and convenient carb-laden foods offered all along our culture's transportation pathways. Let us help you form a plan of attack to carry with you when you go.

On the Road and in the Air

Truck stops, diners, and rest areas bring to mind burgers, colas, french fries—and vending machines filled with chips and candy that reside somewhat incongruously with travel-size toothbrushes and sewing kits. You can also often find entire emporia of fast food just off the highway, selling frozen yogurt, hot pretzels, pizza, pasta, and, of course, burgers, french fries, and onion rings.

Take the roadside food court one step further and you've got the airport's supersize food court. In addition to the concessions you find in rest areas are others that might sell Asian noodle concoctions, foot-long subs, and popcorn in a dozen flavors—and colors—to say nothing of those seemingly ubiquitous fragrant cinnamon buns dripping with sugary frosting. And then there's the food you get on the airplane. It's bound to be a disappointment on all fronts and especially in terms of carb counts. But when you're strapped into a seat at thirty thousand feet, it can be hard to resist even the most tasteless offerings.

The obvious solution is to plan ahead and pack your own food. People who get into the habit of doing this find that it can make traveling much easier in many ways. Avoiding all that junk food means that you don't have to wait in lines, you don't have to pay exorbitant prices for terrible food, you don't retain excess water from eating over-salted foods, and you don't get indigestion to boot. Bring food along in a mini-cooler pack that straps onto your back or a carry-on bag. Try individually wrapped string cheese and rolled-up deli meats or chunks of chicken or beef. Snap-top cans of tuna, salmon, sardines, or chicken are good picks, too. Depending on the food, you might pack a container of toothpicks instead of a fork. Other good ideas for your mini-cooler: berries, nuts, seeds, a small apple, celery sticks (and a small container of cream cheese for dipping), and a plastic cup of salad, hard-boiled eggs, and olives. Carry a few low carb protein bars in your bag or jacket pocket for emergencies.

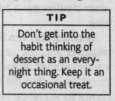

TIP

Don't get into the habit thinking of dessert as an every-night thing. Keep it an occasional treat.

Workers' Compensation: Overindulging at the Office

If you asked someone to name the most common eating danger zones they'd probably cite restaurants, movie theaters, and parties. But probably the number-one danger zone is the workplace. People who work in offices are often saddled with an insidious combination of negative influences: being sedentary and stressed in an environment full of high carb, easy-to-grab food.

The nature of office work is to sit perfectly still in front of a computer, a desk, and a phone. The better worker you are, the more time you spend sitting still. When you do get up, however, you're often looking for a quick stress reliever or energy boost (which is why so many office workers drink coffee all day long)—something nearby to nibble on. Even if you're just on your way to the copy machine or the rest room, you may find yourself walking by a candy dish, a platter of brownies brought in for someone's birthday, or doughnuts or bagels from a morning meeting. And that's before you get to the vending machine full of candy and salty chips. How can you possibly stick to your controlled carb program and still survive at work? The answer is the same as it is with other challenges: a little ingenuity and some advance planning.

Between the vending machine and the coffee cart—and whatever goodies your coworkers have brought in that day—a smorgasbord of carbs confronts you. Don't even consider them! Also, skip the high-octane coffee: Caffeine has been known to stimulate hunger even in people with stable blood sugar. Decaffeinated coffee, tea and herbal tea are all better bets.

Navigating the Fast-Food Jungle

When you're stuck without provisions and you have no other choice but to skip a meal and go hungry (don't do this, ever!), there are ways to eat at junk food joints without letting your nutritional house collapse. Some tips:

- Avoid the nitrates. When possible, limit your intake of hot dogs, bologna, salami, and other meat products that are preserved with nitrates, or keep exposure to the bare minimum.

- Burger, burger. Sandwiches are always a good bet as long as you toss the white-flour bun and avoid sugary sauces such as barbecue or sweet-and-sour (mayo and mustard are okay).

- Avoid low fat. Anything advertised as low fat usually translates to high carb. Pass it by.

- Search for salad. Almost every fast-food place, from the big chains to the little one-man carts, carries salads, often with grilled chicken on top.

- Deconstruct. If you end up with breaded chicken, just use your fork and knife to separate the chicken from the empty carbs.

To avoid being tempted at break time, eat a good, low carb breakfast before you go to work. A breakfast with sufficient protein and fat not only sets you up for a positive and productive day, it keeps you from an energy dip that leaves you ravenous by mid-morning. (See The Breakfast Dilemma on page 139). Also make sure you have your own low carb snacks handy so that you have an alternative if and when you need a snack.

To meet the growing variety of dietary restrictions among employees, most cafeterias offer a good selection of healthy food these days. Skip the fried foods, sandwiches, and desserts. Instead, scrutinize the hot entrées, the salad bar, and the grill section for Atkins-friendly choices. Ask to substitute extra veggies for high carb sides. Or bring your own meals. If a refrigerator is not available, pack your homemade lunch in an insulated bag or mini-cooler. Tuna, chicken, or egg salads can be combined with a container of salad greens. Baked chicken legs, slices of roast beef, cheese, and steamed shrimp are also highly portable.

TIP

Storing sliced bread in the freezer makes it easy to exercise portion control. Just defrost or toast what you need when you need it.

Carbs consumed when working overtime may be the hardest of all to avoid, especially if you weren't able to plan ahead by packing dinner or an extra snack. As your workday stretches into evening, your stress level may rise—bringing with it a desire for something sweet or salty and crunchy. Create an emergency stash of low carb snacks such as nuts and protein bars to keep in a desk drawer so you can dip into that instead of heading to the nearest vending machine. When your coworkers are sending out for dinnertime food, go ahead and join them, making the best choice you can from the available menu. (If it's the ubiquitous pizza, use a fork and eat the toppings but leave the crust. Or order a cheese sandwich and ditch the white roll.)

Delicious Alternatives

Fortunately, if the desire for something sweet or starchy does strike, you can almost always satisfy it with a low carbohydrate alternative—such as a handful of nuts or low carb chocolate bar. In fact, you can even have a stack of low carb pancakes with sugar-free syrup! Today's range of low carb products is truly impressive and growing better all the time. Look for such delectables as muffins, brownies, bread, snack chips, even ice cream and cheesecake. It all boils down to one essential fact. The only way you will maintain a way of eating—and by extension, your weight— is if the food you can eat is enjoyable and the quantities ample enough to keep you from being hungry. On Atkins you will experience both.

Low carb alternatives to high carb products can make managing your weight while still enjoying a variety of foods considerably easier. Just remember that like any tasty food, they can be abused and you need to avoid mindless munching. You may be able to have a larger serving, or at least a guilt-free one, but eating one low carb brownie with 5 grams of carbs is one thing and eating four of them is an entirely different matter!

Carb Creep

If you are under a lot of pressure at work, you may be eating the wrong kinds of food and going too long between meals, thereby triggering blood sugar swings that lead to cravings for high carbohydrate foods. You may feel the only treat you can give yourself is food. This may take the form of binges or simply carb creep, meaning that little by little your carb intake edges up until you are well over your ACE. Our association of food with love can also come into play when a relationship has gone sour. "If he/she no longer loves me, I must be unlovable and do not deserve to be slim and attractive," you may be thinking on a subconscious level. If a loved one has died, you may feel the desire to replace the affection that person gave you with comfort food. On the other hand, we also use food to celebrate good fortune or mark life's milestones, so food becomes a reward. As a child you may have been given a lollipop when you went to the pediatrician, and good behavior may have resulted in a trip to the ice cream parlor. As a result, food has become an integral part of a reward system.

Sometimes You Have to Just Say No

Just as you may have to force yourself to exercise, you will sometimes have to simply give yourself a firm "No!" For many of us, it's easier to ban a food than eat it sparingly. For example, you've probably heard people say no to potato chips, claiming, "If I have one, I'll eat the whole bag."

To keep your reserve of self-control strong and available whenever you need it, it must be rooted in the idea of keeping your eye on the prize. What is that prize, again? Staying slim, feeling good, living a longer and healthier life—that's all. If you start slipping and go back to your old way of eating and behaving, this is the prize you're giving up. Is any food worth that? We think not.

How to Turn Friends and Relatives into Allies

It's one thing when you're alone in a grocery store or at home, making decisions for yourself about what to cook and eat. It becomes easy and pleasurable to control your carb intake. But it can be a very different thing when you're shopping, eating, or entertaining with friends or family members who, at best, don't understand your lifestyle or, at worst, disagree with it and harangue you about it. Either way, you can bring them around.

Denise Lopez, who lost 139 pounds on Atkins, comes from a family whose traditions make it challenging to control her carbs. Her story is typical of people of many cultures in which food plays a multilayered role.

"Everything in my family and in our Hispanic culture revolves around food," says Denise. "Celebrations, accomplishments, awards, sad occasions, even death is surrounded by food! When we were kids, if we did well on our report cards—food! If we received an award at school—food! When Aunt Fela died—food! And Christmastime where I live—in the Rio Grande Valley at the southernmost tip of Texas—means *tamales* [pork filling wrapped in a thin corn dough], *menudo* [a soup filled with hominy, which is made from dried corn], *buñuelos* [fried flour tortillas covered with a sugar-and-cinnamon mixture], and hot chocolate made with milk, real chocolate squares, and cinnamon sticks."

The first few holidays after Denise and Luis, her husband, started doing Atkins were tough. "Thanksgiving dinner that first year was different, to say the least. My mother-in-law is a terrific cook so to pass up dressing and potatoes and all that is an insult to her. Then came Christmas and more carb-laden food. Not being able to eat a single thing that was offered was a problem. But we managed—and as soon as the pounds started melting off, our family became more accepting. Now, five years later, it's easy." In fact, now that the Lopezes are both maintaining their weight, when they feel like having some Mexican food, they do so. They've also educated their friends and family about Atkins so that now, when they go out to other people's houses, there's always a green salad and sugar-free drinks available. Luis and Denise also make a point of eating a protein snack before they leave their own house so that they're not so hungry that they're tempted to eat pretzels and other high carb snack foods at a party.

What Friends and Family Say— and What They Really Mean

When you tell people that you're doing Atkins, chances are good that someone is going to try to talk you out of it. How can you turn these saboteurs into supporters? Here's a guide to reading the real meaning behind friends' and family members' words and how to reply to them.

What they say: You look fine. Why are you still doing Atkins?
What they mean: You aren't the same overweight person I once knew. Shaking things up like that makes me uncomfortable.
What you reply: Now that I have lost weight and feel and look better, I know how I need to continue eating to maintain these positive changes. I'd love your support.

What they say: Nobody can stick with the Atkins approach—it's too restrictive.
What they mean: You've regained weight after following other diets. Why should I think that you'll continue to stick with Atkins?
What you reply: My own experience and everything I've learned from looking into the way Atkins works convinces me it is easier to stick to long-term than low-fat, low-calorie approaches.

What they say: Doing Atkins is bad for your health: It ruins your kidneys, it weakens your bones, and it raises your cholesterol and so on.
What they mean: What I've heard in the media must be the truth, no matter what you say.
What you reply: I've researched Atkins and read a lot about it, and there's just no evidence for what you say. To prove it, why don't you check out the Why Atkins Works section of the Web site (www.atkins.com).

What they say: You'll gain it all back.
What they mean: I don't believe that you can maintain your weight loss on a program that's so easy to do.
What you reply: You don't have to say anything—your improved health and appearance will speak for you.

Family Bonds and Food

Denise's story is an example of one reason some people resist Atkins. Many of the traditional foods people eat at holidays and other occasions are high carb foods. (Back when
most of these traditions began, humans lived very differently
than they do today—and our food supply looked entirely
different, too.) When one family member chooses to stop
eating dishes that are steeped in family history and tradition,
it can feel like a personal affront, especially to the person
who did all the cooking. But just as Denise's story represents
a very common problem, it also illustrates the most common
and effective solution. When her family members saw that
Denise's new lifestyle resulted in a slimmer, healthier, and
happier person, they did an about-face and became her
greatest supporters.

Oftentimes, it's not family traditions that cause resistance
among friends and relatives but misinformation. However,
the shaky theories and half-truths run as deep and are as
strong as the many ancient cultural traditions. This has to do
with the extremely widespread belief that a healthy diet is
one that is extremely low in saturated fat. When friends and
family ask you how you can possibly eat so much meat and
fat, the best thing you can do is be well informed and hope
that they are willing to listen. Often, the best thing you can
do is tell them how great you feel on Atkins, share your improved cholesterol and blood pressure numbers with them,
and then spin around to show off your svelte body.

You should now be armed with the information you need
and the mindset that will assist you in keeping on the straight
and narrow—pun intended—as you pursue the Atkins
lifestyle. In the next chapter, which concludes Part 1 of this
book, we will look at some of the challenges that life can
toss in your way over the years and how you can deal with
them without straying from your commitment to doing
Atkins for life.

Are You Sandbagging Yourself?

Now that you are slim and healthy, why would you want to be anything else? But what our conscious minds believe and what goes on in our subconscious are not always the same. To see whether you might be undermining your chances of permanent weight control, respond to each question with a "yes" or "no."

1. Do you attach too much value to food, using it as a reward when you've done well or a salve when you're suffering?
2. Do you ever tell yourself that you're over the hill and staying slim and attractive is a losing battle, so why bother?
3. Does the thought of suddenly having a more sexually appealing body make you just a little bit afraid?
4. Do you ever feel guilty because you've "left behind" a dear friend or relative who still struggles with a weight problem?
5. Is there one situation, party, or event in which you always succumb to your old (unproductive) eating habits?
6. Do you expect other, unrelated problems to go away once you're at your goal weight?
7. Do you have trouble getting others to respect your way of eating?
8. To some degree, do you measure your own worth by how thin you are?
9. Do you feel that you don't really deserve to have all the things you have wanted?

If you've answered "yes" to any of these questions, you may have some hidden psychological issues that could sandbag your weight-maintenance efforts. To address these issues, you may find it helpful to get these thoughts and feelings out of hiding. Write them down in a journal and talk about them with someone you trust, whether a friend or a therapist. Why do you think you feel this way? What are some things you can do or change to overcome these barriers? Acknowledging such emotions is the first step to overcoming them.

It All Started at the Emergency Room

When low-fat didn't help, Brendan Adams solved his health problems—and slimmed down—by following Atkins.

BRENDAN'S TIPS FOR SUCCESS

Regard your dietary change as a lifestyle decision, not just a diet.

It's easier to stay on track if the whole family eats the same way. Design meals around protein-based main courses such as Cornish game hens or shrimp Parmesan, then add vegetables. The rest of the family can then also have rice, pasta, or potatoes and fruit for dessert.

My ordeal began one summer morning four years ago when I wound up in the emergency room. I had gained 30 pounds in just four months and was retaining a lot of water. My blood pressure was 206/170, my hands and arms were numb, and I was having difficulty breathing. Fortunately, a wise emergency-room doctor didn't believe that a 34-year-old was having a heart attack; she realized something else was causing the problem.

After reviewing my symptoms in depth, she concluded that I suffered from hypothyroidism, or a sluggish thyroid. On her advice, I began seeing an internist for treatment. Although the thyroid condition stabilized over a six-month period, I could not seem to lose weight. My cholesterol skyrocketed, and my liver and kidney functions also registered abnormal. To treat these problems, my physician started me on a regimen of up to seventeen medications a day. He also put me on a low-protein, high-carbohydrate diet that shunned red meat and eggs. Most of my meals consisted of lettuce minus dressing and a variety of other vegetables.

Although I was supposedly doing everything right, my health was not improving. In addition, my blood sugar was unstable, I was experiencing severe headaches, and I had put on another 20 pounds. After months of tests, my internist advised me that I should probably get used to being overweight and taking a lot of medications. This was certainly not what I wanted to hear and, quite frankly, not how I wanted to live my life.

Two years after my trip to the emergency room, in October 1999, I saw a television report on Atkins. I was skeptical; however, I was willing to try anything to get my health back.

I purchased a copy of *Dr. Atkins' New Diet Revolution* and, after reading it from cover to cover, chose to change my eating habits. Within just a few short days of starting Induction, my energy level increased and I was enjoying foods that not only tasted good but also filled me up.

After two and a half weeks, I had lost nearly 15 pounds. This was great, but I had a blood test because I was concerned about my cholesterol and triglyceride levels. My total cholesterol levels had decreased from 520 to 200, my LDL went from 225 to 125, and my triglycerides dropped from 740 to 193. Moreover, my blood-sugar level registered normal. My internist called to give me the good news and asked if I was doing anything differently. When I explained that I was doing Atkins, he said that he would not continue to be my physician if I stayed on the program, so I terminated my relationship with him.

My new doctor was skeptical, but he was open to hearing more about Atkins, and suggested, based on my previous results, that for the time being I stay on the program. He did, however, recommend that I have blood tests done every six weeks. My next results showed that my total cholesterol had decreased to 173, my LDL to 110, and my triglycerides to 119. After about eight weeks on Atkins, I had lost 40 pounds. Six weeks later my test results were even better. Cycling through the four phases of Atkins, I found that I felt better when I chose to maintain my intake at approximately 50 Net Carb grams per day.

Because I was feeling so good, I decided to take up running. I hadn't been much of a runner before, but I wanted to choose a form of exercise that I could do on my own. Imagine my surprise when I could run three or four miles without knee and back pain, unlike my experience in the recent past. My business partner, who is a serious runner, encouraged me to join him in a marathon to benefit the Leukemia Society of America. Had anyone suggested I run a marathon a year earlier, I would have laughed. In those days I couldn't even have run a mile! Not only did I complete the marathon, I finished 1,573 out of the 22,000 runners who completed the course. Interestingly, I did not "carb up" like most runners tell you to do.

Today, I weigh 146 pounds and my blood work continues to be excellent. I only take one medication to control my thyroid, and my headaches are practically gone. People who "diet" are usually not successful long-term; following Atkins requires a complete lifestyle change. I made a decision to have a different life. It's now been more than three years since I started the program, and I like myself a lot more today than I used to. Both my energy level and my outlook are much improved, not just because I'm thinner but because I'm healthier. And now I love keeping up with eighteen-year-olds—in fact, I can run them into the ground!

ACE: 50	WEIGHT AFTER: 146 pounds	TRIGLYCERIDES BEFORE: 740
AGE: 38		
HEIGHT: 5 feet 8½ inches	WEIGHT LOST: 60 pounds	TRIGLYCERIDES AFTER: 60
	LDL BEFORE: 225	TOTAL CHOLESTEROL BEFORE: 520
WEIGHT BEFORE: 206 pounds	LDL AFTER: 86	
		TOTAL CHOLESTEROL AFTER: 147

8 | Looking Forward

When most people think about getting older, they assume that diminishment of mental skills, physical energy, muscle tone, and the like are inevitable. Moreover, they regard heart disease, hypertension, blood sugar imbalances, and even cancer as a part of the aging process. It needn't be that way. We have all met or heard about men and women in their seventies, eighties, and even nineties who are enjoying active, healthy lives. Whether they are ace tennis players, tap dancers, artists, humanitarians, or individuals who are accomplished

TIP

Reward yourself with treats like a massage, a facial, a new pair of running shoes, or a new CD, but not with food. That's what got you into trouble in the first place.

and fulfilled in a variety of other endeavors, such individuals are proof that getting older needn't translate into a catalog of disease and diminishment.

In addition to their role in increasing your risk of heart disease and Type 2 diabetes, excess carbohydrate intake can affect the aging process in another important way. Chronic elevated levels of blood glucose due to high carbohydrate consumption can react with proteins, forming advanced glycosylation end products (AGEs), which can deteriorate organs and vascular function. One result is hardening of the arteries, diminishing the oxygen flow to vital organs, including the brain.[1-5]

How can you increase your chances of having your golden years be numerous and vigorous? Along with having a positive attitude, seeing change as an opportunity, and remaining mentally challenged, the following answers should come as no surprise. They are the same advice that appears elsewhere in this book.

- Eat healthy. Control your carbohydrate intake and select a broad range of nutrient-rich foods.

- Keep your weight under control.

- Stay physically active. Exercise regularly to maintain your energy, oxygenate your body, strengthen your heart, and maintain muscle tone.

- Take nutritional supplements to make up for any deficiencies caused by depleted soil or over-processed food.

To this, we would add: Take a proactive attitude to your health. Find a physician who is open to complementary medicine and who is willing to see you as an active and equal participant in your healthcare. Take note, you thirty-year-olds, this message applies to you as much if not more than it does to the sixty-year-olds reading this book. The sooner you adopt an all-encompassing healthy way of living, the longer you are likely to live and the better the quality of those years.

Aging

Doing Atkins is for life, but your ACE may be subject to change over your lifetime. No matter how careful you are about your diet, fitness program, and overall approach to wellness, life happens. You can be certain of one thing: you will age. What can you do about it? First of all, be in the best shape you can be so that you can fight the aging process; secondly, understand that you may have to make some changes in the face of new challenges.

As we age, our metabolism slows down, which makes it harder to maintain a constant weight. The only way to slow the effects of time is with more vigorous exercise. So while it is never too late to start a fitness program, if you're already a regular exerciser, you're more likely to be able to increase your activity level without injury. If you become more active, you may be able to increase your ACE. If you have an accident that limits your activity level for a while, you may have to decrease your ACE. Perhaps you have retired recently or have gone from walking to work, to commuting by bus. Or perhaps you've left an occupation that required a fair amount of physical effort and are now living a less active life. Or worse, perhaps you recently had surgery and were told not to exercise for

TIP

Celebrate your successes every day. Each morning, take a moment to look at yourself in the mirror and be proud of your accomplishments.

a couple of months. All these situations could mean that your energy output has decreased. You have two options in order to maintain your weight. The first is to up your energy output another way. You may have to develop a more structured exercise program than you used to need. If your mobility is temporarily restricted, you may be able to find a gentler form of exercise you can engage in while on the mend—perhaps water aerobics, stretching, or chair exercises. A physical therapist will be able to tell you what is advisable for your particular condition.

The second approach is to lower your carbohydrate intake. If you were happily maintaining your goal weight on 80 grams of Net Carbs a day, you may need to scale back until you can resume your former activity level. Start by dropping to 70 grams. If you can maintain, fine, this is your new ACE. If you start to gain after a week or so, drop to 60 grams, and so forth. Your new ACE is where you can easily maintain your weight. (This is not to say that we recommend eating fewer carbs as an anti-

TIP

When you stumble don't be too hard on yourself. No one can be 100 percent perfect 100 percent of the time. Instead, learn from your mistakes and move on.

dote to being inactive.) Most people find that a combination of exercise and dropping their ACE works best in a short-term situation.

A Sluggish Thyroid

If you begin to slowly put on weight despite adhering to your ACE and maintaining your fitness regimen, one possibility is that your thyroid function has slowed down. Ask your doctor to do a TSH (thyroid stimulating hormone) test to ascertain whether you are producing a lot of that hormone. If the results are high, it means your body is working hard to overcome a depressed thyroid.

A New Prescription

Sometimes an individual has had his weight under control for years and is humming along happily with an eating and exercise routine that keeps him slim and trim. Then suddenly, without any apparent change in routine, the pounds pile on. What gives? The cause is often a side effect of a new prescription drug. Many pharmaceuticals (see a partial list on page 11) make it harder to control your weight, although this is not necessarily indicated on the information sheet. If your doctor suggests that you start taking a new drug, ask the following questions:

- Is there a lifestyle change or combination of changes I can make instead?

- Is there a natural alternative in the form of a dietary supplement or combination of supplements that I can take instead?

- Will this drug make it harder to control my weight?

- If so, is there another drug I can take that will not have this effect?

- How long will I have to stay on this drug?

If you must take this drug and it does have a weight-gain effect, you might have to increase your activity level and/or decrease your ACE to maintain your weight.

Hormones and Weight Gain

From a weight viewpoint, being female poses special challenges at several phases of your life. Hormonal fluctuations may contribute to weight gain or water retention. Likewise, taking hormones during peri-menopause and menopause can cause a slow and insidious weight gain over time. If taking estrogen causes you to gain weight, discuss alternatives with your doctor. (The most recent research on Prempro, one brand of hormone replacement therapy which uses both estrogen and synthetic progesterone, raises questions about its safety and the long-term risk for breast cancer and heart disease. On the other hand, it does appear to have some protective effect on colon cancer and osteoporosis.)[6]

TIP

Ignore people who try to sabotage your healthy new lifestyle. They often have their own reasons for not wanting to see you take control of your life.

Men are not immune from hormonal changes. As they age, men produce less testosterone, the primary male hormone, so the effects of estrogen are not suppressed as they are when there is sufficient testosterone. The result can be difficulty in maintaining weight.

Stressful Situations

Many people who have struggled with their weight over the years cite a particularly stressful situation as the trigger that signaled the start of their difficulties. It can also be the occasion for backsliding. After years of keeping their weight under control, some people fall off the wagon in response to an

event such as divorce, loss of a job, or death of a spouse. If
you have encountered such an experience, you may have felt
that no matter how much you have been in control of your
health and your weight, this devastating event shows that you
cannot really control what happens to you or those you love.

And so you may find yourself falling
back into old eating habits that promote weight gain.

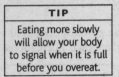

TIP

Eating more slowly
will allow your body
to signal when it is full
before you overeat.

The intimate relationship between
food and emotions is the subject of a
whole field of psychology. Our pur-
pose here is to make you aware that if you previously had a
problem with overeating or eating the wrong things—like a
"dry" alcoholic—you may always be vulnerable to falling
back into these bad habits when life throws you a curveball.

How to Avoid Backsliding

If something happens that pushes your stress buttons and
points you in the direction of the refrigerator, fast-food
restaurant, or candy jar, you need to be immediately aware
of your backsliding. Awareness is the first step to avoiding
a spiral into behavior that in turn triggers self-reproach and
more bingeing. If you have an ongoing or even an occasional history of going off the program when you en-
counter a stressful situation, you need to get a handle on
the time, the circumstances, and the food that have been
your undoing in the past. Otherwise, your behavior could
lead to a pattern of yo-yo dieting. And if you do temporarily fall into the pit of temptation, you need to know that you
can dig yourself out, as you have before. If you find yourself in a stressful situation, try the following tactics:

Do talk to a person you trust, whether a family member,
friend, or therapist. Airing your feelings is the first step to
dealing with them constructively.

Don't wallow in self-pity. If you've been disappointed in love, the real revenge is showing your ex-mate that you have the fortitude to be happy without him or her. If you've found that retiring has made you feel useless, get involved in volunteer activities or start a second career. If you have lost a loved one, reach out to other members of the family, who are also in pain.

Do talk to yourself. Remind yourself of how you have overcome other problems in the past and how you are strong enough to do it again.

Don't fall into the guilt trap of punishing yourself for back-sliding with more inappropriate eating.

Do acknowledge what you did, forgive yourself—and then get right back on the program.

Don't ever allow yourself to gain more than five pounds. Losing that small amount of weight is always doable. (Here we are talking about real weight, not fluctuation throughout the day, which is reflected in an increase in inches as well.)

So long as you take control of your carb intake immediately, you should be able to lose the few pounds you may have piled on, which will make you start feeling better. Meanwhile, give some thought to why you went "off the wagon" and how to avoid doing so again in the future. Was it purely emotional eating? Or were you also letting yourself get too hungry? Are you drinking enough water? Do you keep controlled carb snacks around you at all times? After you eat something you shouldn't or even too much of a perfectly fine food, how do you feel?

Here are some tips to help you avoid behavior you know is destructive:

Know your triggers. If it's a certain bakery you pass every day, take another route. If it's attending a birthday party with tempting birthday cake, make sure you've eaten before you go or bring a low carb substitute you can enjoy while the others overdose on sugar and bleached white flour. If it's going to a newsstand with its tempting array of candy bars, decide ahead of time that you will leave only with your newspaper. If it's social drinking, set a limit on how many drinks you'll have.

Plan your path through the grocery store. Simply avoid the aisles that hawk sodas, snack foods, and other junk food full of empty carbohydrates. You'll be amazed at how quickly you can whiz through the store when you avoid all that unnecessary stuff.

Stay busy. It's obvious but true. When you find yourself opening the fridge for something to do, it's time to find yourself a task. On the other hand, getting so absorbed in an activity that you skip a meal or go too long between meals can lead to a drop in blood sugar and a desperate need to eat the first object in sight.

Start up that food diary again. You may have kept a diary while you were in the weight-loss phases of Atkins. Why not get back in the habit and make it a notebook you can carry with you. In addition to tracking your food intake and any shifts in weight, consider adding the following categories: Mood, Location, Hunger Meter (on scale of 1 to 5). A food diary works on a few different levels. In addition to listing your daily carbs, it interferes with unconscious nibbling and provides a history of your eating habits so you can see what does and doesn't work for you.

Treat yourself. Remember that controlling carbs allows you to eat many of the ultimate luxury foods such as Pineapple Mango Layer Cake and Miso-Glazed Salmon, among the many delicious dishes in the recipe section that follows. Preparing and enjoying such foods will keep you from feeling deprived.

Ten Rules for a Lifetime

1. Count your Net Carbs.

2. Stay at or below your ACE (Atkins Carbohydrate Equilibrium).

3. Adjust **your** ACE as needed.

4. Eat primarily whole, unprocessed foods.

5. Stay away from sugar, bleached white flour, and other junk foods.

6. Don't go more than four to six waking hours without a meal or snack.

7. Exercise regularly.

8. Supplement with vitamins, minerals, and essential fatty acids.

9. Drink a minimum of eight 8-ounce glasses of water.

10. Never let yourself gain more than 5 pounds.

Talking About Atkins to Your Doctor

As part of your overall commitment to good health, you should have an annual physical exam. Of course, if you have any known health problems, you must be seen more often. If you have lost weight by doing Atkins and overall you're feeling more energetic and positive, your doctor is probably willing to acknowledge that you have improved your health. And if he or she has seen that in addition to slimming down, you've improved your blood lipids, brought your blood pressure down, and corrected or improved any blood sugar imbalance, the proof is in the low carb pudding. If you did not share your decision to do Atkins with your physician (which we do not recommend), now that you have achieved your goals and are doing Atkins for life, it would be an excellent time to reveal the reason for your success. If you are just starting to do Atkins for health reasons, you definitely should discuss

TIP

Weigh yourself no more than twice a week.

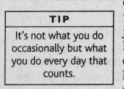

TIP

Eliminating sugar- and white-flour-laden junk food from your home may be the greatest gift you can ever give your children.

your decision with him or her. Also be sure to get baseline blood tests done. When you go in for another checkup—say, in three months— your doctor will likely see that you've improved your blood lipids and blood sugar levels, and brought your blood pressure down. Since you'll also be feeling more energetic and positive, you'll have made your point. Although some doctors still have a knee-jerk anti-Atkins reaction, many others have come to understand that controlling carbohydrate intake is a key component of good health, and they will support your decision once they understand what Lifetime Maintenance entails.

Your doctor may be pleased with your results, but it is up to you to be proactive about why you are doing Atkins for life. First of all, you need to make it clear that this regimen is

TIP

It's not what you do occasionally but what you do every day that counts.

distinct from the Induction phase, which was a short-term phase to jumpstart weight loss. Explain that Lifetime Maintenance is not about eating 20 grams of Net Carbs a day. Rather, it is about finding your individual tolerance for carbs so you can

maintain your goal weight for life. It does not mean eating only steak, bacon, and eggs and eliminating all vegetables and fruit. It is about eating a wide variety of foods, including plenty of nutrient-rich carbohydrates. What it does cut out are foods full of white flour, sugar, and other empty carbohydrates in the form of junk foods.

If your physician is still bothered by the myths he or she has heard about Atkins, here's what you might hear and here's how you can respond:

MYTH #1: Lipolysis/ketosis is dangerous.
How you can respond: Many doctors believe this, but it's not true. What is dangerous is a life-threatening condition known as ketoacidosis, which affects insulin-dependent dia-

betics or alcoholics. The two terms sound similar, but that's the only connection. Ketosis is simply a shorthand way to say your body is burning stored fat instead of glucose as its primary fuel. This desirable and perfectly natural process of using fat instead of glucose to fuel your body happens in the Induction phase of Atkins. In any case, now that you are in Lifetime Maintenance, you burn both fat and carbs for energy so you are no longer in lipolysis/ketosis.

MYTH #2: Eating so much protein leaches calcium from your bones.

How you can respond: This is another myth that has been disproved. It is true that your body will excrete more calcium in the urine than usual when you are in the early part of the Induction phase of Atkins, but studies that looked for bone loss, found none.[7,8] After the first week on Induction, calcium excretion in the urine returns to normal with no long-term effects. And recent research with older adults has shown that eating a high-protein diet not only does not weaken your bones, it actually strengthens them if you also take a calcium supplement—as the Atkins program recommends.[9]

MYTH #3: Doing Atkins will raise your cholesterol.

How you can respond: Just the opposite is true. Almost every Atkins follower sees a drop in LDL cholesterol and a rise in HDL ("good") cholesterol, along with a sharp drop in triglycerides, a type of blood fat that is an important indicator of heart health. If your blood lipid tests show this, the question should never arise. (Several of these studies are referenced in chapter 3.)

MYTH #4: The amount of protein in the Atkins approach is bad for your kidneys.

How you can respond: This may be the biggest myth of all, because there is absolutely no evidence for it—not one single study shows that a high-protein, low carbohydrate diet damages normal kidneys. (There are studies that show that too much protein in concert with too much carbohydrate can be problematic, but you are not consuming excessive carbs when you are doing any phase of Atkins.) If you already have severe kidney disease, of course, you must take the advice of your physician and he/she will probably tell you to sharply restrict your protein intake, as well as intake of other nutrients and even water. But kidney disease cannot be caused by eating protein.

MYTH #5: No one knows the long-term results of eating the low carb way.
How you respond: How could it be unhealthy to eat whole foods such as protein, healthy fats, a variety of vegetables, low glycemic fruits, seeds, and nuts, and modest amounts of legumes and whole grains? And how could it be unhealthy to feel better, be more active, and reduce your need for medicines?

Once you've cleared up some misconceptions about doing Atkins, it's time to provide your doctor with some solid scientific studies that support its underlying principles. There are far too many of these to provide a complete list here. At the end of this book are nine recent studies that you can share with your physician.[10–18] For additional studies whose findings can be applied to the four Atkins Nutritional Principles— weight loss, weight maintenance, good health, and disease prevention—your physician can go to Research Summaries in The Science Behind Atkins on www.atkins.com.

Recipe for a Healthy Life

We hope that reading the first half of this book has provided you with the knowledge and tools that you can use now and in the years to come to enrich your life with health and vitality. If you are like the other Atkins followers to whom we have introduced you, we trust that your feelings of empowerment about your weight and your health will spill over into other areas of your life. And as you read the recipes and re-

view the meal plans that follow in Part 2, we are confident
that you will feel equally empowered in the kitchen. You will
also soon see tangible evidence of the wide variety of tasty,
satisfying foods you can enjoy even as you remain slim,
healthy, and full of boundless energy.

Annual Tune-Up

Maintaining your health, and with it a healthy weight, is an ongoing process. To evaluate where you stand, ask yourself these questions now, a year from now, and every year thereafter. In certain
cases, there can be more than one correct answer to a question.

1. Weight: In the last year,
   I have lost weight
   I have maintained my weight
   I have gained no more than 5 pounds
   I have gained more than 5 pounds
   I have seesawed up and down but basically maintained my
      weight

2. Eating habits: In the last year,
   I ate mostly protein and fat
   I have moderated my intake of protein and fat to include more
      healthy carbs
   I have eaten a variety of carbohydrate foods
   I could eat healthier carb foods than those that I am eating
   I am eating too many carbs overall
   I avoid all white flour and sugar
   I rarely eat white flour and sugar
   I eat some white flour and sugar
   I avoid all fats
   I am careful to avoid trans fats
   I wouldn't know a trans fat if I fell over it

3. Atkins Carbohydrate Equilibrium (ACE): In the last year,
   I have been able to raise my ACE
   I have stayed at the same ACE
   I have had to lower my ACE
   I do not know what my ACE is
   I am able to maintain my weight without worrying about my ACE

continued

4. Fitness: Over the past year,
   I exercise about one hour a day every day
   I exercise regularly but not every day
   I exercise sometimes
   I rarely exercise
   I never exercise
   I exercise more than I did the previous year
   I exercise less than I did the previous year
   I have stepped up my overall fitness level
   My overall fitness level has declined

5. Activities: Over the past year,
   I engaged in aerobic exercise
   I engaged in anaerobic exercise
   I engaged in both aerobic and anaerobic exercise
   I have a regular exercise routine
   I varied my exercise routine
   I am enjoying exercise
   I enjoy exercise more than I used to
   I am exercising because I know it is good for me
   I still hate to exercise but I do it anyway

6. Physical Exam: Over the past year,
   I have had a complete physical
   I have not had a physical

7. Blood Lipids: Over the past year,
   My total cholesterol has risen
   My total cholesterol has dropped
   My total cholesterol has remained the same
   My HDL has risen
   My HDL has dropped
   My HDL has remained the same
   My LDL has dropped
   My LDL has risen
   My LDL has remained the same
   My triglycerides have dropped
   My triglycerides have risen
   My triglycerides have remained the same

8. Other markers: Over the past year,
   My blood pressure has risen
   My blood pressure has dropped

My blood pressure has remained the same
My fasting blood sugar has risen
My fasting blood sugar has dropped
My fasting blood sugar has remained the same

9. Dietary supplements: Over the past year,
    I have not taken any supplements
    I have taken a multivitamin/mineral regularly
    I have taken a multivitamin/mineral when I remembered
    I have taken omega-3 and omega-6 fatty acids regularly
    I have taken omega-3 and omega-6 fatty acids when I
        remembered
    I have followed a regular vitamin and mineral regimen
        tailored to my needs

10. Review of medications: Over the past year,
    I started taking one or more new medications on a regular
        basis
    I continued to take one or more medications on a regular
        basis
    I stopped taking one or more medications
    I increased the dosage of one or more medications
    I decreased the dosage of one or more medications
    I took no medications

PART TWO

Eating for Life

Getting Your Kitchen in Order

Whether you've been doing Atkins for years or are just starting, stack the deck in your favor with the right ingredients and techniques for low carb cooking.

What to Buy

Most of your food shopping will be concentrated in the produce, dairy, poultry, fish, and meat sections of the supermarket.

BUY FRESH. Fresh vegetables, fruits, and protein will still be the basis of your diet. You know by now that many canned goods and packaged products contain hidden carbs and are loaded with trans fats. If your budget permits, buy organic poultry, meat, eggs, and produce. Other items that should be on your grocery list follow.

THINK FISH. Fatty fish such as salmon, tuna, halibut, mackerel, herring, bluefish, and sardines supply protein and B vitamins, but these flavorsome fish also pack plenty of omega-3s, a type of essential fatty acid with disease-fighting properties. Keep canned fish on hand, too, for hurry-up suppers. Canned salmon is higher in calcium than milk. Mash the soft bones with a fork and you'll get 225 milligrams of this bone-building mineral per 3½-ounce serving. Canned sardines are even higher: 3 ounces supply 325 milligrams. Four ounces of milk? A mere 150 milligrams. Look for light tuna packed in olive oil; it tastes better than tuna in water or vegetable oil.

SHOP WITH THE SEASONS. Choose vegetables and fruits at their height of flavor and freshness. You'll save money too: Seasonal produce is generally less expensive. There is no reason to buy asparagus or watermelon in January when broccoli and a host of fruits are readily available.

COLOR MATTERS. Buy as many richly colored foods as possible: Dark leafy greens, orange vegetables, purple grapes, and the like contain more nutrients than their paler cousins. Arugula has almost twice the folate of iceberg lettuce, watercress has about four times the vitamin C, and spinach has nearly thirty times more beta-carotene. Red grapes are higher in anthocyanins than green; and pink grapefruit has 40 times more beta-carotene than white. In general, avoid white foods—with the exception of dairy products, of course. White rice, white flour, sugar, and pale pasta are out. Instead, focus on brown breads and grains, beans, and other legumes.

THE GREENER THE BETTER. From collards and kale to spinach and turnip greens, these nutritional powerhouses are loaded with vitamins A, C, E, folate, and other vitamins; minerals, including calcium and iron; and cancer-fighting compounds such as indoles, sulforaphane, and isocyanate. Many dark greens are at their best in winter—they're fresh and inexpensive when other vegetables are pale and flavorless. Sauté greens with lots of garlic, stir them into soup, or braise them with a bit of bacon.

GO WITH THE GRAIN. Whole grains provide a host of nutrients, but they're dense in carbohydrates. Go beyond brown rice and whole-wheat pasta to find those that are lower in Net Carbs. Oatmeal boasts cholesterol-lowering fiber. Wild rice packs twice the protein of other varieties. Bulgur, a form of whole wheat, is already cooked; simply pour boiling liquid over it and soak it until soft, about 30 minutes.

SCRUTINIZE LABELS. Carbohydrates lurk in foods you might not suspect. Avoid anything that has high-fructose corn syrup or any kind of starch, such as modified potato or rice starch, in the ingredients list. Canned goods and condiments are common culprits. Pay particular attention to fat-free foods, especially salad dressings and marinades. Corn syrup often is used instead of oil because they have similar consistencies. Not only do you end up with unwanted carbs, but also a host of chemicals that are added to mask the sweetness. Instead, use high-flavor condiments that boast healthful ingredients, such as pesto and salsa.

ENJOY ETHNIC SPECIALTIES. If you're fortunate enough to live near an ethnic food market, stock up on spices and condiments—prices are generally lower than at natural foods stores.

THINK SMALL. Purchase dairy products in small quantities and wrap cheeses in a double layer of plastic wrap to ensure freshness.

What to Have on Hand

Unless your supermarket has an unusually well-stocked health food section, you should find a good natural foods supplier nearby or online. Products such as kamut and amaranth (both grains) and many of the others listed below are generally only available at natural foods stores. Here's what you should be looking for:

- Organic stone-ground whole grains, breads, muffins, bagels, crackers, cereals, and flours. Good hot cereal choices are old-fashioned oatmeal, Wheatena, and Atkins™ Hot Cereal. There are now a good number of low carb cold cereals, including Atkins Morning Start™ products.

- Nut flours

- Unsweetened fruit juice concentrates—dilute and sweeten to taste with low carb sweeteners

- Soy products, including tofu in all its forms, soy milk (look for brands without any sugar) soy nuts, etc. Also frozen green soy beans (edamame).

- Sugar-free sauces and salsas—they contain relatively few carbs and add interest to steaks, sautéed chicken breasts, and other simple main dishes.

- Low carbohydrate thickeners, such as ThickenThin™ not/Starch (available at www.atkins.com); low carbohydrate bread and muffin mixes; low carbohydrate soy-based and/or whole-wheat pasta, bake mix, and pancake and waffle mix.

- Low carb tortillas. One brand is La Tortilla Factory.

- Sugar-free macadamia and other nut butters; also soy nut butter. All are lower in carbs than peanut butter.

- Low carb soups in a cup

How to Cook Low Carb

A few simple techniques and cooking habits will make life much easier and help minimize carb intake.

- Prep greens the day you buy them. We know it's easier to make an iceberg lettuce salad than to clean, chop, and sauté kale. Unfortunately, there is no comparison in nutritional value. So, be your own sous chef and wash and cut dark leafy greens when you buy them and store in plastic bags.

- Keep both canned and dried beans on hand. Dried beans are more economical and generally have a better texture when cooked. You can rinse them and soak them overnight, or—

if you forget—cover them with water, bring to a boil, and let them soak for one hour before proceeding with your recipe. Beans and legumes are high in protein, fiber, and iron. Try tuna salad mixed with marinated beans at lunchtime, instead of a tuna sandwich, for a nutritious and delicious change.

- If you're not yet a vegetable fan, try roasting them, which brings out their sweetness and intensifies flavors. Vegetables contain natural sugars that caramelize when roasted. For best results, cut into same-size pieces, arrange in a single layer on a baking sheet, drizzle with olive oil, sprinkle with salt, and pop them in a 425°F. oven until tender.

Sweet Rewards

You will either be buying low carb desserts and candies or making your own. Keep a supply of soy-based flour, Atkins™ Bake Mix, nut flours, sugar-free syrups, jams with no added sugar, unsweetened cocoa powder, sugar-free vanilla and chocolate extracts, and sugar-free chocolate chips in your pantry. Sugar substitutes come in two forms. The granular type, sold in boxes, is particularly useful for baking because it can be substituted cup for cup for sugar in conventional recipes. Sugar substitute in packets is useful for sweetening beverages and frozen desserts. This way you'll have ingredients on hand when you feel the urge to whip up a sweet treat. Make a habit of baking a double batch of low carb cookies, muffins, or cakes and freezing half. It's just a little more work, but you can freeze in portion-controlled packages. On the other hand, if knowing such treats are in the freezer could be a problem for you, ignore this suggestion.

Invest in an ice-cream maker to make your own low carb ice creams and sorbets. Depending on the flavor and degree of sweetness, you can easily control the amount of Net Carb grams per serving. Nut-based and chocolate flavors will generally contain fewer carbs than fruit flavors. As with all treats, portion size is paramount. Look in the frozen food section of your supermarket or natural foods store for low carb ice cream.

- Make your own bread crumbs: Toast low carb or 100 percent whole-grain breads, then tear into pieces and place
  in food processor. Pulse until crumbs form. (If you don't
  own a processor, consider buying a small one—it costs
  about the same as a blender and you will get a lot of use
  out of it.) Store bread crumbs in the freezer to have on
  hand anytime you want to make breaded cutlets. You may
  season bread crumbs by adding Parmesan cheese,
  oregano, paprika, and a dash of garlic powder.

- Sprinkle nuts and seeds on salads and cooked vegetables:
  they add texture, flavor, and B vitamins as well as protein
  and iron. Store nuts and seeds in the freezer to preserve
  freshness.

- Add texture to salads with low carb croutons. Brush low
  carb bread with olive oil, bake in a hot oven until crisp,
  then cut into small cubes.

- Keep a variety of oils on hand, but buy them in small
  quantities. They are essential for cooking and flavoring.
  In addition to olive oil, you will want to have on hand
  canola or grapeseed oil for higher-heat cooking, plus
  some nut and seed oils. Most nut oils are too delicate to
  cook with—they break down over heat—so use them in
  dressings or drizzle over vegetables. (See Smoke and Fire
  on page 192 and Flavorful Oils on page 190 for more
  about culinary oils.)

The Goods on Garlic

Garlic has the highest ratio of antioxidant capacity to carb content
of any food, what we call the Atkins Ratio™. It also contains
dozens of sulfur compounds that are thought to protect against
cancer, fight infections, lower cholesterol, and prevent blood clots.
If you're not fond of garlic, try roasting it, which mellows the flavor considerably. Serve it as a side dish, or mash and mix with olive
oil and wine vinegar for a salad dressing.

- Learn how to sauté properly to ensure moist chops and chicken: Set a heavy skillet (cast-iron is ideal) over high heat for 2 to 3 minutes. Sprinkle salt in the skillet, then add meat. Sear on both sides; if the cut is thick, finish cooking it in a 350°F oven for 5 to 10 minutes.

Smart Snacks

To head off hunger "emergencies," keep plenty of low carb snack fixers on hand. Many of the following can also serve as hors d'oeuvres when you're entertaining:

- Blanched broccoli florets (they have a more pleasant texture than raw broccoli), baby carrots, or zucchini sticks with a sour cream dip

- Berries and cut-up melon

- Olives—avoid the canned black kind, which are pretty tasteless. Instead try fresh kalamatas, gaetas, Sicilians, or Niçoise.

- Low carb soy chips with salsa

- Jarred marinated artichoke hearts and roasted red peppers

- Popcorn (in moderation, of course)

- Cheese cubes

- Pâté

- Nuts, seeds, and soy nuts

- Celery stuffed with nut butter or cream cheese

- Hard-boiled eggs topped with a custom mayonnaise (recipe page 405).

The Leader in Low Carb Foods

Atkins Nutritionals, Inc., has developed an extensive line of low carbohydrate foods and ingredients. In addition to a full line of Atkins Advantage™ bars and Ready to Drink™ Shakes and Endulge™ chocolate candy bars, which can be used to make delicious desserts, the following items make it easier to cook tasty dishes while controlling your carbohydrate intake:

- Atkins Advantage™ shake mixes in chocolate, vanilla, strawberry, and cappuccino flavors (handy for making mousses, granitas, and other desserts)
- Atkins Quick Quisine™ Sugar Free Pancake Syrup (adds brown sugar richness to desserts, marinades, and sauces)
- Atkins Quick Quisine ™ Sugar Free Cherry, Hazelnut, Strawberry, Chocolate, Raspberry, and Vanilla syrups
- Atkins Quick Quisine™ Pancake & Waffle Mix, and Deluxe Buttermilk Pancake Mix
- Atkins Quick Quisine™ Muffin and Bread mixes in corn, blueberry, banana nut, lemon poppy, orange cranberry, and chocolate with chocolate chip flavors
- Atkins™ All-Purpose Batter Mix
- Atkins Quick Quisine™ Bake Mix
- Atkins Quick Quisine™ Fudge Brownie, Chocolate Chip, and Chocolate Chocolate Chip Mixes
- Atkins Kitchen™ Quick & Easy Bread Mix in country white, caraway rye, and sourdough
- Atkins Bakery™ sliced bread in white, rye, and multigrain
- Atkins™ Pasta Cuts in fettuccini, penne, fusilli, and spaghetti
- Atkins Crunchers™ soy chips in BBQ, Nacho, Original, and Sour Cream & Onion (crumble and use to bread fish, shellfish, poultry, or meat; sprinkle over salads; or use in place of croutons in soup)
- Atkins Kitchen™ Ketch-a-Tomato, Barbecue, Steak, and Teriyaki sauces
- Atkins™ Cheesecake

And when you're too busy to cook, consider using the following products:

- Atkins Quick Quisine™ Pasta Sides in Elbows & Cheese, Fettucine Alfredo, and Pesto
- Atkins™ Heat-And-Serve quiches and soufflés
- Atkins™ Enchiladas and Fajitas

The Organic Edge

Eating well isn't just about watching your carbohydrates and eating nutrient-dense whole foods. Another component is minimizing your intake of potentially harmful chemicals. True organic farmers do not use pesticides, fertilizers, hormones, or antibiotics. Instead, they use techniques to maintain nutrients in the soil and protect the health of their livestock. These techniques are labor-intensive, so organic foods often cost more. Because organic produce isn't sprayed or waxed, it might look less appealing. The trade-off? Organic foods are often more flavorful.

Smart Substitutions

To add sparkle to your meals while keeping your carbs under control, try some of these ideas, too.

INSTEAD OF . . .	USE: . . .
Wheat flour or bread crumbs	Naturally low carb soy flour or Atkins™ Bake Mix to "bread" foods before cooking. Or ground nuts, but take care; nut crusts are fragile and can burn easily.
Croutons	Nuts. Toss slivered almonds, chopped walnuts, or pecan pieces into your salad for crunch. Or make croutons from low carb bread.
Barbecue sauce on chicken	Tapenade, an olive paste from Provence, or pesto. Gently lift the skin and rub

continued

INSTEAD OF . . .	USE: . . .
Barbecue sauce on chicken *(continued)*	the paste between skin and breast. (If only barbecue sauce will do, use low carb barbecue sauce.)
Crackers	Bell peppers. Hold upright and cut off the sides into panels; discard the core. Cut the side panels into squares. Top with cheese. Or eat low carb tortillas, cut into wedges and then baked.
White bread	Low carb bread or 100-percent whole-grain bread. Also, serve eggs Benedict on asparagus spears, or burgers between lettuce leaves, in lieu of bread.

Flavorful Oils

There are two kinds of culinary oils, the ones you cook with and the ones you use right out of the bottle as flavorings on salads, vegetables, or bread. Common cooking oils are listed in Smoke and Fire (on page 192). In addition to dark, fruity extra-virgin olive oil for dressing salads and vegetables, nut oils and such exotic options as avocado oil add delicious flavor. Smoky sesame oil added at the end of a stir-fry gives the food that special Asian flavor. The following oils have lower smoke points, meaning they are best unheated and most should be reserved for flavoring. The exception is light olive oil.

TYPE OF OIL	COMMENTS/USE
Extra Virgin Olive Oil (EVOO)	Oil from the first, cold-pressing. Deep in color and aromatic. Expensive so it is

TYPE OF OIL	COMMENTS/USE
Extra Virgin Olive Oil (EVOO) *(continued)*	wasteful to cook with it. Low flash point. Best used cold in salad dressings, dipping sauces, and to dress cooked vegetables.
Virgin Olive Oil/Olive Oil	Both extracted with solvents. Flavor is weaker and color paler than EVOO. We do not recommend using oils processed with solvents.
Superfine Olive Oil/Cold-Pressed Olive Oil	Made from secondary pressings. Best for cold uses and suitable for sautéing at lower temperatures, then finish with EVOO. Flavor less robust. Less expensive than EVOO.
Flaxseed Oil	Use in salad dressings or in smoothies. Do not heat.
Light Olive Oil	Highly filtered; pale in color. Higher flash point than other olive oils and suitable for frying at higher heat. Processing removes most of the olive flavor, making it comparable to canola or grapeseed oil.
Toasted Sesame/Dark Sesame Seed Oil	Adds a smoky flavor to Asian-style stir-fries but use regular sesame for cooking, then add a splash of the toasted oil before serving. Can also make interesting salad dressings.

continued

TYPE OF OIL	COMMENTS/USE
Avocado Oil	Green, full of flavor with a higher flash point than olive oil so it is more suitable for cooking. Expensive. Use like EVOO to dip bread, dress a salad, or finish soup. Avocado contains a compound that helps prevent absorption of LDL cholesterol.
Walnut/Almond/Hazelnut/ Pistachio/Pignoli/Apricot Seed/Macadamia/Pumpkin Seed Oils	These gourmet oils are great for salads and savory finishes. Because they are more flavorful than normal salad oils you can use less of these expensive oils. Heat alters their flavor so don't use in cooking. Try macadamia oil with mashed turnips; pumpkinseed oil in salads garnished with apples or pears; or walnut oil on a spinach salad. Hazelnut oil pairs well with fish such as salmon.

Smoke and Fire

Each oil has a smoke point, or flash point, the temperature at which it begins to smoke or catch fire. (The oil is actually decomposing.) Not only does this ruin your food and smell up your kitchen, but the fats form nitrosamine compounds that can be hazardous to your health. Only certain oils should be used for high-temperature cooking and even they can be overheated. If you burn oil, discard it and thoroughly scour the pan before using it again. You should only use oils with high flash points for quick sautéing or stir-frying at high temperatures. Refined oils have higher smoke points but have been stripped of some of their flavor and nutrients.

OIL	UNREFINED OIL SMOKE POINT	REFINED OIL SMOKE POINT
Grapeseed*	410°F	485°F
Light olive	320°F	468°F
Ghee**	375°F	n/a
Butter	350°F	n/a
Light sesame	350°F	450°F
Peanut	320°F	450°F
Soybean	320°F	450°F
Canola	225°F	400°F
Safflower	225°F	450°F
Sunflower	225°F	450°F
Corn***	320°F	450°F

*Not to be confused with rapeseed oil, grapeseed oil is flavorless and has the highest smoke point of any oil.

**Ghee, which is used in traditional East Indian cuisine, is butter that has had the milk solids removed so that it can be heated to a higher temperature than butter.

***We do not recommend using corn oil because of its imbalance of omega-3 and omega-6 fatty acids.

How to Use These Meal Plans

In the section to follow we offer more than 200 meal plans. The 45 ACE (Atkins Carbohydrate Equilibrium) meal plan (45 grams of Net Carbs) is the core of each plan. Subsequent meal plans at higher ACE levels build on the core through the addition of higher carb foods and substitutions. It is important to note that these meal plans are meant to give you an idea of what a typical day looks like at different carb levels. These four Net Carb gram levels were selected to show the range of possibilities. Since your own ACE may be lower, higher, or somewhere within the 15- to 20-gram span between levels, you may have to add or subtract foods to create an individual plan that fits your ACE to a tee. We have also provided you with 80 different holiday and ethnic menus.

The meal plans also stress healthy choices and showcase the wide variety of foods you can eat when doing Atkins for life. While you certainly may follow them to the letter, we encourage you to make your own substitutions based on personal tastes, budget, and seasonality of produce. If we suggest, for example, whole-grain bread at breakfast, and you prefer whole-grain cereal instead, that's fine. To make comparable substitutions, select similar items from other menus, follow the mix and match lists in Carb Counting Made Easy (page 276), or use the Atkins Glycemic Ranking (AGR) and a carb-gram counter as guides. This will actually give you literally hundreds of menu alternatives. Note that we have been careful not to use too many items with high AGR on a single day. Meal plans don't need to be followed in any particular order, and comparable (in terms of Net Carb counts) breakfasts, lunches, and dinners may be exchanged. And, if you are doing Atkins but your spouse or the rest of the family is not, you may find the higher ACE meal plans helpful in suggesting what you might also prepare to meet the needs of the other members of your family.

There is a 10 percent spread in either direction for total Net Carb counts for a given meal plan for a day because at this point in your dietary regimen a certain amount of flexibility will be the norm. So, if your ACE is 80, you might well consume 70 grams of Net Carbs on one day and 90 the following day. To a certain extent, the numbers in these pages are approximations. The grapefruit half you eat may actually contain 6 grams of Net Carbs or it might be 8, or even more, depending on size and variety.

The meal plans are another of the many tools we have given you to assist you in making intelligent decisions about what foods to eat and when to eat them. Items in bold, blue type indicate recipes found in this book.

General Guidelines

At 45 grams of Net Carbs, a daily meal plan generally includes at least five servings of vegetables and fruits. You can typically include one slice of 100-percent whole-grain bread, or the equivalent, a few times a week. You should probably not be eating more than one serving of an "eat sparingly" food on one day.

At 60 grams of Net Carbs, we recommend adding more vegetables first, then legumes and grains. If you want to have a double-face instead of an open-face sandwich, do not use grains at other meals.

At 80 grams of Net Carbs, two slices of whole-grain breads is usually okay for sandwiches so long as you stay away from other "eat sparingly" foods that day. But don't eat bread and other grains to the exclusion of other "eat sparingly" foods. At this level, you may also be able to add another piece of fruit for three servings (preferably eaten with nuts or cheese).

At 100 grams of Net Carbs, you can comfortably eat

more "eat sparingly" foods, spacing them out throughout the day. You can also substitute whole wheat pasta for soy (low carb) pasta or enjoy a small portion of brown rice.

You can also add a glass of dry wine with dinner a few times a week on all levels.

Substitutions

Besides adding more foods to each meal plan as we increase the ACE, we also provide substitutions, which are indicated in bold type and preceded by the word "or." Remember that you should read across as the substitution refers to the food listed on the same line at a lower ACE. When a food item appears for the first time, say at the 45 ACE level, and we often offer substitutes at higher levels, the carb count number from that original food item is carried through. Therefore, a plum, for example, might be listed as 3 in one place or 4 in another. Don't worry about such inconsistencies. In Lifetime Maintenance, a gram or two of carbs here or there will not impact your weight control efforts. The foods on any given day may be eaten at the suggested mealtimes or at another time in the day. Some people do better on three meals a day; others prefer four, five, or even six mini-meals. Likewise, desserts can be eaten as snacks or snacks can be moved to a meal. This is why we don't list snacks every day.

Ethnic and Holiday Menus

Unlike the meal plans, the 40 ethnic and 40 holiday menus include a single meal that is generally higher in grams of carbs than the equivalent meal on the daily meal plans. Again, the 45 ACE holiday or ethnic meal is the core of each plan; subsequent menus at higher ACE levels build upon it.

The single meals typically comprise about two-thirds the day's intake of carbohydrates: about 30 grams of Net Carbs at an ACE of 45; about 35 grams of Net Carbs at an ACE of 60; about 55 grams of Net Carbs at an ACE of 80; and about 60 grams of Net Carbs at an ACE of 100. To compensate, make sure the other foods that you choose on a day that you prepare one of these meals are somewhat lower in carbs or make adjustments in the days before such a meal.

Certain cuisines are based in large part on foods that are relatively high in carbs—for example, the rice, beans, and corn that are staples of many Latin cultures. To enjoy such food without consuming too many carbs, we suggest that you eat a higher proportion of protein to beans and rice, substitute brown rice for white rice, have small portions of rice and beans—and substitute low carb tortillas for regular tortillas.

Serving Sizes

Remember that now that you are eating more carbohydrates, your intake of fat should have diminished comparably so that you are eating not more food but a different balance of foods.

When it comes to carb foods, a serving of salad greens is typically 1 cup; a serving of cooked vegetables is ½ cup; a serving of vegetable juice is ¾ cup. A serving of fruit is generally ½ cup of berries or chunks of fruit, one small to medium fruit, or half a large one. A quarter cup of cooked legumes is a typical serving. One 1-ounce slice of bread is a serving, as is an ounce of ready-to-eat cereal or a ½ cup of cooked cereals or grains. Consult the food lists in chapter 3 and a carb-gram counter for more specifics.

We have noted serving sizes for most carbohydrate-rich foods on the meal plans and in the holiday and ethnic menus. In most cases, when the item is from a recipe in the book, we have not specified the measurement. Instead, refer

to the recipe to see the serving size. Obviously, grams of Net
Carbs are based upon the same serving size as the one listed
in the recipe. In certain cases, such as muffins or cookies,
where, depending upon your ACE, you might have more
than one portion, we will list the number for perfect clarity.
We do not list portions for foods that are primarily protein
foods, such as poultry, fish, or red meat. Instead, have
moderate-sized portions as discussed earlier. For example,
you might eat one small can of tuna with your salad at lunch
and a 6- to 8-ounce piece of poultry, meat, or fish for dinner.
We do give serving sizes for foods such as cheese that contain both carbs and protein.

Here are a few more pointers to keep in mind.

- Yogurt, milk, cottage cheese, sour cream, and other dairy
  products are assumed to be the full-fat type. Yogurt and
  soy milk should be both unflavored and unsweetened.

- All pasta and legume serving sizes are for cooked food.

- Tuna, egg, chicken, salmon, and other protein salads contain just mayonnaise. Add extra grams of carbs for celery,
  onions, or other additions.

- Products such as granola should have no added sugar or
  other caloric sweeteners including honey, molasses, and
  the like.

- All grains are whole grains, not "instant" or processed
  grains. Portions are for cooked, not raw, grains and cereals.

- All whole-grain breads are 100-percent whole grain.

- When there is a range in carb counts for different brands
  or flavors within a brand, we use the higher number. So,
  for example, while we list flatbread as having 8 grams of

Net Carbs per piece, certain brands may have as few as 4 grams of Net Carbs.

- We specify scallions in many recipes because they are lower in carbs than yellow or white onions. They also have a more delicate flavor.

Thirty Meal Plans at Each Level

MEAL PLAN 1

45 GRAMS NET CARBS		60 GRAMS NET CARBS	
Breakfast			
½ cup Fiber 1 cereal	10	½ cup Fiber 1 cereal	10
½ cup low carb soy milk	1	½ cup whole milk	5
½ cup blueberries	8	½ cup blueberries	8
	19		23
Lunch			
large green salad	6	or Atkins Cole Slaw	6
with dressing, ½ tomato			
hamburger patty	0	hamburger patty	0
Macaroni and Cauliflower Salad	4	**Cauliflower Macaroni Salad**	4
	10		10
Dinner			
Miso-Soy Glazed Salmon	5	**Miso-Soy Glazed Salmon**	5
½ cup green vegetable stir-fry	5	or 1 cup broccoli	5
		¾ cup edamame	9
½ cup raspberries	3	½ cup raspberries	3
	13		22
Snack			
1 ounce macadamia nuts with 2 ounces cheese	3	1 ounce macadamia nuts with 2 ounces cheese	3
Total	45		58

80 GRAMS NET CARBS		100 GRAMS NET CARBS	
½ cup Fiber 1 cereal	10	½ cup Fiber 1 cereal	10
½ cup whole milk	5	¾ cup whole milk	7.5
or ⅓ small banana	8	**or 1 peach**	8
	23		25.5
large green salad w/dressing, ½ tomato	6	**or 1 small red pepper, sliced**	6
hamburger patty	0	hamburger patty	0
		½ whole-grain bun	15
or ⅓ cup green peas	4	**or ½ cup low carb pasta**	4
	10		25
Miso-Soy Glazed Salmon	5	**Miso-Soy Glazed Salmon**	5
½ cup green vegetable stir-fry	5	¾ cup green vegetable stir-fry	7.5
½ cup brown rice	20	½ cup brown rice	20
½ cup raspberries	3	½ cup raspberries	3
Frozen Lemon Mousse	7.5	**Frozen Lemon Mousse**	7.5
	40.5		43
1 kiwifruit	9	**or 1 peach**	9
1 ounce macadamia nuts with 2 ounces cheese	3	**or ½ cup cottage cheese**	3
	85.5		105.5

MEAL PLAN 2

45 GRAMS NET CARBS		60 GRAMS NET CARBS	
Breakfast			
2 slices low carb French toast	8	2 slices low carb French toast	8
sugar-free pancake syrup	0	sugar-free pancake syrup	0
2 slices Canadian bacon	0.5	2 slices Canadian bacon	0.5
½ orange	6.5	**or 1 large plum**	6.5
	15		15
Lunch			
tomato stuffed with shrimp salad	4	tomato stuffed with shrimp salad	4
Chickpea and Vegetable Salad	9.5	**Chickpea and Vegetable Salad**	9.5
		1 peach	9
	13.5		22.5
Dinner			
Braised Short Ribs with Horseradish Sauce	7	**Braised Short Ribs with Horseradish Sauce**	7
½ cup mashed cauliflower	3	⅓ cup pinto beans	10
small green salad with vinaigrette	2	**or small endive salad with vinaigrette**	2
½ cup raspberries	3	½ cup raspberries	3
	15		22
Snack			
2 ounces almonds	2	2 ounces almonds	2
Total	45.5		61.5

80 GRAMS NET CARBS		100 GRAMS NET CARBS	
2 slices low carb French toast	8	2 slices low carb French toast	8
sugar-free pancake syrup	0	sugar-free pancake syrup	0.5
2 slices Canadian bacon	0.5	2 slices Canadian bacon	0
1 orange	13	**or ½ cup mango**	13
	21.5		21.5
tomato stuffed with shrimp salad	4	tomato stuffed with shrimp salad	4
Chickpea and Vegetable Salad	9.5	**Chickpea and Vegetable Salad**	9.5
½ whole-wheat pita	15	1 whole-wheat pita	30
or 3 apricots	9	**or ½ apple**	9
	37.5		52.5
Braised Short Ribs with Horseradish Sauce	7	**Braised Short Ribs with Horseradish Sauce**	7
or ½ cup mashed potatoes	10	**or ½ sweet potato**	10
small green salad with vinaigrette	2	small green salad with vinaigrette	2
or ½ cup strawberries	3	1 peach	9
	22		28
2 ounces almonds	2	2 ounces almonds	2
	83		104

MEAL PLAN 3

45 GRAMS NET CARBS		60 GRAMS NET CARBS	
Breakfast			
1 flatbread	8	2 flatbreads	16
egg salad	1	egg salad	1
	9		17
Lunch			
Smoked Mozzarella, Tomato, and Green Bean Salad	11	**Smoked Mozzarella, Tomato, and Green Bean Salad**	11
grilled chicken	0	grilled chicken	0
½ cup honeydew	7	or 2 small plums	7
	18		18
Dinner			
Not Your Mama's Meat Loaf	3.5	**Not Your Mama's Meat Loaf**	3.5
		Atkins Baked Beans	11.5
½ cup broccoli	3	or ½ bell pepper	3
large green salad with dressing	4	or large spinach salad with dressing	4
½ cup mixed berries	5	½ cup mixed berries	5
	15.5		27
Snack			
2 tbs. hummus with celery sticks	5.5	or ½ cup Crenshaw melon balls with 1 ounce cheese	5.5
Total	48		67.5

80 GRAMS NET CARBS		100 GRAMS NET CARBS	
1 slice pumpernickel	12	2 slices pumpernickel	24
egg salad	1	egg salad	1
1 small tomato	4	1 small tomato	4
½ thinly sliced onion	5	½ thinly sliced onion	5
		decaf latte	5
	22		**39**
Smoked Mozzarella,	**11**	**Smoked Mozzarella,**	**11**
Tomato, and Green Bean		**Tomato, and Green Bean**	
Salad		**Salad**	
grilled chicken	0	grilled chicken	0
2 small whole-wheat	4	2 small whole-wheat	4
sesame breadsticks		sesame breadsticks	
¾ cup honeydew	11	**or 1 cup cantaloupe**	**11**
	26		**26**
Not Your Mama's	**3.5**	**Not Your Mama's**	**3.5**
Meat Loaf		**Meat Loaf**	
Atkins Baked Beans	**11.5**	½ cup mashed potatoes	11.5
½ cup broccoli	3	**or 8 asparagus spears**	**3**
with 1 tbs. walnuts	0.5	with 1 tbs. walnuts	0.5
large green salad	4	large green salad	4
with dressing		with dressing	
½ cup mixed berries	5	**Brown Rice Pudding**	**11**
	27.5		**33.5**
2 tbs. hummus with	5.5	**or 1 bag low carb soy chips**	**5**
celery		1 tbs. green salsa	0.5
	81		**104**

MEAL PLAN 4

45 GRAMS NET CARBS		60 GRAMS NET CARBS	
Breakfast			
½ cup plain whole yogurt	5.5	1 cup plain whole yogurt	11
2 tbs. wheat germ	5	2 tbs. wheat germ	5
½ cup sliced strawberries	4	½ cup sliced strawberries	4
	14.5		**20**
Lunch			
salmon salad with arugula	2	salmon salad with arugula	2
on 1 slice low carb bread	3	on 1 slice whole-grain bread	10
small tomato and hearts of	6	**or Greek Salad**	6
palm salad			
	11		**18**
Dinner			
Chili Blanco	12.5	**Chili Blanco**	12.5
		low carb tortilla	3
large green salad	4	**or Tomato and**	4
with dressing		**Cucumber Salad**	
½ cup watermelon	5	½ cup watermelon	5
	21.5		**24.5**
Snack			
hard-boiled egg	0.5	½ ounce hard cheese	0.5
Total	**47.5**		**63**

80 GRAMS NET CARBS		100 GRAMS NET CARBS	
1 cup plain whole yogurt	11	1 cup plain whole yogurt	11
¼ cup granola	9	¼ cup granola	9
½ cup blueberries	8	or ¾ cup honeydew	8
	28		**28**
salmon salad with arugula on	2	salmon salad with arugula	2
1 slice whole-grain bread	10	or on ½ whole-grain roll	10
small tomato and hearts of palm salad	6	or 1 medium carrot	6
	18		**18**
Chili Blanco	12.5	**Chili Blanco**	12.5
		⅓ cup brown rice	14
1 corn tortilla	11	**or ⅓ cup corn**	11
large green salad with dressing	4	large green salad with dressing	4
Pineapple-Mango Layer Cake	12.5	**or ¾ cup cherries**	12.5
	40		**54**
hard-boiled egg	0.5	**Maple-Chili Trail Mix**	5.5
	86.5		**105.5**

MEAL PLAN 5

45 GRAMS NET CARBS		60 GRAMS NET CARBS	
Breakfast			
1 low carb tortilla	3	or 1 slice low carb bread	3
2 scrambled eggs	1	2 scrambled eggs	1
2 tbs. salsa	2	2 tbs. salsa	2
½ cup strawberries	4	1 kiwi fruit	9
	10		15
Lunch			
Spicy Turkey Club	15	**Spicy Turkey Club**	15
½ cup fresh mushroom salad with dressing	2	**Atkins Cole Slaw**	5.5
	17		20.5
Dinner			
grilled steak	0	grilled steak	0
Broccolini in Sage and Feta Cream	8.5	**Broccolini in Sage and Feta Cream**	8.5
		1 small roast potato	10
large green salad with dressing	4	large green salad with dressing	4
⅓ cup pineapple	5	or 1 small tangerine	5
	17.5		27.5
	44.5		63

80 GRAMS NET CARBS		100 GRAMS NET CARBS	
½ whole-wheat tortilla	10	2 slices whole-grain bread	20
2 scrambled eggs	1	2 scrambled eggs	1
2 tbs. salsa	2	2 tbs. salsa	2
or 1 peach	9	**or ¾ cup papaya**	9
	22		32
Spicy Turkey Club	15	**Spicy Turkey Club**	15
Mexican Chopped Salad	5.5	**or ½ cup green beans**	5.5
or 1 bag low carb soy chips	5	**or 2 apricots**	5
	25.5		25.5
grilled steak	0	grilled steak	0
or 1 cup broccoli	8.5	**or 1 cup okra**	8.5
or oven-baked sweet potato fries from ½ small potato	10	2 small roast potatoes	20
large green salad with dressing	4	large green salad with dressing	4
Almond Flan	7	**Almond Flan**	7
⅓ cup pineapple	5	½ cup cherries	10
	34.5		49.5
	82		107

MEAL PLAN 6

45 GRAMS NET CARBS		60 GRAMS NET CARBS	
Breakfast			
Atkins Banana Nut Muffin*	2	**Morning Muffin**	11.5
2 tbs. cream cheese and 1 tbs. no-added-sugar jam	3	or ½ cup cottage cheese	3
½ cup strawberries	4	or ½ peach	4
	9		18.5
Lunch			
tuna salad	0	tuna salad	0
⅓ cup chickpeas	10	**or 1 slice whole-grain bread**	10
small green salad w/dressing	2	small green salad w/dressing	2
2 plums	8	**or 1 peach**	8
	20		20
Dinner			
Lamb Chops with Tomatoes and Olives	4	**Lamb Chops with Tomatoes and Olives**	4
1 cup grilled zucchini and mushrooms	5	1 cup grilled zucchini and mushrooms	5
½ cup low carb pasta	5	½ cup low carb pasta	5
	14		14
Snack			
1 cup blanched broccoli florets with mayonnaise	2	**or 1 ounce sunflower seeds**	2
Total	45		54.5

*Made from Atkins Quick Quisine™ Banana Nut Muffin and Bread Mix.

80 GRAMS NET CARBS		100 GRAMS NET CARBS	
Morning Muffin	11.5	**2 Morning Muffins**	23
cream cheese and	3	**or ⅓ cup ricotta cheese**	3
no-added-sugar jam			
½ cup strawberries	4	**or 2 apricots**	4
	18.5		30
tuna salad	0	tuna salad	0
2 slices whole-grain bread	20	**or ⅔ cup navy beans**	20
small green salad	2	small green salad	2
w/dressing		w/dressing	
or 3 apricots	8	**or ½ cup honeydew**	8
	30		30
Lamb Chops with	4	**Lamb Chops with**	4
Tomatoes and Olives		**Tomatoes and Olives**	
or ¾ cup green beans	5	**or 1 cup broccoli**	5
Brown Rice Pilaf	12	**Brown Rice Pilaf**	12
1 Chocolate Chip	7.5	½ small banana	10
Oatmeal Cookie			
	28.5		31
celery stuffed with	3.5	**or 1 ounce mixed**	3.5
1 tbs. sugar-free		**nuts with 2 ounces**	
peanut butter		**cheese**	
	80.5		94.5

MEAL PLAN 7

45 GRAMS NET CARBS		60 GRAMS NET CARBS	
Breakfast		**Breakfast**	
spinach and feta omelet	3	spinach and feta omelet	3
1 small tomato	4	1 small tomato	4
1 slice low carb bread	3	1 slice low carb bread	3
	10		**10**
Lunch		**Lunch**	
Lobster Salad	6.5	**Lobster Salad**	6.5
large green salad with dressing	4	**or 1 small sliced cucumber with vinaigrette**	4
½ cup cantaloupe	6	**or 2 apricots**	6
	16.5		**16.5**
Dinner		**Dinner**	
Sesame Tofu with Snow Peas and Peppers	9	**Sesame Tofu with Snow Peas and Peppers**	9
½ cup low carb pasta	5	⅓ cup brown rice	14
½ cup strawberries	4	1 peach	9
	18		**32**
Snack			
½ Haas avocado	2	½ cup pepper and jicama sticks with 2 tbs. sour cream dip	6
turkey and ham roll-ups	0		
Total	**46.5**		**64.5**

80 GRAMS NET CARBS		100 GRAMS NET CARBS	
spinach and feta omelet	3	spinach and feta omelet	3
1 small tomato	4	1 small tomato	4
1 slice light rye bread	7	1 slice whole-grain bread	10
	14		17
Lobster Salad	6.5	**Lobster Salad**	6.5
large green salad with dressing	4	**or large spinach salad with dressing**	4
		1 flatbread	8
or ⅓ cup pineapple	6	1 cup cantaloupe	13
	16.5		31.5
Asian Vegetable Bowl	5.5	**or consommé with 1 small chopped tomato**	5.5
Sesame Tofu with Snow Peas and Peppers	9	**Sesame Tofu with Snow Peas and Peppers**	9
½ cup brown rice	20	½ cup brown rice	20
or 1 kiwifruit	9	**or Chocolate-Custard Pecan Bar**	9
	43.5		43.5
½ cup pepper and jicama sticks with 2 tbs. sour cream dip	6	½ apple with 1 ounce nuts	10
	80		102

MEAL PLAN 8

45 GRAMS NET CARBS		60 GRAMS NET CARBS	
Breakfast			
½ cup low carb hot cereal	5	½ cup old-fashioned oatmeal	11
½ cup low carb soy milk	1	½ cup low carb soy milk	1
½ cup blueberries	8	**or ½ chopped apple**	8
hard-boiled egg	0.5	hard-boiled egg	0.5
	14.5		**20.5**
Lunch			
ham salad	2	**or salmon salad**	2
Macaroni and Cauliflower Salad	4	**Macaroni and Cauliflower Salad**	4
2 ounces Swiss cheese	2	2 ounces Swiss cheese	2
		1 slice Olive Cheese Bread	11
	8		**19**
Dinner			
Roasted Red Pepper Soup	10.5	**or 1 cup tomato juice**	10.5
Fish with Flavored Butter	0.5	**Fish with Flavored Butter**	0.5
½ cup roasted green beans	3	½ cup roasted baby carrots	6
large green salad with dressing	4	large green salad with dressing	4
	18		**21**
Snack			
½ cup boysenberries with 2 tbs. whipped cream	6	**or ½ cup mixed berries with whipped cream**	6
Total	**46.5**		**66.5**

80 GRAMS NET CARBS		100 GRAMS NET CARBS	
½ cup old-fashioned oatmeal	11	¾ cup old-fashioned oatmeal	16
1 tablespoon raisins	8	or 3 tbs. wheat germ	8
½ cup low carb soy milk	1	½ cup low carb soy milk	1
or 1 peach	8	or ⅓ banana	8
hard-boiled egg	0.5	hard-boiled egg	0.5
	28.5		33.5
ham salad with ⅓ cup green peas	7	ham salad or with ⅓ cup corn	7
Macaroni and Cauliflower Salad	4	or chopped broccoli salad	4
2 ounces Swiss cheese	2	2 ounces Swiss cheese	2
or 1 slice whole-grain bread	11	**1 slice Olive Cheese Bread**	11
	24		24
or Minestrone Soup	10.5	**Roasted Red Pepper Soup**	10.5
		½ whole-grain roll	10
Fish with Flavored Butter	0.5	**Fish with Flavored Butter**	0.5
or ¼ cup brown rice	10	**or ½ cup mashed potatoes**	10
large green salad with dressing	4	large green salad with dressing	4
	25		35
or 1 plum with 2 tbs. hulled sunflower seeds	6	**or 1 stalk celery stuffed with 2 tbs. peanut butter**	6
	83.5		98.5

Meal Plan 9

45 grams Net Carbs		60 grams Net Carbs	
Breakfast		**Breakfast**	
Pecan Buttermilk Waffle	7	**Pecan Buttermilk Waffle**	7
sugar-free pancake syrup	0	sugar-free pancake syrup	0
½ cup raspberries	3	1 peach	9
	10		16
Lunch		**Lunch**	
Eggplant, Mushroom, and	9.5	**Eggplant, Mushroom, and**	9.5
Goat Cheese Sandwich		**Goat Cheese Sandwich**	
chicken consommé	1	**Spring Vegetable Soup**	8.5
	10.5		18
Dinner		**Dinner**	
Bistro Skillet Steak	4	**Bistro Skillet Steak**	4
½ cup sautéed spinach	2	**Tomato, Zucchini,**	8.5
		and Mushroom Gratin	
large mesclun salad	4	large mesclun salad	4
with dressing		with dressing	
½ baked pear	12	**or ½ baked apple**	12
with 1 tbs.		**with cinnamon**	
toasted nuts			
	22		28.5
Total	42.5		62.5

80 GRAMS NET CARBS		100 GRAMS NET CARBS	
Pecan Buttermilk Waffle	7	**Pecan Buttermilk Waffle**	7
sugar-free pancake syrup	0	sugar-free pancake syrup	0
or ½ small banana	9	or ¾ cup cantaloupe	9
	16		16
Eggplant, Mushroom, and	9.5	**Eggplant, Mushroom, and**	9.5
Goat Cheese Sandwich		**Goat Cheese Sandwich**	
or ¾ cup tomato juice	8.5	or vegetable beef soup	8.5
		Chunky Mocha Ice Cream	7
	18		25
Bistro Skillet Steak	4	**Bistro Skillet Steak**	4
Tomato, Zucchini,	8.5	or 1 cup steamed	8.5
and Mushroom Gratin		snow peas	
1 whole-grain roll	20	or ½ cup brown rice	20
large mesclun salad	4	large mesclun salad	4
with dressing		with dressing	
½ baked pear	12	1 baked pear	22
with 1 tbs. toasted nuts		with 1 tbs. toasted nuts	
	48.5		58.5
	82.5		99.5

Meal Plan 10

45 grams Net Carbs		60 grams Net Carbs	
Breakfast			
1 slice Lemon Zucchini Bread	9	1 slice Lemon Zucchini Bread	9
1 soft-boiled egg	0.5	1 soft-boiled egg	0.5
		½ cup ricotta cheese	4
	9.5		**13.5**
Lunch			
Not Your Mama's Meat Loaf	3.5	Not Your Mama's Meat Loaf	3.5
on 1 slice low carb bread	3	on 1 slice whole-grain bread	10
large green salad with dressing	4	large green salad with dressing	4
1 small tangerine	6	or 1 large plum	6
	16.5		**23.5**
Dinner			
Jerk Shrimp (without pineapple)	4	Jerk Shrimp (with pineapple)	8
Garden Pasta	7	Garden Pasta	7
1 cup sautéed escarole with garlic	5	or 1 cup collard greens	5
½ cup raspberries	3	½ cup cantaloupe	6
	19		**26**
Totals	**45**		**63**

80 GRAMS NET CARBS		100 GRAMS NET CARBS	
or 1 slice light rye bread	9	2 slices Lemon Zucchini Bread	18
1 soft-boiled egg	0.5	1 soft-boiled egg	0.5
or cottage cheese	4	or cream cheese with no-sugar-added jam	4
2 prunes	10	or 1 small orange	10
	23.5		32.5
Not Your Mama's Meat Loaf	3.5	Not Your Mama's Meat Loaf	3.5
or with ½ small sweet potato	10	on 1 slice whole-grain bread	10
large green salad with dressing	4	or Atkins Cole Slaw	4
or ½ orange	6	or ½ cup watermelon	6
	23.5		23.5
Jerk Shrimp (with pineapple)	8	Jerk Shrimp (with pineapple)	8
or ¼ cup chickpeas	7	⅓ cup brown rice	14
1 cup sautéed escarole with garlic	5	1 cup sautéed escarole	5
Coconut Ice Cream	4.5	Coconut Ice Cream	4.5
or ⅓ cup pineapple	6	½ cup mango	13
	30.5		44.5
	77.5		100.5

MEAL PLAN 11

45 GRAMS NET CARBS		60 GRAMS NET CARBS	
Breakfast			
Zucchini Frittata	4	Zucchini Frittata	4
1 small sliced tomato	4	1 small sliced tomato	4
		1 slice flatbread	8
	8		16
Lunch			
Chicken and Sun-Dried Tomato Quesadilla	10	Chicken and Sun-Dried Tomato Quesadilla	10
¾ cup cucumber and radish salad with dressing	4	Mexican Chopped Salad	6
	14		16
Dinner			
Baihian Halibut	5.5	Baihian Halibut	5.5
1 cup sautéed spinach	4.5	or 1 cup steamed broccoli	4.5
large green salad with dressing	4	large green salad with dressing	4
½ cup mixed berries with cream	6	or 2 apricots	6
	20		20
Snack			
1 celery stalk stuffed with cream cheese	3	4 ounces tomato juice with 4 tbs. walnuts	6
Total	**45**		**58**

80 GRAMS NET CARBS		100 GRAMS NET CARBS	
Zucchini Frittata	4	Zucchini Frittata	4
or ½ red pepper	4	1 small sliced tomato	4
1 slice flatbread	8	1 slice rye bread	10
½ cup grapefruit	8	or ½ cup honeydew	8
		decaf latte	5
	24		**31**
Chicken and Sun-Dried Tomato Quesadilla	10	Chicken and Sun-Dried Tomato Quesadilla	10
or 1 chopped carrot	6	Mexican Chopped Salad	6
		with ⅓ cup chickpeas	10
	16		**26**
Baihian Halibut	5.5	Baihian Halibut	5.5
1 cup sautéed spinach	4.5	1 cup sautéed spinach	4.5
½ cup whole-wheat couscous	17	¾ cup whole-wheat pasta	25
large green salad with dressing	4	large green salad with dressing	4
or ⅓ cup cherries	6	or Lime Granita	6
	37		**45**
1 bag low carb soy chips with 2 tbs. green salsa and 1 ounce melted Monterey jack cheese	6	or ½ cup strawberries with ¼ cup cottage cheese	5.5
	83		**107.5**

Meal Plan 12

45 grams Net Carbs		60 grams Net Carbs	
Breakfast			
cheese and green pepper omelet	4	**or cheese and tomato omelet**	4
1 slice low carb toast	3	1 slice low carb toast	3
1 small tangerine	6	**or ½ orange**	6
	13		13
Lunch			
consommé with sliced mushrooms	2	**Barley Vegetable Soup**	12
grilled chicken breast	0	**or turkey cutlet**	0
Custom Mayonnaise	0.5	**or green salsa**	0.5
small green salad with dressing	2	small green salad with dressing	2
	4.5		14.5
Dinner			
grilled salmon	0	grilled salmon	0
Asian Vegetable Stir-Fry	5.5	**Asian Vegetable Stir-Fry**	5.5
¾ cup edamame	9	½ cup steamed lentils	12
½ cup pineapple	8.5	**or 1 peach**	8.5
	23		26
Snack			
1 bag low carb soy chips	5	**or Coconut Ice Cream**	5
Total	45.5		58.5

80 grams Net Carbs		100 grams Net Carbs	
cheese and green pepper omelet	4	or cheese and mushroom omelet	4
1 slice light rye toast	7	1 slice whole-grain toast	10
1 orange	13	or ½ cup grapes	13
		decaf latte	5
	24		32
or Minestrone soup	12	Barley Vegetable Soup	12
grilled chicken breast	0	grilled chicken breast	0
Custom Mayonnaise	0.5	Custom Mayonnaise	0.5
green salad with dressing	2	green salad with dressing	2
½ whole-grain roll	10	1 whole-grain roll	20
	24.5		34.5
grilled salmon	0	grilled salmon	0
Asian Vegetable Stir-Fry	5.5	or 1 cup sautéed spinach	5.5
or ½ cup chickpeas	12	½ cup steamed lentils	12
⅔ cup pineapple	10	or ½ pear	10
	27.5		27.5
or Maple Chili Trail Mix	5	1 bag low carb soy chips	5
	81		99

MEAL PLAN 13

45 GRAMS NET CARBS		60 GRAMS NET CARBS	
Breakfast			
Breakfast Smoothie	9	**Breakfast Smoothie**	9
1 slice low carb toast	3	**Morning Muffin**	11.5
	12		**20.5**
Lunch			
ham and cheese rolled around asparagus	6	**Grilled Ham and Cheese with Asparagus**	8
green salad with dressing	2	green salad with dressing	2
½ cup raspberries	3	1 tangerine	6
	11		**16**
Dinner			
Broccoli Rabe and Sausage Pasta	11	**Broccoli Rabe and Sausage Pasta**	11
Italian-Style Green Beans	5	**or 1 cup sautéed escarole**	5
⅓ cup blueberries with 2 tbs. cream	6	**Mixed Berry Shortcake**	10.5
	22		**26.5**
Snack			
hard-boiled egg	0.5	hard-boiled egg	0.5
Total	**45.5**		**63.5**

80 GRAMS NET CARBS		100 GRAMS NET CARBS	
or ¾ cup milk	9	Breakfast Smoothie	9
Morning Muffin	11.5	or 1 slice whole-grain toast with ½ cup cottage cheese	14.5
	20.5		23.5
Grilled Ham and Cheese with Asparagus	22	Grilled Ham and Cheese with Asparagus	22
on 2 slices whole-grain bread		on 2 slices whole-grain bread	
		Gazpacho	10.5
green salad with dressing	2	or 1 small sliced cucumber	2
or ⅓ cup pineapple	6	or 2 apricots	6
	30		40.5
Broccoli Rabe and Sausage Pasta	11	Broccoli Rabe and Sausage Pasta	11
or ½ cup green peas	5	or 1 medium tomato	5
or ½ small banana	10.5	or ¾ cup honeydew	10.5
	26.5		26.5
1 bag low carb soy chips	5	or Maple-Chili Trail Mix	5
	82		93.5

Meal Plan 14

45 grams Net Carbs		60 grams Net Carbs	
Breakfast			
Florentine Omelet	4	or cheese omelet	4
½ cup grapefruit	8	or 1 large tomato	8
	12		12
Lunch			
2 tbs. sugar-free peanut butter and 2 tbs. no-added-sugar jam sandwich on 2 slices low carb bread	14	2 tbs. sugar-free peanut butter and 2 tbs. no-added-sugar jam sandwich on 2 slices low carb bread	14
½ cup carrot and celery sticks	3	½ cup carrot and celery sticks	3
		½ cup whole milk	5.5
	17		22.5
Dinner			
broiled steak	0	broiled steak	0
with Flavored Butter	0.5	**with Flavored Butter**	0.5
small mesclun salad with dressing	2	small mesclun salad topped with ¼ cup marinated navy beans	11
Warm Zucchini Mint Salad	5.5	**Warm Zucchini Mint Salad**	5.5
½ cup cantaloupe	7	or 2 apricots	7
	15		24
Snack			
Total	44		58.5

80 GRAMS NET CARBS		100 GRAMS NET CARBS	
Florentine Omelet	4	**Florentine Omelet**	4
1 orange	13	or 1 cup pineapple	13
	17		17
2 tbs. sugar-free peanut butter and 2 tbs. no-added-sugar jam sandwich on 2 slices low carb bread	14	2 tbs. sugar-free peanut butter and 2 tbs. no-added-sugar jam sandwich on 2 slices whole-grain bread	28
½ cup carrot and celery sticks	3	**or medium salad with dressing**	3
or 1 bag low carb soy chips	5.5	½ cup whole milk	5.5
	22.5		36.5
broiled steak	0	broiled steak	0
with Flavored Butter	0.5	**with Flavored Butter**	0.5
small mesclun salad topped with ¼ cup marinated navy beans	11	**or Caesar salad**	11
or ¾ cup green beans	5.5	**or 1 cup sautéed spinach**	5.5
1 small potato	10	**or ½ small sweet potato**	10
or 1 tangerine	7	½ cup cantaloupe	7
Almond Flan	7	**Almond Flan**	7
	41		41
		Maple-Chili Trail Mix	5.5
	80.5		100

MEAL PLAN 15

45 GRAMS NET CARBS		60 GRAMS NET CARBS	
Breakfast			
low carb tortilla with 2 scrambled eggs	4	low carb tortilla with 2 scrambled eggs	4
2 tbs. salsa	2	2 tbs. salsa	2
½ Haas avocado	2	¾ cup cantaloupe	10
	8		16
Lunch			
Roast Beef Sandwich on 1 slice low carb bread	6	**Roast Beef Sandwich**	9
Tomato and Cucumber Salad	3.5	or medium spinach salad with vinaigrette	3.5
2 apricots	6	or 1 large plum	6
	15.5		18.5
Dinner			
Spanish Chicken over Penne	13	**Spanish Chicken over Penne**	13
½ cup green beans	3	or ½ cup sautéed spinach	3
small salad with dressing	2	small salad with dressing	2
½ cup mixed berries	5	**Brown Rice Pudding**	11
	23		29
Snack			
2 ounces macadamia nuts	2	or 2 ounces hard cheese	2
Total	**46.5**		**65.5**

80 GRAMS NET CARBS		100 GRAMS NET CARBS	
2 scrambled eggs with	11	2 scrambled eggs	11
½ whole-wheat tortilla		**or 1 slice whole-grain bread**	
or no-added-sugar jam	2	or herb cream cheese	2
or 1 kiwifruit	10	or ⅔ cup honeydew	10
	23		23
Roast Beef Sandwich	9	**Roast Beef Sandwich**	9
Tomato and Cucumber Salad	3.5	**Tomato and Cucumber Salad**	3.5
or 1 bag low carb soy chips	6	**or 1 Chocolate Chip Oatmeal Cookie**	6
	18.5		18.5
Spanish Chicken over Penne	13	**Spanish Chicken over** ½ cup whole-wheat pasta	25
or ½ cup broccoli	3	½ cup green beans	3
small salad with dressing	2	small salad with dressing	2
Brown Rice Pudding	11	or 1 cup yogurt	11
with 1 tbs. raisins	8	or with 1 tbs. dried cherries	8
	37		49
2 ounces macadamia nuts	2	½ cup blueberries with 6 ounces low carb vanilla yogurt	12
	80.5		**102.5**

Meal Plan 16

45 grams Net Carbs		60 grams Net Carbs	
Breakfast			
"Dutch Baby" Baked Pancake	7.5	"Dutch Baby" Baked Pancake	7.5
sugar-free pancake syrup	0	sugar-free pancake syrup	0
½ cup ricotta cheese	4	or ½ cup cottage cheese	4
	11.5		11.5
Lunch			
turkey burger	0	turkey burger	0
		Atkins Baked Beans	11.5
Atkins Cole Slaw	5.5	or ¾ cup green beans	5.5
½ cup watermelon	5	½ cup watermelon	5
	10.5		22
Dinner			
grilled tuna with	0	grilled tuna with	0
Custom Mayonnaise	0.5	**Custom Mayonnaise**	0.5
Broccoli, Daikon, and Pepper Salad	5	or 1 cup broccoli and mushroom salad with dressing	5
½ cup low carb pasta with butter	5	½ cup low carb pasta with butter	5
2 small plums	7	2 small plums	7
		Chunky Mocha Ice Cream	7
	17.5		24.5
Snack			
½ cup carrot and zucchini sticks with sour cream onion dip	6	or Mexican Chopped Salad	6
Total	45.5		64

80 GRAMS NET CARBS		100 GRAMS NET CARBS	
"Dutch Baby"	7.5	"Dutch Baby"	7.5
Baked Pancake		Baked Pancake	
with Apple Filling	7	with Apple Filling	7
½ cup ricotta cheese	4	½ cup ricotta cheese	4
		sugar-free hot cocoa	3
	18.5		21.5
turkey burger	0	turkey burger	0
½ whole-grain bun	12	½ whole-grain bun	12
or sweet potato fries	11.5	Atkins Baked Beans	11.5
from ½ sweet potato		or ½ small baked potato	
Atkins Cole Slaw	5.5	Atkins Cole Slaw	5.5
or 1 plum	5	¾ cup honeydew	10
	34		39
grilled tuna with	0	grilled tuna with	0
Custom Mayonnaise	0.5	Custom Mayonnaise	0.5
or large spinach salad	5	or 10 cherry tomatoes	5
with dressing			
or 1/3 cup steamed winter	5	½ cup brown rice	20
squash			
or 1 small tangerine	7	or ½ cup cantaloupe	7
Chunky Mocha Ice Cream	7	Chunky Mocha Ice Cream	7
	24.5		39.5
or 2 ounces nuts and	6	or 1 bag low carb soy chips	6
2 ounces cheese		with 2 tbs. green salsa	
	83		106

Meal Plan 17

45 grams Net Carbs		60 grams Net Carbs	
Breakfast			
½ cup low carb hot cereal	5	½ cup old-fashioned oatmeal	11
Rhubarb Applesauce	6.5	1 peach	9
hard-boiled egg	0.5	hard-boiled egg	0.5
	12		20.5
Lunch			
Roasted Red Pepper Soup	10.5	or Gazpacho	10.5
tuna salad with pepper	2	tuna salad with pepper	2
		1 slice low carb bread	3
		½ cup cherries	8.5
	12.5		24
Dinner			
Veal Milanese	5.5	**Veal Milanese**	5.5
small arugula salad with shaved parmesan and vinaigrette	3	**or medium green salad with vinaigrette**	3
		1 slice low carb garlic bread	3
¾ cup broccoli with garlic	5	**or ¾ cup green beans**	5
2 poached apricots	6	**or ½ cup mixed berries with cream**	6
	19.5		22.5
Total	44		67

80 GRAMS NET CARBS		100 GRAMS NET CARBS	
½ cup old-fashioned oatmeal	11	¾ cup Wheatena	16
1 tablespoon raisins	8	or 1 tablespoon chopped dried apricots	8
or ½ cup blueberries	9	or ¾ cup cantaloupe	9
hard-boiled egg	0.5	hard-boiled egg	0.5
	28.5		33.5
Roasted Red Pepper Soup	10.5	**Roasted Red Pepper Soup**	10.5
tuna salad with pepper	2	tuna salad with pepper	2
1 slice low carb bread	3	1 slice whole-grain bread	10
or ¾ cup watermelon	8.5	or ½ cup pineapple	8.5
	24		31
Veal Milanese	5.5	**Veal Milanese**	5.5
small arugula salad with shaved parmesan and vinaigrette	3	or medium endive salad with vinaigrette	3
Polenta Triangles	12	or ⅓ cup whole-wheat pasta	12
¾ cup broccoli with garlic	5	¾ cup broccoli with garlic	5
or 1 grilled peach half with chopped almonds	6	**4 Chocolate Almond Biscotti**	12
	31.5		37.5
	84		102

Meal Plan 18

45 grams Net Carbs		60 grams Net Carbs	
Breakfast			
smoked salmon and	2	smoked salmon and	2
cream cheese on 1 slice	3	cream cheese on ½ low	6
low carb bread		carb bagel	
1 sliced small tomato	4	1 sliced small tomato and	8
		¼ sliced onion	
	9		**16**
Lunch			
Cajun-spiced chicken breast	0	Cajun-spiced chicken breast	0
Caribbean Black	11.5	**or ⅓ cup chickpeas**	11.5
Bean Salad		**with vinaigrette**	
½ cup raspberries	3	¾ cup fruit salad	9
	14.5		**20.5**
Dinner			
Spiced Beef and	7.5	**Spiced Beef and**	7.5
Asparagus Stir-Fry		**Asparagus Stir-Fry**	
½ cup low carb pasta	5	½ cup low carb pasta	5
with sesame oil		with sesame oil	
Asian Carrot and	5.5	**or large green salad**	5.5
Zucchini Salad		**with pumpkin seeds**	
		and dressing	
		Lime Granita	5
	18		**23**
Snack			
½ cup whole strawberries	6	**or ½ Florida avocado with**	6
with 6 ounces of low carb		**1 tbs. vinaigrette**	
vanilla yogurt			
Total	**47.5**		**65.5**

80 GRAMS NET CARBS		100 GRAMS NET CARBS	
smoked salmon and	2	smoked salmon and	2
cream cheese on 1 low	12	cream cheese on small	
carb bagel		pumpernickel bagel	36
or ¾ cup tomato juice	8	or ½ cup blueberries	8
	22		46
Cajun-spiced chicken breast	0	Cajun-spiced chicken breast	0
Mixed Veggie Potato	14.5	or ½ sweet potato	14.5
Salad			
or ½ cup cherries	9	or ½ apple	9
	23.5		23.5
Spiced Beef and	7.5	**Spiced Beef and**	7.5
Asparagus Stir-Fry		**Asparagus Stir-Fry**	
½ cup whole-wheat pasta	17	or ⅓ cup brown rice	17
or ¾ cup red pepper	5.5	**Asian Carrot and**	5.5
		Zucchini Salad	
Lime Granita	5	or ½ cup mixed berries	5
	35		35
or ½ cup creamed cottage	6	or 3 tbs. pumpkin seeds	6
cheese with 2 tbs. pistachios			
	86.5		110.5

Meal Plan 19

45 grams Net Carbs		60 grams Net Carbs	
Breakfast			
Blueberry Silver Dollar Pancakes	14.5	**Blueberry Silver Dollar Pancakes**	14.5
Canadian bacon	0.5	or baked ham slices	0.5
	15		15
Lunch			
poached salmon with Custom Mayo	1	poached salmon with Custom Mayo	1
small green salad with vinaigrette	2	**Mexican Chopped Salad**	6
		½ whole-grain roll	10
½ orange	6.5	1 kiwifruit	9
	9.5		26
Dinner			
grilled pork chops	0	grilled pork chops	0
Atkins Baked Beans	11.5	⅓ cup cooked navy beans	11.5
½ cup sauerkraut	2	½ cup sauerkraut	2
½ cup mixed berries	5	¾ cup mixed berries	7
	18.5		20.5
Snack			
½ cup zucchini sticks	2	or ½ cup jicama sticks	2
Total	45		63.5

80 GRAMS NET CARBS		100 GRAMS NET CARBS	
Blueberry Silver Dollar Pancakes	14.5	**Blueberry Silver Dollar Pancakes**	14.5
Canadian bacon	0.5	**or turkey sausage**	0.5
1 small tangerine	6	1 orange	13
	21		28
poached salmon with Custom Mayo	1	**poached salmon with Custom Mayo**	1
or Atkins Cole Slaw	6	**or large salad with creamy dressing**	6
or 1 slice whole-grain bread	10	1 whole-wheat roll	20
or 1 peach	9	**or ½ cup cherries**	9
	26		36
grilled pork chops	0	grilled pork chops	0
or ½ sweet potato with olive oil	11.5	**Atkins Baked Beans**	11.5
½ cup sauerkraut	2	**or ½ cup sauteed escarole**	2
⅓ cup grapes	9	**or Blackberry-Orange Sorbet**	11
	22.5		24.5
½ apple with 1 ounce nuts	10	**or Maple-Chili Trail Mix**	10
		with ½ cup plain whole yogurt	
	79.5		98.5

MEAL PLAN 20

45 GRAMS NET CARBS		60 GRAMS NET CARBS	
Breakfast			
poached egg, Canadian	1.5	poached egg, Canadian	1.5
bacon, sliced cheese		bacon, sliced cheese	
on 1 slice low carb bread	3	on low carb tortilla	3
1 small tangerine	6	1 orange	13
	10.5		17.5
Lunch			
½ Haas avocado filled with	2	½ Haas avocado filled with	2
Lobster Salad	6.5	**Lobster Salad**	6.5
small green salad	2	small green salad	2
with dressing		with dressing	
		½ whole-grain roll	10
	10.5		20.5
Dinner			
ham steak	0	ham steak	0
Sweet Potato and	5.5	**Sweet Potato and**	5.5
Spinach Salad		**Spinach Salad**	
Red Swiss Chard and Bacon	4	or 1 cup sautéed escarole	4
¾ cup blackberries	9	or 1 grilled peach	9
	18.5		18.5
Snack			
1 bag low carb soy chips	5	or 2 tbs. hummus	5
		with celery	
Total	**44.5**		**61.5**

80 GRAMS NET CARBS		100 GRAMS NET CARBS	
poached egg, Canadian bacon, sliced cheese	1.5	poached egg, Canadian bacon, sliced cheese	1.5
on 1 slice low carb bread	3	on 1 slice low carb bread	3
or ½ cup grapes	13	**or ¾ cup grapefruit**	13
	17.5		17.5
½ Haas avocado filled with	2	**or tomato filled with**	2
or tuna and veggie salad	6.5	**Lobster Salad**	6.5
small green salad with dressing	2	small green salad with dressing	2
1 whole-grain roll	20	1 whole-grain roll	20
		⅔ cup pineapple	12
	30.5		42.5
ham steak	0	ham steak	0
¾ cup sweet potato salad	8	**or 1 small roast potato**	8
or ½ cup green beans	4	**Red Swiss Chard and Bacon**	4
Chocolate Pecan Bar	9.5	**or ½ cup cherries**	9.5
	21.5		21.5
2½ cups buttered popcorn	12	**or 4 Chocolate Biscotti**	12
		decaf latte	5
	81.5		98.5

MEAL PLAN 21

45 GRAMS NET CARBS		60 GRAMS NET CARBS	
Breakfast			
Creamy Baked Eggs	2.5	**or scrambled eggs**	2.5
1 slice low carb toast	3	1 slice low carb toast	3
½ cup grapefruit	8	**or ½ orange**	8
	13.5		**13.5**
Lunch			
turkey, Swiss cheese, and tomato slices rolled in lettuce leaves	2	turkey, Swiss cheese, and tomato slices rolled in lettuce leaves	6
Atkins Cole Slaw	5.5	**or carrot salad**	5.5
½ cup strawberries	4	½ cup strawberries	4
	11.5		**15.5**
Dinner			
sliced roast pork	0	**Southwestern-Style Pork Fajitas**	11
Pineapple-Pepper Salsa	4.5	**Pineapple-Pepper Salsa**	4.5
Caribbean Black Bean Salad	11.5	**Caribbean Black Bean Salad**	11.5
small green salad with dressing	2	small green salad with dressing	2
Lime Granita	5	**Lime Granita**	5
	23		**34**
Snack			
2 ounces walnuts	2	**or 2 ounces almonds**	2
Total	**50**		**65**

80 GRAMS NET CARBS		100 GRAMS NET CARBS	
Creamy Baked Eggs	2.5	**Creamy Baked Eggs**	2.5
1 slice low carb toast	3	1 slice whole-grain toast	10
1 kiwifruit	9	**or 1 peach**	9
		½ cup milk	5.5
	14.5		27
turkey, Swiss cheese, and tomato slices on whole-grain bread	12	turkey, Swiss cheese, and tomato slices or on ½ whole-grain roll	12
or steamed green peas	5.5	**or 1 small chopped carrot**	5.5
1 peach	9	1 apple	17
	26.5		34.5
Southwestern-Style Pork Fajitas	11	**Southwestern-Style Pork Fajitas**	11
Pineapple-Pepper Salsa	4.5	**Pineapple-Pepper Salsa**	4.5
or sweet potato fries from ½ potato	11.5	**or ½ cup steamed lentils with olive oil and lemon juice**	11.5
or ½ cup sautéed zucchini	2	small green salad with dressing	2
Almond Flan	7	**or ½ cup blackberries**	7
	36		36
2 ounces walnuts	2	**2 tbs. hulled sunflower seeds**	2
	79		99.5

MEAL PLAN 22

45 GRAMS NET CARBS		60 GRAMS NET CARBS	
Breakfast			
Atkins Blueberry Muffin*	3	**Cherry Muffin**	8
2 tbs. cream cheese	1	2 tbs. cream cheese	1
soft-boiled egg	0.5	soft-boiled egg	0.5
1 small tangerine	6	**or 1 fig**	6
	10.5		15.5
Lunch			
corned beef	0	corned beef	0
on 1 slice low carb rye bread	3	on 2 slices low carb rye bread	6
½ cup sauerkraut	2	**Atkins Cole Slaw**	5.5
		½ cup strawberries	4
	5		15.5
Dinner			
Escarole and Chickpea Stew	21.5	**Escarole and Chickpea Stew**	21.5
		½ cup low carb pasta	5
½ cup strawberries with 2 tbs. whipped cream	5	**or ¾ cup raspberries** with 2 tbs. whipped cream	5
	26.5		31.5
Snack			
½ cup broccoli florets with sour cream dip	3	**or ½ cup cucumber with sour cream**	3
Total	45		65.5

*Made from Atkins Quick Quisine™ Blueberry Muffin and Bread Mix.

80 GRAMS NET CARBS		100 GRAMS NET CARBS	
Cherry Muffin	8	**Cherry Muffin**	8
½ cup cottage cheese	3	**or ½ cup ricotta cheese**	3
soft-boiled egg	0.5	soft-boiled egg	0.5
or 2 apricots	6	1 small tangerine	6
	17.5		17.5
Golden Onion Soup	15	**or ⅔ cup tomato soup**	15
corned beef	0	corned beef	0
on 2 slices low carb rye bread	6	on 2 slices light rye bread	14
Atkins Cole Slaw	5.5	**Atkins Cole Slaw**	5.5
or ½ cup mixed berries	4	1 peach	9
	30.5		43.5
Escarole and Chickpea Stew	21.5	**Escarole and Chickpea Stew**	21.5
½ cup low carb pasta	5	**Olive Cheese Bread**	11
Chocolate Chip Oatmeal Cookie	7.5	**or ½ cup blueberries with 2 tbs. whipped cream**	7.5
	34		40
or 1 ounce macadamia nuts with 2 ounces cheese	3	**or ½ Haas avocado**	3
	85		104

MEAL PLAN 23

45 GRAMS NET CARBS		60 GRAMS NET CARBS	
Breakfast			
Pecan Buttermilk Waffle	7	Pecan Buttermilk Waffle	7
½ cup mixed berries	5	or ⅓ banana	5
	12		12
Lunch			
bell pepper stuffed with chicken salad	7 0	bell pepper stuffed or with tuna salad	7 0
½ orange	6.5	or 1 small peach	6.5
	13.5		13.5
Dinner			
Seafood Chowder	7.5	Seafood Chowder	7.5
blackened catfish	2	Bronzed Catfish	11.5
1 cup sautéed broccoli and cauliflower florets	4	½ small baked sweet potato	10
small green salad with dressing	2	small green salad with dressing	2
	15.5		31
Snack			
2 ounces cheese	2	or 2 ounces almonds	2
Total	43		58.5

80 GRAMS NET CARBS		100 GRAMS NET CARBS	
Pecan Buttermilk Waffle	7	**Pecan Buttermilk Waffle**	7
½ cup ricotta cheese	4	**or ½ cup cottage cheese**	4
½ cup mixed berries	5	**or ¾ cup raspberries**	5
		1 cup sugar-free hot cocoa	3
	16		19
or tomato stuffed	7	**or ½ Haas avocado**	7
with chicken salad	0	**with chicken salad**	0
1 slice whole-grain bread	10	**or ½ whole-grain roll**	10
or 1 small tangerine	6.5	**or ½ cup cantaloupe**	6.5
	23.5		23.5
Seafood Chowder	7.5	**Seafood Chowder**	7.5
Bronzed Catfish	11.5	**Bronzed Catfish**	11.5
or ⅓ cup corn	10	1 small baked sweet potato	20
½ cup sautéed spinach	2	small green salad with	2
		dressing	
Frozen Lemon Mousse	7.5	**or Almond Flan**	7.5
	38.5		48.5
2 ounces cheese and	4	4 ounces of tomato juice	6
2 ounces almonds		with 4 tbs. walnuts	
	82		97

Meal Plan 24

45 grams Net Carbs		60 grams Net Carbs	
Breakfast			
1 slice low carb toast	3	**Ricotta Strawberry**	13
½ cup ricotta cheese	4	**Breakfast Sandwich**	
½ cup strawberries	4	½ cup strawberries	4
	11		**17**
Lunch			
chicken consommé	1	**Gazpacho**	10.5
Vegetable Quiche	13.5	**Vegetable Quiche**	13.5
large green salad with creamy dressing	6	or 1 cup green beans with vinaigrette	6
	20.5		**30**
Dinner			
grilled shrimp kebabs	0	grilled shrimp kebabs	0
½ cup cooked low carb pasta	5	**or 1 cup cauliflower purée**	5
Italian-Style Green Beans	5	**or 1 cup sautéed escarole**	5
	10		**10**
Snack			
1 small tangerine	6	1 bag low carb soy chips with 1 ounce melted Monterey Jack cheese	6
hard-boiled egg	0.5	hard-boiled egg	0.5
Total	**48**		**63.5**

80 GRAMS NET CARBS		100 GRAMS NET CARBS	
Ricotta Strawberry Breakfast Sandwich	13	Ricotta Strawberry Breakfast Sandwich	13
or ⅓ cup pineapple	4	or 1 apricot	4
		decaf latte	5
	17		22
or 1 cup tomato juice	10.5	Gazpacho	10.5
Vegetable Quiche	13.5	Vegetable Quiche	13.5
or large spinach salad with vinaigrette	6	large green salad with creamy dressing	6
		¼ cup cooked chickpeas	8
1 fresh fig	6	or ½ cup cantaloupe	6
	36		44
grilled shrimp kebabs	0	grilled shrimp kebabs	0
Brown Rice Pilaf	12	or 1 cup winter squash	12
or ¾ cup sautéed broccoli with garlic	5	Italian-Style Green Beans	5
Orange Walnut Cake	12	or 1 cup cantaloupe	12
	29		29
or 2 apricots	6	or Maple-Chili Trail Mix	6
hard-boiled egg	0.5	hard-boiled egg	0.5
	88.5		101.5

Meal Plan 25

45 grams Net Carbs		60 grams Net Carbs	
Breakfast			
2 eggs with Canadian bacon	1.5	or 2 eggs with sausage	1.5
1 small tangerine	6	1 orange	13
	7.5		**14.5**
Lunch			
low carb vegetable soup in a cup	5	Lentil Soup	11.5
muenster cheese melt on 1 slice low carb bread	4	muenster cheese melt on 1 slice low carb bread	4
large green salad with dressing	4	or sliced tomato and cucumber with dressing	4
	13		**19.5**
Dinner			
Stuffed Chicken Breast	8.5	**Stuffed Chicken Breast**	8.5
1 cup sautéed zucchini and mushrooms	5	Tomato, Zucchini, and Mushroom Gratin	8.5
½ cup blackberries with 2 tbs. whipped cream	6	Blackberry-Orange Sorbet	11
	19.5		**28**
Snack			
½ cup red pepper and cucumber strips with mayonnaise and bleu cheese	5	1 plum with ¼ cup whole milk ricotta cheese	5
Total	**45**		**67**

80 GRAMS NET CARBS		100 GRAMS NET CARBS	
or 2 eggs with Canadian bacon	1.5	or 2 eggs with turkey bacon	1.5
or ⅔ cup pineapple	13	1 orange	13
1 slice whole-grain toast	10	or ½ whole-grain roll	10
		decaf latte	5
	24.5		**29.5**
or ⅓ cup cooked chickpeas with olive oil and parsley	11.5	Lentil Soup	11.5
muenster cheese melt on 1 slice low carb bread	4	muenster cheese melt on 1 slice pumpernickel	12
Greek Salad	4	large green salad with dressing	4
		¾ cup watermelon	7.5
	19.5		**35**
Stuffed Chicken Breast	8.5	Stuffed Chicken Breast	8.5
or ¾ cup Brussels sprouts	8.5	or ¾ cup green peas	8.5
or 1 grilled peach	11	or ½ baked apple with chopped walnuts	11
	28		**28**
½ cup blueberries with ¼ cup plain whole yogurt	11	or ⅔ cup Maple-Chili Trail Mix	11
	83		**103.5**

Meal Plan 26

45 grams Net Carbs		60 grams Net Carbs	
Breakfast			
Atkins Lemon Poppy Muffin*	3	**1 slice Lemon Zucchini Bread**	9
hard-boiled egg	0.5	hard-boiled egg	0.5
½ cup raspberries	3	½ cup blueberries	8
½ cup cottage cheese	4	½ cup plain whole yogurt	5.5
	10.5		23
Lunch			
Roast Beef and Tomato Sandwich on 1 slice low carb bread	6	Roast Beef and Tomato Sandwich on 1 slice low carb bread	6
Macaroni and Cauliflower Salad	4	**or Atkins Cole Slaw**	4
	10		10
Dinner			
Chili Blanco	12.5	**Chili Blanco**	12.5
small salad with dressing	2	**or 2 marinated artichoke hearts**	2
½ cup roasted green beans	3	½ cup roasted green beans	3
½ cup watermelon	5	**or 2 apricots**	5
	22.5		22.5
Snack			
Lime Granita	5	**or 2 ounces nuts and 2 ounces cheese**	5
Total	45		60.5

*Made from Atkins Quick Quisine™ Lemon Poppy Muffin Mix.

80 GRAMS NET CARBS		100 GRAMS NET CARBS	
or 1 slice rye toast	9	**2 slices Lemon Zucchini Bread**	18
hard-boiled egg	0.5	hard-boiled egg	0.5
or 1 cup strawberries	8	**or 1 small peach**	8
½ cup yogurt	5.5	**or decaf latte**	5.5
	23		32
Roast Beef and Tomato Sandwich on 1 slice whole-grain bread	13	Roast Beef and Tomato Sandwich on whole-grain roll	23
or large green salad w/dressing	4	**or Greek Salad**	4
1 kiwifruit	9	**or ½ cup cherries**	9
	26		36
Chili Blanco	12.5	**Chili Blanco**	12.5
or sliced tomato	2	small salad with dressing	2
½ cup roasted green beans	3	½ cup sautéed spinach	3
1 fresh fig	6.5	**Almond Flan**	7.5
	24		25
Lime Granita	5	**3 Pinwheel Cookies**	7.5
		½ cup milk	5.5
	78		106

MEAL PLAN 27

45 GRAMS NET CARBS		60 GRAMS NET CARBS	
Breakfast			
ham and cheese omelet	2	ham and cheese omelet	2
		½ low carb bagel	6
½ cup strawberries	4	or ⅔ cup raspberries	4
decaf latte	5	or sugar-free hot cocoa	5
	11		17
Lunch			
Panini	10	**Panini**	10
Greek Salad	3.5	**or Tomato and Cucumber Salad**	3.5
	13.5		13.5
Dinner			
roast chicken	0	roast chicken	0
1 cup roasted asparagus and carrots	5	**Braised Leeks and Fennel**	15.5
large green salad with dressing	4	large green salad with dressing	4
2 poached apricots with toasted almonds	6	broiled peach with toasted almonds	9
	15		28.5
Snack			
1 bag low carb soy chips	5	1 bag low carb soy chips	5
Total	44.5		64

80 GRAMS NET CARBS		100 GRAMS NET CARBS	
or spinach omelet	2	ham and cheese omelet	2
1 slice rye bread	10	½ pumpernickel bagel	18
or ½ tangerine	4	**or 1 sliced tomato**	5
decaf latte	5	decaf latte	
	21		29
Panini	10	**Panini**	10
or ½ cup green beans	3.5	**Greek Salad**	3.5
	13.5		13.5
roast chicken	0	roast chicken	0
Braised Leeks and Fennel	15.5	**or ½ cup leeks gratin**	15.5
or large endive and tomato salad with dressing	4	large green salad with dressing	4
		⅓ cup brown rice	14
or ½ baked pear	9	broiled peach with toasted almonds	9
Coconut Ice Cream	4.5	**Coconut Ice Cream**	4.5
	33		47
½ cup mango with 2 tbs. whipped cream	13	**½ cup unsweetened applesauce with 2 tbs. cream**	13
	80.5		102.5

MEAL PLAN 28

45 GRAMS NET CARBS		60 GRAMS NET CARBS	
Breakfast			
1 slice low carb bread	3	1 slice low carb bread	3
1 slice Swiss cheese	1	1 slice Swiss cheese	1
		1 small tomato	3
½ cup grapefruit	8	or ½ orange	8
	12		15
Lunch			
antipasti plate:	8	antipasti plate:	8
2 ounces cheese,		2 ounces cheese,	
salami, olives,		salami, olives,	
4 artichoke hearts,		4 artichoke hearts,	
½ roasted pepper		½ roasted pepper	
		1 slice Olive Cheese Bread	11
	8		19
Dinner			
Chickpea and Vegetable Salad	9.5	or Tabbouleh	9.5
lamb burgers	0	lamb burgers	0
Greek Salad	3.5	**or large green salad with vinaigrette**	3.5
	13		13
Snack			
¾ cup cantaloupe	9	**or 1 Chocolate Pecan Bar**	9
1 bag low carb soy chips	5	**or ½ cup mixed berries**	5
Total	47		61

80 GRAMS NET CARBS		100 GRAMS NET CARBS	
1 slice whole grain bread	10	½ pumpernickel bagel	18
1 slice Swiss cheese	1	1 slice Swiss cheese	1
or ¼ sliced onion	3	1 small tomato	3
or 1 tangerine	8	or ½ small papaya	8
	22		30
or ½ cup marinated mushrooms and carrots and ½ cup grilled eggplant	8	antipasti plate: 2 ounces cheese, salami, olives, 4 artichoke hearts, ½ roasted pepper	8
1 slice Olive Cheese Bread	11	or 1 slice whole-grain bread	11
1 small slice honeydew	6	or ½ cup blueberries	6
	25		25
Chickpea and Vegetable Salad	9.5	Brown Rice Pilaf	12
or turkey burgers	0	lamb burgers	0
Greek salad	3.5	or 1 small steamed artichoke	3.5
Orange Walnut Cake	12	or Baked Pear Fan	12
	25		27.5
or ¾ cup fruit salad	9	or 1 peach	9
1 bag low carb soy chips	5	or Maple-Chili Trail Mix	5
	86		96.5

MEAL PLAN 29

45 GRAMS NET CARBS		60 GRAMS NET CARBS	
Breakfast			
2 slices low carb cinnamon toast	6	**Cinnamon Crumb Coffeecake**	16
½ cup plain whole yogurt	5.5	½ cup plain whole yogurt	5.5
½ cup raspberries	3	½ cup blueberries	8
	14.5		29.5
Lunch			
turkey, ham and cheese strips over	4	**Croque Monsieur**	7
large green salad with dressing	4	large green salad with dressing	4
	8		11
Dinner			
grilled steak	0	grilled steak	0
roasted Portobello mushroom	4	**or 8 spears roasted asparagus**	4
Broccoli, Daikon, and Pepper Salad	5	**or tomato and endive salad with dressing**	5
	9		9
Snack			
2 prunes stuffed with almonds	10	**1 fresh fig with 6 ounces low carb vanilla yogurt**	10
Total	41.5		59.5

80 GRAMS NET CARBS		100 GRAMS NET CARBS	
Cinnamon Crumb Coffeecake	16	or 2 slices light rye toast	16
or decaf latte	5.5	½ cup plain whole yogurt	5.5
or ¾ cup cantaloupe	8	½ cup blueberries	8
	29.5		29.5
Croque Monsieur	7	Croque Monsieur on whole-grain bread	21
Chickpea and Vegetable salad	9.5	or large green salad with ¼ cup beans	9.5
	16.5		30.5
grilled steak	0	grilled steak	0
Brown Rice Pilaf	12	or ⅓ cup whole-wheat pasta	12
Broccoli, Daikon, and Pepper Salad	5	or ¾ cup broccoli with garlic	5
		Pineapple-Mango Layer Cake	9.5
	17		26.5
or ½ pear	10	or 1 kiwifruit	10
½ cup carrot and zucchini sticks with sour cream onion dip	6	or 2 tbsp. hummus with celery	6
	79		102.5

MEAL PLAN 30

45 GRAMS NET CARBS		60 GRAMS NET CARBS	
Breakfast			
2 scrambled eggs with bacon	1	2 scrambled eggs with bacon	1
		1 slice low carb toast	3
½ orange	6.5	**or 1 tangerine**	6.5
	7.5		10.5
Lunch			
low carb soup in a cup	5	**Lentil Soup**	11.5
chicken salad with celery	2	or tuna salad with celery	2
in ½ Haas avocado	2	in ½ Haas avocado	2
	9		15.5
Dinner			
small Caesar salad	4	large Caesar salad	8
Lamb Chops with	4	**Lamb Chops with**	4
Tomatoes and Olives		**Tomatoes and Olives**	
1 cup green beans	6	**or 1 cup broccoli**	6
½ cup honeydew	7	**or ½ cup cantaloupe**	7
	21		25
Snack			
2 tbs. hummus with	7.5	1 ounce macadamia nuts	11
carrot sticks		with ½ apple	
Total	45		62

80 GRAMS NET CARBS		100 GRAMS NET CARBS	
2 scrambled eggs with bacon	1	2 scrambled eggs with bacon	1
1 slice whole-grain toast	10	**or ½ whole-grain roll**	10
½ orange	6.5	1 orange	13
		decaf latte	5
	17.5		**29**
Lentil Soup	11.5	**or Barley Vegetable Soup**	11.5
chicken salad with celery	2	chicken salad with celery	2
in ½ Haas avocado	2	in ½ Haas avocado	2
1 sliced tomato	5	**or ¾ cup steamed snow peas**	5
	20.5		**20.5**
large Caesar salad	8	large Caesar salad	8
Lamb Chops with Tomatoes and Olives	4	**Lamb Chops with Tomatoes and Olives**	4
1 cup green beans	6	**or 1 cup sautéed escarole**	6
½ cup low carb pasta	5	½ cup low carb pasta	5
or ½ cup pineapple	7	1 tbs. raisins over	8
		Brown Rice Pudding	11
	30		**42**
or Baked Pear Fan	11	**or 2 ounces cheese with 1 flat bread**	11
	79		**102.5**

Twenty Meal Plans for Special Occasions

10 Holiday Menus

45 GRAMS NET CARBS		60 GRAMS NET CARBS	
Christmas			
Crab Deviled Eggs	1	**Crab Deviled Eggs**	1
Perfect Filet Mignon with Wine Sauce	5.5	**Filet Mignon with Wine Sauce**	5.5
Salad with Brie and Spicy Nuts	6	**Salad with Brie and Spicy Nuts**	6
½ flatbread	4	½ flatbread	4
¾ cup mixed sautéed vegetables	8	¾ cup mixed sautéed vegetables with 1 new potato	8
			10
Christmas Yule Log	5.5	**Christmas Yule Log**	5.5
	30		40
Easter			
Vegetable Quiche	13.5	**Vegetable Quiche**	13.5
Fresh Baked Easter Ham	2.5	**Fresh Baked Easter Ham**	2.5
¾ cup roasted asparagus and carrots	8	**or ¾ cup peas**	8
		steamed new potato with butter	10
small mixed spring green salad with dressing	2	small mixed spring green salad with dressing	2
Citrus Chiffon Cake	5.5	**Citrus Chiffon Cake**	5.5
	31.5		41.5

80 GRAMS NET CARBS		100 GRAMS NET CARBS	
Crab Deviled Eggs	1	Crab Deviled Eggs	1
Filet Mignon with Wine Sauce	5.5	Perfect Filet Mignon with Wine Sauce	5.5
Salad with Brie and Spicy Nuts	6	Salad with Brie and Spicy Nuts	6
½ whole-grain roll	10	1 whole-grain roll	20
¾ cup mixed sautéed vegetables	8	¾ cup mixed sautéed vegetables with 1 new potato	18
or with ½ sweet potato	10		
Christmas Yule Log	5.5	Christmas Yule Log	5.5
	46		56
Vegetable Quiche	13.5	Vegetable Quiche	13.5
Fresh Baked Easter Ham	2.5	Fresh Baked Easter Ham	2.5
¾ cup roasted asparagus and carrots	8	¾ cup roasted asparagus and carrots	8
2 steamed new potatoes with butter	20	or 1 whole-wheat roll	20
small mixed spring green salad with dressing	2	small mixed spring green salad with dressing	2
Citrus Chiffon Cake	5.5	Citrus Chiffon Cake	5.5
		with ¾ cup fruit salad	9
	51.5		60.5

45 GRAMS NET CARBS		60 GRAMS NET CARBS	
Valentine's Day			
Roasted Red Pepper Soup	10.5	Roasted Red Pepper Soup	10.5
Cornish Hens with Wild Rice	14.5	Cornish Hens with Wild Rice	14.5
baby greens with creamy dressing	4	baby greens with creamy dressing	4
		1 flatbread	8
Chocolate Soufflé	4.5	or Coconut Ice Cream	4.5
	33.5		41.5
July 4th Cookout			
Chili-Cheese Roll-Ups	2.5	Chili-Cheese Roll-Ups	2.5
mixed grill	0	mixed grill	0
Mixed Veggie Potato Salad	14.5	Mixed Veggie Potato Salad	14.5
		with ½ cup peas	6.5
		Atkins Cole Slaw	5.5
Mixed Berry Shortcake	10.5	Mixed Berry Shortcake	10.5
	27.5		39.5
Memorial Day Picnic			
Tomato and Cucumber Salad	3.5	Tomato and Cucumber Salad with ¼ cup navy beans	13.5
chicken salad with olives	3	or ham salad with olives	3
Macaroni and Cauliflower Salad	4	or crudités	4
1 thin slice whole-grain baguette	5	1 thin slice whole-grain baguette	5
½ cup watermelon chunks	5	½ cup watermelon chunks	5
Chunky Mocha Ice Cream	7	Chunky Mocha Ice Cream	7
	27.5		37.5

80 GRAMS NET CARBS		100 GRAMS NET CARBS	
Roasted Red Pepper Soup	10.5	Roasted Red Pepper Soup	10.5
Cornish Hens with Wild Rice	14.5	Cornish Hens with Wild Rice	14.5
		with 1 tbs. dried fruit in stuffing	8
baby greens with creamy dressing	4	baby greens with chopped nuts and creamy dressing	6
or 2 stoned-wheat crackers	8	1 flatbread	8
Chocolate Soufflé	4.5	Chocolate Soufflé	4.5
½ cup cherries	8.5	½ cup cherries	8.5
	50		60
Chili-Cheese Roll-Ups	2.5	Chili-Cheese Roll-Ups on corn tortilla	10.5
mixed grill	0	mixed grill	0
or 1 grilled potato	21	Mixed Veggie Potato Salad	14.5
		with ½ cup peas	6.5
½ ear corn	8.5	1 small ear corn	14
or salad with creamy dressing	5.5	or Tomato and Cucumber Salad	5.5
Mixed Berry Shortcake	10.5	or 4 Pinwheel Cookies	10.5
	48		61.5
Tomato and Cucumber Salad or with ⅓ cup corn	13.5	Tomato and Cucumber Salad with ¼ cup navy beans	13.5
or crab salad with olives	3	chicken salad with olives	3
Macaroni and Cauliflower Salad	4	Macaroni and Cauliflower Salad	4
½ whole-grain bun	15	1 whole-grain bun	30
or ¾ cup strawberries	5	or 4 Chocolate Coconut Macaroons	5
Chunky Mocha Ice Cream	7	Chunky Mocha Ice Cream	7
	47.5		62.5

45 GRAMS NET CARBS		60 GRAMS NET CARBS	
New Year's Eve Buffet			
3 Polenta Triangles	12	**3 Polenta Triangles**	12
Salmon-Stuffed Zucchini	1	**Salmon-Stuffed Zucchini**	1
Mushroom Crostini	9	**Mushroom Crostini**	9
Eggplant Stack	7.5	**Eggplant Stack**	7.5
assorted cheese platter	3	assorted cheese platter	3
		½ cup carrot sticks	6
1 glass champagne	1	1 glass champagne	1
	33.5		**39.5**
Super-bowl Sunday			
1 bag low carb soy chips with onion dip	8	1 bag low carb soy chips with onion dip	8
Chili Blanco	12.5	**Chili Blanco**	12.5
Savory Cornbread Muffin	9	**Savory Cornbread Muffin**	9
green salad with creamy dressing	4	green salad with creamy dressing	4
		Chunky Mocha Ice Cream	7
	33.5		**40.5**
Thanksgiving			
		½ cup crudites with dip	6
Country-Style Stuffed Turkey	16.5	**Country-Style Stuffed Turkey**	16.5
¾ cup Brussels sprouts with browned butter	8	**or 1 cup roasted green beans**	8
Cranberry Relish	8	**Cranberry Relish**	8
Pumpkin Pie with Pecan Crust	12.5	**Pumpkin Pie with Pecan Crust**	12.5
	45		**51**

80 GRAMS NET CARBS		100 GRAMS NET CARBS	
3 Polenta Triangles	12	**3 Polenta Traingles**	12
Salmon-Stuffed Zucchini	1	**Salmon-Stuffed Zucchini**	1
Mushroom Crostini	9	**Mushroom Crostini**	9
on whole-grain toast points	10	**or on 1 piece flatbread**	10
Eggplant Stack	7.5	**Eggplant Stack**	7.5
assorted cheese platter	3	assorted cheese platter	3
⅓ cup grapes	9	¾ cup grapes	20
1 glass champagne	1	1 glass champagne	1
	52.5		63.5
or ½ cup carrot sticks with onion dip	8	1 bag low carb soy chips with onion dip	8
Chili Blanco	12.5	**Chili Blanco**	12.5
or 1 slice whole-grain bread	9	**2 Savory Cornbread Muffins**	18
green salad with creamy dressing	4	green salad with creamy dressing	4
Chunky Mocha Ice Cream	7	**Chunky Mocha Ice Cream**	7
3 Chocolate Almond Biscotti	9	**3 Chocolate Almond Biscotti**	9
	49.5		58.5
½ cup crudites with dip	6	½ cup crudites with dip	6
Country-Style Stuffed Turkey	16.5	**Country-Style Stuffed Turkey**	16.5
¾ cup Brussels sprouts with browned butter	8	¾ cup Brussels sprouts with browned butter	8
		Savory Cornbread Muffin	9
or Rhubarb Applesauce	8	**Cranberry Relish**	8
Pumpkin Pie with Pecan Crust	12.5	**Pumpkin Pie with Pecan Crust**	12.5
½ baked apple with cinnamon	8.5	½ baked apple with cinnamon	8.5
	59.5		68.5

45 GRAMS NET CARBS		60 GRAMS NET CARBS	
Chanukah			
Barley Vegetable Soup	12	Barley Vegetable soup	12
Brisket with Porcini Mushrooms	6	Brisket with Porcini Mushrooms	6
		½ whole-grain roll	10
Sweet Potato and Zucchini Latkes	8	Sweet Potato and Zucchini Latkes	8
Rhubarb Applesauce	6.5	Rhubarb Applesauce	6.5
	32.5		42.5
Mother's Day Brunch			
decaf latte	5	decaf latte	5
Creamy Baked Eggs	2.5	Creamy Baked Eggs	2.5
		1 small broiled tomato	4
1 slice low carb toast	3	1 slice low carb toast	3
Cinnamon Crumb Coffeecake	16	Cinnamon Crumb Coffeecake	16
½ cup fruit salad	6	¾ cup fruit salad	9
	32.5		39.5

80 GRAMS NET CARBS		100 GRAMS NET CARBS	
Barley Vegetable Soup	12	Barley Vegetable Soup	12
Brisket with Porcini	13	Brisket with Porcini	13
Mushrooms,		Mushrooms,	
with 1 small carrot		with 1 small carrot	
½ whole-grain roll	10	whole-grain roll	20
or ⅓ cup kasha	8	Sweet Potato-Zucchini	8
		Latkes with carrots	
Rhubarb Applesauce	6.5	Rhubarb Applesauce	6.5
Chocolate Coconut	2.5	Chocolate Coconut	2.5
Macaroons		Macaroons	
	52		62
decaf latte	5	decaf latte	5
Creamy Baked Eggs	2.5	Creamy Baked Eggs	5.5
1 small broiled tomato	4	1 small broiled tomato	4
1 slice whole-grain toast	10	whole-grain English muffin	22
Cinnamon Crumb	16	Cinnamon Crumb	16
Coffeecake		Coffeecake	
or ½ orange	9	¾ cup fruit salad	9
	46.5		61.5

10 Ethnic Menus

45 grams Net Carbs		60 grams Net Carbs	
Italian			
salad with Italian dressing	2	**Minestrone Soup**	12
Veal Milanese	5.5	**Veal Milanese**	5.5
½ cup low carb pasta	5	½ cup low carb pasta	5
¼ cup low carb tomato sauce	2.5	¼ cup low carb tomato sauce	2.5
3 Chocolate Almond Biscotti	9	**3 Chocolate Almond Biscotti**	9
	24		34
French			
consommé with mushrooms	2	**Golden Onion Soup**	15
Bistro Skillet Steak	4	**Bistro Skillet Steak**	4
large green salad with vinaigrette	4	or endive and tomato salad	4
small slice whole-grain baguette	7	small slice whole-grain baguette	7
½ cup mixed berries with 2 tbs. whipped cream	6	½ cup mixed berries with 2 tbs. whipped cream	6
	23		36
Mexican			
salsa with ½ cup crudités	6	**Mexican Bean Dip** with ½ cup crudités	14
Southwestern-Style Pork Fajitas	11	**Southwestern-Style Pork Fajitas**	11
low carb tortilla	3	low carb tortilla	3

80 GRAMS NET CARBS		100 GRAMS NET CARBS	
Minestrone Soup	12	**Minestrone Soup**	12
Veal Milanese	5.5	**Veal Milanese**	5.5
⅓ cup whole-wheat pasta	12	½ cup whole-wheat pasta	17
¼ cup low carb tomato	2.5	¼ cup low carb tomato	2.5
sauce		sauce	
3 Chocolate Almond Biscotti	9	**3 Chocolate Almond Biscotti**	9
		Lime Granita	3
	41		49
Golden Onion Soup	15	**Golden Onion Soup**	15
Bistro Skillet Steak	14	**Bistro Skillet Steak**	14
with ½ cup roasted		with ½ cup roasted	
root vegetables		root vegetables	
		and 1 small roast potato	10
large green salad with	4	large green salad with	4
vinaigrette		vinaigrette	
or 2 breadsticks	7	small slice whole-grain	7
		baguette	
½ cup mixed berries with	6	½ cup mixed berries with	6
2 tbs. whipped cream		2 tbs. whipped cream	
	46		56
Mexican Bean Dip	14	**Mexican Bean Dip**	14
with ½ cup crudités		with ½ cup crudités	
Southwestern-Style	11	**Southwestern-Style**	11
Pork Fajitas		**Pork Fajitas**	
low carb tortilla	3	corn tortilla	11

45 GRAMS NET CARBS		60 GRAMS NET CARBS	
Almond Flan	7	**Almond Flan**	7
	27		35
Asian			
Asian Vegetable Bowl	5.5	**Asian Vegetable Bowl**	5.5
Spiced Beef and	7.5	**Spiced Beef and**	7.5
Asparagus Stir-Fry		**Asparagus Stir-Fry**	
½ cup low carb pasta w/sesame oil	5	⅓ cup brown rice	14
Coconut Ice Cream	4.5	**Coconut Ice Cream**	4.5
	22.5		31.5
Indian			
Cucumber Raita	4	**Cucumber Raita**	4
Coconut Chicken	10	**Coconut Chicken**	10
		1 flatbread	8
⅓ cup mango	9	⅓ cup mango	9
	23		31
Greek			
Spinach Phyllo Triangles	11	**Spinach Phyllo Triangles**	11
grilled fish with lemon, oregano, and olive oil	1	grilled fish with lemon, oregano, and olive oil	1
Greek Salad	3.5	**Greek Salad**	3.5
½ cup honeydew	7	**Orange Walnut Cake**	12
	22.5		27.5

80 GRAMS NET CARBS		100 GRAMS NET CARBS	
Almond Flan	7	**Almond Flan**	7
with ½ small broiled banana	10	with ½ small broiled banana	10
	45		53
Asian Vegetable Bowl	5.5	**Asian Vegetable Bowl**	5.5
Spiced Beef and Asparagus Stir-Fry	7.5	**Spiced Beef and Asparagus Stir-Fry**	7.5
or ⅓ cup whole-wheat pasta	14	⅔ cup brown rice	27
Coconut Ice Cream	4.5	**Coconut Ice Cream**	4.5
½ cup pineapple	9	½ cup pineapple	9
	40.5		53.5
Cucumber Raita	4	**Cucumber Raita**	4
Coconut Chicken	10	**Coconut Chicken**	10
¼ cup grilled peppers	4	⅓ cup grilled peppers	4
		¼ cup grilled onions	4
½ whole-wheat pita	15	or ⅓ cup basmati rice	15
or ⅔ cup pineapple	9	½ cup mango	13
	42		50
Spinach Phyllo Triangles	11	**Spinach Phyllo Triangles**	11
grilled fish with lemon, oregano, and olive oil	1	grilled fish with lemon, oregano and olive oil	1
1 small new potato	10	1 small new potato	10
		½ cup grilled fennel	2
Greek Salad	3.5	or 1 large salad with olive oil and vinegar	3.5
		with whole-wheat pita wedge	8
Orange Walnut Cake	12	**Orange Walnut Cake**	12
	37.5		47.5

45 GRAMS NET CARBS		60 GRAMS NET CARBS	
Middle Eastern			
Tabbouleh	8	Tabbouleh	8
Grilled Roast Lamb with Yogurt Sauce	11	Grilled Roast Lamb with Yogurt Sauce	11
½ cup grilled mixed vegetables	6	or ½ cup grilled eggplant	6
		1 almond stuffed date	7
	25		32
Caribbean			
Jerk Shrimp	8	Jerk Shrimp	8
Caribbean Black Bean Salad	11.5	Caribbean Black Bean Salad	11.5
Tomato and Cucumber Salad	3.5	Tomato and Cucumber Salad	3.5
		½ cup tropical fruit salad	10
	23		33
Southern			
Bronzed Catfish	11.5	Bronzed Catfish	11.5
Atkins corn muffin*	3	Atkins corn muffin*	3
Atkins Cole Slaw	5.5	Atkins Cole Slaw	5.5
Chocolate Pecan Bar	9.5	or 1 cup watermelon	9.5
	29.5		29.5
Brazilian			
¼ papaya drizzled with lemon juice	3	¼ papaya drizzled with lemon juice	3
Baihian Halibut	5.5	Baihian Halibut	5.5

80 GRAMS NET CARBS		100 GRAMS NET CARBS	
Tabbouleh	8	Tabbouleh	8
Grilled Roast Lamb with Yogurt Sauce	11	Grilled Roast Lamb with Yogurt Sauce	11
2 small grilled tomatoes	8	or 1 grilled pepper	8
½ cup grilled mixed vegetables	6	½ cup grilled mixed vegetables	6
or 1 fresh fig	7	2 fresh figs	14
	40		47
Jerk Shrimp	8	Jerk Shrimp	8
Caribbean Black Bean Salad	11.5	Caribbean Black Bean Salad	11.5
with ¼ cup brown rice	10	with ½ cup brown rice	20
Tomato and Cucumber Salad	3.5	Tomato and Cucumber Salad	3.5
or Pineapple-Mango Layer Cake	10	½ cup tropical fruit salad	10
	43		53
Bronzed Catfish	11.5	Bronzed Catfish	11.5
Atkins corn muffin*	3	Atkins corn muffin*	3
Atkins Cole Slaw	5.5	Atkins Cole Slaw	5.5
½ baked sweet potato	10	1 baked sweet potato	20
Chocolate Pecan Bar	9.5	Chocolate Pecan Bar	9.5
	39.5		49.5
or ¼ cup cantaloupe	3	¼ papaya drizzled with lemon juice	3
Baihian Halibut	5.5	Baihian Halibut	5.5

continued

45 GRAMS NET CARBS	60 GRAMS NET CARBS
Brazilian *(continued)*	
small hearts of palm 4 salad with tomato	small hearts of palm 4 salad with tomato
	1 new potato with butter 10
Blackberry-Orange Sorbet 11	or ⅔ cup pineapple 11
23.5	33.5

*Made from Atkins Quick Quisine™ Corn Muffin and Bread Mix.

80 GRAMS NET CARBS		100 GRAMS NET CARBS	
small hearts of palm salad with tomato	4	small hearts of palm salad with tomato	4
2 new potatoes	20	**or ½ cup brown rice**	**20**
		½ whole-grain roll	10
Blackberry-Orange Sorbet	**11**	**Blackberry-Orange Sorbet**	**11**
	43.5		53.5

Carb Counting Made Easy

The following items and their carb counts will help you plan meals and can be mixed and matched as substitutions in the preceding meal plans.

5 Grams

Each of the following contains approximately 5 grams of Net Carbs:

Vegetables

1 cup cooked spinach	1 cup cooked broccoli
½ cup cooked Brussels sprouts	½ cup cooked spaghetti squash
⅔ cup chopped red peppers	⅔ cup cooked green beans
½ cup chopped onions	⅓ cup coleslaw
1 cup cooked yellow squash	5 ounces raw portobello mushrooms
1 medium tomato	⅔ cup raw snow peas
12 medium asparagus spears	

Note: Almost all salad greens contain well below 5 grams of Net Carbs per 1-cup serving.

Dairy

5 ounces farmer's cheese or pot cheese

¾ cup whole-milk cottage cheese

⅔ cup whole-milk ricotta cheese

¾ cup heavy cream

½ cup whole milk

½ cup whole-milk plain yogurt

Note: Almost all aged cheeses, such as Brie, Parmesan, provolone, Swiss, and Cheddar include less than 1 gram of Net Carbs per ounce.

Berries
Each portion contains approximately 5 grams of Net Carbs. Note that the frozen berries must be unsweetened to qualify for this carb count

Blackberries:
Fresh   ½ cup
Frozen   ⅓ cup

Blueberries:
Fresh   ⅓ cup
Frozen   ⅓ cup

Boysenberries:
Fresh   ½ cup
Frozen   ½ cup

Raspberries:
Fresh   ¾ cup
Frozen   ½ cup

Strawberries:
Fresh   ¾ cup whole
Frozen   ½ cup

Nuts and Seeds

Because nuts and seeds are so rich and generally low in carbs, the following servings provide no more than 3 grams of Net Carbs:

Macadamias, 10 to 12 nuts

Walnuts, 14 halves

Almonds, 14 nuts

Pecans, 14 halves

Hulled sunflower seeds, 3 tablespoons

Dry-roasted peanuts,* 26 nuts

Cashews, 2 tablespoons

2 tablespoons natural chunky peanut butter

Filberts (hazelnuts), 14 nuts

Pine nuts (pignoli), 3 tablespoons

Shelled pistachios, 14 nuts

Pumpkinseeds, 3 tablespoons

Sesame seeds, 3 tablespoons

*Note: Peanuts are actually legumes, rather than nuts, which grow on trees.

10 Grams

All the portions below contain approximately 10 grams of Net Carbs:

Higher Carb Vegetables

¾ cup cooked carrots

⅓ cup steamed parsnips

½ cup baked acorn squash

½ small baked potato

½ small baked sweet potato

1 cup cooked pumpkin

⅔ cup cooked peas

¾ cup cooked mashed turnip

¼ cup cooked green plantain

¾ cup water chestnuts

1 cup canned beets

Beans and Legumes
Note: All figures are for cooked beans and legumes.

⅓ cup lentils

⅓ cup great northern beans

⅓ cup kidney beans

⅓ cup chickpeas (garbanzos)

⅓ cup black beans

¼ cup fava beans

¼ cup navy beans

⅓ cup pinto beans

⅓ cup baby lima beans

¾ cup green soybeans (edamame)

Fruits

½ large apple

3 small plums

11 sweet cherries

½ small banana

1 medium peach

1 cup guava

12 Thompson green grapes

⅓ cup mango

½ medium grapefruit

2 fresh dates

1 medium kiwi

½ cup pineapple

1 cup watermelon balls

1 medium tangerine

¼ small cantaloupe (or ¾ cup balls)

½ medium pear

Grains

Note: All measurements are for cooked grains.

¼ cup grain brown rice	¼ cup barley
⅓ cup wild rice	⅓ cup whole-wheat couscous
⅓ cup kasha (buckwheat groats)	⅓ cup bulgur
½ cup plain (old-fashioned) oatmeal	¼ cup whole-wheat pasta
⅓ cup whole-wheat cereal (Wheatena)	⅓ cup corn kernels

125 Recipes for Success

APPPETIZERS AND SNACKS	NET CARBS (IN GRAMS)
Bruschetta	3
Chili-Cheese Roll-Ups	2.5
Crab Deviled Eggs	1
Eggplant Stacks	7.5
Maple-Chili Trail Mix	5.5
Mexican Bean Dip	11.5
Mushroom Crostini	9
Salmon-Stuffed Zucchini	1
Spicy Shrimp Pâté	5.5
Spinach Phyllo Triangles	11

BREAKFAST AND BRUNCH	NET CARBS (IN GRAMS)
Blueberry Silver Dollar Pancakes	14.5
Breakfast Smoothies	9
Cherry Muffins	8
Cinnamon Crumb Coffee Cake	16
Creamy Baked Eggs	2.5
"Dutch Baby" Baked Pancake	14.5
Florentine Omelets	4

Lemon Zucchini Bread	9
Morning Muffins	11.5
Pecan Buttermilk Waffles	7
Ricotta-Strawberry Breakfast Sandwich	13
Vegetable Quiche	13.5
Zucchini Frittata	4

SOUPS AND SANDWICHES	NET CARBS (IN GRAMS)
Asian Vegetable Bowl	5.5
Barley Vegetable Soup	12
Chicken and Sun-Dried Tomato Quesadillas	10
Croque Monsieur	7
Eggplant, Mushroom, and Goat Cheese Sandwiches	9.5
Gazpacho	10.5
Golden Onion Soup	15
Grilled Ham and Cheese with Asparagus	8
Lentil Soup	11.5
Mediterranean Sandwiches	12.5
Minestrone Soup	12
Panini	10
Roast Beef Sandwiches	9
Roasted Chicken and Feta Cheese Wrap	12

Roasted Red Pepper Soup	10.5
Seafood Chowder	7.5
Spicy Turkey Club	15
Spring Vegetable Soup	8.5

ENTREES	NET CARBS (IN GRAMS)
Baihian Halibut	5.5
Bistro Skillet Steak	4
Braised Short Ribs with Horseradish Sauce	7
Brisket with Porcini Mushrooms	6
Broccoli Rabe and Sausage over Penne	12.5
Bronzed Catfish	11.5
Chili Blanco	12.5
Coconut Chicken	10
Cornish Hens with Wild Rice	14.5
Country-Style Stuffed Turkey	16.5
Escarole and Chickpea Stew	21.5
Fresh Baked Easter Ham	2.5
Grilled Lamb Roast with Yogurt Sauce	11
Jerk Shrimp	8
Lamb Chops with Tomatoes and Olives	4

Miso-Soy Glazed Salmon	5
Not Your Mama's Meat Loaf	3.5
Pasta with Fresh Tomatoes, Lemon, and Feta	13.5
Perfect Filet Mignon with Red Wine Sauce	5.5
Sesame Tofu with Snow Peas and Peppers	9
Southwestern-Style Pork Fajitas	11
Spanish Chicken over Penne	13
Spiced Beef and Asparagus Stir-Fry	7.5
Stuffed Chicken Breast	8.5
Veal Milanese	5.5

SALADS	NET CARBS (IN GRAMS)
Asian Carrot and Zucchini Salad	5.5
Atkins Cole Slaw	5.5
Broccoli, Daikon, and Pepper Salad	5
Caribbean Black Bean Salad	11.5
Chickpea and Vegetable Salad	9.5
Greek Salad	3.5
Lobster Salad	6.5

Macaroni and Cauliflower Salad	4
Mexican Chopped Salad	6
Mixed Veggie Potato Salad	14.5
Salad with Brie and Spicy Nuts	6
Smoked Mozzarella, Tomato, and Green Bean Salad	11
Sweet Potato and Spinach Salad	5.5
Tabbouleh	8
Tomato and Cucumber Salad	3.5

SIDE DISHES	NET CARBS (IN GRAMS)
Asian Vegetable Stir-Fry	5.5
Atkins Baked Beans	11.5
Braised Leeks and Fennel	15.5
Broccolini in Sage and Feta Cream	8.5
Brown Rice Pilaf	12
Garden Pasta	7
Grilled Eggplant with Cilantro Sauce	7.5
Italian-Style Green Beans	5
Olive Cheese Bread	11
Polenta Triangles	4
Red Swiss Chard and Bacon	4

Savory Cornbread Muffins	9
Sweet Potato and Zucchini Latkes	8
Tomato, Zucchini, and Mushroom Gratin	8.5
Warm Zucchini Mint Salad	5.5

SAUCES AND CONDIMENTS	NET CARBS (IN GRAMS)
Cranberry Relish	8
Cucumber Raita	4
Custom Mayonnaises	0.5
Faux Pickled Vegetables	5.5
Flavored Butters	0.5
Homemade Tomato Sauce	6.5
Pineapple-Pepper Salsa	4.5
Quick Velouté and Variations	1.5
Rhubarb Applesauce	6.5

DESSERTS	NET CARBS (IN GRAMS)
Almond Flans with "Sugared" Almonds	7
Baked Pear Fans	11
Blackberry-Orange Sorbet	11
Brown Rice Pudding	11
Chocolate Chip Oatmeal Cookies	7.5

Chocolate Almond Biscotti	3
Chocolate Coconut Macaroons	2.5
Chocolate Pecan Bars	9.5
Chocolate Soufflé	4.5
Christmas Yule Log	5.5
Chunky Mocha Ice Cream	7
Citrus Chiffon Cake	5.5
Coconut Ice Cream	4.5
Frozen Lemon Mousse	7.5
Lime Granita	5
Mixed Berry Shortcakes	10.5
Orange Walnut Cake	12
Pineapple-Mango Layer Cake	12.5
Pinwheel Cookies	2.5
Pumpkin Pie with Pecan Crust	12.5

Recipes for Success

Bruschetta

Even in winter, tomatoes dressed in extra-virgin olive oil with fresh basil leaves can be delicious (in the height of summer, few food combinations are better). If ripe plum tomatoes aren't available, use 1½ cups diced cherry tomatoes instead. To thinly slice basil, stack the leaves, roll up lengthwise, and slice across at one-eighth-inch intervals.

PREP TIME: 15 minutes
BAKE TIME: 5 to 6 minutes
6 servings (2 pieces of toast per serving)

> 3 slices low carb white bread or 12 quarter-inch-thick round slices whole-wheat baguette
> 3 plum tomatoes, roughly diced
> 8 large basil leaves, very thinly sliced
> 1 medium garlic clove, pushed through a press
> 6 pitted kalamata olives, finely chopped
> 1 tablespoon extra-virgin olive oil
> 1 teaspoon balsamic vinegar
> ¼ teaspoon salt
> ⅛ teaspoon pepper

1. Heat oven to 350° F. For white bread only: Remove crusts and cut into quarters on the diagonal to form triangles. Bake bread on a baking sheet 5 to 6 minutes, turning once, until lightly golden.
2. Meanwhile, combine the remaining ingredients in a bowl. Spread each toast with about 1 tablespoon of topping.

Per serving:

CARBOHYDRATES:	NET CARBS:	FIBER:	PROTEIN:	FAT:	CALORIES:
5.5 grams	3 grams	2.5 grams	4 grams	4 grams	68

Chili-Cheese Roll-Ups

Poblano chilies are dark green and about 3½ to 4 inches long. They have a mild to slightly hot taste and a deep, complex flavor. In a pinch, you may substitute bell peppers.

PREP TIME: 15 minutes
CHILL TIME: 10 minutes
COOK TIME: 2 minutes
10 servings (2 pieces per serving)

Filling:
2 poblano chilies, roasted, seeded, peeled, and chopped
1 (8-ounce) package cream cheese, softened
1 tablespoon minced scallion
2 teaspoons fresh lime juice

olive oil
4 low carb garlic herb tortillas

1. With a wooden spoon, mix all filling ingredients in a bowl. Cover and chill until firm.
2. Lightly brush tortillas with oil. Toast about 30 seconds per side in nonstick skillet just until golden and softened. Cool slightly.
3. Spread each tortilla with ⅓ cup filling to edges. Roll up and cut each across into five 1-inch-thick pieces.

Per serving:

CARBOHY-DRATES:	NET CARBS:	FIBER:	PROTEIN:	FAT:	CALORIES:
7 grams	2.5 grams	4.5 grams	4 grams	9 grams	113

Crab Deviled Eggs

A classic appetizer that never goes out of style, this version is flavored with a touch of Old Bay Seasoning and filled with crab. Use leftovers as a super sandwich filling or a dip for celery sticks and endive spears.

PREP TIME: 10 minutes
COOK TIME: 10 minutes
12 servings (2 egg halves per serving) with 1 cup leftover filling

> 1 dozen large eggs, hard-boiled
> ½ cup mayonnaise
> 1 tablespoon coarse-grain mustard
> 1 teaspoon Old Bay Seasoning
> 1 to 2 teaspoons red-hot sauce
> 1 refrigerated (6-ounce) container Special White
>   crabmeat, picked over
> ¼ cup finely diced red onion

1. Cut eggs in half lengthwise and remove yolk. In a food processor, process yolks with half the mayonnaise, the mustard, bay seasoning, and hot sauce until smooth. Transfer to a bowl and stir in crabmeat, remaining mayonnaise, and red onion.
2. Spoon or pipe filling into hollow of egg whites, forming small mounds. Serve cold or at room temperature.

TIP: Follow these steps for perfect hard-boiled eggs: Put the eggs in a large saucepan and add water to cover by one inch. Cover the pan and bring the water to a boil; then remove from the heat and let stand 15 minutes. Drain water; jiggle eggs in pan to crack shells, then peel and rinse under cold water.

Per serving:

CARBOHY-DRATES:	NET CARBS:	FIBER:	PROTEIN:	FAT:	CALORIES:
1 gram	1 gram	0 grams	7 grams	8.5 grams	110

Eggplant Stacks

It may look like a long recipe, but this beautiful first course is made up of three simple parts, and can be partially made ahead of time. Both the eggplant and the pesto can be prepared up to 8 hours in advance. (Grill the eggplant, wrap in foil and let stand at room temperature until ready to assemble.) For convenience—if not quite the flavor—pesto in a jar may be substituted for the homemade version.

PREP TIME: 20 minutes
MARINATING TIME: 1 hour
GRILL TIME: 10 minutes
4 servings (1 stack per serving)

Marinade:
1½ tablespoons extra-virgin olive oil
3 tablespoons red wine vinegar
1 large garlic clove, pushed through a press
1 teaspoon dried oregano
½ teaspoon salt
½ teaspoon pepper
8 half-inch-thick slices eggplant

Pesto:
1 cup packed basil leaves
¼ cup grated Parmesan cheese
¼ cup toasted pine nuts or pumpkin seeds
¼ cup extra-virgin olive oil

1 tablespoon extra-virgin olive oil
1 teaspoon balsamic vinegar
½ teaspoon salt
⅛ teaspoon pepper
1 large tomato, cut into 12 very thin slices
4 ounces fresh mozzarella, cut into 8 thin
   slices

1. Combine marinade ingredients in a large bowl, add eggplant, toss well, and let stand 1 hour, turning eggplant occasionally.

2. Prepare a medium-hot grill; oil grill; cook eggplant, covered, 5 minutes per side until tender and grill marks appear. Wrap stacked in foil until ready to assemble.

3. In a food processor, blend all pesto ingredients until a smooth paste forms. Transfer to bowl and cover entire surface with plastic wrap.

4. Combine oil, vinegar, salt, and pepper in a pie plate; add tomato and turn to coat. To assemble each stack: Arrange 3 tomato slices in a slightly overlapping triangle. Top with 1 eggplant slice and spread ½ tablespoon pesto over eggplant. Top with 1 mozzarella slice. Add another layer of eggplant, pesto, and cheese. Drizzle any extra tomato juices around each stack.

TIP: You may broil eggplant instead of grilling it. Broil 6 inches from heat source.

Per serving:

CARBOHY-DRATES:	NET CARBS:	FIBER:	PROTEIN:	FAT:	CALORIES:
11 grams	7.5 grams	3.5 grams	10.5 grams	30 grams	347

Maple-Chili Trail Mix

Our homemade trail mix features sweet and savory seasonings that make it an irresistible snack at any time of day. Keep portions in mind though: a single serving is ⅓ cup. Wheat nuts are available in natural foods stores.

PREP TIME: 15 minutes
BAKE TIME: 25 to 30 minutes
18 servings (⅓ cup per serving)

Syrup:
¼ cup sugar-free pancake syrup
2 tablespoons butter, cut up
1 tablespoon chili powder
½ teaspoon salt
¼ teaspoon ground cinnamon

3 cups air-popped popcorn
3 cups unsalted mixed nuts
1½ cups original Kashi cereal
1 cup wheat nuts
⅓ cup dried no-sugar-added blueberries

1. Heat oven to 300° F. Combine syrup ingredients in saucepan and bring to a simmer, stirring frequently, to melt the butter.
2. Toss popcorn, nuts, Kashi, wheat nuts, and blueberries in a large broiler pan. Pour syrup over all and toss well to coat. Bake 25 to 30 minutes, stirring once halfway through baking time, until golden.
3. Scrape out mix onto large sheet of wax paper to cool. Spread out mix pieces for a crisper texture. Store in an airtight container for up to 2 weeks.

Per serving:

CARBOHY-DRATES:	NET CARBS:	FIBER:	PROTEIN:	FAT:	CALORIES:
8 grams	5.5 grams	2.5 grams	4 grams	12.5 grams	152

Mexican Bean Dip

Removing the gills from the underside of Portobellos keeps the mushrooms from releasing dark liquid when cooked.

PREP TIME: 15 minutes
COOK TIME: 5 minutes
8 servings (3 tablespoons per serving)

   2 tablespoons extra-virgin olive oil
   2 Portobello mushroom caps, (about 4 ounces), dark
     gills removed with side of spoon (and discarded),
     coarsely chopped
   ¼ cup finely chopped shallot
   ¼ teaspoon dried oregano
   ¼ teaspoon ground cumin
   1 (15-ounce) can pink beans, rinsed and drained
   2 tablespoons mayonnaise
   1 tablespoon sherry vinegar
   ½ teaspoon salt
   2 tablespoons finely diced plum tomato
   1 small jalapeño pepper, seeded and minced

1. Heat oil in a large skillet over medium-high heat. Cook mushrooms and shallot 4 minutes until starting to brown. Sprinkle with oregano and cumin; cook 1 to 2 minutes more until well browned.
2. In a food processor, process beans, mushroom mixture, mayonnaise, vinegar, and salt to a chunky purée, adding 1 to 2 tablespoons water to thin, if necessary. Transfer to bowl and stir in tomato and jalapeño, reserving a teaspoon of this combination to garnish. Sprinkle remaining tomato pepper mixture over the top.

TIP: For a super-quick quesadilla, spread dip over a low carb tortilla, top with tomatoes and cheese, fold in half, and pan-grill.

Per serving:

CARBOHY-DRATES:	NET CARBS:	FIBER:	PROTEIN:	FAT:	CALORIES:
14 grams	11.5 grams	2.5 grams	4.5 grams	6.5 grams	126

Mushroom Crostini

Though mushrooms are available year-round, their peak season is spring. The exotic varieties used in this recipe are more intensely flavored than button, or white, mushrooms.

PREP TIME: 15 minutes
COOK TIME: 30 minutes
4 servings (4 triangles per serving)

    4 slices low carb white bread, crusts trimmed
    2 tablespoons olive oil
    2 garlic cloves, pushed through a press
    ½ teaspoon oregano
    10 ounces button mushrooms, sliced
    10 ounces assorted wild mushrooms (shiitake, morels,
       cremini, oyster), cleaned and sliced
    2 tablespoons chopped sun-dried tomatoes in oil, lightly
       drained
    2 tablespoons chopped fresh parsley
    salt and pepper

1. Heat oven to 350° F. Toast bread 10 minutes, until crispy throughout. Cut each slice in half diagonally, then in half again to form four triangles.
2. Heat oil in a large skillet over medium heat. Add garlic and oregano; cook until garlic is lightly colored, about 30 seconds. Add mushrooms and cook 10 minutes or until brown.

3. Mix in sun-dried tomatoes and parsley. Season to taste with salt and pepper. Divide mixture over toast points and serve.

TIP: Freeze bread crusts until you want to make bread crumbs. Defrost, then spread crusts on a baking sheet. Bake in a 350° F. oven for 10 minutes, until golden and crisp. Transfer to a food processor and process until crumbs form. Bread crumbs may be frozen for up to two weeks.

Per serving:

CARBOHY-DRATES:	NET CARBS:	FIBER:	PROTEIN:	FAT:	CALORIES:
16 grams	9 grams	7 grams	16.5 grams	13.5 grams	238

Salmon-Stuffed Zucchini

You may prepare these colorful appetizers up to 6 hours ahead. To get even stripes along the length of the zucchini, peel one half at a time: it will give you greater control. Smoked whitefish, available at the deli counter, may be substituted for salmon.

PREP TIME: 20 minutes
8 servings (2 pieces per serving)

2 medium or 3 small zucchini, scrubbed
1 (6-ounce) can salmon, drained and flaked
2 tablespoons mayonnaise
1 teaspoon Dijon mustard
1 teaspoon chopped dill
Dash Worcestershire sauce
1 tablespoon finely chopped red bell pepper

1. With a vegetable peeler, peel strips ¼-inch apart down length of zucchini (to create a striped pattern of dark and

light green). Cut zucchini into ¾-inch rounds; remove seeds, discard, and hollow out zucchini slightly with a spoon. Arrange in rows on a serving plate.

2. Mix salmon, mayonnaise, mustard, dill, and Worcestershire. Fill zucchini hollows with salmon mixture. To garnish, sprinkle red pepper on top of stuffed zucchini rounds.

Per serving:

CARBOHYDRATES:	NET CARBS:	FIBER:	PROTEIN:	FAT:	CALORIES:
1.5 grams	1 gram	0.5 grams	4.5 grams	4 grams	60

Spicy Shrimp Pâté

Serrano chilies are small and slightly pointed. They are quite hot, so it's wise to wear gloves when handling them, or to wash your hands very well after. Dairy products, like the cream cheese in this pâté, help to tame their heat.

PREP TIME: 18 minutes
COOK TIME: 7 to 8 minutes
6 servings (2 toasts per serving)

   2 tablespoons butter, divided
   ⅓ cup chopped shallot
   1 to 2 serrano chilies, seeded and finely chopped
   1 pound large shrimp, peeled and deveined
   1 teaspoon grated fresh ginger
   1½ ounces cream cheese
   2 teaspoons rum
   ¼ teaspoon salt
   6 slices low carb white bread, crusts removed, toasted, and cut in half diagonally

1. Melt 1 tablespoon of the butter in a medium skillet over medium-high heat. Cook shallot and chilies 2 minutes, until

shallot is lightly browned. Add shrimp and ginger; cook about 5 minutes, turning once, until shrimp is just cooked through.

2. Spoon shrimp mixture into a food processor. Add remaining tablespoon butter, cream cheese, and rum; process mixture to a paste. Pack into decorative cup or crock. Serve immediately or cover and refrigerate up to 24 hours in advance. Bring to room temperature before serving. Serve with toasts or as open-face sandwich.

Per serving:

CARBOHYDRATES:	NET CARBS:	FIBER:	PROTEIN:	FAT:	CALORIES:
9.5 grams	5.5 gram	4 grams	23 grams	9.5 grams	216

Spinach Phyllo Triangles

Crunchy, creamy, and delicious, this spinach appetizer or side dish can be made and then frozen for up to 1 month before baking. If freezing, line a heavy aluminum jelly-roll pan or baking sheet with parchment or use disposable nonreactive aluminum-rimmed cookie sheets without lining.

PREP TIME: 45 minutes
COOK TIME: 12 to 15 minutes
8 servings (3 triangles per serving)

   1 (10-ounce) microwavable bag of fresh spinach, washed, or frozen chopped spinach thawed, and squeezed dry
   ½ cup (1 stick) butter, melted
   1 tablespoon extra-virgin olive oil
   2 garlic cloves, minced or pushed through a press
   ⅓ cup whole-milk ricotta cheese
   1 cup crumbled feta cheese (4 ounces)

⅛ teaspoon salt
⅛ teaspoon pepper
10 sheets spelt or whole-wheat phyllo dough
1½ teaspoons each sweet paprika and dried crumbled
  parsley, combined

1. Heat oven to 375° F. Brush a jelly-roll pan or baking sheet lightly with butter.
2. Cook spinach according to bag directions; squeeze dry, chop and place in a bowl. Combine oil and garlic in microwavable cup and microwave 30 to 40 seconds, just until garlic is aromatic; add to spinach. Mix in ricotta, feta, salt, and pepper in bowl; stir until ingredients are well combined.
3. Arrange phyllo sheets atop one another and cut crosswise into thirds. Cover 2 stacks with plastic wrap and a kitchen towel to keep them from drying out. Separate one strip from the exposed stack and brush it lightly with melted butter; fold in half lengthwise to form a narrow strip. Place a scant tablespoon of filling at one end and fold up flag-style to form a triangular pastry. Place on prepared sheet. Repeat process to make 28 triangles (you will have 2 phyllo strips left over). Brush tops and sides of triangles with butter every time you finish a row, and sprinkle lightly with paprika mixture. (If freezing, cover with plastic wrap, then heavy-duty foil, crimping edges tightly. Remove both coverings before baking, but do not defrost.)
4. Bake triangles 12 to 15 minutes (or 20 to 25 minutes if frozen) until golden and slightly puffed in centers.

TIP: Spelt, an ancient type of wheat, contains a more digestible type of gluten than modern wheat hybrids. Spelt phyllo is made from 100 percent spelt flour.

Per serving:

CARBOHY-DRATES:	NET CARBS:	FIBER:	PROTEIN:	FAT:	CALORIES:
12.5 grams	11 grams	1.5 grams	5.5 grams	17 grams	222

Blueberry Silver Dollar Pancakes

These are best hot off the griddle. However, leftovers can be frozen and warmed in a toaster oven. If you love banana pancakes, replace the blueberries with 1 small chopped banana, which adds an insignificant amount to the carb count.

PREP TIME: 10 minutes
COOK TIME: 4 minutes per batch
7 servings (4 pancakes per serving)

⅓ cup soy flour
⅓ cup whole-grain pastry flour
⅓ cup whole-wheat flour
¼ cup cornmeal
1 tablespoon granular sugar substitute
1½ teaspoons baking powder
¼ teaspoon salt
1 large egg
½ cup heavy cream mixed with ⅔ cup of water
2 tablespoons sour cream
2 tablespoons unsalted butter, melted
1 cup blueberries

1. Heat griddle over moderate heat. In a large bowl whisk together soy flour, pastry flour, whole-wheat flour, cornmeal, sugar substitute, baking powder, and salt.
2. In a bowl, whisk together the egg, cream mixture, sour cream, and butter. Pour wet ingredients into flour mixture. Mix just to combine (the batter can be a little lumpy). Stir in blueberries.
3. Lightly grease griddle. For each pancake, dollop out a heaping tablespoon of batter onto the griddle. Cook about 3 minutes, until bubbles appear on surface. Flip pancakes and cook 1 minute more.

Per serving:

CARBOHY-DRATES:	NET CARBS:	FIBER:	PROTEIN:	FAT:	CALORIES:
17 grams	14.5 grams	2.5 grams	5 grams	15.5 grams	192

Breakfast Smoothies

This creamy-rich smoothie is an easy, delicious way to add soy to your diet. Each serving provides about 8 milligrams of isoflavones, the hormonelike compounds that researchers believe help protect against some forms of cancer and heart disease, and which also alleviate symptoms of menopause. Silken tofu comes in a variety of consistencies; soft is your best option for smoothies.

PREP TIME: 5 minutes
4 servings (⅔ cup per serving)

> 1 cup plain whole-milk yogurt
> 2½ cups sliced strawberries (1 quart)
> 4 ounces silken tofu
> 2 packets sugar substitute, or more, to taste
> 8 ice cubes

1. In a blender, purée all ingredients, except ice cubes, on high until smooth.
2. Add cubes one at a time through feed tube, using ice-crusher feature on blender; blend until smooth.

Per serving:

CARBOHY-DRATES:	NET CARBS:	FIBER:	PROTEIN:	FAT:	CALORIES:
11.5 grams	9 grams	2.5 grams	4 grams	3 grams	86

Cherry Muffins

Freshly diced cherries add a nice fruitiness to these golden not-too-sweet muffins. Or use blueberries, if you prefer.

PREP TIME: 15 minutes
BAKE TIME: 25 to 30 minutes
8 servings

1 cup Atkins™ Bake Mix
½ cup whole-wheat flour
3 packets sugar substitute
2 teaspoons baking powder
½ teaspoon salt
½ teaspoon cinnamon
⅔ cup water
¼ teaspoon almond extract
½ cup (1 stick) unsalted butter
2 large eggs, at room temperature
½ cup pitted and diced fresh sweet cherries

1. Heat oven to 350° F. Coat 8 compartments of a nonstick muffin pan with cooking spray or grease; set aside. Whisk together bake mix, flour, sugar substitute, baking powder, salt, and cinnamon in bowl. Whisk water and extract in another bowl.
2. Beat butter with an electric mixer on medium-high speed until light and fluffy. Add eggs, one at a time; beat until smooth, about 1 to 2 minutes per egg. With mixer on medium, add flour and water mixtures in three additions, starting and ending with flour. Fold in cherries.
3. Divide batter in muffin compartments evenly. Bake 25 to 30 minutes until golden on top and toothpick inserted in centers comes out clean. Cool in pan 5 minutes; remove muffins with a small spatula.

Per serving:

CARBOHY-DRATES:	NET CARBS:	FIBER:	PROTEIN:	FAT:	CALORIES:
10.5 grams	8 grams	2.5 grams	12 grams	14 grams	210

Cinnamon Crumb Coffee Cake

This is an adaptation of a traditional Jewish sour cream coffee cake that's less easy to make. The combination of flours gives the cake a tender texture, and adding the crunchy sweet topping in two layers provides pockets of extra flavor throughout.

PREP TIME: 30 minutes
BAKE TIME: 40 minutes
12 servings

Cake:
¾ cup whole-grain pastry flour
¾ cup soy flour
½ cup whole-wheat flour
1 teaspoon baking powder
1 teaspoon baking soda
½ teaspoon salt
2 large eggs
1 teaspoon vanilla extract
1 cup sour cream
½ cup (1 stick) unsalted butter
1 cup granular sugar substitute

Topping:
½ cup quick-cooking oatmeal
1 cup granular sugar substitute
1½ cups pecans, coarsely chopped
¾ cup unsalted butter, softened
2 teaspoons ground cinnamon

1. Heat oven to 350° F. Grease a 9 × 13-inch baking pan. In a medium bowl, whisk together pastry flour, soy flour, whole-wheat flour, baking powder, baking soda, and salt. In a large liquid measuring cup whisk eggs, vanilla, and sour cream until well combined.

2. In a mixing bowl, with an electric mixer on medium, beat butter until smooth. Beat in sugar substitute. Alternately add the flour mixture and egg mixture to the butter, beginning and ending with the flour mixture.

3. For topping: with a fork, mix oatmeal, sugar substitute, pecans, butter, and cinnamon until well combined.

4. Spread two-thirds of the batter into the prepared pan. Sprinkle half the topping over batter and lightly swirl with a knife to create pockets of topping within the batter. Spoon remaining batter over topping, and sprinkle evenly with remaining topping. Bake about 40 minutes, or until a knife inserted in the center comes out clean.

5. Cool cake in pan set over a wire rack; serve warm or at room temperature. Cut into twelve pieces. Cake may be stored at room temperature 2 days, or frozen up to 2 months.

Per serving:

CARBOHY-DRATES:	NET CARBS:	FIBER:	PROTEIN:	FAT:	CALORIES:
20 grams	16 grams	4 grams	7.5 grams	36.5 grams	422

Creamy Baked Eggs

Baked, or shirred, eggs are incredibly easy to make and taste delicious. Once you've cracked them into the skillet you needn't worry about breaking the yolks. Because the oven's heat is constant, there's little chance they'll burn. The skillet will retain heat and continue to cook the eggs after they're out of the oven, so it's better to undercook them just slightly.

PREP TIME: 5 minutes
COOK TIME: 10 minutes
4 servings (2 eggs per serving)

> ¼ cup half-and-half
> 8 large eggs
> salt and pepper
> 1 cup grated Jarlsberg cheese, or other semisoft cheese

1. Heat oven to 450° F.
2. Pour cream into a 9-inch ovenproof skillet. Carefully crack the eggs into the skillet. Season with salt and pepper. Sprinkle evenly with cheese.
3. Bake about 10 minutes, until eggs are set. If you prefer soft yolks, remove the eggs after 9 minutes; for firmer yolks, 11 minutes is sufficient.

Per serving:

CARBOHY-DRATES:	NET CARBS:	FIBER:	PROTEIN:	FAT:	CALORIES:
2.5 grams	2.5 grams	0 grams	21 grams	19.5 grams	277

"Dutch Baby" Baked Pancake

A "Dutch Baby" is a cross between a giant baked pancake and a popover. If you've never made one, you're in for a treat. This is a great brunch dish and always a crowd pleaser as it emerges golden and puffed from the oven. The apple filling is wonderful, but you can do without it if you want to reduce the Net Carbs by 7.5 grams per serving.

PREP TIME: 15 minutes
BAKE TIME: 15 minutes
6 servings

> 3 tablespoons unsalted butter, divided
> 3 large eggs
> ½ cup whole-grain pastry flour
> ¼ cup soy flour
> ¼ teaspoon salt
> ½ cup heavy cream
> 5 tablespoons granular sugar substitute, divided
> ½ teaspoon cinnamon
> 2 Golden Delicious apples, peeled, cored, and cut into
>   thin slices

1. Heat oven to 425° F. Place 2 tablespoons of the butter in a 12-inch nonstick ovenproof skillet; set aside. Whisk eggs, pastry flour, soy flour, salt, cream, 3 tablespoons of the sugar substitute, and ¼ cup water together until smooth.
2. Place skillet in oven until butter melts. Pour batter into skillet. Bake 15 minutes.
3. While pancake is baking, melt remaining tablespoon of butter in a medium skillet over medium heat. Add remaining 2 tablespoons sugar substitute, cinnamon, and ¼ cup water. Bring to a boil; add apples. Cook 15 minutes over a low heat, stirring occasionally, until apples are tender and most of the liquid has evaporated.
4. After removing pancake from the oven, spoon apples into the center. Serve immediately.

Per serving:

CARBOHY-DRATES:	NET CARBS:	FIBER:	PROTEIN:	FAT:	CALORIES:
17.5 grams	14.5 grams	3 grams	6.5 grams	16.5 grams	240

Florentine Omelets

You might be tempted to make one big omelet and divide it into four servings, but don't yield to it. Omelets should always be made individually. Smaller omelets cook more evenly, and they are easier to fold.

PREP TIME: 10 minutes
COOK TIME: 8 to 12 minutes
4 servings

Filling:
2 (7 to 10 ounces each) microwavable bags spinach
leaves, cooked according to bag directions
1 tablespoon butter
¼ cup chopped onion
1 garlic clove, minced
½ teaspoon salt
¼ teaspoon pepper
4 ounces diced Italian fontina or Asiago Fresco cheese

4 tablespoons butter
8 large eggs
½ cup water
1 teaspoon salt

1. For the filling, drain cooked spinach, then squeeze dry on paper towels. Transfer spinach to a bowl. Heat butter in a 10-inch nonstick skillet over medium heat, add onion, and cook 3 minutes until lightly browned. Add garlic, salt, and pepper and cook 30 seconds more. Stir into spinach, then toss in cheese, and stir again.
2. Wipe out skillet. Melt 1 tablespoon of the butter over medium heat. Whisk 2 eggs with 2 tablespoons water and ⅛ teaspoon salt in small bowl. Pour egg mixture into the skillet and cook 1 minute until bottom is set. Push back on one side

of egg and allow loose egg to flow into exposed skillet. Cook 1 to 2 minutes until top is set. Add one-quarter of filling on one side of omelet, run knife around edge and fold over to cover filling; slide out onto platter. Repeat steps three more times for a total of 4 omelets. Serve immediately.

TIP: The protein in an egg is complete—it provides the eight essential amino acids that the human body cannot produce. Because eggs provide them in balanced proportions, they are used as the standard for evaluating proteins in other foods. Eggs also contain omega-3 fatty acids.

Per serving:

CARBOHY-DRATES:	NET CARBS:	FIBER:	PROTEIN:	FAT:	CALORIES:
8 grams	4 grams	4 grams	24 grams	34.5 grams	428

Lemon Zucchini Bread

The addition of lemon zest, instead of the usual cinnamon, gives this tea bread a summery flavor. Be sure to use only the yellow part of the peel; the white pith underneath tastes bitter.

PREP TIME: 15 minutes
BAKE TIME: 55 minutes
12 servings

¾ cup whole-grain pastry flour
¾ cup granular sugar substitute
½ cup soy flour
¼ cup whole-wheat flour
2 teaspoons baking powder
½ teaspoon baking soda
½ teaspoon salt
1 zucchini, coarsely grated (about 1½ cups)

1 teaspoon freshly grated lemon rind
⅓ cup canola oil
2 eggs

1. Heat oven to 350° F. Grease an 8 × 4-inch loaf pan. In a bowl whisk together pastry flour, sugar substitute, soy flour, whole-wheat flour, baking powder, baking soda, and salt to combine. Stir in zucchini and rind.
2. In a small bowl whisk oil and eggs. With a rubber spatula, combine egg and flour mixtures until flour is completely incorporated.
3. Spoon into prepared pan and bake 55 minutes or until a toothpick inserted in center comes out clean. Cool in pan on wire rack 10 minutes. Turn out onto rack to cool completely. Cut into 12 slices.

Per serving:

CARBOHY- DRATES:	NET CARBS:	FIBER:	PROTEIN:	FAT:	CALORIES:
10.5 grams	9 grams	1.5 grams	4 grams	8 grams	124

Morning Muffins

These muffins will have you leaping out of bed in the morning! Lightly sweet, chewy, and studded with currants, they're perfect with cream cheese and low carb preserves. Store at room temperature for 2 days, or wrap and freeze for up to 2 months.

PREP TIME: 15 minutes
BAKE TIME: 20 minutes
12 servings (1 muffin per serving)

½ cup whole-grain pastry flour
¾ cup whole-wheat flour
¼ cup sugar substitute

1½ teaspoons baking soda
1 cup heavy cream
¼ cup vegetable oil
1 large egg
2 medium carrots, grated
¼ cup currants

1. Heat oven to 375° F. Line a 12-compartment muffin pan with cupcake liners. Whisk together pastry flour, whole-wheat flour, sugar substitute, and baking soda. In a large measuring cup, mix cream, oil, and egg.
2. Pour wet ingredients into flour mixture; stir just to combine. Stir in carrots and currants.
3. Pour batter into muffin pan. Bake about 20 minutes or until a toothpick inserted in the center of a muffin comes out clean. Let rest 5 minutes, turn out onto a rack to cool completely.

Per serving:

CARBOHYDRATES:	NET CARBS:	FIBER:	PROTEIN:	FAT:	CALORIES:
13.5 grams	11.5 grams	2 grams	3 grams	12.5 grams	172

Pecan Buttermilk Waffles

As this batter sits, it gets stiffer and thicker. If necessary, stir in water, 1 tablespoon at a time, to return batter to a pourable consistency. Waffles may be frozen and crisped in a toaster oven to reheat.

PREP TIME: 10 minutes
COOK TIME: 5 to 7 minutes per batch
Yield: 8 waffles

½ cup pecans
1½ cups soy flour

2 tablespoons granular sugar substitute
1 tablespoon baking powder
1 teaspoon baking soda
½ teaspoon salt
1 cup buttermilk
1 cup heavy cream
4 tablespoons unsalted butter, melted
3 eggs, lightly beaten

1. Heat nonstick waffle iron. In a food processor, process all dry ingredients until pecans are finely ground. Transfer to a bowl.
2. Stir buttermilk, cream, butter, and eggs into the flour mixture to combine.
3. For each waffle, pour about ½ cup batter in center of waffle iron. Cook according to manufacturer's instructions, until no more steam appears and waffle is crisp. Repeat with remaining batter.

Per serving:

CARBOHY-DRATES:	NET CARBS:	FIBER:	PROTEIN:	FAT:	CALORIES:
9 grams	7 grams	2 grams	10.5 grams	27 grams	312

Ricotta-Strawberry Breakfast Sandwich

Better than strawberry-stuffed French toast—and there is no need to soak this stuffed sandwich, just dip and pan-grill. Draining the ricotta thickens it, providing a better texture for cooking.

PREP TIME: 15 minutes
COOK TIME: 4 minutes
4 servings

1 cup whole-milk ricotta cheese
2 large eggs
¼ cup heavy cream
3 tablespoons granular sugar substitute divided
½ teaspoon ground cinnamon
8 slices low carb white bread
4 tablespoons no-sugar-added strawberry jam (such as
   Steele's)
1 tablespoon butter

1. Spoon ricotta onto triple thickness of paper towels, fold paper over top, and let stand 10 minutes.
2. Whisk eggs, cream, and 2 tablespoons of the sugar substitute in a pie plate or shallow bowl.
3. Scrape ricotta off paper towels into bowl, stir in remaining 1 tablespoon sugar substitute, and cinnamon. Spread ¼ cup ricotta filling onto each of 4 slices bread, and spread jam on remaining slices. Close sandwiches, by placing inverted jam slices over filling.
4. Melt 1½ teaspoons of the butter in a 12-inch nonstick skillet over medium heat. Dip both sides and edges of each sandwich into egg mixture; let excess drain. Cook sandwiches for 2 minutes, until golden. Flip sandwiches; add remaining butter, and cook 2 minutes more. Cut sandwiches in half diagonally and serve immediately.

Per serving:

CARBOHY-DRATES:	NET CARBS:	FIBER:	PROTEIN:	FAT:	CALORIES:
21 grams	13 grams	8 grams	24.5 grams	23 grams	387

Vegetable Quiche

Quiches are menu chameleons: They fit in anywhere and are perfect for breakfast, lunch, or as a side dish at dinner. They are also good hot, cold, or at room temperature. This one is beautiful as well, with its variety of vegetables forming a colorful mosaic.

PREP TIME: 30 minutes
BAKE TIME: 1 hour
6 servings

½ cup whole-grain pastry flour
½ cup soy flour
¼ cup whole-wheat flour
½ cup (1 stick) cold unsalted butter, cut into 16 pieces
2 tablespoons ice water
2 slices bacon
¼ pound sliced mushrooms
1 small onion, chopped
¼ red bell pepper, chopped
1 cup heavy cream
3 eggs
¼ teaspoon salt
¼ teaspoon ground black pepper
¼ cup chopped parsley
½ cup (2 ounces) Cheddar cheese, grated
1 medium beefsteak tomato, thinly sliced

1. Heat oven to 425° F. In a large bowl whisk together flours. Cut butter in with a pastry blender or two knives until pieces are the size of peas. Add ice water; stir to combine.
2. Transfer crust mixture to a 9-inch pie plate and press along bottom and sides to form a crust. Place in freezer to harden, about 15 minutes. Bake covered with aluminum foil for 15 minutes. Remove from oven; take off foil. Reduce oven temperature to 325° F.
3. While crust is baking, cook bacon in a large skillet over medium heat for 5 minutes or until crisp. Drain on paper towels; crumble and set aside. Add mushrooms and onion to skillet. Cook on medium high heat about 8 minutes, until most of the liquid has evaporated. Add red pepper; cook 2 minutes more.

4. In a bowl whisk cream, eggs, salt, pepper, and parsley. Stir in cheese and bacon. Spoon cooked vegetables on bottom of partially baked crust. Pour in egg mixture. Top with tomato slices. Bake quiche 45 minutes or until middle is just set. If the crust seems to be over-browning, cover edges of crust with foil. Cut into six wedges.

Per serving:

CARBOHYDRATES:	NET CARBS:	FIBER:	PROTEIN:	FAT:	CALORIES:
16 grams	13.5 grams	2.5 grams	9.5 grams	23 grams	306

Zucchini Frittata

This Old World Italian dish is a staple in many Italian American homes. Easy does it when cooking eggs though: Overcooking makes them tough and rubbery. Serve with buttered low carb or whole-wheat toast.

PREP TIME: 10 minutes
COOK TIME: 20 to 25 minutes
4 servings

    2 tablespoons olive oil
    2 medium zucchini, cut in ¼-inch-thick rounds
    ½ cup sliced scallions
    1 teaspoon salt
    ¼ teaspoon crushed red pepper
    8 large eggs, lightly beaten with 2 tablespoons water
    4 ounces goat cheese, crumbled
    ¼ cup packed basil leaves, thinly sliced

1. Heat oven to 350° F. Heat 1 tablespoon of the oil in a 12-inch nonstick ovenproof skillet over medium-high heat. Cook zucchini 10 minutes, turning slices as they brown. Add

scallions; sprinkle with ½ teaspoon of the salt and crushed red pepper. Cook 2 to 4 minutes, until zucchini is golden and tender; transfer to a bowl. Wipe down skillet.

2. Heat broiler with rack in upper level (but not the closest to heat source). Whisk eggs, water, goat cheese, basil, and remaining ½ teaspoon salt in a bowl. Heat remaining 1 tablespoon oil in skillet over medium-high heat; add egg mixture and cook 1½ minutes to set bottom. Spoon zucchini mixture evenly over top; reduce heat to medium-low, cover, and cook 5 to 6 minutes until edge is set and puffed. Uncover, transfer to broiler, and broil 1 to 1½ minutes just until top is set and lightly golden. Cut into four wedges. Serve immediately.

Per serving:

CARBOHY-DRATES:	NET CARBS:	FIBER:	PROTEIN:	FAT:	CALORIES:
5.5 grams	4 grams	1.5 grams	19 grams	23.5 grams	310

Asian Vegetable Bowl

Most Asian soups are light, filling, and take very little time to prepare. If you enjoy a little heat, add a few drops of Asian chili oil before serving.

PREP TIME: 10 minutes
COOK TIME: 10 minutes
6 servings (1⅓ cups per serving)

    6 cups reduced-sodium chicken broth
    2 tablespoons lite (reduced-sodium) soy sauce
    2 cups sliced bok choy (Chinese cabbage; use half
      leaves and half stems)
    1 (4-ounce) package exotic mixed sliced mushrooms
    2 quarter-size slices fresh ginger

1 garlic clove, very thinly sliced
1 Thai or Serrano chili, seeded and minced
1 cup diced tomatoes
½ cup green onions, sliced
½ of 1 (12.3-ounce) box tofu cut into ½-inch dice
1 medium carrot, peeled and shredded
4 teaspoons chopped fresh cilantro, optional

1. In a large saucepan, bring broth and soy sauce to a boil. Reduce heat; add bok choy, mushrooms, ginger, garlic, and chili; simmer 5 minutes until bok choy is tender-crisp and mushrooms are tender.
2. Add tomatoes, green onions, tofu, and carrot; heat through for 1 minute. Sprinkle with cilantro, if desired.

TIP: All ingredients for this soup can be found in your supermarket. If you can't find a prepacked shiitake-oyster mushroom combo, mix 2 ounces of each type of mushroom or simply substitute with a 4-ounce package of sliced shiitake mushrooms.

Per serving:

CARBOHY-DRATES:	NET CARBS:	FIBER:	PROTEIN:	FAT:	CALORIES:
7 grams	5.5 grams	1.5 grams	6.5 grams	2.5 grams	71

Barley Vegetable Soup

Barley, like all whole grains, is a concentrated source of carbohydrates. Adding it to a soup is an ideal way to enjoy it while keeping your carbs under control. The ¼ cup in this recipe cooks up to ½ cup and provides 26 grams of Net Carbs, meaning a manageable 4 grams per serving.

PREP TIME: 20 minutes
COOK TIME: 1 hour
6 servings (1 cup per serving)

¼ cup raw pearl barley
1 tablespoon butter
2 cups sliced mushrooms
1 cup chopped onion
1 garlic clove, chopped
4 cups reduced-sodium chicken broth
½ cup diced tomato
2 cups coarsely chopped kale

1. Bring 1½ cups water to boil in saucepan; add barley, cover, and reduce heat. Simmer 30 minutes until liquid is absorbed and barley is tender but not mushy.
2. Melt butter in large saucepan over medium heat. Add mushrooms and onion; cook 4 to 5 minutes until vegetables are tender. Add garlic; cook 1 minute more.
3. Stir in broth, diced tomato and barley, bring to a boil, and reduce heat to low. Cover and cook 15 minutes. Add kale and simmer 5 minutes more until kale is tender.

TIP: This soup may be kept up to 5 days in the refrigerator or frozen up to 2 months. Cool soup and store in airtight container.

Per serving:

CARBOHY-DRATES:	NET CARBS:	FIBER:	PROTEIN:	FAT:	CALORIES:
14.5 grams	12 grams	2.5 grams	5 grams	3.5 grams	100

Chicken and Sun-Dried Tomato Quesadillas

If you don't have cooked chicken in the fridge, just pick up a small rotisserie chicken at the supermarket. Since prepared chickens contain varying amounts of salt, start with the smaller amount indicated in the recipe, and adjust accordingly.

PREP TIME: 10 minutes
BAKE TIME: 10 minutes
4 servings

3 tablespoons mayonnaise
3 tablespoons sun-dried tomato pesto
½ cup finely diced sweet onion
1½ teaspoons fresh lime juice
¼ to ½ teaspoon salt
1½ cups shredded pepper jack cheese
3 cups sliced or shredded cooked chicken
8 low carb garlic-herb tortillas

1. Heat oven to 425° F. Combine mayonnaise, pesto, onion, lime juice, and salt in a large bowl. Fold in chicken and cheese until evenly mixed.

2. Lightly brush one side of each tortilla with olive oil or lightly spray with nonstick cooking spray. Place 4 tortillas oiled side down on a baking sheet. Divide chicken mixture evenly over tortillas (about ¾ cup per tortilla). Top with remaining tortillas, oiled side up. Bake 10 minutes until golden. Serve hot.

TIP: For variety, substitute regular basil pesto for sun-dried tomato pesto and replace pepper jack cheese with provolone.

Per serving:

CARBOHY-DRATES:	NET CARBS:	FIBER:	PROTEIN:	FAT:	CALORIES:
28.5 grams	10 grams	18.5 grams	49.5 grams	32 grams	558

Croque Monsieur

We've put a new twist on the classic French snack sandwich by adding sauerkraut for a spicier taste and using smoked gouda instead of Gruyère cheese.

PREP TIME: 5 minutes
COOK TIME: 8 minutes
4 servings

    1 tablespoon butter
    1½ teaspoons whole-wheat flour
    ¼ cup heavy cream
    1 cup coarsely shredded smoked gouda
    8 slices low carb rye or white bread
    1 cup sauerkraut, well drained
    ¼ pound sliced ham
    4 teaspoons spicy mustard

1. Melt butter in small saucepan over low heat, stir in flour, and cook 30 seconds. Whisk in cream. Bring to a boil; boil 1 minute. Cool mixture slightly; stir in cheese.

2. Spread all bread slices with cheese mixture. Top four slices with sauerkraut then with ham. Spread mustard on top of ham. Close sandwiches with remaining bread slices.

3. Heat large nonstick skillet over medium heat; lightly coat with cooking spray. Add sandwiches, and cook 2 minutes per side, until golden in color and cheese has melted. Remove pan from heat. Let stand 1 minute more if necessary, to fully melt cheese. Cut sandwiches in half and serve.

Per serving:

CARBOHYDRATES:	NET CARBS:	FIBER:	PROTEIN:	FAT:	CALORIES:
12 grams	7 grams	5 grams	19.5 grams	19.5 grams	294

Eggplant, Mushroom, and Goat Cheese Sandwiches

Small Italian eggplants or slender Japanese ones work best in this recipe because they are mild-tasting and do not need to be presalted to draw out the bitter juices as larger eggplants do. Pairing eggplant with mushrooms brings out its mellowness; goat cheese provides a tangy flavor accent.

PREP TIME: 15 minutes
COOK TIME: 15 minutes
4 servings

> 2 tablespoons extra-virgin olive oil
> 3 cups diced eggplant
> 1 (3.5-ounce) package shiitake mushrooms, stems removed and discarded
> 1 large garlic clove, pushed through a press
> Scant ½ teaspoon salt
> Freshly ground pepper to taste
> 4 ounces Montrachet (fresh) goat cheese
> 8 slices low carb white bread, lightly toasted

1. Heat oil in a 12-inch nonstick skillet over medium heat. Add eggplant and mushrooms. Cover and cook 9 to 10 minutes, stirring once, halfway through cooking time. Add garlic and sprinkle with salt and a few twists of the peppermill. Cook, uncovered, 2 minutes more or until eggplant is very tender and lightly browned.
2. Spread 2 tablespoons goat cheese on each of four slices of toast. Top cheese evenly with eggplant mixture (about ¼ cup) and cover with remaining slices of toast. Serve warm.

TIP: If you are not partial to the taste of goat cheese, substitute herb-flavored cream cheese.

Per serving:

CARBOHYDRATES:	NET CARBS:	FIBER:	PROTEIN:	FAT:	CALORIES:
19.5 grams	9.5 grams	10 grams	20.5 grams	17 grams	302

Gazpacho

This version of the classic dish features a smooth purée studded with sweet diced tomatoes and a topping of finely diced pepper and cucumber. For the smoothest possible texture, start your blender on low and gradually increase speed.

PREP TIME: 20 minutes
4 servings (1½ cups per serving)

1 slice low carb white bread, crust removed
1 cucumber, peeled and seeded
3 cups diced ripe tomatoes, divided
½ cup coarsely chopped red bell pepper
1 medium onion, chopped and rinsed in colander under
  hot tap water for 20 seconds
1 large garlic clove
2 tablespoons extra-virgin olive oil
2 tablespoons white balsamic vinegar
1 to 2 teaspoons minced jalapeño pepper
½ teaspoon salt
¼ cup finely diced green bell pepper
4 teaspoons minced fresh cilantro

1. Soak bread with water and squeeze out excess. Coarsely chop half the cucumber and purée with half the tomato, red bell pepper, onion, garlic, soaked bread, oil, vinegar, jalapeño, and salt in a blender until smooth.
2. Finely dice the remaining half-cucumber.
3. Pour purée into 4 bowls and evenly divide remaining

diced tomatoes on top. Sprinkle centers with finely diced cucumber, green bell pepper, and cilantro. Serve cold or at room temperature.

Per serving:

CARBOHY-DRATES:	NET CARBS:	FIBER:	PROTEIN:	FAT:	CALORIES:
14.5 grams	10.5 grams	4 grams	4 grams	8 grams	134

Golden Onion Soup

To live up to its name, this delicious soup uses chicken broth instead of the more typical beef broth. Slowly cooking the onions allows them to caramelize, which produces a sweet, intense flavor.

PREP TIME: 10 minutes
COOK TIME: 50 to 55 minutes
4 servings (1⅓ cups per serving)

2 tablespoons butter
4 medium onions, thinly sliced
4 cups reduced-sodium chicken broth
½ teaspoon minced fresh rosemary or ¼ teaspoon dried
½ teaspoon salt
⅛ teaspoon freshly ground black pepper
8 slices low carb white bread, crusts removed
½ pound Gruyère cheese, coarsely shredded

1. Melt butter in a large saucepan over medium heat until it just begins to color. Add onions, reduce heat to medium-low, and cook, stirring occasionally, 30 to 35 minutes until onions are very wilted, golden, and tender.
2. Add broth, rosemary and salt; bring to a boil. Reduce heat, cover, and simmer 20 minutes.

3. During last 5 minutes of soup-cooking time, heat broiler. Arrange bread slices on a baking sheet. Toast bread under broiler, 4 inches from heat source, 20 to 40 seconds per side. Turn broiler off. Top each toasted slice with cheese. Return baking sheet to hot oven until cheese melts (about 30 to 50 seconds).

4. To serve: Place 1 bread slice in bottom of each soup bowl, ladle in soup, and top with another bread slice.

Per serving:

CARBOHYDRATES:	NET CARBS:	FIBER:	PROTEIN:	FAT:	CALORIES:
25 grams	15 grams	10 grams	35.5 grams	30 grams	498

Grilled Ham and Cheese with Asparagus

This hearty sandwich makes a great quick dinner when paired with soup or a salad. Look for medium-thin asparagus; if unavailable, split the thicker variety in half lengthwise.

PREP TIME: 10 minutes
COOK TIME: 10 minutes
4 servings

    1½ tablespoons mayonnaise
    1 tablespoon finely chopped fresh parsley
    8 slices low carb bread
    ½ pound thinly sliced baked ham or any deli ham
    4 ounces fontina cheese, cut into 4 slices
    1 bunch (about 8 spears) medium thin asparagus,
      trimmed and steamed 4 to 5 minutes until tender

1. Combine mayonnaise and parsley in cup; spread on one side of bread and place 4 slices, spread side down, on waxed paper.

2. Arrange ham on plain side of the 4 slices, top with asparagus and cheese, and cover with remaining bread, spread side up.

3. Heat a large nonstick skillet over medium heat. Pan-grill sandwiches 1½ to 2 minutes per side until golden and cheese has melted. If cheese is not completely melted, remove skillet from heat and let sandwiches stand 1 minute more. Serve.

TIP: If asparagus is not in season, roasted red peppers (preferably homemade), cut in half, would make a tasty and colorful substitute.

Per serving:

CARBOHY-DRATES:	NET CARBS:	FIBER:	PROTEIN:	FAT:	CALORIES:
16.5 grams	8 grams	8.5 grams	32 grams	19 grams	353

Lentil Soup

Swiss chard paired with lentils makes this soup tasty—and both are an excellent source of potassium, fiber, and iron.

PREP TIME: 15 minutes
COOK TIME: 40 minutes
6 servings (1 scant cup per serving)

1 tablespoon butter
1 medium onion, chopped
1 celery stalk, finely diced
1 garlic clove, pushed through a press
1 (32-ounce) container reduced-sodium chicken broth
¾ cup lentils
4 cups chopped Swiss chard
1 small tomato, chopped

1 teaspoon red wine vinegar
½ teaspoon salt
Grated Parmesan cheese, optional

1. Melt butter in 3-quart saucepan over medium heat. Cook onion and celery, covered, 4 minutes, until just golden; add garlic and cook 30 seconds more.
2. Add broth and lentils and bring to a boil. Reduce heat and simmer, covered, 20 minutes until lentils are almost tender. Add Swiss chard and tomato, cover, and cook 15 to 18 minutes more until lentils and chard are tender. Stir in vinegar and salt. Sprinkle with cheese, if desired.

TIP: Adding a splash of any type of vinegar to most soups just before serving perks up the flavor without being detectable.

Per serving:

CARBOHYDRATES:	NET CARBS:	FIBER:	PROTEIN:	FAT:	CALORIES:
17.5 grams	11.5 grams	6 grams	9 grams	3.5 grams	130

Mediterranean Sandwiches

Puréed cannellini beans may seem like an unusual sandwich ingredient, but wait till you try them! Pepper jack cheese adds creamy spiciness and roasted peppers provide color and texture in this hearty, filling vegetarian sandwich. If you can, use extra-virgin olive oil—its fruity flavor adds just the right note.

PREP TIME: 10 minutes
COOK TIME: 1 minute
4 servings

2 teaspoons extra-virgin olive oil
1 medium garlic clove, minced or pushed through a
  press
¼ teaspoon cumin seeds
½ cup cannellini beans, rinsed and drained
1 cup shredded pepper jack cheese
8 slices low carb white bread, lightly toasted
4 roasted red pepper halves (jarred are fine; pat dry
  before using)

1. Heat broiler. In a microwavable cup, microwave oil, garlic, and cumin seeds until aromatic, 20 to 30 seconds. Combine oil with beans in a food processor, and blend to a thick paste.
2. Mix bean paste with cheese in a bowl. Mixture will be thick. Spread evenly on 4 slices of toast. Arrange on a baking sheet and broil 4 inches from heat source for 30 to 50 seconds, just until golden. Top with enough roasted pepper pepper halves (or pieces) to cover in a single layer; top with remaining toast slices. Serve at room temperature.

Per serving:

CARBOHY-DRATES:	NET CARBS:	FIBER:	PROTEIN:	FAT:	CALORIES:
22 grams	12.5 grams	9.5 grams	21.5 grams	14 grams	289

Minestrone Soup

Ready in less than half an hour, this hearty soup is made primarily with ingredients kept in most pantries. Adding the zucchini after bringing the soup to a boil and cooking it for only 5 minutes keeps its color bright green.

PREP TIME: 10 minutes
COOK TIME: 15 minutes
4 servings (1⅓ cups per serving)

2 slices bacon, chopped
½ tablespoon olive or canola oil
1 medium onion, chopped
2 cups sliced mushrooms (5 ounces)
3 cups reduced-sodium chicken broth
2 cups coarsely chopped escarole
1 cup cannellini beans, rinsed and drained
2 plum tomatoes, cut into ¼-inch dice
1 small zucchini, cut into ¼-inch dice
Grated Parmesan cheese

1. In a large skillet, cook bacon in oil until crisp. Add onion and cook 2 to 3 minutes until softened. Add mushrooms and cook 5 minutes until softened.
2. Add broth, escarole, beans, and tomato. Bring to a boil. Reduce heat, add zucchini, and simmer 5 minutes. Sprinkle with cheese before serving.

TIP: Minestrone lends itself to variations, and you may substitute ingredients depending on what you have on hand: spinach or chard instead of escarole or pink beans instead of cannellini, for example.

Per serving:

CARBOHY-DRATES:	NET CARBS:	FIBER:	PROTEIN:	FAT:	CALORIES:
17 grams	12 grams	5 grams	8 grams	5 grams	141

Panini

Panini are grilled and pressed sandwiches native to Italy. They are perfect for lunch or a light supper. Roasting the onions gives them a sweet, deep flavor. Any leftovers would be delicious with grilled meats.

PREP TIME: 5 minutes
BAKE TIME: 25 minutes
COOK TIME: 5 minutes
4 servings

1 red onion, cut into 1-inch chunks
2 teaspoons olive or canola oil
8 slices low carb white bread, crusts removed
8 tablespoons artichoke or basil pesto
16 very thin slices prosciutto or Genoa salami
4 ounces Asiago fresco, fontina, or mozzarella cheese,
    cut in ¼-inch-thick slices

1. Heat oven to 425° F. Toss onion with 1 teaspoon of the oil in a broiler pan. Bake 25 minutes, stirring once, until charred in spots and tender. Cool.

2. Spread bread slices with pesto (about 1 tablespoon per slice). Top 4 bread slices with one-quarter of the onions, one-quarter of the prosciutto, and one-quarter of the cheese. Cover with remaining bread slices.

3. Heat remaining 1 teaspoon oil in a 12-inch nonstick skillet over medium heat. Add sandwiches and cook 2 to 2½ minutes per side, pressing down frequently with a spatula, until cheese has melted and sandwiches are deep golden in color. Cut each sandwich in half diagonally and serve.

TIP: Serve with cream of broccoli or tomato soup or a salad of radicchio and arugula.

Per serving:

CARBOHY-DRATES:	NET CARBS:	FIBER:	PROTEIN:	FAT:	CALORIES:
19.5 grams	10 grams	9.5 grams	31 grams	30.5 grams	458

Roast Beef Sandwiches

Spicy and hearty, these sandwiches include marinated artichoke hearts and fresh ripe tomato. The quantity of meat
and veggies is balanced in this recipe, but feel free to add
more roast beef if you prefer.

PREP TIME: 10 minutes
4 servings

> 2 tablespoons mayonnaise
> 1 tablespoon chopped sun-dried tomatoes in oil, well
>   drained
> ½ cup marinated artichoke hearts, well drained and
>   chopped
> 1 small tomato, chopped
> 8 slices low carb white bread, toasted
> ½ pound sliced roast beef

1. Combine mayonnaise and sun-dried tomato in a cup. In a
separate bowl, combine the artichoke and tomato.
2. Spread mayonnaise evenly on 4 slices of bread. Top with
roast beef, then artichoke mixture; cover with remaining
bread. Cut sandwiches in half and serve.

TIP: This recipe works equally well with sliced chicken or
turkey. To reduce the Net Carb count by 3 grams, make
open-face sandwiches.

Per serving:

CARBOHY-DRATES:	NET CARBS:	FIBER:	PROTEIN:	FAT:	CALORIES:
18 grams	9 grams	9 grams	26.5 grams	12 grams	277

Roasted Chicken and Feta Cheese Wrap

These wraps are both tasty and colorful. For maximum flavor and texture purchase a premium salsa.

PREP TIME: 10 minutes
COOK TIME: 10 minutes
4 servings

1 tablespoon olive oil
1 medium red onion, cut into thin wedges
1 medium red pepper, cut into thin strips
½ cup corn kernels
1 roasted chicken breast half, skin and bones removed
   and chicken torn into large shreds (about 1 cup)
⅓ cup roasted tomatillo or roasted green salsa
¾ cup crumbled feta cheese (about 3 ounces)
4 low carb flour tortillas

1. Heat oil in a 12-inch nonstick skillet over medium-high heat. Add onion and pepper; cook 4 minutes. Add corn and cook 2 to 4 more minutes until charred in spots and peppers are tender. Cool slightly and transfer to a bowl. Wipe down skillet.
2. Toss vegetables with chicken, salsa, and feta cheese.
3. Cook tortillas, two at a time, in the skillet over medium-high heat for 40 to 60 seconds until crisp on one side only. Remove from pan and divide filling among tortillas. Place on crisped side and fold up. Return the folded, filled tortillas to the skillet and cook 1 to 2 minutes, turning once, until golden and lightly crisped on both sides.

TIP: This is a great way to use leftover cooked chicken. If you don't have any on hand, look for Cryovac-packaged roasted chicken breast in the refrigerator case at your supermarket.

Per serving:

CARBOHY-DRATES:	NET CARBS:	FIBER:	PROTEIN:	FAT:	CALORIES:
23 grams	11 grams	12 grams	20 grams	11.5 grams	248

Roasted Red Pepper Soup

Roasting intensifies the flavor and sweetness of most vegetables. The peppers and tomatoes can be peeled after roasting or, for even easier removal of the skins, after simmering. (The peels will slip right off when pulled with a fork.) Red peppers are high in vitamin C and tomatoes are an excellent source of lycopene.

PREP TIME: 10 minutes
BAKE TIME: 30 minutes
COOK TIME: 12 minutes
4 servings (about ¾ cup per serving)

    3 large red bell peppers
    2 plum tomatoes, halved lengthwise
    1 onion, quartered
    3 large garlic cloves, peeled
    1 tablespoon canola oil
    1 (15-ounce) can reduced-sodium chicken broth
    1 teaspoon balsamic vinegar
    ¾ teaspoon salt
    ⅛ teaspoon black pepper
    1 tablespoon heavy or whipping cream
    ¼ cup very thinly sliced basil, for garnish

1. Heat oven to 425° F. Toss peppers, tomatoes, onion, and garlic with oil. Spread on a broiler pan in a single layer. Roast 30 minutes, until vegetables are tender and caramelized.

2. Transfer vegetables to saucepan and add broth; bring to a simmer. Cover and cook 10 minutes. Remove peels.

3. Transfer to a blender; add vinegar, salt, and pepper. Purée on low for 30 seconds. Increase speed to high; puree until smooth. Add cream and pulse just to blend. Return to saucepan until just heated through. Garnish with a small nest of basil in center of soup, if desired, before serving.

Per serving:

CARBOHYDRATES:	NET CARBS:	FIBER:	PROTEIN:	FAT:	CALORIES:
14 grams	10.5 grams	3.5 grams	3.5 grams	6 grams	118

Seafood Chowder

This is a delicate chowder, lighter than most. It features a lively-tasting clam broth enriched with cream and studded with big chunks of tender white fish.

PREP TIME: 20 minutes
COOK TIME: 30 minutes
6 servings (about 1 cup each)

1 dozen cherrystone clams, scrubbed
4 slices bacon
1 medium onion, chopped
½ medium carrot, finely diced
2 large garlic cloves, minced or pushed through a press
½ cup dry white wine
1 (27-ounce) can or 3 cups bottled clam broth
¾ cup cubed Yukon Gold potatoes (about ½-inch dice)
1 teaspoon minced fresh thyme or ½ teaspoon dried
1 pound haddock or halibut fillet, cut into 2-inch chunks
½ cup heavy cream

1. Place clams and 1 cup of water in a nonreactive stockpot with a tight-fitting lid. Set over high heat and cook 7 to 9 minutes, stirring once halfway through, until clams open. Cool. Remove clams from shells and chop. Strain pan juice through fine sieve into a bowl, add clams to bowl, and set aside.

2. Cook bacon in a large saucepan until crisp. Remove, chop, set aside. Add onion and carrot to drippings; cook 6 to 8 minutes over medium heat. Add garlic, cook 30 seconds. Add wine and boil 1 minute. Add canned clam broth and potatoes; bring to a boil. Reduce heat and simmer 10 minutes until potatoes are tender.

3. Add fish and thyme; cover and simmer 5 minutes. Add cream and reserved clams with their juice. Cook 1 to 2 minutes until clams are lightly cooked and tender and soup is heated through. Divide among 6 bowls and sprinkle with bacon.

Per serving:

CARBOHYDRATES:	NET CARBS:	FIBER:	PROTEIN:	FAT:	CALORIES:
8.5 grams	7.5 grams	1 gram	25 grams	14.5 grams	281

Spicy Turkey Club

Our updated version of an old classic uses a spicy garlic-lime mayonnaise, which tastes great with any one of the various flavors of sliced turkey breast now available in the supermarket: pepper turkey, natural roasted, or honey baked. If you wish to reduce the Net Carb count by 3 grams, use two slices of bread per sandwich, instead of three.

PREP TIME: 15 minutes
4 servings

    ½ cup mayonnaise
    3 tablespoons sliced scallions

1 tablespoon fresh lime juice
1 tablespoon Asian chili garlic sauce (sambal oelek)
Radicchio leaves
1 pound deli roasted turkey breast, divided evenly
12 slices low carb white bread, toasted

1. Combine mayonnaise, scallions, lime juice, and chili sauce in small bowl. Spread bread slices with mayonnaise.
2. Lay 2 to 3 turkey slices on top of 4 bread slices, then cover turkey with a large leaf of radicchio or several small ones. Repeat layering once and then cover with the last 4 bread slices. Insert toothpicks to hold sandwiches in place before slicing.

TIP: If you prefer a more traditional sandwich, swap the garlic-lime mayo for a mustard and mayo combo. This sandwich pairs well with Atkins Cole Slaw (recipe page 370).

Per serving:

CARBOHY-DRATES:	NET CARBS:	FIBER:	PROTEIN:	FAT:	CALORIES:
27 grams	15 grams	12 grams	40 grams	31 grams	536

Spring Vegetable Soup

Choose the smallest leeks and yellow squash you can find; both become woody in texture as they grow larger. When buying asparagus, look at the bottom of the spears to be sure they are rounded; flatter spears tend to be tougher. The soup may be stored in the refrigerator for up to 3 days.

PREP TIME: 15 minutes
COOK TIME: 15 minutes
8 servings (1 cup per serving)

3 tablespoons canola oil
4 leeks (white part only), washed well and chopped

½ pound asparagus, cut into ½-inch pieces
1 small yellow squash, cut into ½-inch pieces
4 ounces snow peas
½ teaspoon salt
¼ teaspoon pepper
3 (14½-ounce) cans reduced-sodium chicken broth, plus
   1 can water
¼ cup chopped fresh parsley
1 teaspoon freshly grated lemon peel

1. Heat oil in a large soup pot over medium-high heat. Add leeks and cook 2 minutes, until softened, stirring occasionally. Add asparagus and cook 2 minutes, until color brightens. Add squash and pea pods and cook 2 minutes, or until squash begins to soften.
2. Add salt, pepper, broth, and water; bring to a boil. Reduce heat to low and simmer 5 minutes, until vegetables are tender. Just before serving, stir in parsley and lemon peel.

TIP: Get in the habit of using the scale in the produce section of the supermarket. It's a great help in learning about size/weight proportions.

Per serving:

CARBOHY-DRATES:	NET CARBS:	FIBER:	PROTEIN:	FAT:	CALORIES:
10.5 grams	8.5 grams	2 grams	5.5 grams	6 grams	113

Baihian Halibut

Need a fast and company-worthy dish? Make this delicious Brazilian fish entrée, which pairs tender, moist halibut with coconut milk, peppers, and garlic. Serve it Brazilian style—with a splash of hot sauce.

PREP TIME: 10 minutes
COOK TIME: 10 minutes
4 servings

  2 tablespoons extra-virgin olive oil
  2 tablespoons fresh lime juice
  4 (1-inch-thick) halibut steak halves (about 2 pounds)
  1 small onion, chopped
  1 cup chopped green bell pepper
  1 teaspoon salt
  2 large garlic cloves, thinly sliced
  1 serrano chili or jalapeño pepper, seeded and minced*
  ½ cup unsweetened coconut milk
  1 medium tomato, diced

1. With a fork, whisk 1 tablespoon of the oil and lime juice
on large platter, add fish, and turn to coat.
2. Heat remaining tablespoon oil in a 12-inch nonstick skillet over medium heat. Add onion and pepper. Cook 6 minutes until onion is translucent and pepper is just tender.
3. Sprinkle ½ teaspoon of the salt over fish, add fish to skillet; pour coconut milk over fish and add tomato. Reduce heat
to medium-low and simmer 8 to 9 minutes, turning fish
halfway through cooking time. Stir remaining salt into
sauce, spoon over fish a few times, and serve immediately.

*Add the seeds of the chili to the recipe for more heat.

Per serving:

CARBOHY-DRATES:	NET CARBS:	FIBER:	PROTEIN:	FAT:	CALORIES:
7.5 grams	5.5 grams	2 grams	49 grams	18 grams	394

Bistro Skillet Steak

A simple topping of cherry tomatoes plus hot or sweet cherry peppers turns plain steaks into a memorable dish. Having a repertoire of quick and tasty toppings can enliven any basic protein food.

PREP TIME: 8 minutes
COOK TIME: 15 minutes
4 servings

2 teaspoons olive or canola oil
1 onion, cut into thin wedges
1 (2-pound) boneless sirloin steak
¾ teaspoon salt
½ teaspoon freshly ground pepper
¾ cup reduced-sodium chicken broth
12 cherry tomatoes, halved
⅓ cup jarred sliced hot or mild cherry peppers, as preferred

1. Heat oil in a 12-inch nonstick skillet over medium-high heat. Add onion and cook 7 to 8 minutes, until browned and almost tender; transfer to a plate.
2. Sprinkle both sides of steak with salt and pepper. Add steak to hot skillet; cook 5 minutes per side for medium rare. (Cook 7–8 minutes per side for medium.) Remove steak from skillet and keep warm.
3. Add broth, tomatoes, peppers, and onions to skillet; cook 1 to 2 minutes until sauce thickens slightly. Slice steak into thin strips and top with sauce. Serve immediately.

TIP: For two other quick toppings for basic dishes, use:

• One tablespoon of canned caponata (an eggplant spread) per fish fillet.

• One tablespoon of prepared pesto mixed with a grating of lemon rind per chicken breast.

Per serving:

CARBOHY-DRATES:	NET CARBS:	FIBER:	PROTEIN:	FAT:	CALORIES:
5.5 grams	4 grams	1.5 grams	52.5 grams	15 grams	297

Braised Short Ribs with Horseradish Sauce

Short ribs are a fatty cut, which makes the meat tender and succulent. Ask your butcher to cut the ribs for you into 2½- to 3-inch pieces. To remove excess fat easily, make the dish a day ahead: The fat will rise and congeal, making it easy to spoon off.

PREP TIME: 10 minutes
COOK TIME: 15 minutes
BAKE TIME: 2¼ hours (largely unattended)
4 servings

  3 pounds short ribs, cut into 2½- to 3-inch lengths
  ½ teaspoon salt
  ¼ teaspoon black pepper
  1½ teaspoons canola oil
  1 cup chopped fennel
  1 medium carrot, finely diced
  2 large garlic cloves, minced or pushed through a press
  ½ cup plus 2 tablespoons dry red wine
  1 (14½-ounce) can beef broth
  ¼ teaspoon ground allspice
  2 tablespoons whole-wheat flour

  Horseradish Cream:
  ½ cup sour cream
  1 tablespoon prepared white horseradish, well drained
  1 tablespoon thinly sliced scallions

1. Heat oven to 325° F. Heat a Dutch oven over medium-high heat. Sprinkle ribs with salt and pepper; add half to Dutch oven. Brown well, about 3 to 4 minutes per side. Transfer to a plate. Repeat with remaining ribs.

2. Reduce heat to medium, add oil, fennel, and carrot to Dutch oven. Cook 3 minutes until vegetables are slightly golden; add garlic and cook 1 minute more. Add ½ cup wine and simmer 1 minute. Return ribs to Dutch oven; stir in broth and allspice. Bring to a boil. Cover, transfer to oven, and bake 2¼ to 2½ hours until meat is tender enough to fall off the bone.

3. Prepare horseradish cream by stirring together sour cream, horseradish, and scallions. Set aside in fridge.

4. Transfer ribs to bowl. (May be made up to one day ahead up to this point. Cool and refrigerate.) Spoon as much of the fat as possible off top of liquid and discard. Stir remaining 2 tablespoons wine into flour. Whisk mixture into liquid in pot; bring to a boil on the stovetop. Cook 1 to 2 minutes, stirring frequently, until thickened. Return ribs to pot and heat through a few minutes. Serve with dollop of horseradish cream.

Per serving:

CARBOHY-DRATES:	NET CARBS:	FIBER:	PROTEIN:	FAT:	CALORIES:
9 grams	7 grams	2 grams	30.5 grams	24 grams	402

Brisket with Porcini Mushrooms

A small handful of dried mushrooms adds lots of flavor to this comforting main course. If you are a real mushroom fan, add a cup of sliced sautéed mushrooms to your plate just before serving.

PREP TIME: 15 minutes
COOK TIME: 2½ hours (largely unattended)
6 servings

   1 ounce dried porcini mushrooms
   1 tablespoon canola oil
   1 4- to 5-pound beef brisket
   2 medium onions, thinly sliced
   3 garlic cloves, pushed through a press
   1 (14½-ounce) can reduced-sodium beef broth
   1 bay leaf
   ½ teaspoon salt
   ¼ teaspoon pepper

1. Place mushrooms in a small microwavable bowl with ¾ cup of water. Microwave on high until water boils; remove and let mushrooms cool to room temperature.
2. Heat oil in a large Dutch oven over medium heat. Brown brisket on one side. Turn and add onions; continue browning. When onions are brown, add garlic; cook 1 minute more.
3. Remove mushrooms from water and reserve liquid. Rinse mushrooms and chop. Strain soaking liquid through a coffee filter to remove grit.
4. Pour beef broth and mushroom liquid into Dutch oven. Add bay leaf, salt, and pepper. Cover, reduce heat to low, and cook 2½ to 3 hours, until brisket is tender. Transfer brisket to a cutting board. Let beef rest 10 minutes before slicing.
5. Increase heat to high and cook until juices thicken slightly. Remove bay leaf. Cut brisket against the grain into thin slices and serve with cooking juices.

Per serving:

CARBOHY-DRATES:	NET CARBS:	FIBER:	PROTEIN:	FAT:	CALORIES:
7.5 grams	6 grams	1.5 grams	66 grams	68 grams	921

Broccoli Rabe and Sausage over Penne

Italian-style pork sausage is used in this dish for its full flavor, which is nicely balanced by the slightly bitter taste of broccoli rabe.

PREP TIME: 10 minutes
COOK TIME: 25 minutes
4 servings

> 1 pound Italian-style pork sausage, sweet or spicy
> 3 large garlic cloves, pushed through a press
> ¼ teaspoon crushed red pepper
> 1¼ cups reduced-sodium chicken broth
> 1 bunch (about 14 ounces) broccoli rabe, tough stems removed
> ½ pound low carb soy penne pasta, cooked according to package directions and drained
> Fresh grated *ricotta salata* cheese, optional

1. Place sausage in a 12-inch nonstick skillet with 2 tablespoons water and cook 12 to 14 minutes over medium heat until browned on both sides, but not cooked through; center should be slightly pink when cut. Cool slightly and slice.
2. Add garlic and pepper to skillet and cook just until aromatic, about 20 seconds. Add broth, broccoli rabe, and sausage. Bring to a boil, reduce heat, cover, and simmer 8 minutes until sausage is no longer pink and greens are tender. Serve over pasta. Sprinkle with cheese, if desired.

TIP: *Ricotta salata* is a semi-firm, pure white sheep's milk cheese from Italy, and is now available in well-stocked supermarkets. If you can't find it, a sprinkling of freshly grated Parmesan would work as well.

Per serving:

CARBOHY-DRATES:	NET CARBS:	FIBER:	PROTEIN:	FAT:	CALORIES:
21.5 grams	12.5 grams	9 grams	52 grams	18.5 grams	454

Bronzed Catfish

Spiced cornmeal-coated catfish takes on a "bronzed" color (as opposed to "blackened" which is a method that uses many spices and flour), if prepared correctly. Be sure your skillet is hot before adding the fish, and don't move the fillets until they develop a deeply colored crust. The lemony tartar sauce is the perfect accompaniment.

PREP TIME: 10 minutes
Standing time: 15 minutes
COOK TIME: 6 to 8 minutes
4 servings

1 egg
2 tablespoons water
7 tablespoons yellow cornmeal
1 tablespoon Old Bay Seasoning
½ teaspoon salt
¼ teaspoon cayenne pepper
1½ pounds catfish fillets
2 tablespoons canola oil

Lemony-Scallion Tartar Sauce:
½ cup mayonnaise
2 tablespoons chopped scallions
1 tablespoon fresh lemon juice
½ teaspoon freshly grated lemon peel

1. Whisk egg with 2 tablespoons water. Combine cornmeal, seasoning, salt, and pepper on a piece of wax paper. Dust fillets *lightly* in cornmeal. Dip each fillet in egg, then cornmeal again. Let stand to dry on a cake cooling rack about 15 minutes.
2. Heat 1 tablespoon of the oil in a 12-inch nonstick skillet over medium-high heat. Add half the fish and cook, without moving, 3 to 4 minutes, until bronze or deep golden in color.

Turn and cook 3 to 4 minutes more. Remove carefully with a spatula. Repeat with remaining fish.

3. To prepare tartar sauce, combine all remaining ingredients. Serve 2 tablespoons of sauce per serving of fish.

TIP: The best tool for quickly grating citrus peel is a microplane grater, available in specialty cookware stores.

Per serving:

CARBOHY-DRATES:	NET CARBS:	FIBER:	PROTEIN:	FAT:	CALORIES:
12.5 grams	11.5 grams	1 gram	29.5 grams	43.5 grams	563

Chili Blanco

The name chili blanco, or white chili, refers to the fact that this recipe contains no tomatoes. We brown the pork until the meat is caramelized, a process that produces a richer flavor. If you can find them, use red jalapeños or a Fresno chili for added color.

PREP TIME: 15 minutes
COOK TIME: 25 minutes
4 servings (about 1¼ cups per serving)

2 pounds ground pork
1 cup chopped onion
1 cup chopped fennel
1 cup green bell pepper, cut into ¼-inch dice
1 to 2 red or green jalapeño peppers, seeded and finely chopped
1 teaspoon ground cumin
2 garlic cloves, pushed through a press
1 (15-ounce) can cannellini beans, rinsed and drained
1 cup reduced-sodium chicken broth

½ teaspoon salt
Sour cream and chopped cilantro for garnish

1. Heat a 12-inch nonstick skillet over medium-high heat. Add pork, onion, and fennel. Cook, breaking up clumps with side of spoon, 10 to 13 minutes until pork begins to brown. Add bell pepper, jalapeño, and cumin. Cook about 4 minutes more until pork is browned. Add garlic; cook 1 minute more.
2. Add beans, broth, and salt. Bring to a simmer; mash some of the beans in the pan with a potato masher. Cook 3 minutes until sauce is slightly thickened. Serve with sour cream and chopped cilantro, if desired.

Per serving:

CARBOHY-DRATES:	NET CARBS:	FIBER:	PROTEIN:	FAT:	CALORIES:
20 grams	12.5 grams	7.5 grams	48.5 grams	34 grams	588

Coconut Chicken

Coconut milk and ginger give this dish a mellow, spicy flavor. If you enjoy hot foods, add the seeds of the chili. Small red chilies, such as the Fresno or Thai, add both heat and color. This dish can also be made with pork tenderloin, cut into 1½-inch pieces.

PREP TIME: 10 minutes
COOK TIME: 30 minutes
4 servings

1¾ pounds boneless, skinless chicken thighs, cut in half
1 teaspoon salt
2 garlic cloves, pushed through a press
1 tablespoon grated fresh ginger
1 onion, chopped

1 jalapeño pepper, seeded and minced
¾ cup unsweetened coconut milk
1 zucchini, cut in half lengthwise and sliced into ½-inch moons
1¾ cups frozen green peas, cooked according to box directions

1. Heat a 12-inch nonstick skillet over medium-high heat for 1 minute. Sprinkle chicken with salt; add to skillet. Cook without moving 3 minutes until browned. Turn and repeat. Push chicken to one side; add garlic and ginger, fry 1 minute.
2. Stir in onion and jalapeño; cook 8 minutes until onion is lightly browned and tender. Add coconut milk; reduce heat and simmer 7 minutes.
3. Stir in zucchini, cover, and simmer 7 minutes more or until zucchini is just tender but still bright green. Stir in cooked peas. Serve hot.

Per serving:

CARBOHY-DRATES:	NET CARBS:	FIBER:	PROTEIN:	FAT:	CALORIES:
14.5 grams	10 grams	4.5 grams	44 grams	17 grams	390

Cornish Hens with Wild Rice

This recipe is a bit lengthy, but the steps are simple and the stuffing can be made ahead (simply store in the refrigerator and bring to room temperature before proceeding). If you have a high ACE, you can add a couple of tablespoons of raisins or dried chopped apricots to the other stuffing ingredients.

PREP TIME: 40 minutes
COOK TIME: 45 minutes
BAKE TIME: 45 minutes
4 servings

Stuffing:
¼ cup raw wild rice
2 slices low carb white bread, cut into ½-inch dice
2 tablespoons shelled toasted, salted pumpkin seeds
2 tablespoons butter
1 carrot, finely diced
1 (4-ounce) link mild Italian sausage, casing removed
1 egg, lightly beaten
¼ cup chopped scallion
1 large garlic clove, pushed through a press
1 teaspoon salt
½ cup very hot chicken broth

4 Cornish game hens, (about 1 pound each, giblets removed), rinsed and patted dry
¼ teaspoon black pepper
½ cup no-added-sugar apricot jam (such as Steele's)
2 tablespoons dry sherry

1. Bring 1 cup water to a boil in small saucepan, add rice, cover, and reduce heat. Simmer 40 to 50 minutes until grains have tenderized, slightly split, and liquid is absorbed.
2. While rice is cooking, toast bread on a baking sheet in a 350° F. oven 5 to 7 minutes until just golden. Remove from oven. Increase oven temperature to 375° F.
3. Melt 1 tablespoon butter in skillet over medium heat; add carrot and cook 4 minutes until golden. Transfer to a large bowl. Crumble sausage into skillet and increase heat slightly; cook, breaking up clumps, until browned. Add to bowl with carrots. Mix in rice, bread, pumpkin seeds, egg, scallion, garlic, and ½ teaspoon of the salt. Toss well, until ingredients are evenly mixed, adding broth as you go.
4. Place hens breast-side up directly on a large broiler pan. Fill cavities evenly with stuffing (about ⅔ cup per hen) and close with a toothpick through skin. Dot tops with remaining tablespoon butter and sprinkle with remaining ½ teaspoon salt and pepper.

5. Roast hens 40 to 45 minutes until an instant-read thermometer inserted in the thigh (not touching bone) registers 180° F and juices run clear. Remove hens from oven. Remove any cloudy bits from juices at the bottom of the pan. Increase heat to broil.

6. Stir together jam and sherry. Spoon mixture evenly over hens. Broil hens in middle of oven 3 to 4 minutes until golden, turning pan around once for even broiling. Transfer hens to platter. Strain juices into gravy boat.

Per serving:

CARBOHY-DRATES:	NET CARBS:	FIBER:	PROTEIN:	FAT:	CALORIES:
18 grams	14.5 grams	3.5 grams	75 grams	64.5 grams	984

Country-Style Stuffed Turkey

Turkey dinner just isn't the same without stuffing, but some stuffing recipes provide as many as 35 grams of carbohydrates per serving. In this recipe, low carbohydrate bread helps to lower it; studding the stuffing with chunks of sausage, mushrooms, and apples adds flavor and texture.

PREP TIME: 35 minutes
COOK TIME: 20 minutes
BAKE TIME: 3 hours
12 servings

Stuffing:
4 slices low carb rye bread, cut into ½-inch dice
4 slices low carb white bread, cut into ½-inch dice
1 package (12 ounces) maple-flavored breakfast sausage
1 package (10 ounces) white mushrooms, chopped
(about 4 cups)
1 medium onion, chopped

2 tablespoons butter
2 Granny Smith apples, peeled, cored, and diced
3 large garlic cloves, pushed through a press
1 teaspoon minced fresh thyme leaves
1½ cups chicken broth
1 teaspoon salt
¼ teaspoon black pepper
2 large eggs, lightly beaten
1 12-pound turkey, giblets removed, rinsed and patted dry
salt and pepper

Gravy:
½ cup dry white wine
1½ cups reduced-sodium chicken broth
3 tablespoons whole-wheat flour

1. Heat oven to 350° F. Bake bread on large jelly-roll pan 10 to 14 minutes, stirring once, until deep golden. Transfer to large bowl.
2. Cook sausage in skillet until deep brown and cooked through; coarsely chop and add to bowl.
3. Add mushrooms and onion to skillet and cook 10 to 12 minutes over medium-high heat until browned; add to bowl. Melt butter in skillet, add apples, and cook 4 minutes, until lightly caramelized. Add garlic, cook 30 seconds, then add broth and thyme; bring to a boil. Pour mixture into bowl, add salt and pepper, and toss to combine all ingredients evenly. Stir in eggs.
4. Reduce oven temperature to 325° F. Fill turkey cavities with stuffing and secure with 6-inch metal skewers. Place in large shallow roasting pan. Sprinkle all over with salt and pepper. Bake 1½ hours; pour 1 cup water over top of turkey and baste occasionally during next 1½ to 1¾ hours, covering top with foil during last hour of baking. An instant-read thermometer inserted into the thickest part of the thigh, not touching bone, should register 175° to 180° F, when done. Transfer turkey to a cutting board and let stand 20 minutes before carving.

5. To prepare the gravy, place roasting pan on stovetop over two burners. Add wine; cook 30 seconds. Add 1 cup of the broth and bring to a boil, scraping up browned bits on bottom of pan. Strain gravy through a fine sieve into a saucepan. Skim off fat. Whisk flour into remaining ½ cup broth, add to saucepan, and continue whisking. Bring to a boil for 1 minute. Transfer stuffing to a large serving bowl. Carve turkey and serve with hot gravy.

TIP: Place leftover turkey in the fridge before you serve the dessert course, to inhibit the growth of bacteria.

Per serving:

CARBOHY-DRATES:	NET CARBS:	FIBER:	PROTEIN:	FAT:	CALORIES:
20 grams	16.5 grams	3.5 grams	83.5 grams	35.5 grams	746

Escarole and Chickpea Stew

Delicious and quick to make, this vegetarian entrée is a high-fiber, vitamin-rich meal in a bowl. Cooking the garlic slowly releases all of its flavor into the oil. If you want to reduce the amount of Net Carbs by 5 grams, omit the potato.

PREP TIME: 15 minutes
COOK TIME: 20 minutes
4 servings (1¼ cups per serving)

3 garlic cloves, pushed through a press
2 tablespoons olive oil
1 medium tomato, diced
½ teaspoon crushed red pepper
2 cups chicken or vegetable broth
1 (1¼-pound) head escarole, trimmed and coarsely chopped (8 cups)
1 small potato, peeled and cut into ½-inch dice (½ cup)

1 cup canned chickpeas, rinsed and drained
½ cup diced fontina, Asiago fresco, or provolone cheese

1. Add garlic to cold oil in large saucepan; heat over medium heat just until garlic sizzles and begins to color, about 4 minutes. Add tomato and pepper; cook 4 minutes until oil is orange colored and tomato has softened.
2. Add broth, escarole, potato, and chickpeas; bring to a boil. Reduce heat, cover, and simmer 10 minutes until potato is tender. Stir in cheese, allow to melt, and serve immediately.

TIP: Dark leafy greens such as escarole, chicory, and mustard greens are delicious in soups and stews. When preparing greens, cut out the fibrous middle ribs if they are especially thick.

Per serving:

CARBOHY-DRATES:	NET CARBS:	FIBER:	PROTEIN:	FAT:	CALORIES:
28.5 grams	21.5 grams	7 grams	11.5 grams	13 grams	268

Fresh Baked Easter Ham

Fresh ham is simply the shank or butt cut of fresh pork. Mild-tasting and adaptable to many types of seasoning, it's a nice change from cured ham. Apricot jam and sherry vinegar add a piquant sweetness to the glaze.

PREP TIME: 15 minutes
BAKE TIME: 3 to 3¼ hours
10 servings

1 fresh ham shank (9 pounds), skin on
10 large sage leaves
2 large garlic cloves
1 teaspoon salt

1 (10-ounce) jar no-sugar-added apricot jam (such as Steele's)

2 tablespoons sherry vinegar

⅛ to ¼ teaspoon ground white pepper

1. Heat oven to 325° F. Make ten 1-inch-wide slits on the skin side of the ham (not the cut side) as deep as blade of knife can go. Process sage, garlic, and salt together in a minichopper or hand-chop to a chunky paste. Press into slits, pushing in with a butter knife; reserve 1 teaspoon to spread over top of roast. Place in heavy roaster pan, cover tightly with foil, and bake 2 hours. Uncover, increase temperature to 375° F., and bake 30 minutes.

2. Bring jam, vinegar, and pepper to a boil in small saucepan, cook 2 minutes. Spoon half the jam mixture over the top of the ham. Pour 2 cups water in the bottom of pan. Bake 30 to 45 minutes more or until an instant-read thermometer inserted into thickest part of ham, away from bone, registers 150° F. and the outside is golden. Transfer ham to a cutting board.

3. Transfer pan to stovetop; place over 2 burners. Add remaining jam mixture to pan and bring to a boil, scraping up browned bits on bottom; cook 2 minutes. Pour into a bowl and skim off fat. Slice ham and serve with glaze.

Per serving:

CARBOHYDRATES:	NET CARBS:	FIBER:	PROTEIN:	FAT:	CALORIES:
2.5 grams	2.5 grams	0 grams	55 grams	43.5 grams	645

Grilled Lamb Roast with Yogurt Sauce

For ultra convenience, look for a rolled and tied boneless lamb roast in the supermarket meat case. Or ask your butcher to bone and tie a leg of lamb that will weigh 2 pounds after boning.

PREP TIME: 15 minutes
Marinate time: 4 hours
COOK TIME: 1 hour 20 minutes
6 servings

Marinade:
2 tablespoons olive oil
2 large garlic cloves, pushed through a garlic press
1 tablespoon finely chopped fresh rosemary
1 tablespoon ground coriander
½ cup red wine

2 pounds boneless lamb from the leg, tied for roasting
1 teaspoon kosher salt
4 large red onions
1 tablespoon olive oil

Yogurt Sauce:
2 cups whole-milk yogurt
3 tablespoons chopped mint
1 large garlic clove, pushed through a garlic press

1. Combine marinade ingredients in a large zipper-lock plastic bag. Add lamb and refrigerate 4 hours or overnight. Remove lamb from bag and sprinkle with salt.
2. Prepare a medium-heat grill with an area for indirect heat (turn off one burner on a gas grill, or make a space without coals in a charcoal grill). Place lamb on the unheated portion of grill, cover, and cook 1 hour. Turn every 20 minutes for an even, golden color.
3. When an instant-read thermometer registers 125° F., remove lamb from grill. Wrap completely in foil and let stand 20 minutes for a medium-rare center. Increase standing time for a more well-done roast. Unwrap, slice, and transfer to a large platter; pour juices over meat.
4. With stem end down, cut onions to within a half inch of stem end into eight wedges (onion remains attached at stem end). Brush with oil. Add to grill over direct heat during the

last 20 minutes of lamb cooking time. Grill onions stem side down 5 minutes, turn, press lightly to open wedges, and grill 5 to 8 minutes more until outside is charred. Remove and discard the tough, charred outer layers. Coarsely chop onions. Sprinkle with salt and scatter over sliced lamb.

5. To prepare Yogurt Sauce, combine all remaining ingredients in a medium bowl. Serve ⅓ cup per serving with lamb.

Per serving:

CARBOHY-DRATES:	NET CARBS:	FIBER:	PROTEIN:	FAT:	CALORIES:
13 grams	11 grams	2 grams	31 grams	19 grams	352

Jerk Shrimp

Spicy and flavorful, this Jamaican specialty is great year-round. Broil or grill, but remember, if you're using wooden skewers, soak them in water for 30 minutes first to avoid burning them. If you want to reduce the carb count in this recipe, simply use less pineapple or none at all for a truly traditional dish.

PREP TIME: 15 minutes
Marinate time: 1 hour
COOK TIME: 5 minutes
4 servings (6 shrimp per serving)

Marinade:
4 scallions, quartered crosswise
2 garlic cloves, pushed through a press
1 tablespoon soy sauce
1 tablespoon canola oil
1-inch piece of fresh ginger, quartered
1 teaspoon ground allspice
½ teaspoon dried thyme

24 peeled and deveined jumbo shrimp (1–1½ pounds)
1¼ cups pineapple chunks

1. Process all marinade ingredients in a food processor until a chunky paste is formed. Transfer to zipper-lock plastic storage bag. Add shrimp to bag; toss to coat. Refrigerate 1 hour.
2. Skewer shrimp and pineapple on 8 wooden or metal skewers (use 3 shrimp per skewer).
3. Broil on a broiler pan 3 to 4 inches from heat source or grill on a medium-hot grill 1½ to 2 minutes per side, or just until shrimp are cooked through (do not overcook shrimp—they will become rubbery).

Per serving:

CARBOHY-DRATES:	NET CARBS:	FIBER:	PROTEIN:	FAT:	CALORIES:
8.5 grams	8 grams	0.5 grams	35 grams	4 grams	215

Lamb Chops with Tomatoes and Olives

Turn plain lamb chops into an exciting entrée with the addition of a few pantry ingredients. This dish can be made ahead and gently reheated.

PREP TIME: 10 minutes
COOK TIME: 6 minutes
4 servings (2 chops per serving)

8 lamb shoulder chops, trimmed
salt and pepper to taste
2 tablespoons olive oil
⅓ cup dry white wine
1 (14½-ounce) can chopped peeled tomatoes with juice
½ cup sliced pimiento-stuffed olives

½ packet sugar substitute
2 tablespoons chopped fresh parsley

1. Season chops with salt and pepper. In a large skillet, heat oil over medium-high heat. Cook chops 2 to 3 minutes per side, in two batches. Transfer to a platter and tent with foil.
2. Pour wine into skillet and scrape up brown bits. Stir in tomatoes, olives, and sugar substitute. Reduce heat to medium. Cook 5 minutes or until sauce thickens slightly.
3. Season to taste with salt and pepper. Spoon sauce over chops. Sprinkle with parsley and serve.

TIP: This recipe works equally well with pork chops. Simply increase cooking time, depending on the thickness of the chops.

Per serving:

CARBOHY-DRATES:	NET CARBS:	FIBER:	PROTEIN:	FAT:	CALORIES:
5 grams	4 grams	1 gram	48 grams	24 grams	448

Miso-Soy Glazed Salmon

Miso (soybean paste) can be found in the refrigerated case of well-stocked supermarkets or in Asian groceries. In this recipe, we used red miso. However, any miso may be substituted (the lighter the color, the milder the taste).

PREP TIME: 5 minutes
COOK TIME: 5 minutes
BAKE TIME: 6 minutes
4 servings

4 teaspoons lite (reduced-sodium) soy sauce
1 tablespoon sugar-free maple syrup
2 teaspoons red miso

1 garlic clove, pushed though a press
½ teaspoon sesame oil
4 center-cut salmon fillets, 2 inches wide and 1 inch
thick (about 1½ pounds)

1. Heat oven to 450° F. Combine all ingredients except the salmon in a bowl. Stir to dissolve miso; set aside.
2. Heat a large ovenproof nonstick skillet over medium-high heat. Add fillets, skin side down. Press down lightly with a spatula to sear skin; cook 3 to 4 minutes until skin is crisped.
3. Spoon half the sauce over fish. Transfer skillet to oven. Bake 6 minutes for medium-rare doneness (bake longer, if desired). Spoon remaining sauce over hot fish and serve.

TIP: Try this dish with Asian Vegetable Stir-Fry (page 386), and low carb pasta tossed with sesame oil and red pepper flakes.

Per serving:

CARBOHY-DRATES:	NET CARBS:	FIBER:	PROTEIN:	FAT:	CALORIES:
5 grams	5 grams	0 grams	34.5 grams	19 grams	339

Not Your Mama's Meat Loaf

A purée of roasted red bell pepper and plum tomato gives this meat loaf a rich, savory flavor and an attractive glaze. As with most meat loaves, leftovers make great sandwiches the next day.

PREP TIME: 15 minutes
BAKE TIME: 60 to 65 minutes
6 servings

1 medium red bell pepper, halved and seeded
1 plum tomato, halved lengthwise
2 slices low carb white bread or 1 cup reserved low carb
  bread crumbs from freezer
2 pounds meat loaf mix (ground beef, pork, and veal)
¼ cup chopped onion
1 large egg, lightly beaten
2 tablespoons coarse-grain mustard
2 tablespoons chopped fresh parsley or dried
1 large garlic clove, pushed through a press
1 teaspoon salt

1. Broil pepper and tomato, cut sides down, on a foil-lined broiler pan, 4 inches from heat, 8 to 10 minutes, turning pan if necessary, until vegetables are evenly charred and tender. Wrap foil around vegetables and let stand until cool, about 15 minutes. Remove skin from vegetables.
2. Heat oven to 350° F. Pulse bread in a food processor until crumbs form; set aside. Purée pepper and tomato in processor until smooth.
3. In a large bowl, gently combine ground meat with half the pepper puree, 3 tablespoons water, bread crumbs, onion, egg, mustard, parsley, garlic, and salt.
4. Lightly grease a broiler pan; form meat mixture into a 9 × 4-inch-wide oblong loaf directly on pan. Bake 50 minutes. Spread remaining purée over top and bake 10 to 15 minutes more until meat is browned and an instant-read thermometer registers 160° F.

TIP: Try this meat loaf with puréed cauliflower, which is a great low carb stand-in for mashed potatoes. Leftover meat loaf makes tasty open-face sandwiches.

Per serving:

CARBOHYDRATES:	NET CARBS:	FIBER:	PROTEIN:	FAT:	CALORIES:
5.5 grams	3.5 grams	2 grams	36 grams	26 grams	403

Pasta with Fresh Tomatoes, Lemon, and Feta

All tomatoes work equally well in this dish—from summer beefsteaks to winter grape tomatoes. Uncooked tomato sauce highlighted with lemon and the tang of feta cheese makes a nice change of pace from the usual cooked sauces.

PREP TIME: 20 minutes
COOK TIME: 7 minutes
4 servings

  3 medium tomatoes (about 18 ounces), cut into ½-inch dice
  1 small red onion, chopped
  1 tablespoon fresh lemon zest
  ½ teaspoon salt
  ½ teaspoon freshly ground pepper
  1 cup crumbled feta cheese
  8 ounces low carb fettuccine pasta

1. In a medium bowl combine tomatoes, onion, zest, salt, and pepper. Let sit at room temperature at least 30 minutes.
2. Cook pasta according to package directions. Drain and toss with tomato mixture. Sprinkle with feta. Serve warm or at room temperature.

TIP: For an easy variation, and about the same number of carbs, substitute ½ cup oil-cured black olives for the feta cheese.

Per serving:

CARBOHY-DRATES:	NET CARBS:	FIBER:	PROTEIN:	FAT:	CALORIES:
24.5 grams	13.5 grams	11 grams	43 grams	11.5 grams	367

Perfect Filet Mignon with Red Wine Sauce

The perfect wine to use in this dish is an inexpensive, spicy Syrah. The technique of wrapping the tenderloin in foil after roasting and letting it stand continues the cooking process and guarantees uniform doneness.

PREP TIME: 10 minutes
COOK TIME: 1 hour (largely unattended)
BAKE TIME: 30 to 35 minutes
8 servings

4 tablespoons butter
2 large shallots, chopped (½ cup)
1 carrot, chopped
1 small stalk celery, chopped
2 large garlic cloves, minced
1 tablespoon dried porcini mushroom pieces, rinsed well
1 bottle Syrah red wine
½ to ⅔ cup reduced-sodium chicken broth
1½ tablespoons whole-wheat flour

1 (5- to 5½-pound) trimmed and tied whole filet mignon*
1½ teaspoons salt
¾ teaspoon pepper

1. Heat oven to 425° F. Melt 2 tablespoons of the butter in a 2- to 3-quart saucepan over medium heat, add shallot, carrot, and celery and cook 3 minutes until shallot is translucent. Add garlic and porcini and cook 2 to 3 minutes more. Add wine and bring to a boil. Reduce heat and simmer 45 minutes until wine is reduced to 1⅓ to 1½ cups. Strain wine into a 2-cup measure; add enough broth to equal 2 cups.

*Most butchers, including those who work in supermarkets, will trim and tie prepackaged tenderloins upon request.

2. Meanwhile, sprinkle roast evenly with salt and pepper. Place on large broiler pan and roast in upper third of oven, 30 to 35 minutes for rare or about 10 to 15 minutes longer for more well done (see temperature guidelines below). Wrap tightly in aluminum foil; let stand 15 to 30 minutes before slicing.

3. Transfer roasting pan to stovetop; place over 2 burners. Melt remaining 2 tablespoons butter in pan with drippings over medium heat. Add flour and cook, stirring, 1 minute. Whisk in strained red wine–broth mixture and simmer, scraping up browned bits, for 2 to 3 minutes. Unwrap beef and add juices to pan, whisking. Slice beef and serve with wine sauce.

TIP: For rare beef, remove roast from oven when a thermometer registers 120° F, for medium-rare 125° F, and medium 130° F.

Per serving:

CARBOHY-DRATES:	NET CARBS:	FIBER:	PROTEIN:	FAT:	CALORIES:
6.5 grams	5.5 grams	1 gram	63.5 grams	28 grams	607

Sesame Tofu with Snow Peas and Peppers

This dish pairs sesame-coated tofu with a colorful mélange of savory stir-fried veggies, flavored with a light sauce that just about evaporates, leaving only a light coating. Tofu is high in protein, iron, phosphorous, and potassium.

PREP TIME: 15 minutes
Standing time: 30 minutes
COOK TIME: 15 minutes
4 servings

   1 pound firm tofu, drained and cut into 16 (½-inch) slices

6 tablespoons sesame seeds
3 tablespoons canola oil
1 leek, white part only, rinsed and chopped
1 cup snow peas, cut into matchsticks
1 large red bell pepper, cut into matchsticks
2 teaspoons finely chopped fresh ginger

Sauce:
1 tablespoon dry sherry
1½ teaspoons lite (reduced-sodium) soy sauce
⅛ teaspoon sugar substitute

1. To remove excess moisture from tofu, arrange slices between triple layers of paper towels set between two baking sheets. Place 2 cans over top baking sheet to lightly weight the tofu for 30 minutes. Spread sesame seeds on a plate. Remove tofu, pat dry, and press each slice into sesame seeds to coat.

2. Heat 1 tablespoon of the oil in a 12-inch nonstick skillet over medium-high heat. Add half the tofu, and fry about 2 minutes per side until golden, turning carefully with a small spatula. Transfer to a platter; repeat with remaining tofu. While tofu is cooking, combine sauce ingredients in a small bowl.

3. Add remaining tablespoon of oil to skillet; stir-fry leek 1 minute, add snow peas, pepper, and ginger, and cook 2 minutes more until vegetables are tender-crisp. Mix sauce ingredients and pour over vegetables; cook stirring, 30 to 60 seconds more just until sauce is absorbed. Pour vegetable mixture over tofu and serve.

Per serving:

CARBOHYDRATES:	NET CARBS:	FIBER:	PROTEIN:	FAT:	CALORIES:
15 grams	9 grams	6 grams	21.5 grams	27 grams	369

Southwestern-Style Pork Fajitas

A lively salsa made with corn, green onion, and lime juice gives a Southwestern accent to these hearty fajitas. Unless you really prefer food on the mild side, don't omit the green hot sauce: It adds more flavor than heat. Toasting the tortilla adds a nice nuttiness and crisp texture.

PREP TIME: 15 minutes
COOK TIME: 20 minutes
4 servings

½ teaspoon salt
½ teaspoon garlic powder
1 package (about 1½ pounds) pork tenderloins, cut into ½-inch strips
2 tablespoons canola oil

Salsa:
½ cup corn
2 tablespoons fresh lime juice
½ cup sliced green onion
¼ teaspoon salt

8 low carb tortillas
cooking spray
½ cup shredded Mexican-blend or cheddar cheese
8 teaspoons green hot sauce

1. Combine salt and garlic powder and sprinkle evenly over pork strips; toss to coat. Heat ½ tablespoon of the canola oil in a 12-inch nonstick skillet over high heat. Add one-quarter of the pork; stir-fry 3 minutes until lightly browned. Transfer to a bowl. Repeat 3 more times with remaining pork.
2. Add corn to hot skillet and cook just 1 minute to brown; cool. Toss corn with remaining salsa ingredients in a bowl.
3. Clean skillet; heat over medium heat. Spray tortillas lightly with cooking spray and toast 2 at a time (on one side

only), 1 to 2 minutes, until golden. Evenly divide pork, salsa, and cheese over toasted sides of tortillas; top each with a teaspoon of hot sauce. Fold tortillas in half and toast in skillet 1 to 2 minutes per side, until cheese is melted and tortilla is lightly toasted and crisped.

TIP: To make your own cooking spray, fill a spray bottle with canola or olive oil.

Per serving:

CARBOHY-DRATES:	NET CARBS:	FIBER:	PROTEIN:	FAT:	CALORIES:
30 grams	11 grams	19 grams	50 grams	21.5 grams	465

Spanish Chicken over Penne

Boneless, skinless chicken thighs are richer in flavor than chicken breasts. Although white meat is marginally higher in most vitamins and minerals, dark meat is slightly higher in iron and has more than twice the vitamin A.

PREP TIME: 15 minutes
COOK TIME: 30 minutes
4 servings

1½ pounds boneless, skinless chicken thighs, cut into
  1-inch chunks
½ teaspoon salt
½ medium onion, chopped
½ cup finely diced green bell pepper
½ cup finely diced celery
1 large garlic clove, pushed through a press
2 teaspoons ground cumin
¼ teaspoon crushed red pepper
½ cup dry sherry
1 cup canned diced tomatoes in juice

¼ cup reduced-sodium chicken broth
1 tablespoon butter
8 ounces low carb soy penne pasta, cooked according to
  package directions and drained

1. Sprinkle chicken with salt. Heat a 12-inch nonstick skillet over medium-high heat; add chicken and brown 4 minutes, turning once halfway through cooking time.
2. Stir in onion, pepper, and celery. Reduce heat to medium and cook 4 minutes until vegetables are tender. Add garlic, cumin, and crushed red pepper; cook 1 minute. Add sherry, let bubble about 10 seconds, then add tomatoes and broth; bring to a boil.
3. Reduce heat, cover, and simmer 12 to 15 minutes until chicken is no longer pink in center. Stir in butter until melted. Serve over pasta.

Per serving:

CARBOHY-DRATES:	NET CARBS:	FIBER:	PROTEIN:	FAT:	CALORIES:
24 grams	13 grams	11 grams	71.5 grams	13 grams	520

Spiced Beef and Asparagus Stir-Fry

Besides being a tender cut of meat, shell, or strip, steak is the perfect shape to cut into stir-fry slices. Freezing the steaks for 10 to 15 minutes firms the meat, making slicing easier. Even though we use a scant ¼ teaspoon in this recipe, Chinese five-spice powder is worth purchasing. Its distinctive blend of cloves, anise, pepper, fennel, and cinnamon adds a lot of flavor and can be used in any stir-fry dish when you want an Asian accent.

PREP TIME: 15 minutes
Marinate time: 1 hour

COOK TIME: 10 minutes
4 servings

3 shell or strip steaks, 1-inch thick (about 1½ pounds)

Marinade:
2 tablespoons soy sauce
1 tablespoon grated fresh ginger
1 large garlic clove, pushed through a press
1 tablespoon dry sherry
1½ teaspoons no-sugar-added apricot preserves (such as Steele's)
1½ teaspoons sesame oil
¼ teaspoon Chinese five-spice powder

4 teaspoons canola oil
24 asparagus spears, trimmed
2 tablespoons sesame seeds
24 cherry tomatoes

1. Remove any hard fat from around edge of steaks. Cut steaks crosswise into thin slices.
2. Combine marinade ingredients in a zipper-lock plastic bag or baking dish, add beef, and toss to coat evenly. Refrigerate 1 to 4 hours.
3. Heat 1 teaspoon of the oil in a 12-inch nonstick skillet over high heat until very hot. Add one-third of the beef. Stir-fry 1½ to 2 minutes until no longer pink and transfer to a large shallow serving bowl. Repeat twice with remaining beef.
4. Add remaining teaspoon of oil to skillet along with asparagus and sesame seeds. Stir-fry 3 minutes. Add tomatoes and stir to heat through, 1 minute. Toss vegetables with meat and accumulated juices. Serve immediately.

Per serving:

CARBOHY-DRATES:	NET CARBS:	FIBER:	PROTEIN:	FAT:	CALORIES:
10.5 grams	7.5 grams	3 grams	40 grams	20 grams	339

Stuffed Chicken Breast

A delicious sauté of shiitake mushrooms and onion with pancetta (Italian bacon) makes this a great chicken dish for company. You can prepare the chicken a day ahead, then bake it the next day for carefree entertaining. You'll find sealed packages of presliced pancetta in the cold cuts section of the supermarket or at the deli counter.

PREP TIME: 15 minutes
COOK TIME: 25 minutes
BAKE TIME: 20 minutes
4 servings

   3 slices low carb white bread
   2 tablespoons finely chopped fresh parsley
   4 ounces thinly sliced pancetta, chopped
   1 (3.5-ounce) package or ¼ pound shiitake mushrooms,
      chopped (stems discarded)
   1 medium onion, finely chopped
   ¾ cup shredded Asiago fresco, fontina, or mozzarella
      cheese
   4 large (about 7 ounces each) boneless chicken breast
      halves
   2 tablespoons whole-wheat flour
   ½ teaspoon salt
   ¼ teaspoon black pepper
   2 large eggs, lightly beaten with 2 tablespoons water
   2 tablespoons olive oil

1. Heat oven to 350° F. Pulse bread in a food processor until crumbs form. Spread crumbs on a baking sheet. Bake 4 to 6 minutes, stirring once, until golden. Cool, transfer to a plate, and mix in parsley. Set aside.
2. Meanwhile, heat a 12-inch nonstick ovenproof skillet over medium-high heat. Add pancetta, mushrooms, and onion. Cook 8 to 9 minutes until liquid has evaporated and

mixture is lightly browned. Transfer to a bowl; cool slightly and stir in cheese.

3. Make a 3- to 4-inch slit lengthwise along the thick side of each chicken breast, cutting almost to the other side to form pocket. Stuff each pocket with one-quarter of the pancetta mixture (about ½ cup). Press each pocket closed.

4. Toss flour with salt and pepper. Press chicken breast first into flour mixture and then into egg mixture. Allow excess to drip off and then press breasts into bread crumb mixture to coat. (Crumbs are coarse so they will not coat the chicken completely.)

5. Wipe out skillet. Heat 1 tablespoon of the oil over medium-high heat. Add the chicken and cook 3 minutes until deep golden brown, turn, add remaining tablespoons oil (tilting pan to spread oil), and brown 3 minutes more. (Chicken may be made to this point up to 1 day ahead.)

6. Heat oven to 350° F. Transfer skillet* (or place chicken on baking sheet) to oven and bake 18 to 23 minutes until chicken is no longer pink inside pocket.

Per serving:

CARBOHY-DRATES:	NET CARBS:	FIBER:	PROTEIN:	FAT:	CALORIES:
13 grams	8.5 grams	4.5 grams	63 grams	25 grams	539

Veal Milanese

The bread crumbs for this dish are homemade and not as fine as commercial products. They will not coat as completely, but will form a wonderfully crisp crust with great texture. Letting the cutlets stand before cooking ensures a perfect finished product.

*Most skillets are ovenproof to 350° F. If not sure, wrap handle in double layer of foil.

PREP TIME: 10 minutes
BAKE TIME: 6 minutes
COOK TIME: 10 minutes
4 servings

Crumbs:
3 slices low carb white bread, torn into pieces
⅓ cup finely shredded Parmesan cheese
2 tablespoons chopped fresh parsley
¾ teaspoon dried oregano, crumbled
½ teaspoon salt
½ teaspoon black pepper
1 garlic clove, pushed through a press

1½ pounds veal cutlets for scallopini (pounded very thin, 6 to 8 cutlets)
2 tablespoons whole-wheat flour
2 large eggs, lightly beaten with 3 tablespoons water
2 tablespoons olive or canola oil

1. To prepare crumbs, heat oven to 350° F. Pulse bread in a food processor until coarse crumbs form. Spread crumbs on a jelly-roll pan and bake 4 to 6 minutes, stirring once, until medium gold in color. Transfer to a bowl and mix with cheese, parsley, oregano, salt, pepper, and garlic (crumble garlic with fingers to evenly distribute).
2. On waxed paper, dust veal slices in flour, dip in egg, and then coat both sides in bread-crumb mixture, pressing to make crumbs stick (coat once, there will be spaces between crumbs). Let stand to dry on a cooling rack or cutting board 15 minutes.
3. Heat 1 tablespoon of the oil in a 12-inch nonstick skillet over medium-high heat. Add half the cutlets. Cook 1½ to 2 minutes per side until deep golden. Repeat with remaining cutlets.

Per serving:

CARBOHY-DRATES:	NET CARBS:	FIBER:	PROTEIN:	FAT:	CALORIES:
9 grams	5.5 grams	3.5 grams	52 grams	36 grams	576

Asian Carrot and Zucchini Salad

Blanching carrots gives them a tender-crisp bite and super bright color. For even more crunch, drain an 8-ounce can of sliced water chestnuts and mix them into this salad. (You'll add 3 grams of carbohydrates, 2 grams Net Carbs, and 1 gram of fiber per serving.)

PREP TIME: 15 minutes
COOK TIME: 1 minute
4 servings (¾ cup each)

Dressing:
1 tablespoon seasoned rice wine vinegar
2 teaspoons canola oil
2 teaspoons lite (reduced-sodium) soy sauce
2 teaspoons minced fresh ginger
¼ teaspoon salt

2½ medium carrots, cut into 2-inch matchsticks
1 zucchini, halved lengthwise and thinly sliced
3 tablespoons sliced scallions
3 tablespoons chopped peanuts or toasted almonds

1. Combine dressing ingredients in a large bowl.
2. Blanch carrots in boiling water 30 seconds; drain and rinse under cold water.
3. Add carrots, zucchini, and green onions to dressing and toss well. Top with nuts.

TIP: When buying ginger, look for firm, plump pieces with smooth skin. Fresh ginger can be peeled easily with a vegetable peeler.

Per serving:

CARBOHY-DRATES:	NET CARBS:	FIBER:	PROTEIN:	FAT:	CALORIES:
8 grams	5.5 grams	2.5 grams	3 grams	6 grams	109

Atkins Cole Slaw

Cabbage supplies generous amounts of vitamins A and C, fiber, and the cancer-fighting compounds called indoles. Try this recipe with red cabbage. It's higher in vitamin C and anthocyanins than green, and it gives this salad a lovely purple color. Whichever you choose, our slaw contains none of the sugar found in most deli slaws.

PREP TIME: 15 minutes
CHILL TIME: 30 minutes
8 servings (¾ cup per serving)

> 1 medium cabbage (about 1½ pounds), halved and cored
> 2 carrots
> ¼ cup mayonnaise
> ½ cup sour cream
> 2 tablespoons cider vinegar
> 2 packets sugar substitute
> 1 teaspoon celery seed
> 1 teaspoon salt

1. Cut cabbage halves in half and thinly slice lengthwise. Transfer to a large bowl. Coarsely grate carrots into cabbage and mix well.
2. In a small bowl, whisk together remaining ingredients to make the dressing for the slaw. Pour dressing over vegetables. Toss until thoroughly combined. Refrigerate at least 30 minutes before serving for flavors to blend. Serve cold or at room temperature.

Per serving:

CARBOHY-DRATES:	NET CARBS:	FIBER:	PROTEIN:	FAT:	CALORIES:
8 grams	5.5 grams	2.5 grams	2 grams	19.5 grams	211

Broccoli, Daikon, and Pepper Salad

This healthful, colorful salad can be prepped ahead but don't dress it until it's ready to serve. Vinegar and fruit juices break down the color of green vegetables so they lose their vividness—and their bright taste—when allowed to stand for too long.

PREP TIME: 15 minutes
COOK TIME: 6 minutes
4 servings

> 1 pound broccoli florets
> 1 cup daikon (Japanese radish) cut into matchsticks, or
>   sliced radish
> ½ small red onion, very thinly sliced
> ½ cup finely diced yellow pepper
>
> Dressing:
> 1 tablespoon sesame oil
> 1 tablespoon water
> 1 tablespoon lite (reduced-sodium) soy sauce
> 1 tablespoon sherry vinegar
> ¾ teaspoon granular sugar substitute
> ¾ teaspoon salt
> ½ teaspoon grated fresh ginger

1. Steam broccoli florets until crisp-tender, about 6 minutes. Cool to room temperature.
2. Place broccoli, daikon, onion, and pepper in a large bowl. In a small bowl, whisk together dressing ingredients.
3. Pour dressing over vegetables; toss well to coat. Salad may be served room temperature or cold.

Per serving:

CARBOHY-DRATES:	NET CARBS:	FIBER:	PROTEIN:	FAT:	CALORIES:
9.5 grams	5 grams	4.5 grams	4 grams	4 grams	78

Caribbean Black Bean Salad

English, or hothouse, cucumbers grow up to 20 inches long; they have thin skins, so they are usually wrapped in plastic, and have very few seeds. They provide some vitamin C and folate, and if you leave the skin on you'll get some vitamin A as well.

PREP TIME: 10 minutes
4 servings

Dressing:
2 tablespoons fresh lime juice
1 tablespoon extra-virgin olive oil
½ teaspoon salt
¼ teaspoon ground cumin

Salad:
1 (15-ounce) can black beans, rinsed and drained
half an English cucumber, cut into ¼-inch dice
¾ cup chopped red pepper
½ cup chopped green pepper
¼ cup sliced scallion or diced red onion
1 small jalapeño pepper, seeded and chopped

1. In a large bowl, whisk lime juice, oil, salt, and cumin to blend.
2. Mix in remaining ingredients and serve.

TIP: Canned beans are convenient, but they're quite high in sodium. Rinsing removes some of the salt, but if it is a concern for you, prepare dried beans. Pick over a pound of beans, put them in a pot, and add water to cover by 2 inches; let stand overnight or "quick-soak" the beans by bringing the water to a boil. Let boil 2 minutes, then cover, remove from heat, and let stand for 1 hour. Drain off the soaking liquid (this removes most of the indigestible sugars), then cover the beans with fresh water by 2 inches and bring back to a boil. Reduce the heat, partially cover the pot, and simmer until the beans are tender; start checking after an hour. One pound of dried beans will yield 5 to 6 cups cooked beans, and you need one and a half cups for this recipe. Divide the leftover beans into freezer-proof bags and stack them in your freezer, where they'll keep for up to 6 months.

Per serving:

CARBOHYDRATES:	NET CARBS:	FIBER:	PROTEIN:	FAT:	CALORIES:
18.5 grams	11.5 grams	7 grams	6 grams	4 grams	127

Chickpea and Vegetable Salad

If you like, make this salad a couple of hours ahead so the flavors can blend. Combine all the ingredients except the asparagus, which should be added at the last minute, and refrigerate. Bring to room temperature before serving for the best flavor.

PREP TIME: 10 minutes
COOK TIME: 6 minutes (for asparagus)
8 servings (½ cup per serving)

Dressing:
4 teaspoons extra-virgin olive oil
2 teaspoons red wine vinegar
1 teaspoon Asian chili sauce
¼ teaspoon salt
½ small red onion, very thinly sliced

12 spears asparagus, trimmed, steamed, and cut
   crosswise into thirds
1 (15½-ounce) can chickpeas, rinsed and drained
1 red pepper, cut into 1-inch squares

1. Combine dressing ingredients in a medium bowl. Let stand 5 minutes.
2. Add remaining ingredients and toss well to coat. Serve at room temperature.

TIP: Chickpeas are a good source of iron, but iron from plant sources (called "nonheme" iron) is not absorbed by the body as readily as iron from animal foods (called "heme" iron). Foods that are high in vitamin C, such as red peppers, help the body to absorb nonheme iron.

Per serving:

CARBOHY-DRATES:	NET CARBS:	FIBER:	PROTEIN:	FAT:	CALORIES:
12 grams	9.5 grams	2.5 grams	2.5 grams	2.5 grams	82

Greek Salad

Kalamata olives are a deep purplish-black and have a meaty texture. To pit them, measure out the amount needed, dump them onto a sheet of wax paper (to keep your counter or cutting board clean), and gently press them with the flat side of a large knife or a small skillet. This loosens the flesh so you'll be able to pick out the pits easily.

PREP TIME: 10 minutes
4 servings

Dressing:
¼ cup olive oil
2 tablespoons red wine vinegar
2 teaspoons chopped fresh dill
1 teaspoon salt
½ teaspoon freshly ground black pepper

6 cups romaine lettuce, torn into bite-size pieces
1 cup cherry tomatoes, halved

1 small cucumber, sliced
½ cup feta cheese, crumbled (2 ounces)
¼ cup Kalamata olives
8 anchovy fillets (optional)

1. In a large bowl, whisk olive oil, vinegar, dill, salt, and pepper until combined.
2. Add lettuce, tomatoes, and cucumber to bowl; toss until vegetables are coated with dressing. Divide salad on 4 plates. Sprinkle with feta cheese and olives. Crisscross 2 anchovies atop each salad (if using).

Per serving:

CARBOHYDRATES:	NET CARBS:	FIBER:	PROTEIN:	FAT:	CALORIES:
6 grams	3.5 grams	2.5 grams	4.5 grams	19 grams	203

Lobster Salad

This recipe has only a few ingredients, yet is lush in flavor. You can use frozen thawed lobster meat, but if your supermarket runs specials on freshly steamed lobsters note that four 1¼-pound lobsters yield approximately 1 pound of tail meat.

PREP TIME: 25 minutes
4 servings

Dressing:
½ cup buttermilk
3 tablespoons mayonnaise
2 teaspoons fresh lime juice
½ teaspoon salt
¼ teaspoon red hot sauce (optional)

4 cups very thinly sliced green cabbage
¼ cup very thinly sliced red onion, plus 1 tablespoon finely chopped
1 pound cooked lobster tail meat, cut in bite-size pieces
1 tablespoon sliced scallion for garnish

1. Whisk dressing ingredients in a medium-sized bowl. Transfer half of the dressing to a large bowl. Add cabbage and sliced red onion to large bowl and toss well. Let stand 15 minutes.

2. Add remaining minced onion to dressing in medium bowl; add lobster and toss. To serve, divide cabbage salad on 4 plates; mound one-quarter of the lobster salad in the center of each and top with scallion slices.

TIP: If you are purchasing live lobsters, choose active ones, whose tails curl inward when picked up. Cook lobsters the same day you purchase them and make sure they are still alive before cooking. (Dead lobsters develop bacteria.)

Per serving:

CARBOHY-DRATES:	NET CARBS:	FIBER:	PROTEIN:	FAT:	CALORIES:
8.5 grams	6.5 grams	2 grams	25.5 grams	9.5 grams	221

Macaroni and Cauliflower Salad

Mixing pasta and cauliflower gives this twist on the traditional summer dish a fresher flavor and more interesting texture than the original.

PREP TIME: 20 minutes
COOK TIME: 25 minutes
4 servings (1 cup per serving)

1½ cups low carb elbow pasta
2 cups cauliflower, broken into small florets
½ cup mayonnaise
2 tablespoons Dijon mustard
1 packet sugar substitute
⅓ cup chopped celery
¼ cup chopped dill pickle
¼ cup pimiento-filled green olives, sliced
salt and pepper, to taste

1. Prepare pasta according to package directions. During the last 8 minutes of cooking, add cauliflower florets. When pasta and cauliflower are tender, drain in a colander and rinse under cold water.
2. In a large serving bowl, mix mayonnaise, mustard, and sugar substitute. Add celery, pickle, and olives. Fold in pasta and cauliflower. Turn gently until all ingredients are combined. Season to taste with salt and pepper.

TIP: If you have a high ACE, you may substitute whole-wheat pasta for low carb. The exchange will add another 10 Net Carbs per serving.

Per serving:

CARBOHY-DRATES:	NET CARBS:	FIBER:	PROTEIN:	FAT:	CALORIES:
9.5 grams	4 grams	5.5 grams	16 grams	24 grams	314

Mexican Chopped Salad

Easy does it with this simple chopped salad. If corn is in season and you have an extra minute, add fresh pan-fried corn (instead of canned). Cut kernels from the cob and cook in ½ teaspoon canola oil just 1 minute until lightly charred.

PREP TIME: 15 minutes
4 servings (1½ cups per serving)

Dressing:
2 tablespoons canola oil
1 tablespoon fresh lime juice
½ teaspoon ground cumin
½ teaspoon salt

4 cups packed chopped romaine lettuce
1 Haas avocado, pitted, peeled, and cut in ½-inch dice
½ cup canned corn, drained
2 hard-boiled eggs, chopped
1 small plum tomato, diced
¼ cup chopped red onion

1. Combine dressing ingredients in a large bowl and whisk together.
2. Add romaine, avocado, and corn; toss to coat.
3. Arrange salad on a large platter and top with eggs, tomato, and red onion.

TIP: When purchasing avocados, choose pebbly-skinned Haas over smooth-skinned Florida varieties; their flavor is creamier and more intense. Haas are also lower in carbs.

Per serving:

CARBOHY-DRATES:	NET CARBS:	FIBER:	PROTEIN:	FAT:	CALORIES:
10.5 grams	6 grams	4.5 grams	6 grams	18 grams	212

Mixed Veggie Potato Salad

This salad calls to mind traditional potato salad, but it contains more vitamins and fiber, and is more colorful as well. Red potatoes are a good choice here because their texture is waxy rather than dry. This salad is perfect for a picnic or as an accompaniment to grilled foods.

PREP TIME: 25 minutes
COOK TIME: 15 minutes
9 servings (about ⅔ cup per serving)

  1 pound red potatoes, cut into 1-inch chunks
  2 carrots, grated
  4 stalks celery, chopped
  2 medium yellow squash, cut into ½-inch dice
  ½ red onion, chopped
  ⅓ cup chopped parsley
  ½ cup mayonnaise
  ¼ cup sour cream
  ¾ teaspoon salt
  ¼ teaspoon freshly ground black pepper

1. Place potatoes in a medium pot with enough water to cover. Bring to a boil; lower heat and simmer 20 minutes or until potatoes are tender. Drain and cool.
2. In a large bowl, toss together potatoes, carrots, celery, squash, onion, and parsley. In a small bowl, combine mayonnaise, sour cream, salt, and pepper.
3. Add the dressing to the vegetables. Toss gently until evenly coated. Serve warm, at room temperature, or cold.

TIP: To transport picnic foods safely, use a cooler packed with plenty of ice packs. Keep the cooler in a shady spot, and store leftovers promptly.

Per serving:

CARBOHY-DRATES:	NET CARBS:	FIBER:	PROTEIN:	FAT:	CALORIES:
17 grams	14.5 grams	2.5 grams	2.5 grams	12 grams	174

Salad with Brie and Spicy Nuts

St. André is a triple-crème cheese, meaning it is at least 75 percent butterfat. As you might imagine, it's very rich, and it has a mild flavor. Brie, on the other hand, is a soft-ripened cheese. Despite its creamy texture, Brie is actually lower in fat than Gouda, Cheddar, or Parmesan cheese.

PREP TIME: 10 minutes
BAKE TIME: 20 minutes
4 servings

Sweet and Spicy Nuts:
1 egg white
½ teaspoon water
2 tablespoons granular sugar substitute
½ teaspoon salt
¼ teaspoon Chinese five-spice powder
¼ teaspoon ground ginger
¼ teaspoon cayenne pepper
½ cup pecan halves

Salad:
3 slices low carb white bread
1½ ounces Brie or St. André cheese
3 tablespoons olive oil
1 tablespoon red wine vinegar
6 ounces mixed baby greens
salt and pepper

1. Heat oven to 325° F. Line a baking sheet with aluminum foil; spray with nonstick cooking spray.

2. In a large bowl, mix egg white, water, sugar substitute, salt, five-spice powder, ginger, and cayenne. Add nuts; mix until evenly coated.

3. Spread nuts in a single layer on the prepared baking sheet. Bake 20 minutes until fragrant and golden brown. Set aside.

4. Toast the bread. Spread each slice with about 2 teaspoons cheese. Cut into crouton-size pieces.

5. Place oil and vinegar in a mixing bowl; whisk to combine. Add greens and toss to coat. Season to taste with salt and pepper. Divide greens on 4 salad plates. Top with cheese croutons and nuts.

Per serving:

CARBOHYDRATES:	NET CARBS:	FIBER:	PROTEIN:	FAT:	CALORIES:
11 grams	6 grams	5 grams	10 grams	25 grams	301

Smoked Mozzarella, Tomato, and Green Bean Salad

Walnuts add more than just crunch to this salad: they are an excellent source of omega-3 fatty acids and sterols, both of which contribute to cardiovascular health, and ellagic acid, which may inhibit the growth of cancer cells.

PREP TIME: 10 minutes
COOK TIME: 10 minutes
2 servings

½ pound thin green beans
4 marinated artichoke hearts, drained and patted dry

2 plum tomatoes, thinly sliced
6 ounces smoked mozzarella cheese, cut into ¼-inch
  slices
¼ cup walnut halves

Dressing:
3 tablespoons extra-virgin olive oil
2 teaspoons red wine vinegar
½ teaspoon Dijon mustard
½ teaspoon salt
¼ teaspoon freshly ground black pepper

1. Cook green beans in a large pot of lightly salted boiling water 8 minutes, or until crisp-tender. Drain and refresh under cold water.
2. To assemble salad: Place artichoke hearts in the center of each plate. Encircle with the tomato slices. Then arrange green beans and cheese slices around the artichokes. Sprinkle each plate with walnuts.
3. To make the dressing: Whisk olive oil, vinegar, mustard, salt, and pepper until well combined. Spoon dressing over salad.

Per serving:

CARBOHY-DRATES:	NET CARBS:	FIBER:	PROTEIN:	FAT:	CALORIES:
17 grams	11 grams	6 grams	23.5 grams	51.5 grams	609

Sweet Potato and Spinach Salad

This salad dressing is less acidic than most, allowing the orange flavor to come through. To make ahead, prep your ingredients the night before, chilling the dressing in an airtight container and the vegetables in separate sandwich bags.

PREP TIME: 15 minutes
COOK TIME: 10 minutes
4 servings (1¼ cups per serving)

Dressing:
⅓ cup very thinly sliced onion
1 tablespoon canola oil
1 tablespoon orange juice
1½ teaspoons rice vinegar (not sweetened or seasoned)
¾ teaspoon salt

1 medium sweet potato, peeled and cut into ½-inch dice
4 cups packed spinach leaves
1 small red bell pepper, cut into matchsticks

1. Combine dressing ingredients in a bowl with a whisk or fork.
2. Put potato in a small saucepan with enough water to cover and bring to a boil; cook 7 to 8 minutes until tender but not mushy. Drain in colander and rinse briefly under cold water to stop the cooking.
3. Toss dressing with potato, spinach, and pepper. Serve immediately.

TIP: This salad is chock full of vitamins and minerals. Sweet potatoes provide beta-carotene (a precursor of vitamin A), vitamin C, and potassium. Spinach contributes iron and vitamin B_2.

Per serving:

CARBOHY-DRATES:	NET CARBS:	FIBER:	PROTEIN:	FAT:	CALORIES:
7 grams	5.5 grams	1.5 grams	1 gram	2.5 grams	51

Tabbouleh

Bulgur is made from whole-wheat kernels that are specially processed into coarse, medium, or fine grinds. It is a staple ingredient in this traditional Middle Eastern salad. Bulgur must be well rinsed in a sieve before use to rid the grains of dust.

PREP TIME: 15 minutes
Standing time: 15 minutes
4 servings

⅓ cup medium or fine bulgur, rinsed and drained
¾ cup boiling water
1 tablespoon extra-virgin olive oil
1 tablespoon fresh lemon juice
½ teaspoon grated fresh lemon peel
1 tablespoon finely chopped fresh cilantro or mint
½ teaspoon salt
1 cup English cucumber, cut into ¼-inch dice
¼ cup finely diced green pepper
¼ cup finely diced onion

1. In a medium bowl, pour ¾ cup boiling water over bulgur; cover and let stand until tender and liquid is absorbed, 10 to 15 minutes (drain, if necessary).
2. Make the dressing: Whisk oil, lemon juice, peel, and salt with a fork. Add bulgur, cucumber, pepper, and onion. Mix well. Transfer to a bowl and serve.

Per serving:

CARBOHY-DRATES:	NET CARBS:	FIBER:	PROTEIN:	FAT:	CALORIES:
10.5 grams	8 grams	2.5 grams	2 grams	3.5 grams	77

Tomato and Cucumber Salad

This light, refreshing salad is sure to make frequent appearances at your table. Take care, though, that you don't make it too far in advance or in large quantities thinking that it will keep—the scallions can become overpowering if they stand more than a day.

PREP TIME: 15 minutes
Marinate time: 30 minutes
4 servings

> 1 English cucumber or 2 small regular cucumbers
> 3 tablespoons red wine vinegar
> 2 packets sugar substitute
> ½ teaspoon salt, plus more to taste
> 2 small tomatoes, seeded and coarsely chopped
> ½ cup chopped scallions
> ¼ cup chopped fresh mint
> 2 tablespoons olive oil
> pepper, to taste

1. Peel cucumber, cut in half lengthwise and scoop out seeds with a small spoon. Cut cucumber into ½-inch slices and transfer to a large serving bowl. Toss with vinegar, sugar substitute, and salt. Let sit 30 minutes.
2. Add tomatoes, scallions, mint, and olive oil to bowl. Gently mix to combine all ingredients. Season to taste with additional salt and pepper.

TIP: One half-teaspoon of salt doesn't sound like much, but it has the power to have a considerable effect on this dish. Cucumbers can be bitter; letting them stand for 30 minutes in the salty-sweet vinegar helps to make them more palatable. Salt will pull the juice from the tomatoes and boosts their flavor. If the tomatoes at your market look pale and wan, halve or quarter cherry tomatoes instead.

Per serving:

CARBOHY-DRATES:	NET CARBS:	FIBER:	PROTEIN:	FAT:	CALORIES:
5.5 grams	3.5 grams	2 grams	1 gram	7 grams	86

Asian Vegetable Stir-Fry

Bok choy and red peppers are both good tasty sources of vitamin C, which is destroyed by heat. Quickly stir-frying the vegetables limits their exposure to heat and to nutrient loss.

PREP TIME: 20 minutes
COOK TIME: 5 minutes
4 servings

> 1 tablespoon sesame oil
> 2 cups sliced shiitake mushrooms (stems removed and discarded)
> 4 cups sliced bok choy
> 1 cup short, thin strips of red bell pepper
> ½ of 1 medium onion, sliced
> 1 large garlic clove, pushed through a press
> 1 tablespoon lite (reduced-sodium) soy sauce
> 2 to 3 teaspoons sambal oelek (hot chili paste)

1. Heat oil in 12-inch nonstick skillet over high heat. Add mushrooms and stir-fry 1 minute; add bok choy, red bell peppers, onion, and garlic and stir-fry 2 minutes.
2. Stir in soy and chili sauces and stir-fry 1 minute more for tender-crisp vegetables. Serve hot.

TIP: Sambal oelek is a fiery-hot seasoning paste made of chilies, brown sugar, and salt. It is used in the cuisines of southern India, Indonesia, and Malaysia. If you cannot find it in your supermarket or specialty foods store but have access to fresh red chilies, make your own. Set a skillet over high heat. After 2 or 3 minutes, reduce the heat to medium and put in 4 ounces fresh chilies. Roast, stirring, 2 minutes. Cool, then chop (wear gloves to protect hands, and remove the seeds for a milder paste) and combine with ½ teaspoon salt and ½ teaspoon brown sugar. Refrigerate any leftovers for up to 1 week.

Per serving:

CARBOHYDRATES:	NET CARBS:	FIBER:	PROTEIN:	FAT:	CALORIES:
8 grams	5.5 grams	2.5 grams	3 grams	4 grams	70

Atkins Baked Beans

Beans are a terrific source of iron, fiber, and protein. When you are on Lifetime Maintenance, they should be a regular part of your diet. Delicious homemade beans are easier to prepare than you may think, and most of the cooking time is unattended. Our recipe contains only 11.5 Net Carbs per serving, versus 28 grams for store-bought beans.

PREP TIME: 5 minutes
COOK TIME: 10 minutes
BAKE TIME: 50 minutes (plus bean cooking time)
6 servings (⅔ cup per serving)

1½ cups small white beans, soaked and cooked according to package directions (see page 372)
2 slices applewood-smoked thick-cut bacon
1 onion, chopped
2 garlic cloves, pushed through a press
1 (8-ounce) can tomato sauce
¼ cup sugar-free pancake syrup
⅓ cup chicken broth

1. Heat oven to 400° F. Cook bacon in a skillet until crisp; remove and chop. Add onion and cook over medium heat 6 minutes until very tender; add garlic and cook 30 seconds more. Add tomato sauce, syrup, and broth. Bring to a boil.

2. Place cooked beans in a 3-quart baking dish; pour sauce over beans. Cover tightly with foil and bake 50 to 60 minutes until hot throughout and sauce is caramelized on top.

TIP: Baked beans freeze well—so make a double batch. Transfer cooked beans to low, wide two-cup containers. Cool uncovered in the refrigerator, then cover and place in the freezer. Small containers freeze food more quickly and are convenient for defrosting.

Per serving:

CARBOHY-DRATES:	NET CARBS:	FIBER:	PROTEIN:	FAT:	CALORIES:
26 grams	11.5 grams	14.5 grams	10 grams	7.5 grams	160

Braised Leeks and Fennel

Roasting vegetables slowly mellows and sweetens their flavor. Leeks are the sweetest-tasting member of the onion family, and they are a good source of iron and fiber. This side dish goes beautifully with roast chicken or fish.

PREP TIME: 15 minutes
COOK TIME: 45 minutes
8 servings

1 small fennel bulb (½ pound)
4 medium leeks (½ pound each)
1 cup reduced-sodium chicken broth
½ teaspoon salt
¼ teaspoon pepper

3 tablespoons unsalted butter
1 tablespoon lemon juice
⅓ cup chopped parsley

1. Heat oven to 450° F. Trim fennel leaving 1 inch of the stalk. Quarter bulb; remove center core. Cut crosswise into thin (⅛-inch) slices.
2. Cut roots off leeks and trim, leaving 4 inches of green parts. Cut in half lengthwise and thoroughly wash under running water. Place vegetables in a 11 × 9-inch pan. Pour in broth. Sprinkle with salt and pepper and dot with butter.
3. Cover pan with aluminum foil; bake 25 minutes. Uncover; stir lightly. Bake uncovered 20 minutes more, until vegetables are very tender and liquid is almost all gone. Mix in lemon juice and parsley. Serve warm.

TIP: Leeks can be stored up to five days in the refrigerator. Be sure to wash them thoroughly before using because their tightly-wound layers trap soil and sand.

Per serving:

CARBOHY-DRATES:	NET CARBS:	FIBER:	PROTEIN:	FAT:	CALORIES:
18.5 grams	15.5 grams	3 grams	3 grams	5 grams	122

Broccolini in Sage and Feta Cream

A simply flavored cream sauce, tangy feta, and almost any steamed veggie (we chose broccolini here) produces a three-star side dish. Fresh feta in brine (sold at deli counters) is especially creamy and delicious.

PREP TIME: 5 minutes
COOK TIME: 15 minutes
4 servings

½ cup heavy cream
½ cup reduced-sodium chicken broth
8 large fresh sage leaves
1 pound broccolini (2 small bunches), trimmed
½ cup crumbled feta

1. Bring cream, broth, and sage to a boil in a medium saucepot. Reduce heat and cook at a low boil about 10 minutes until reduced to ½ cup.
2. Steam broccolini just until tender but bright green, about 5 minutes.
3. Sprinkle feta over hot broccolini and pour cream sauce over top. Serve.

TIP: If you substitute broccoli in this recipe, use one medium bunch. Cut heads into florets. Peel stems with a vegetable peeler, and cut into ¼-inch slices. Blue cheese may be substituted for the feta, if you prefer.

Per serving:

CARBOHYDRATES:	NET CARBS:	FIBER:	PROTEIN:	FAT:	CALORIES:
10 grams	8.5 grams	1.5 grams	7.5 grams	15 grams	204

Brown Rice Pilaf

To get more carb mileage out of this pilaf, we added lots of low carb mushrooms and celery. The vegetables complement the nutty flavor of brown rice and make a small quantity of rice go a long way. A handful of toasted walnuts rounds out the dish.

PREP TIME: 15 minutes
COOK TIME: 1 hour
6 servings (⅔ cup per serving)

6 tablespoons butter, divided
½ cup brown rice
4 stalks celery, peeled and thinly sliced
1 teaspoon salt, divided
20 ounces white or cremini mushrooms, sliced
¼ teaspoon black pepper
½ cup walnuts, coarsely chopped

1. In a medium pot, melt 1 tablespoon of the butter over medium heat. Add rice and celery and cook 5 minutes, stirring occasionally, until rice begins to brown slightly. Add 1 cup plus 2 tablespoons water and ¼ teaspoon salt. Bring to boil. Cover and simmer 45 minutes, until liquid is absorbed. Remove from heat and let stand 5 minutes.
2. In a large skillet melt the remaining 5 tablespoons butter over medium-high heat. Add mushrooms, remaining ¾ teaspoon salt, and pepper. Cook 15 minutes, stirring occasionally, until mushrooms begin to brown and almost all liquid has evaporated. Remove from heat, and set aside.
3. In the same skillet over medium heat toast walnuts for 5 minutes, stirring occasionally, until golden.
4. Stir mushrooms and walnuts into cooked rice. Serve.

Per serving:

CARBOHY-DRATES:	NET CARBS:	FIBER:	PROTEIN:	FAT:	CALORIES:
13.5 grams	12 grams	1.5 grams	4 grams	16 grams	206

Garden Pasta

Soy pasta tastes best when freshly made. The trick to making good pasta salads is using a high ratio (1:1) of vegetables to pasta. You can vary the flavor of this salad by substituting parsley for the cilantro and using red wine vinegar instead of lime juice.

PREP TIME: 15 minutes
COOK TIME: 15 minutes
6 servings

Dressing:
2 tablespoons canola oil
3 tablespoons fresh lime juice
¾ teaspoon salt
1 large garlic clove, pushed through a press

½ pound low carb soy fusilli pasta, cooked according to
    package directions, rinsed under cold water, and
    drained well
1 cup shredded green cabbage
½ cup diced yellow pepper
½ cup cooked green peas
½ cup cilantro leaves, coarsely chopped
¼ cup sliced red onion

1. Combine the oil, lime juice, salt, and garlic in a large bowl.
2. Add the cooked pasta, cabbage, pepper, green peas, cilantro, and onion. Toss well and serve.

TIP: Serve this refreshing and colorful salad at room temperature.

Per serving:

CARBOHY-DRATES:	NET CARBS:	FIBER:	PROTEIN:	FAT:	CALORIES:
14.5 grams	7 grams	7.5 grams	25.5 grams	7 grams	217

Grilled Eggplant with Cilantro Sauce

Cool, creamy cilantro sauce pairs perfectly with the smoky taste of grilled eggplant. Select eggplants that are light for their size (they'll have fewer seeds and taste milder), and are also smooth and plump. If you aren't partial to the taste of cilantro, parsley is a fine substitute.

PREP TIME: 15 minutes
COOK TIME: 25 minutes
6 servings

Sauce:
¾ cup whole-milk yogurt
2 tablespoons sour cream
½ cup freshly chopped cilantro
4 scallions, chopped
¼ teaspoon salt
⅛ teaspoon ground pepper

2 pounds eggplant, cut into ½-inch slices
1 large garlic clove, halved
¼ cup olive oil
½ teaspoon salt
¼ teaspoon ground pepper

1. In a medium bowl mix yogurt, sour cream, cilantro, scallion, salt, pepper, and garlic to combine. Let stand 20 minutes for flavors to blend.
2. Heat grill to medium and lightly oil. Rub cut sides of eggplant with garlic and brush with oil. Sprinkle with salt and pepper. Cook about 20 to 25 minutes, turning once halfway through cooking time, until eggplant is fork tender and lightly browned. Serve warm or at room temperature. Add dollop of sauce to your plate and serve.

Per serving:

CARBOHY-
DRATES: NET CARBS: FIBER: PROTEIN: FAT: CALORIES:
11.5 grams   7.5 grams   4 grams   3 grams   11 grams   151

Italian-Style Green Beans

This super-easy side dish is packed with flavor, and pretty to boot. The beans can be cooked ahead, cooled, and refrigerated. When ready to serve, simply warm them in the microwave and toss with dressing.

PREP TIME: 10 minutes
COOK TIME: 6 minutes
4 servings

> 3 cups (¾ pound) trimmed green beans
> 1 tablespoon extra-virgin olive oil
> 1 large garlic clove, thinly sliced
> ¼ cup marinated artichokes in oil, drained and chopped
> 1 plum tomato, cut into ¼-inch dice
> ½ teaspoon salt

1. Bring a large saucepan two-thirds filled with water to a boil, add beans, and cook 6 minutes until tender-crisp and still bright green. Drain and rinse briefly under cold water.
2. Place oil and garlic in a small microwave-safe dish. Cook on low 30 seconds or until garlic begins to color. Toss with beans, artichokes, tomato, and salt. Serve warm.

TIP: Pair this side dish with Veal Milanese (page 367) and low carb pasta topped with marinara sauce for a delicious Italian-themed meal.

Per serving:

CARBOHY-DRATES:	NET CARBS:	FIBER:	PROTEIN:	FAT:	CALORIES:
8 grams	5 grams	3 grams	2 grams	4 grams	70

Olive Cheese Bread

Substitute your own favorite olives and cheese if you prefer. A great accompaniment to almost any entrée, this bread also makes tasty open-faced sandwiches. Toast a slice and top with sliced grilled beef or chicken and roasted onions or peppers. Add a salad, and lunch or dinner is ready.

PREP TIME: 15 minutes
BAKE TIME: 50 minutes
12 servings

   ¾ cup soy flour
   ¾ cup whole-wheat flour
   ¾ cup whole-grain pastry flour
   2½ teaspoons baking powder
   ½ teaspoon salt
   1 cup shredded Cheddar cheese
   ½ cup olives, chopped (about 12 olives)
   2 large eggs
   ½ cup heavy cream
   ½ cup water
   ¼ cup olive oil

1. Heat oven to 350° F. In a large bowl whisk together soy flour, whole-wheat flour, pastry flour, baking powder, and salt. Add cheese and olives; toss to combine.
2. In a small bowl whisk eggs, cream, water, and olive oil. Pour egg mixture into flour mixture; stir to combine. Spoon into an 8 × 4-inch loaf pan.

3. Bake 50 minutes or until a wooden skewer inserted in the center comes out clean. Cool in pan on wire rack 10 minutes. Turn out onto rack to cool completely. Cut into 12 slices and store in an air-tight container or the freezer for up to one month.

Per serving:

CARBOHY-DRATES:	NET CARBS:	FIBER:	PROTEIN:	FAT:	CALORIES:
13.5 grams	11 grams	2.5 grams	7.5 grams	14 grams	205

Polenta Triangles

Creamy, savory, and firm enough to be cut into triangles, these cornmeal-based treats can be eaten as a finger food or fried and eaten with a fork. When fried, the outside will be crispy and the inside creamy.

PREP TIME: 10 minutes
Standing time: 30 minutes
COOK TIME: 25 minutes
12 servings

    1⅔ cups reduced-sodium chicken broth
    ¼ cup heavy cream
    ½ cup yellow cornmeal
    ⅓ cup grated Parmesan cheese
    9 pitted Kalamata olives, finely chopped
    1 tablespoon chopped sun-dried tomatoes in oil
    ¼ teaspoon salt

1. Bring broth and cream to a boil in a heavy 3-quart saucepan. Whisking constantly, gradually add cornmeal. Reduce heat to medium-low and cook, stirring with a wooden spoon, 15 to 20 minutes until thick and creamy.

2. Stir in remaining ingredients. Pour mixture into an oiled 9 × 13-inch baking pan; spread evenly. Top with plastic wrap and press to level. Cool 30 minutes.

3. Remove wrap; turn out polenta onto a cutting board. Cut loaf into thirds crosswise, then lengthwise through middle to form squares. Cut squares diagonally to form 12 triangles. Serve immediately (or rewarm in the microwave 30 seconds).

If you wish, triangles may be fried in two batches. Cook in 1 tablespoon oil in a 12-inch nonstick skillet 1 minute per side until golden and caramelized.

Per serving:

CARBOHY-DRATES:	NET CARBS:	FIBER:	PROTEIN:	FAT:	CALORIES:
4.5 grams	4 grams	0.5 grams	2 grams	3.5 grams	55

Red Swiss Chard and Bacon

Beta-carotene-rich chard, like most dark greens, tastes wonderful when paired with smoky bacon. If the chard stems are very thick, blanch them before adding them to the skillet. To turn this savory vegetable side dish into a complete meal for two, toss with low carb pasta.

PREP TIME: 10 minutes
COOK TIME: 10 minutes
4 servings

   4 slices thick-sliced bacon
   2 cloves garlic, chopped
   1 bunch red Swiss chard, about ¾ pound, leaves cut into
      1-inch pieces, stems thinly sliced (4 cups)
   ½ cup navy beans, drained and rinsed
   ¼ teaspoon salt
   ⅛ teaspoon ground pepper

1. In a large skillet over moderate heat, cook bacon 5 minutes or until crisp. Drain on paper towels. Coarsely chop.
2. Remove all but 1 tablespoon of bacon fat from the skillet. Over moderate heat cook garlic 30 seconds, stirring constantly, until fragrant. Add chard and beans. Cook, stirring occasionally, until chard is wilted and beans are warmed through, about 3 minutes. Season with salt and pepper.
3. Transfer to a serving dish with a slotted spoon. Sprinkle bacon on top. Serve.

Per serving:

CARBOHY- DRATES:	NET CARBS:	FIBER:	PROTEIN:	FAT:	CALORIES:
6 grams	4 grams	2 grams	4.5 grams	4.5 grams	114

Savory Cornbread Muffins

A blend of flours plus cornmeal give these muffins a great texture. If you can't find thick-cut applewood smoked bacon, use 3 slices of regular bacon instead. If you are using a 12-compartment muffin tin, fill the empty 4 compartments halfway with water for even baking.

PREP TIME: 10 minutes
COOK TIME: 3 minutes
BAKE TIME: 20 minutes
8 servings

2 slices thick-cut applewood smoked bacon, or three slices regular bacon
½ cup Atkins™ Bake Mix
½ cup cornmeal
¼ cup whole-wheat flour
1 tablespoon baking powder
2 packets sugar substitute
½ teaspoon salt

¼ teaspoon cayenne
¾ cup water
¼ cup heavy cream
1 large egg
2 tablespoons bacon drippings or canola oil
¼ cup sliced scallions
½ cup shredded Mexican-blend or Cheddar cheese

1. Heat oven to 350° F. Line 8 standard muffin cups with paper cupcake liners.
2. Cook bacon until crisp. Reserve drippings and finely chop bacon.
3. Whisk together bake mix, cornmeal, flour, baking powder, sugar substitute, salt, and cayenne in bowl.
4. In a separate bowl, whisk water, cream, egg, and drippings. Add the dry ingredients and mix with wooden spoon. Fold in cheese. Spoon batter into prepared cups. Bake 18 to 21 minutes until muffins feel set and toothpick inserted in centers comes out clean. Cool in pan 10 minutes; transfer to wire rack. Can be eaten warm or at room temperature.

TIP: These muffins can be made ahead and frozen. They are a terrific accompaniment to Southwestern and Mexican food or as a breakfast dish.

Per serving:

CARBOHY-DRATES:	NET CARBS:	FIBER:	PROTEIN:	FAT:	CALORIES:
11 grams	9 grams	2 grams	9 grams	12 grams	185

Sweet Potato and Zucchini Latkes

A traditional side dish at Jewish holidays, latkes (savory pancakes) are usually made with white potatoes. Our sweet potato version is a lighter, more colorful, and lower-carb offering. For a crisp texture, be sure the oil is hot before adding the potato mixture. Cooked latkes can be kept warm in a 200° F. oven until ready to serve.

PREP TIME: 15 minutes
COOK TIME: about 12 minutes
4 servings

　　1 medium zucchini
　　1 medium sweet potato, peeled and coarsely shredded
　　1 egg
　　1½ teaspoons whole-wheat flour
　　½ teaspoon salt
　　¼ teaspoon onion powder
　　¼ teaspoon cumin
　　⅛ teaspoon cayenne
　　¼ cup canola oil

1. Coarsely shred zucchini onto a triple layer of paper towels. Cover with more towels and press down to squeeze out all excess moisture. Transfer to a bowl and mix in potato, egg, flour, salt, onion powder, cumin, and cayenne.

2. Heat 2 teaspoons of the oil in a large nonstick skillet over medium-high heat until hot. For each latke, use a packed (but level) measuring tablespoonful of potato mixture. Cook 6 latkes at a time, 1½ to 2 minutes per side, until deep golden. Remove and keep warm; repeat twice more with remaining potato mixture. Serve with sour cream, if desired.

Per serving:

CARBOHYDRATES:	NET CARBS:	FIBER:	PROTEIN:	FAT:	CALORIES:
9.5 grams	8 grams	1.5 grams	2.5 grams	15.5 grams	184

Tomato, Zucchini, and Mushroom Gratin

Like most gratins, this hearty side dish or light main course has a crunchy topping and a creamy sauce. You can assemble it up to a day ahead.

PREP TIME: 20 minutes
COOK TIME: 10 minutes
BAKE TIME: 25 minutes
6 servings

1½ slices rye bread
2 tablespoons chopped parsley
2 tablespoons butter, divided, plus extra for pan
3 cups sliced button mushrooms
2 large garlic cloves, pushed through a press
½ cup heavy cream
3 medium zucchini, sliced
2 small tomatoes, thinly sliced
½ cup shredded Swiss cheese

1. Heat oven to 375° F. Pulse bread in a food processor to form coarse crumbs. Mix with parsley in a small bowl.
2. Melt 1 tablespoon of the butter in a large skillet over medium-high heat, add mushrooms, and cook 5 minutes until browned. Transfer mushrooms to a plate. Add remaining tablespoon butter to skillet and cook garlic just until aromatic; pour in cream. Cook a few minutes or until cream is reduced to ⅓ cup.
3. Butter a 13 × 9-inch glass baking dish. Arrange zucchini in three overlapping rows lengthwise. Arrange tomato slices evenly over zucchini and cover tomatoes with mushrooms.
4. Sprinkle cheese over vegetables. Drizzle with cream sauce and sprinkle bread crumbs over surface in an even layer. Bake uncovered 25 to 30 minutes, until cream around vegetables is bubbly, zucchini is tender, and crumbs are golden.

Per serving:

CARBOHY-DRATES:	NET CARBS:	FIBER:	PROTEIN:	FAT:	CALORIES:
11 grams	8.5 grams	2.5 grams	6 grams	14 grams	188

Warm Zucchini Mint Salad

The warm dish brings out the flavor of the dressing. If desired, vary the dressing by substituting different herbs; instead of mint, try marjoram or basil. Be sure to leave enough room on the baking sheets so that the zucchini pieces brown rather than steam.

PREP TIME: 15 minutes
COOK TIME: 10 minutes
6 servings

   5 tablespoons olive oil, divided
   2 tablespoons rice wine vinegar
   3 tablespoons chopped mint or 2 teaspoons dried
   2 tablespoons minced shallots
   2 teaspoons freshly grated lemon rind
   1 teaspoon Dijon mustard
   ½ teaspoon salt, divided
   ¼ teaspoon pepper, divided
   pinch ground cinnamon (optional)
   2½ pounds (about 6 small) zucchini, halved lengthwise
      and cut in ½-inch-wide semicircles
   ½ cup slivered almonds, toasted

1. Heat broiler. In a large serving bowl, whisk together 4 tablespoons of the oil, vinegar, mint, shallots, lemon rind, mustard, ¼ teaspoon of the salt, and ⅛ teaspoon of the pepper.
2. Sprinkle zucchini with remaining salt and pepper; toss with remaining tablespoon of oil. Arrange zucchini in a sin-

gle layer on two baking sheets. Place one sheet 5 inches from heat source. Broil 10 minutes, turning halfway through cooking time, until zucchini are browned and tender. Repeat with remaining baking sheet.

3. Transfer the warm zucchini to bowl; gently toss with vinaigrette to coat. Sprinkle with almonds.

Per serving:

CARBOHY-DRATES:	NET CARBS:	FIBER:	PROTEIN:	FAT:	CALORIES:
9 grams	5.5 grams	3.5 grams	4.5 grams	17.5 grams	202

Cranberry Relish

You can make this delicious, quick homemade relish up to three days ahead, but add the walnuts an hour before serving, to preserve their crunchy texture. Cranberries are a great source of vitamin C. If you want to reduce the carb count by 2 Net Carbs grams per portion, omit the orange.

PREP TIME: 10 minutes
COOK TIME: 10 minutes
8 servings

    1 small navel orange
    1 (12-ounce) bag fresh cranberries, rinsed
    3 tablespoons water
    ¾ cup granular sugar substitute
    ½ cup chopped walnuts

1. Grate orange; set orange rind aside. With a small sharp knife, peel off the pith (the white part underneath the rind) and inner white membranes between orange segments. Chop orange into ½-inch pieces.

2. Place cranberries, water, orange rind, and sugar substitute in a small saucepan. Bring to a boil over medium heat.

Cook 10 minutes, stirring occasionally, until cranberries pop open. Remove from heat; transfer to a bowl.
3. Mix in orange pieces and walnuts. Chill one hour to blend flavors.

TIP: Don't save cranberry relish just for Thanksgiving. It's also wonderful paired with roast pork or duck.

Per serving:

CARBOHYDRATES:	NET CARBS:	FIBER:	PROTEIN:	FAT:	CALORIES:
10.5 grams	8 grams	2.5 grams	1.5 grams	5 grams	87

Cucumber Raita

Traditionally used in Indian cuisine to cool down spicy dishes, this fresh creamy salad/sauce is great with curries or as a side dish. Pair it with strongly flavored grilled meats such as lamb and venison, too.

PREP TIME: 20 minutes
4 servings

1 medium cucumber, peeled, split lengthwise, and seeded
½ teaspoon salt
1 cup plain whole-milk yogurt
3 tablespoons chopped fresh mint
1½ teaspoons fresh lime juice
1 large garlic clove, minced
pinch sugar substitute

1. Lightly sprinkle both sides of cucumber with ¼ teaspoon salt. Lay on a double thickness of paper towels to drain 15 minutes. Meanwhile, combine remaining ingredients in a bowl.

2. Pat cucumber dry and cut into ½-inch dice. Stir into sauce. Serve cold.

Per serving:

CARBOHY-DRATES:	NET CARBS:	FIBER:	PROTEIN:	FAT:	CALORIES:
4.5 grams	4 grams	0.5 gram	2.5 grams	2 grams	46

Custom Mayonnaises

Custom-flavored mayonnaises are delicious in sandwiches and also make terrific condiments for meats, fish, and poultry. They also work magic with simple tuna or ham salads. Mayos may be refrigerated for up to five days.

PREP TIME: 5 minutes
16 servings (1 tablespoon per serving)

Faux Remoulade:
1 cup mayonnaise
2 tablespoons capers, drained and chopped
1 tablespoon ketchup
1 anchovy, minced

Combine all ingredients in bowl. Serve with poached fish or chicken.

Orange Basil Mayo:
1 cup mayonnaise
2 tablespoons chopped fresh basil
2 tablespoons orange juice
1 teaspoon freshly grated orange rind
1 small garlic clove, minced

Combine all ingredients in bowl. Serve on cooked vegetables or with ham or turkey.

Horseradish Mayo:
1 cup mayonnaise
2 tablespoons jarred drained horseradish
2 tablespoons Chinese mustard sauce

Combine all ingredients in bowl. Serve with roast beef, burgers, or on BLT sandwiches.

Note: The nutritional data for the variations is minimal; therefore only one set of data is given.

Per serving:

CARBOHY-DRATES:	NET CARBS:	FIBER:	PROTEIN:	FAT:	CALORIES:
0.5 gram	0.5 gram	0 grams	0 grams	11 grams	102

Faux Pickled Vegetables

Blanching veggies in an acidic broth for a brief period imparts flavor and makes quick work of "pickling." They are delicious as is—especially when served cold, but they also work well with a light dressing, such as garlicky olive oil.

PREP TIME: 15 minutes
COOK TIME: 3 minutes
4 servings

⅔ cup unsweetened rice vinegar
⅓ cup water
2 (1 × 2-inch) strips lemon peel
1 packet sugar substitute
3 cups cauliflower florets
1 large carrot, peeled and sliced on the diagonal
1 large red bell pepper, cut into 2-inch triangles

Dressing:
1 tablespoon extra-virgin olive oil
1 medium garlic, pushed through a press
2 tablespoons finely chopped cilantro
¼ teaspoon salt

1. Bring vinegar, water, lemon peel, and sugar substitute to a boil in a nonreactive stockpot. Add cauliflower, carrot, and pepper. Cook 3 minutes until crisp-tender. Drain in colander and rinse with cold water until cooled. Drain well.
2. Combine dressing ingredients in large bowl; add vegetables and toss well. Serve.

TIP: For quick Korean-style kimchee, substitute one medium cabbage—cut in eight wedges—for the vegetables. Use white wine instead of vinegar, and omit the cilantro in the dressing.

Per serving:

CARBOHY-DRATES:	NET CARBS:	FIBER:	PROTEIN:	FAT:	CALORIES:
8.5 grams	5.5 grams	3 grams	2 grams	3.5 grams	69

Flavored Butters

Use these compound butters for flavoring vegetables as well as toppings for grilled or broiled meats, poultry, or fish. Store in a decorative cup in the refrigerator if using at the table, or form a log for cutting into pats. Butter logs may be frozen and used as needed.

PREP TIME: 10 minutes
8 servings per flavor (1 tablespoon per serving)

Aromatic Oregano Butter:
½ cup (1 stick) butter at room temperature
2 tablespoons fresh oregano leaves, finely chopped
½ teaspoon freshly grated lemon peel
1 small clove garlic, pushed through a press

Ginger Garlic Butter:
½ cup (1 stick) butter at room temperature
1 tablespoon grated fresh ginger
1 large garlic clove, pushed through a press
2 tablespoons finely chopped fresh parsley or cilantro
1 teaspoon grated fresh lemon peel

Double Chili Butter:
½ cup (1 stick) butter at room temperature
2 teaspoons chili powder
2 teaspoons hot red chili sauce with garlic or chili sauce

For each type of butter, beat all ingredients together in bowl with a wooden spoon. Spoon into an airtight container and chill. Or, chill loosely covered with plastic wrap on a plate until set, then form into a 1-inch-thick log with a piece of plastic wrap or wax paper.

Note: The nutritional data for the variations is minimal; therefore only one set of data is given.

Per serving:

CARBOHY-DRATES:	NET CARBS:	FIBER:	PROTEIN:	FAT:	CALORIES:
0.5 gram	0.5 gram	0 grams	0 grams	11.5 grams	104

Homemade Tomato Sauce

Easy to make and ready in 30 minutes, this sauce is light, fresh in flavor, and much lower in carbs than most commercial products. Be sure to buy tomatoes in purée with no sweeteners (such as corn syrup). The sauce may be kept refrigerated for up to 5 days—or double the recipe and freeze a batch. Tomato sauce is not only for pasta; it makes a great addition to soups, stews, and over fish.

PREP TIME: 10 minutes
COOK TIME: 35 minutes
8 servings (½ cup per serving)

1 (28-ounce) can whole plum tomatoes in purée
¼ cup olive oil
1 medium onion, chopped
3 large garlic cloves, chopped
½ cup red wine
1 (8-ounce) can tomato sauce
¼ cup basil leaves, chopped
1 tablespoon fresh oregano, finely chopped
½ teaspoon salt
¼ teaspoon pepper

1. Process tomatoes with their purée in a food processor until smooth. Or, if you like a chunkier sauce, use your hands to break apart each tomato—first pour into a bowl, then dig in with clean hands.
2. Heat oil in saucepan over medium heat. Add onion and cook 3 minutes until translucent; add garlic and cook 1 minute more. Add wine and boil 1 minute. Add pureed tomatoes and tomato sauce. Bring to a boil, reduce heat, partially cover, and cook 30 minutes. Stir in basil, oregano, salt, and pepper.

Per serving:

CARBOHY-DRATES:	NET CARBS:	FIBER:	PROTEIN:	FAT:	CALORIES:
8 grams	6.5 grams	1.5 grams	1.5 grams	7 grams	104

Pineapple-Pepper Salsa

This fruit-based salsa is a nice change of pace from traditional tomato versions. The sweet taste of pineapple is balanced by the pleasant tartness of lime juice and the fresh flavor of cilantro. Red pepper adds color, and jalapeño a bit of heat. Serve with grilled pork, beef kebabs, or roast chicken.

PREP TIME: 20 minutes
CHILL TIME: 30 minutes
5 servings (⅓ cup per serving)

>   1 cup diced fresh pineapple
>   1 tablespoon cilantro leaves, finely chopped
>   2 teaspoons finely chopped red onion
>   ¾ cup finely diced red bell pepper
>   1½ teaspoons fresh lime juice
>   1 jalapeño pepper, seeded and minced

Combine all ingredients in bowl. Refrigerate 30 minutes for flavors to blend. Serve cold or at room temperature.

TIP: Mild and sweet, red bell peppers contain more beta-carotene than green peppers. All peppers are a good source of vitamin C, and they are a tasty snack food. Keep a bag of pepper strips in the refrigerator at all times and you'll have a nutritious nibble whenever you get the urge to munch.

Per serving:

CARBOHYDRATES:	NET CARBS:	FIBER:	PROTEIN:	FAT:	CALORIES:
5.5 grams	4.5 grams	1 gram	0.5 gram	0 grams	23

Quick Velouté and Variations

The classic preparation of this French master sauce calls for simmering stock a long time to intensify its flavor, but our version uses canned chicken broth and vegetables and cooks in a mere 30 minutes. You'll be surprised how rich and delicious this quick fix is. Use on any roasted pork or poultry dish, as well as with game.

PREP TIME: 15 minutes
COOK TIME: 30 minutes
5 servings (3 tablespoons per serving)

2 tablespoons butter, divided
½ cup finely diced shallot
1 medium carrot, finely diced
1 cup chopped celery
1 small bay leaf
2 cups reduced-sodium chicken broth
1 tablespoon whole-wheat flour

1. Melt 1 tablespoon of the butter in a medium saucepan. Add shallot, carrot, and celery; cover, and cook over medium heat 10 minutes, stirring once, until lightly caramelized.
2. Add bay leaf and broth; bring to a boil. Reduce heat and simmer uncovered 20 minutes until reduced to about 1 cup. Strain stock, pressing on solids. Discard solids and set stock aside.
3. Melt remaining tablespoon of butter in the same saucepan, add flour, and cook, stirring, over medium heat 1 minute

until flour looks dissolved and mixture foams when not stirred. Gradually whisk in reserved stock and bring to a boil. Reduce heat slightly and cook 1 minute. The sauce should be very smooth (if it isn't, simply strain it once more).

Mushroom Velouté:

Prepare Quick Velouté. Melt 1 teaspoon butter in a small saucepan over medium-high heat and add ½ cup diced shitake mushroom caps. Cook 3 minutes until browned. Pour in Quick Velouté; simmer 1 minute to soften mushrooms and infuse sauce with their flavor.

Herb Velouté:

Prepare Quick Velouté. Add ½-inch sprig each of fresh rosemary and thyme; simmer 1 minute. Stir in pinch of ground white pepper. Remove herbs.

TIP: Store leftover sauce in small containers in refrigerator for up to three days. Re-heat gently.

Note: For Mushroom Velouté, add 1 gram Net Carb.

Velouté and Herb Velouté per serving:

CARBOHY-DRATES:	NET CARBS:	FIBER:	PROTEIN:	FAT:	CALORIES:
1.5 grams	1.5 grams	0 grams	1.5 grams	5 grams	58

Rhubarb Applesauce

More interesting—and lower in carbs—than regular applesauce, our version gets its lovely rosy hue from rhubarb and its soft mellowness from butter. A versatile dish, it makes a great snack, dessert, pancake topping, or condiment for pork or chicken. (It's also great with oatmeal!) Rhubarb is actually a vegetable, not a fruit.

PREP TIME: 20 minutes
COOK TIME: 45 minutes
8 servings (⅓ cup per serving)

4 cups fresh or (unsweetened) frozen rhubarb cut into ½-inch pieces
2 medium apples, peeled and coarsely chopped
2 tablespoons granular sugar substitute
2 tablespoons unsalted butter
1 teaspoon vanilla

1. In a medium saucepan mix rhubarb, apples, sugar substitute, and 1 cup water. Cook over moderate heat 45 minutes, stirring occasionally, until rhubarb is broken down and very soft.
2. Remove from heat and stir in butter and vanilla. Serve cold or at room temperature. Keeps in refrigerator for 5 days.

TIP: If you've ever tasted unsweetened rhubarb you know how tart it is. The same acids that give it its distinctive tang can react with certain metals to give this dish an unpleasant flavor and color. Be sure to use a saucepan made of stainless steel, anodized aluminum, or enamel; cast iron and regular aluminum are reactive.

Per serving:

CARBOHY-DRATES:	NET CARBS:	FIBER:	PROTEIN:	FAT:	CALORIES:
8 grams	6.5 grams	1.5 grams	0.5 gram	3 grams	60

Almond Flans with "Sugared" Almonds

To give these flans an intense almond flavor, steep toasted almonds in warm cream for half an hour. Baking in a "bain marie," or water bath, ensures even cooking and a creamy texture.

PREP TIME: 20 minutes
COOK TIME: 30 minutes
BAKE TIME: 55 minutes
CHILL TIME: 4 hours
6 servings

  2 cups heavy cream
  1 cup slivered almonds, toasted
  ½ cup plus 2 tablespoons granular sugar substitute, divided
  5 eggs
  ⅛ teaspoon salt
  1 teaspoon vanilla extract
  ½ teaspoon almond extract
  2 teaspoons unsalted butter

1. In a medium saucepan, bring cream and 1 cup water to a simmer. Add almonds and let steep 30 minutes. Pour cream through a sieve into a large bowl; reserve almonds.
2. Heat oven to 325° F. Whisk ½ cup sugar substitute, eggs, salt, and vanilla and almond extract into cream.
3. Place 6 (6-ounce) custard cups in a roasting pan. Evenly divide the cream mixture among the cups. Place the pan in oven and pour in boiling water to halfway up the sides of the cups. Cover with foil.
4. Bake 50 minutes to 1 hour, until flans are set on outer rim and a little jiggly in the centers. Cool in water bath to room temperature. Cover with plastic wrap, then transfer to refrigerator. Chill at least 4 hours.

5. To sugar nuts: In medium skillet over moderate heat, melt butter. Add almonds and remaining 2 tablespoons sugar substitute. Cook until almonds are golden brown, about 4 minutes. Cool and serve over flan.

Per serving:

CARBOHYDRATES:	NET CARBS:	FIBER:	PROTEIN:	FAT:	CALORIES:
9 grams	7 grams	2 grams	11 grams	44 grams	467

Baked Pear Fans

Beautiful, easy, and elegant, this fruit dessert is festive enough to end a company meal—especially if you top the pear fan with a dollop of whipped, lightly sweetened mascarpone cheese. When you first put the pears in the baking pan don't try to fan them out. After they cook and soften you'll be able to be fan them out easily, without breaking them.

PREP TIME: 10 minutes
COOK TIME: 40 minutes
4 servings

    2 pears, peeled, halved, and cored
    1 tablespoon unsalted butter
    1 tablespoon freshly squeezed lemon juice
    ¼ teaspoon ground pepper
    ¼ teaspoon ground ginger
    ¼ teaspoon ground cinnamon
    ¼ teaspoon vanilla extract

1. Heat oven to 375° F. To make pear fans: make ¼-inch lengthwise slices along length of each half-pear, starting

⅓-inch from the stem end and cutting all the way down toward the rounded end.

2. Place butter in a 9-inch-square baking pan and melt in the oven. Add lemon juice, pepper, ginger, cinnamon, and 2 tablespoons water to butter; mix well. Place pears in the pan, rounded sides up. Cover with aluminum foil. Bake until pears are fork tender, about forty minutes; turn once halfway through baking time.

3. With a slotted spoon, transfer pear halves onto serving plates and carefully fan them out. Stir vanilla into sauce in pan. Place pan on stovetop and cook 1 minute to reduce slightly. Spoon sauce over pears. Serve warm or at room temperature.

Per serving:

CARBOHYDRATES:	NET CARBS:	FIBER:	PROTEIN:	FAT:	CALORIES:
13 grams	11 grams	2 grams	0.5 gram	3 grams	77

Blackberry-Orange Sorbet

To balance the intense flavor of blackberries, we added buttermilk, making this sorbet more like a sherbet. This recipe can be doubled easily. If fresh blackberries aren't available, frozen ones work equally well. You will need an ice-cream maker for this recipe.

PREP TIME: 20 minutes
CHILL TIME: 4 hours
4 servings (½ cup per serving)

2¼ cups blackberries
⅓ cup granular sugar substitute
1 teaspoon freshly grated orange rind
1 cup buttermilk

1. In a medium saucepan, bring blackberries, sugar substitute, 2 tablespoons water, and orange rind to a boil. Reduce heat and simmer, covered, for 15 minutes, stirring occasionally, until berries break down.
2. Place berry mixture in a food processor. Process until smooth. Press through a fine strainer into a bowl. Stir in buttermilk. Chill in refrigerator 1 hour or until cold.
3. Pour into an ice-cream maker and run according to manufacturer's directions. Transfer to a bowl and freeze 2 to 3 hours before serving.

TIP: To make blueberry-lemon sorbet, substitute blackberries and orange rind with equal amounts of blueberries and lemon rind, which will add 3 more grams of Net Carbs per serving. The sorbet can be frozen for up to two weeks—if it lasts that long!

Per serving:

CARBOHY-DRATES:	NET CARBS:	FIBER:	PROTEIN:	FAT:	CALORIES:
15.5 grams	11 grams	4.5 grams	2.5 grams	1 gram	76

Brown Rice Pudding

The use of heavy cream and egg yolks makes this delicious, homey rice pudding extra creamy and rich. If your daily carb count permits an extra 8 grams of Net Carbs, stir a tablespoon of plumped raisins into each serving.

PREP TIME: 30 minutes
COOK TIME: 1 hour 35 minutes
CHILL TIME: 4 hours
8 servings (½ cup per serving)

1½ cups heavy cream
1¼ cups water
½ cup short-grain brown rice
¼ teaspoon salt
3 egg yolks
¼ cup granular sugar substitute
½ teaspoon ground cinnamon
1 tablespoon unsalted butter
2 teaspoons vanilla extract

1. In a heavy saucepan over moderate heat, bring the cream, water, rice, and salt to a boil. Reduce heat to low. Cover and simmer 1½ hours, until rice is very tender and liquid is almost absorbed.

2. In a medium bowl whisk yolks, sugar substitute, and cinnamon. Slowly pour egg mixture into rice pan on stove, stirring constantly. Stir about 6 minutes until thickened. Remove from heat; stir in butter and vanilla. Refrigerate at least 4 hours to chill completely.

Per serving:

CARBOHYDRATES:	NET CARBS:	FIBER:	PROTEIN:	FAT:	CALORIES:
11.5 grams	11 grams	0.5 gram	3 grams	20 grams	238

Chocolate Almond Biscotti

If you like your biscotti the traditional way—meaning dry and light for dunking in espresso—don't add the optional sour cream. Do add it if you prefer a softer cookie. We used sugar substitute packets in this recipe instead of granular substitute because the packets have more condensed sweetness.

PREP TIME: 20 minutes
BAKE TIME: 35 minutes
32 servings (1 biscotti per serving)

1 cup almonds
⅓ cup unsweetened cocoa
½ cup whole-grain pastry flour
½ cup whole-wheat flour
18 packets sugar substitute
1 teaspoon baking powder
2 large eggs
2 tablespoons sour cream (optional)
¾ cup unsalted butter, cut into small pieces

1. Heat oven to 350° F. Line a baking sheet with parchment paper; set aside. In a food processor, process nuts and cocoa until nuts are finely ground. Add pastry flour, whole-wheat flour, sugar substitute, and baking powder; pulse to combine.
2. With processor running, add eggs 1 at a time. Scrape down sides of processor, as needed. Add butter and optional sour cream; pulse to combine.
3. Remove dough from machine and divide in half. Form dough into two 8-inch-long logs directly on baking sheet. Bake 20 minutes. Remove from oven and let cool 5 minutes.
4. On a cutting board, with a serrated knife, cut logs into ½-inch slices on a slight diagonal. Arrange cookies on baking sheet; bake 12 to 14 minutes or until firm. Cool on baking sheet before storing in an airtight container.

Per serving:

CARBOHY-DRATES:	NET CARBS:	FIBER:	PROTEIN:	FAT:	CALORIES:
4.5 grams	3 grams	1.5 grams	2 grams	7 grams	87

Chocolate Coconut Macaroons

These bite-size morsels have a chewy texture and rich chocolate flavor. They keep well for several days in an airtight container. You can make larger macaroons by using a scant tablespoonful measure, instead of a teaspoonful. In that case, a single serving is 1 macaroon, not 2.

PREP TIME: 10 minutes
BAKE TIME: 15 minutes
12 servings (2 macaroons per serving)

    4 large egg whites
    1 cup granular sugar substitute
    ½ teaspoon coconut extract
    ½ teaspoon chocolate extract
    3 tablespoons unsweetened cocoa
    1½ cups unsweetened coconut flakes, chopped

1. Heat oven to 325° F. Line two baking sheets with parchment paper.
2. In a bowl, with an electric mixer on medium speed, beat egg whites until soft peaks form. With the beater on, slowly add sugar substitute and continue to beat until stiff. Stir in coconut and chocolate extracts.
3. Mix cocoa with coconut flakes. Stir into egg mixture. Drop batter onto prepared baking sheets in slightly rounded teaspoons. Bake 12 to 15 minutes until set.

Per serving:

CARBOHY-DRATES:	NET CARBS:	FIBER:	PROTEIN:	FAT:	CALORIES:
5 grams	2.5 grams	2.5 grams	2 grams	7.5 grams	93

Chocolate Pecan Bars

Instead of pecan pie, try these easy-to-make bars instead. We've replaced the traditional corn syrup with sugar-free pancake syrup and added chocolate for texture and flavor. This dessert is rich and dense, so a small serving is sufficient.

PREP TIME: 15 minutes
BAKE TIME: 50 minutes
12 servings (1 square per serving)

Crust:
½ cup whole-grain pastry flour
½ cup whole-wheat flour
½ cup (1 stick) butter
1 teaspoon vanilla extract

Filling:
3 ounces unsweetened chocolate, finely chopped
¼ cup (½ stick) unsalted butter, cut into small pieces
¼ cup heavy cream
1 cup sugar-free pancake syrup
3 eggs
¾ cup granular sugar substitute
1 teaspoon vanilla extract
½ teaspoon salt
1¼ cups pecans, coarsely chopped

1. Heat oven to 325° F. In a large bowl, whisk together pastry and whole-wheat flours. Cut in butter with a pastry blender or two knives, until dough stays together when pressed with your hands. Stir in vanilla. Press onto the bottom and 1 inch up the sides of a 9-inch-square baking pan. Prick all over with a fork. Bake until set and dried, about 20 minutes. Cool slightly.
2. In a small pan over moderate heat, melt chocolate in the butter and cream, stirring occasionally. In a large bowl,

whisk syrup, eggs, sugar substitute, vanilla, and salt to combine.

3. Pour chocolate mixture into syrup mixture; mix well. Stir in nuts. Pour filling into prepared crust. Bake until just set, about 30 minutes. Cool on wire rack before cutting into twelve 3-inch-by-2¼-inch squares.

Per serving:

CARBOHY-DRATES:	NET CARBS:	FIBER:	PROTEIN:	FAT:	CALORIES:
13 grams	9.5 grams	3.5 grams	5 grams	28 grams	302

Chocolate Soufflé

It's a stretch to call chocolate a health food, but chocolate can actually be good for you. It is high in flavonoids, the same beneficial compounds in red wine, tea, and some fruits and vegetables. By combining unsweetened chocolate with sugar substitute, this soufflé gives you chocolate's benefits without candy's pitfalls.

PREP TIME: 15 minutes
COOK TIME: 5 minutes
BAKE TIME: 30 minutes
6 servings

  3 tablespoons butter, plus 1 teaspoon for buttering dish
  ½ cup cream mixed with ½ cup water
  3 tablespoons Atkins™ Bake Mix
  2 ounces unsweetened chocolate, finely chopped
  4 eggs, separated
  1 teaspoon vanilla extract
  14 packets sugar substitute

1. Heat oven to 350° F. Butter a 1½-quart soufflé dish. Melt butter in a medium saucepan; add bake mix and cook over

medium heat 3 minutes, stirring constantly. Add cream mixture slowly. Bring to a boil. Stir in chocolate. Remove from heat.

2. Pour mixture into a large bowl. Whisk in egg yolks and vanilla. With an electric mixer on high, beat egg whites and sugar substitute until stiff peaks form. Fold one-third of the egg whites into the chocolate mixture, then fold in the rest. Transfer to prepared dish. Bake 30 minutes until puffed and set but still slightly wobbly in center.

Per serving:

CARBOHY-DRATES:	NET CARBS:	FIBER:	PROTEIN:	FAT:	CALORIES:
6.5 grams	4.5 grams	2 grams	6 grams	23 grams	251

Christmas Yule Log

This Christmas classic was made over and turned into a perfect Atkins dessert. But don't wait till Christmas to make this delicious cake roll, it's great any time of year. For a simpler version, omit the frosting.

PREP TIME: 20 minutes
COOK TIME: 25 minutes
8 servings

    Cake:
    1 cup granular sugar substitute
    ¼ cup unsweetened cocoa powder
    2 tablespoons Atkins™ Bake Mix
    9 eggs, separated
    ¼ teaspoon salt

Filling:
1 cup (½ pint) heavy cream
2 packets sugar substitute

Frosting:
2 ounces unsweetened chocolate, melted and cooled
⅓ cup heavy cream
1 stick (8 tablespoons) unsalted butter, softened
8 packets sugar substitute
1 tablespoon unsweetened cocoa powder
½ teaspoon vanilla extract

1. Grease a jelly-roll pan, line it with parchment, leaving a 2-inch border, and grease again. Set aside. Heat oven to 375° F. Sift sugar substitute, cocoa powder, and bake mix into a bowl.

2. In a large bowl, with an electric mixer on high speed, beat egg yolks until pale yellow and fluffy. Beat in cocoa mixture on low just until blended.

3. Beat egg whites with salt until stiff peaks form. Fold one-third of the whites into the yolk mixture to lighten it, then fold in the rest. Spread batter evenly in the prepared pan. Bake 12 to 15 minutes, until cake springs back when lightly touched. Cool cake in pan on wire rack.

4. While cake is cooling make the filling: Whip cream and sugar substitute until medium peaks form. (Do not over-beat.) When cake is cool, slide cake from pan with parchment underneath. Place on countertop.

5. Spread filling over cake, leaving a ½-inch border. Roll up cake from narrow end, using parchment to help. Cut 1-inch diagonal pieces from each end. Transfer roll to a serving platter; place cut diagonal pieces on either side to form log "stumps." Slip pieces of waxed paper underneath roll.

6. Make the frosting: In a large mixing bowl gradually whisk cream into melted chocolate. With an electric mixer on medium speed, beat in butter, sugar substitute, cocoa powder, and vanilla extract. Beat until smooth and fluffy.

Spread frosting over log. Run fork tines through frosting to make a barklike texture.

Per serving:

CARBOHY-DRATES:	NET CARBS:	FIBER:	PROTEIN:	FAT:	CALORIES:
7.5 grams	5.5 grams	2 grams	16 grams	24 grams	314

Chunky Mocha Ice Cream

This is for chocolate and coffee lovers! Creamy mocha ice cream, studded with chewy morsels of Mocha Crunch Bars, makes this a dessert to delight in. We used sugar substitute in packets in this recipe, instead of granular sugar substitute, for better texture.

PREP TIME: 10 minutes
COOK TIME: 5 minutes
CHILL TIME: 4 hours
8 servings

- 1 teaspoon unflavored gelatin
- 1 cup water
- 6 egg yolks
- 18 packets sugar substitute
- 2½ cups heavy cream
- ½ cup unsweetened cocoa
- 4 teaspoons instant decaffeinated coffee
- 1 teaspoon vanilla extract
- 3 (2.11-ounce) Advantage™ Chocolate Mocha Crunch Bars, chopped

1. Sprinkle gelatin over water and let soften, about 5 minutes.
2. In a medium bowl, whisk yolks and sugar substitute to combine. In a medium pot, mix cream, gelatin mixture,

cocoa powder, and coffee. Cook over medium-low heat, stirring occasionally, until cocoa and coffee granules have dissolved and mixture has begun to simmer.

3. Slowly pour 1 cup of the hot cocoa mixture over the egg yolk mixture, whisking constantly. Pour mixture back into pot. Cook, stirring constantly, until mixture is thick enough to coat the back of a spoon. Remove from heat. Stir in vanilla. Chill mixture 4 hours.

4. Pour mixture into ice-cream maker. Process according to manufacturer's directions. About 5 minutes before ice cream is finished, add the chopped bars.

Per serving:

CARBOHY-DRATES:	NET CARBS:	FIBER:	PROTEIN:	FAT:	CALORIES:
16 grams	7 grams	5 grams	12.5 grams	36 grams	415

Citrus Chiffon Cake

Chiffon cakes differ from sponge cakes in that oil, not butter, is combined with egg yolks and then added to the dry ingredients. The oil coats the proteins in the flour with fat, and helps to make the cake tender.

PREP TIME: 15 minutes
COOK TIME: 55 minutes
10 servings

1¾ cups Atkins™ Bake Mix
1 cup granular sugar substitute
¼ teaspoon salt
2 teaspoons grated orange rind
1 teaspoon grated lemon rind
9 large egg yolks
¾ cup cold water
½ cup canola oil

12 large egg whites at room temperature
½ teaspoon cream of tartar

1. Heat oven to 325° F. In a large bowl, whisk bake mix, sugar substitute, salt, and orange and lemon rinds. In a medium bowl, mix yolks, water, and oil. Slowly add liquid to dry mixture. Mix gently with a spatula to combine.

2. With an electric mixer on high, beat whites and cream of tartar until stiff, about 4 minutes. Fold one-third of the egg whites into the batter to lighten it. Gently fold in remaining egg whites.

3. Pour batter into an ungreased 10-inch tube pan. Bake 55 minutes or until a toothpick inserted in the center comes out clean. Cool completely upside down. To unmold, run knife around center and outside of cake. Cut into 10 slices.

Per serving:

CARBOHYDRATES:	NET CARBS:	FIBER:	PROTEIN:	FAT:	CALORIES:
7.5 grams	5.5 grams	2 grams	8 grams	17 grams	260

Coconut Ice Cream

Coconut milk imparts a silky texture to this ice cream, in contrast to the crunchy bits of coconut dispersed throughout.

PREP TIME: 5 minutes
COOK TIME: 5 minutes
CHILL TIME: 4 hours
8 servings

6 egg yolks
14 packets sugar substitute
2 cups heavy cream
1 (13.5-ounce) can unsweetened coconut milk
2 teaspoons coconut extract

1 teaspoon vanilla extract
1 cup shredded unsweetened coconut, lightly toasted

1. In a medium bowl whisk yolks and sugar substitute to combine. In a medium pot, bring heavy cream to a simmer over medium-low heat.
2. Slowly pour 1 cup of the cream into the yolk mixture, whisking constantly. Pour yolk mixture back into pot. Cook, stirring constantly, until mixture is thick enough to coat the back of a spoon. Remove from heat. Stir in coconut milk and coconut and vanilla extracts. Chill 4 hours.
3. Pour ice cream mix into ice-cream maker. Process according to manufacturer's directions. About 5 minutes before ice cream is finished, add the toasted coconut.

TIP: You can buy unsweetened shredded coconut in health food stores. To toast coconut, spread on a baking sheet and bake at 350° F. for 5 minutes. Watch it carefully though; coconut goes from browned to burned in a matter of seconds. Coconut extract is available in supermarkets.

Per serving:

CARBOHY-DRATES:	NET CARBS:	FIBER:	PROTEIN:	FAT:	CALORIES:
6 grams	4.5 grams	1.5 grams	4 grams	32 grams	326

Frozen Lemon Mousse

There's a scientific reason for adding a little vodka to this sparkling citrus dessert. Because alcohol freezes at temperatures far below 32° F. (the exact temperature varies depending on the alcohol content), the liquor keeps the mousse from getting too hard. If you don't have vodka, light rum will also work. If you prefer to avoid alcohol altogether, simply omit it from the recipe.

PREP TIME: 10 minutes
COOK TIME: 5 minutes
6 servings (½ cup per serving)

3 eggs
3 egg yolks
½ cup fresh lemon juice
1 cup granular sugar substitute
½ stick unsalted butter
2 tablespoons vodka
1 tablespoon grated lemon peel
1 teaspoon vanilla extract
1 cup heavy cream

1. In a medium bowl, whisk eggs and egg yolks; set aside. In a medium saucepan heat lemon juice, sugar substitute, butter, and vodka. Gradually whisk lemon mixture into eggs. Return mixture to saucepan; cook 3 minutes, stirring constantly, over medium heat until mixture thickens. Do not boil. Remove from heat. Stir in lemon peel and extract. Transfer to a large bowl. Cover with a piece of plastic wrap touching surface; chill at least 1 hour.
2. With an electric mixer on medium speed, beat cream until peaks form. In two additions, fold whipped cream into lemon custard. Transfer to a 1-quart dessert dish. Freeze until solid, at least 2 hours. To serve, spoon into individual dessert plates and garnish with fresh berries, if desired.

Per serving:

CARBOHY-DRATES:	NET CARBS:	FIBER:	PROTEIN:	FAT:	CALORIES:
7.5 grams	7.5 grams	0 grams	5.5 grams	27.5 grams	308

Lime Granita

Simple and simply refreshing, this granita is a little on the tart side; if you prefer a sweeter dessert, add a few more packets of sugar substitute, to taste.

PREP TIME: 5 minutes
FREEZE TIME: 1 hour
6 servings (½ cup per serving)

15 packets sugar substitute
pinch salt
4 teaspoons freshly grated lime peel
⅔ cup lime juice (from about 5 limes)

In a small saucepan over high heat bring to a boil 2⅓ cups water, sugar substitute, salt, and lime peel. Pour through strainer into a metal 9-inch-square baking pan. Stir in lime juice. Freeze 1 hour, scraping surface occasionally with a fork to break up ice crystals.

Per serving:

CARBOHY-DRATES:	NET CARBS:	FIBER:	PROTEIN:	FAT:	CALORIES:
5 grams	5 grams	0 grams	0 grams	0 grams	31

It used to be just ices . . . but now we have granitas, sorbets, and sherbets.

A quick guide:

Granitas are usually flavored with coffee or citrus fruits. During the freezing process they are stirred occasionally with a fork, which gives them a coarse, grainy texture.

Sherbets are usually flavored with fruit and they often have milk, egg white, or gelatin added. Sherbets have a very smooth texture.

Sorbets can be sweet or savory (herb-flavored sorbets are served between courses as a palate cleanser). Like granitas, sorbets never include milk; like sherbets, sorbets are very smooth.

Mixed Berry Shortcakes

These mixed berry shortcakes are perfect in summer, when berries are at their peak. But you may enjoy short-cakes any time of year, substituting seasonal fruit or simply topping with lots of fresh butter. The dough may be prepared ahead of time, but for best results, bake just before serving.

PREP TIME: 15 minutes
COOK TIME: 17 minutes
6 servings

  1 cup Atkins™ Bake Mix
  ½ cup pecan halves
  3 tablespoons plus 2 teaspoons granular sugar substitute, divided
  ¼ teaspoon salt
  6 tablespoons cold butter, cut into small pieces
  1⅔ cups heavy cream, divided
  ¼ cup sour cream
  1 egg
  3 cups mixed fresh berries, such as strawberries, blueberries, raspberries

1. In a food processor, pulse bake mix, pecans, 3 table-spoons sugar substitute, and salt until nuts are finely ground. (If you don't have a food processor, grind the nuts in a nut or coffee grinder.) Add the butter and pulse until butter pieces are the size of peas.
2. In a liquid measuring cup or bowl, whisk ⅔ cup of the heavy cream, sour cream, and egg. Pour evenly over dry mixture and pulse just until combined. Transfer dough to a baking sheet.
3. Separate dough into 12 equal-size pieces (you'll need about 3½ tablespoons of dough for each piece). Pat each piece into a disk measuring 2½ to 3 inches across. Space

disks evenly on baking sheet; refrigerate for 30 minutes. (Dough may be prepared up to 1 day ahead.)

4. Heat oven to 375° F. Bake shortcakes about 17 minutes, until bottoms are golden brown. Cool on baking sheet set on a wire rack.

5. With an electric mixer on medium speed, beat remaining cup of heavy cream with remaining 2 teaspoons sugar substitute until soft peaks form.

6. To assemble: spoon ¼ cup whipped cream on 6 shortcakes, top with ½ cup berries, and cover with remaining shortcakes.

Per serving:

CARBOHY-DRATES:	NET CARBS:	FIBER:	PROTEIN:	FAT:	CALORIES:
16 grams	10.5 grams	5.5 grams	16 grams	49.5 grams	558

Chocolate Chip Oatmeal Cookies

Oats are an excellent source of fiber, and help to lower the number of grams of Net Carbs in these cookies to 7.5 per cookie. (The typical chocolate chip cookie weighs in at around 13 grams.)

PREP TIME: 20 minutes
BAKE TIME: 14 minutes per batch
35 servings (1 cookie per serving)

1¼ cups granular sugar substitute
¾ cup unsalted butter
1 large egg
2 tablespoons sugar-free pancake syrup
½ teaspoon vanilla extract
1½ cups oatmeal
¼ cup soy flour

¼ cup whole-wheat flour
¼ cup whole-grain pastry flour
1 teaspoon baking powder
¼ teaspoon ground cinnamon
½ teaspoon salt
½ cup sugar-free chocolate chips

1. Heat oven to 350° F. In a large bowl, mix butter and sugar substitute with a wooden spoon until well combined. Add egg, pancake syrup, and vanilla; mix well.
2. In a bowl whisk together oatmeal, soy flour, whole-wheat flour, pastry flour, baking powder, cinnamon, and salt. Add dry ingredients to butter mixture; mix well. Fold in chips.
3. Drop dough by tablespoonfuls onto ungreased baking sheets. Space dough 1½ inches apart and flatten with the palm of your hand.
4. Bake 14 minutes or just until cookies begin to turn golden brown. Cool on sheets for 5 minutes before transferring to cooling racks to cool completely.

Per serving:

CARBOHY-DRATES:	NET CARBS:	FIBER:	PROTEIN:	FAT:	CALORIES:
8.5 grams	7.5 grams	1 gram	2 grams	5.5 grams	86

Orange Walnut Cake

A low carb version of a traditional Greek cake, its distinctive flavor comes from ground walnuts and an orange-zest-infused syrup, which is poured over the cake.

PREP TIME: 15 minutes
BAKE TIME: 25 minutes
16 servings

2 cups walnuts
1 cup whole-grain pastry flour
¾ cup whole-wheat flour
1½ teaspoons baking powder
½ teaspoon baking soda
1 cup (2 sticks) unsalted butter, softened to room
  temperature
1½ cups granular sugar substitute, divided
6 large eggs
3 tablespoons freshly grated orange peel, divided
½ cup buttermilk
whipped cream (optional)

1. Heat oven to 350° F. In a food processor, pulse walnuts, pastry flour, whole-wheat flour, baking powder, and baking soda until nuts are finely ground. Add butter, 1 cup of the sugar substitute, eggs, 2 tablespoons of the orange peel, and buttermilk. Process until combined, stopping to scrape down sides, as needed.

2. Pour batter into a 9 × 13-inch baking pan; level surface with an offset spatula. Bake 25 minutes or until a toothpick inserted in the center comes out clean.

3. Meanwhile, in a small pot bring to a boil ¾ cup water, ½ cup sugar substitute, and 1 tablespoon orange peel. Remove from heat and let peel infuse syrup.

4. When cake is removed from the oven, pour syrup evenly over the surface. Cool completely in pan on a cooling rack before cutting into 16 squares. Serve with whipped cream, if desired.

Per serving:

CARBOHY-DRATES:	NET CARBS:	FIBER:	PROTEIN:	FAT:	CALORIES:
14.5 grams	12 grams	2.5 grams	7 grams	23.5 grams	286

Pineapple-Mango Layer Cake

This cake is a variation of a classic chiffon cake. If you like richer cakes, use melted and cooled butter in place of the vegetable oil. For a taste of the tropics, we've topped the cake with mango and pineapple.

PREP TIME: 30 minutes
BAKE TIME: 15 to 20 minutes
8 servings

   ½ cup whole-grain pastry flour
   ½ cup soy flour
   1½ teaspoons baking powder
   ½ teaspoon salt
   6 large eggs, separated
   ¾ cup plus 1 tablespoon sugar substitute
   ¼ cup vegetable oil
   ½ cup heavy cream
   ½ mango, thinly sliced
   ¼ pineapple, thinly sliced

1. Heat oven to 350° F. Grease and flour 2 (8-inch-round) cake pans. In a large bowl, whisk together pastry flour, soy flour, baking powder, and salt.
2. Beat egg whites with an electric mixer on medium speed until soft peaks form. Slowly add sugar substitute; continue beating until firm peaks form.
3. Combine yolks and oil. Pour yolk mixture into dry ingredients; mix well. With an electric mixer, beat one-third of the whites into the batter; beat until very smooth, about 4 minutes. Fold in remaining whites with a spatula, in two additions.
4. Divide batter in prepared pans; smooth tops. Bake 20 minutes or until a toothpick inserted in centers comes out clean. Cool on wire rack in pans 5 minutes; then turn out to cool completely.

5. Whip heavy cream with remaining tablespoon of sugar substitute until soft peaks form. To assemble: Place one cake layer on a serving plate. Spread half the whipped cream over cake. Place second layer over whipped cream. Top with remaining whipped cream. Starting at the edge of the cake, arrange fruit in concentric circles, alternating pineapple and mango.

Per serving:

CARBOHY-DRATES:	NET CARBS:	FIBER:	PROTEIN:	FAT:	CALORIES:
14.5 grams	12.5 grams	2 grams	8 grams	17.5 grams	244

Pinwheel Cookies

This recipe features an easy-to-make cream cheese dough wrapped around a delicious chocolate-nut filling. These easy "rolled" cookies are fun for children to slice and bake.

PREP TIME: 15 minutes
COOK TIME: 17 minutes
28 servings (1 cookie per serving)

Dough:
1 cup Atkins™ Bake Mix
4 ounces cream cheese, softened
2 tablespoons butter, softened
2 tablespoons sour cream
2 packets sugar substitute

Filling:
¼ cup finely chopped walnuts
¼ cup sugar-free chocolate chips
¼ teaspoon ground cinnamon

1. Heat oven to 350° F. Line two baking sheets with aluminum foil; set aside. Using an electric mixer on low, beat bake mix, cream cheese, butter, sour cream, and sugar substitute until well combined. Form dough into a rectangle, cover with plastic wrap, and refrigerate for 20 minutes.

2. While dough is chilling, combine walnuts, chocolate chips, and cinnamon.

3. Roll dough between two pieces of plastic wrap to form a rectangle measuring 10 × 14 inches. Remove top layer of plastic wrap. Sprinkle filling evenly over dough, leaving a ½-inch border. Roll dough up jelly-roll style, beginning with the long side and using bottom sheet of plastic wrap to help roll the dough into a cylinder. With a sharp knife, cut roll into ½-inch slices.

4. Arrange slices on prepared sheets. Bake 17 minutes, or until lightly golden and set.

Per serving:

CARBOHYDRATES:	NET CARBS:	FIBER:	PROTEIN:	FAT:	CALORIES:
3 grams	2.5 grams	0.5 gram	6.5 grams	5 grams	66

Pumpkin Pie with Pecan Crust

This pie is so good it's a shame to serve it only once a year at Thanksgiving! The ingredient list is a bit long, so be your own sous-chef and assemble everything before you start. Like most pumpkin pies, this one tastes even better with a dollop of whipped cream.

PREP TIME: 15 minutes
BAKE TIME: 55 minutes
COOLING TIME: 4 hours
8 servings

Crust:
⅔ cup soy flour
½ cup pecans, finely ground
⅓ cup whole-grain pastry flour
¼ cup granular sugar substitute
6 tablespoons chilled butter, cut into 12 pieces
2 tablespoons ice water

Filling:
1 (15-ounce) can puréed pumpkin
¾ cup granular sugar substitute
1 teaspoon ground cinnamon
¾ teaspoon ground ginger
¼ teaspoon ground cloves
¼ teaspoon salt
2 large eggs
1¼ cups heavy cream

1. Heat oven to 425° F. In a large bowl whisk together soy flour, pecans, pastry flour, and sugar substitute. Cut in butter with a pastry blender or 2 knives until butter pieces are about the size of peas. Add the ice water; stir to combine.
2. Transfer crust mixture to a 9-inch pie plate. Press along bottom and sides of pie plate to form a crust. Place in freezer to harden, about 15 minutes.
3. Cover crust with aluminum foil and bake 15 minutes; remove from oven and take off foil. Reduce oven to 375° F.
4. In a bowl, whisk pumpkin, sugar substitute, cinnamon, ginger, cloves, and salt to combine. Mix in eggs, 1 at a time. Add heavy cream and mix well.
5. Pour filling into partially baked piecrust. Cover crust edge with aluminum foil. Bake 40 minutes, or until filling is set but still a little jiggly in the middle. Cool on a wire rack.

Per serving:

CARBOHY-DRATES:	NET CARBS:	FIBER:	PROTEIN:	FAT:	CALORIES:
16 grams	12.5 grams	3.5 grams	7 grams	31 grams	354

References

2. A Lifetime of Health

1. Westman, E. C., Yancy, W. S., Edman, J. S., et al., "Effect of 6-Month Adherence to a Very Low Carbohydrate Diet Program," *American Journal of Medicine,* 113(1), 2002, pages 30-36.

2. Dreon, D. M., Fernstrom, H. A., Miller, B., et al., "Low-Density Lipoprotein Subclass Patterns and Lipoprotein Response to a Reduced-Fat Diet in Men," *The FASEB Journal,* 8(1), 1994, pages 121–126.

3. Dreon, D. M., Fenstrom, H. A., Campos, H., et al., "Change in Dietary Saturated Fat Intake Is Correlated with Change in Mass of Large Low-Density-Lipoprotein Particles in Men," *The American Journal of Clinical Nutrition,* 67(5), 1998, pages 828–836.

4. Tseng, M., Everhart, J. E., Sandler, R. S., "Dietary Intake and Gallbladder Disease: A Review," *Public Health Nutrition,* 1999, 2(2), pages 161–172.

5. Institute of Medicine of the National Academies, "Dietary Reference Intakes for Energy, Carbohydrates, Fiber, Fat, Fatty Acids, Cholesterol, Protein, and Amino Acids," available at: http://books.nap.edu/books/0309085373/html/index.html, accessed on April 9, 2004.

6. Heaney, R. P., "Dietary Protein and Phosphorous Do not Affect Calcium Absorption," *The American Journal of Clinical Nutrition,* 72(3), 2000, pages 758–761.

7. Promislow, J. H., Goodman-Gruen, D., Slymen, D. J., et al., "Protein Consumption and Bone Mineral Density in the Elderly: The Rancho Bernardo Study," *American Journal of Epidemiology,* 155(7), 2002, pages 636–644.

8. Skov, A. R., Haulrik, N., Toubro, S., et al., "Effect of Protein Intake on Bone Mineralization During Weight Loss: A 6-Month Trial," 10(6), 2002, *Obesity Research,* pages 432–438.

9. Spencer, H., Kramer, L., "Osteoporosis, Calcium Requirement, and Factors Causing Calcium Loss," *Clinical Geriatric Medicine,* 3(2), 1987; pages 389–402.

10. Spencer, H., Kramer, L., Osis, D., "Do Protein and Phosphorus Cause Calcium Loss?" *The Journal of Nutrition,* 118(6), 1998, pages 657–660.

11. McCullough, M. L., Feskanich, D., Stampfer, M. J., et al., "Diet Quality and Major Chronic Disease Risk in Men and Women: Moving toward Improved Dietary Guidance," *American Journal of Clinical Nutrition,* 76(6), 2002, pages 1261–1271.

3. Yes, You Can Eat Carbs!

1. Havel, P. J., "Peripheral Signals Conveying Metabolic Information to the Brain: Short-Term and Long-Term Regulation of Food Intake and Energy Homeostasis," *Experimental Biology and Medicine,* 226(11), 2001, pages 963–977.

2. Talalay, P., Fahey, J. W., "Phytochemicals from Cruciferous Plants Protect Against Cancer by Modulating Carcinogen Metabolism," *The Journal of Nutrition,* 131(11 suppl), 2001, pages 3027S–3333S.

3. Murillo, G., Mehta, R. G., "Cruciferous Vegetables and Cancer Prevention," *Nutrition and Cancer,* 41(1–2), 2001, pages 17–28.

4. Conaway, C. C., Yang, Y. M., Chung, F. L., "Isothiocyanates as Cancer Chemopreventive Agents: Their Biological Activities and Metabolism in Rodents and Humans," *Current Drug Metabolism,* 3(3), 2002, pages 233–255.

5. Bernstein, P. S., Khachik, F., Carvalho, L. S., et al., "Identification and Quantitation of Carotenoids and

Their Metabolites in the Tissues of the Human Eye," *Experimental Eye Research*, 72(3), 2001, pages 215–223.
6. Beatty, S., Murray, I. J., Henson, D. B., et al., "Macular Pigment and Risk for Age-Related Macular Degeneration in Subjects from a Northern European Population," *Investigative Ophthalmology and Visual Science*, 42(2), 2001, pages 439–446.

4. The Skinny on Fat and Protein

1. Taubes, G., "Nutrition. The Soft Science of Dietary Fat," *Science*, 291(5513), 2001, pages 2536–2545.
2. Dreon, D. M., Fernstrom, H. A., Miller, B., et al., "Low-Density Lipoprotein Subclass Patterns and Lipoprotein Response to a Reduced-Fat Diet in Men," *The FASEB Journal*, 8(1), 1994, pages 121–126.
3. Dreon, D. M., Fernstrom, H. A., Williams, P. T., et al., "A Very-Low-Fat Diet Is Not Associated with Improved Lipoprotein Profiles in Men with a Predominance of Large, Low-Density Lipoproteins," *American Journal of Clinical Nutrition*, 68(3), 1999, pages 411–418.
4. Tribble, D. L., Rizzo, M., Chait, A., et al., "Enhanced Oxidative Susceptibility and Reduced Antioxidant Content of Metabolic Precursors of Small, Dense Low-Density Lipoproteins," *American Journal of Medicine*, 110(2), 2001, pages 103–110.
5. Austin, M. A., Breslow, J. L., Hennekens, C. H., et al., "Low-Density Lipoprotein Subclass Patterns and Risk of Myocardial Infarction," *Journal of the American Medical Association*, 260(13), 1988, pages 1917–1921.
6. Festa, A., D'Agostino, R., Jr., Mykkanen, L., et al., "LDL Particle Size in Relation to Insulin, Proinsulin, and Insulin Sensitivity. The Insulin Resistance Atherosclerosis Study," *Diabetes Care*, 22(10), 1999, pages 1688–1693.
7. Friedlander, Y., Kidron, M., Caslake, M., et al., "Low Density Lipoprotein Particle Size and Risk Factors of

Insulin Resistance Syndrome," *Atherosclerosis*, 148(1), 2000, pages 141–149.

8. Lichtenstein, A. H., Van Horn, L., "Very Low Fat Diets," *Circulation*, 98(9), 1998, pages 935–939.

9. McLaughlin, T., Abbasi, F., Lamendola, C., et al., "Carbohydrate-Induced Hypertriglyceridemia: An Insight into the Link Between Plasma Insulin and Triglyceride Concentrations," *Journal of Clinical Endocrinology and Metabolism*, 85(9), 2000, pages 3085–3088.

10. Westman, E. C., Yancy, W. S., Edman, J. S., et al., "Effect of 6-Month Adherence to a Very Low Carbohydrate Diet Program," *American Journal of Medicine*, 113(1), 2002, pages 30–36.

11. Volek, J. S., Gómez, A. L., Kraemer, W. J., "Fasting Lipoprotein and Postprandial Triacylglycerol Responses to a Low-Carbohydrate Diet Supplemented With N-3 Fatty Acids," *Journal of the American College of Nutrition*, 19(3), 2000, pages 383–391.

12. Foster, G. D., Wyatt, H. R., Hill, J. O., et al., "Evaluation of the Atkins Diet: A Randomized Controlled Trial," *Obesity Research*, 9(53), abstract # 01329, 2001.

13. Stern, L., Iqbal, N., Chiceno, K., et al., "The V.A. Low Carbohydrate Intervention Diet (VALID) Study," *Journal of General Internal Medicine*, 17(S1), 2002, pages 147–148 (abstract #51080).

14. Brehm B. J., Seeley, R. J., D'Alessio, D. A., et al., "Effects of a Low Carbohydrate Diet on Body Weight and Cardiovascular Risk Factors," *Obesity Research*, 9 (3S), 2001, page 170S.

15. Sondike, S. B., Copperman, N. M., Jacobson, M. S., "Low Carbohydrate Dieting Increases Weight Loss but not Cardiovascular Risk in Obese Adolescents: A Randomized Controlled Trial," *Journal of Adolescent Health*, 26, 2000, page 91.

16. Westman, E. C., Yancy, W. S., Guyton, J. S., "Effect of a Low Carbohydrate Ketogenic Diet Program on Fasting Lipid Subfractions," *Circulation*, 106(19 SII), 2002, page 727 (abstract #3582).

17. Expert Panel on Detection, Evaluation, and Treatment of High Blood Cholesterol in Adults, "Executive Summary of the Third Report of the National Cholesterol Education Program (NCEP) Expert Panel on Detection, Evaluation, and Treatment of High Blood Cholesterol in Adults (Adult Treatment Panel III)," *Journal of the American Medical Association,* 285(19), 2001, pages 2486–2497.

18. Braunwald, E., "Shattuck Lecture—Cardiovascular Medicine at the Turn of the Millennium: Triumphs, Concerns, and Opportunities," *New England Journal of Medicine*, 337(19), 1997, pages 1360–1369.

19. Alarcon de la Lastra, C., Barranco, M.D., Motilva, V., et al., "Mediterranean Diet and Health: Biological Importance of Olive Oil," *Current Pharmaceutical Design*, 7(10), 2001, pages 933–950.

20. Massaro, M., Carluccio, M.A., De Caterina, R., "Direct Vascular Antiatherogenic Effects of Oleic Acid: A Clue to the Cardioprotective Effects of the Mediterranean Diet," *Cardiologia*, 44(6), 1999, pages 507–513.

21. Kris-Etherton, P.M., Pearson, T.A., Wan, Y., et al., "High-Monounsaturated Fatty Acid Diets Lower Both Plasma Cholesterol and Triacylglycerol Concentrations," *American Journal of Clinical Nutrition*, 70(6), 1999, pages 1009–1015.

22. Grimble, R.F., Tappia, P.S., "Modulation of Pro-Inflammatory Cytokine Biology by Unsaturated Fatty Acids," *Zeitschrift für Ernahrungswissenschaft*, 37(S1), 1998, pages 57–65.

23. Maedler, K., Spinas, G., Dyntar, D., et al., "Distinct Effects of Saturated and Monounsaturated Fatty Acids on B-Cell Turnover and Function," *Diabetes*, 50(1), 2001, pages 69–76.

24. Gillman, M.W., Cupples, L.A., Millen, B.E., et al., "Inverse Association of Dietary Fat with Development of Ischemic Stroke in Men," *Journal of the American Medical Association*, 278(24), 1997, pages 2145–2150.

25. Oliver, M.F., "It Is More Important to Increase the Intake of Unsaturated Fats Than to Decrease the Intake of

Saturated Fats: Evidence from Clinical Trials Relating to Ischemic Heart Disease," *American Journal of Clinical Nutrition*, 66(4S), 1997, pages 980S–986S.

26. Garg, A., Grundy, S. M., "Management of Dyslipidemia in NIDDM," *Diabetes Care*, 13(2), 1990, pages 153–169.

27. Parker, B., Noakes, M., Luscombe, N., et al., "Effect of a High-Protein, High-Monounsaturated Fat Weight Loss Diet on Glycemic Control and Lipid Levels in Type 2 Diabetes," *Diabetes Care*, 25(3), 2002, pages 425–430.

28. Masella, R., Giovannini, C., Vari, R, et al., "Effects of Dietary Virgin Olive Oil Phenols on Low Density Lipoprotein Oxidation in Hyperlipidemic Patients," *Lipids*, 36(11), 2001, pages 1195–1202.

29. Zambon, D., Sabate, J., Munoz, S., et al., "Substituting Walnuts for Monounsaturated Fat Improves the Serum Lipid Profile of Hypercholesterolemic Men and Women. A Randomized Crossover Trial," *Annals of Internal Medicine*, 132(7), 2000, pages 538–546.

30. Albert, C. M., Gaziano, J. M., Willett, W. C., et al., "Nut Consumption and Decreased Risk of Sudden Cardiac Death in the Physicians' Health Study," *Archives of Internal Medicine*, 162(12), 2002, pages 1382–1387.

31. Hu, F. B., Manson, J. E., Willett, W. C., "Types of Dietary Fat and Risk of Coronary Heart Disease: A Critical Review," *Journal of the American College of Nutrition*, 20(1), pages 5–9.

32. Hu, F. B., Stampfer, M. J., Manson, J. E., et al., "Frequent Nut Consumption and Risk of Coronary Heart Disease in Women: Prospective Cohort Study," *BMJ*, 317(7169), 1998, pages 1341–1345.

33. Enig, Mary, *Know Your Fats: The Complete Primer for Understanding the Nutrition of Fats, Oils, and Cholesterol*, Bethesda Press, 2000, pages 113–152.

34. Clevidence, B. A., Judd, J. T., Schaefer, E. J., "Plasma Lipoprotein (a) Levels in Men and Women Consuming Diets Enriched in Saturated, Cis-, or Trans-Monounsaturated Fatty Acids," *Arteriosclerosis, Throm-*

bosis, and Vascular Biology, 17(9), 1997, pages 1657–1661.

35. Ascherio, A., Katan, M.B., Zock, P.L., et al., "Trans Fatty Acids and Coronary Heart Disease," *New England Journal of Medicine,* 340(25), 1999, pages 1994–1998.

36. Salmerón, J., Hu, F.B., Manson, J.E., et al., "Dietary Fat Intake and Risk of Type 2 Diabetes in Women," *American Journal of Clinical Nutrition,* 73(6), 2001, pages 1019–1026.

37. Weiland, S.K., von Mutius, E., Husing, A., et al., "Intake of Trans Fatty Acids and Prevalence of Childhood Asthma and Allergies in Europe. ISAAC Steering Committee," *Lancet,* 353(9169), 1999, pages 2040–2041.

38. Stampfer, M.J., Hu, F.B., Manson, J.E., et al., "Primary Prevention of Coronary Heart Disease in Women Through Diet and Lifestyle," *New England Journal of Medicine,* 343(1), 2000, pages 16–22.

39. Kohlmeier, L., "Biomarkers of Fatty Acid Exposure and Breast Cancer Risk," *American Journal of Clinical Nutrition,* 66(6S), 1997, pages 1548S–1556S.

40. Smith, R.E., "Dietary Fat and Breast Cancer," *Cancer Detection and Prevention,* 10(3–4), 1987, pages 193–196.

41. Kohlmeier, L., Simonsen, N., van't Veer, P., et al., "Adipose Tissue Trans Fatty Acids and Breast Cancer in the European Community Multicenter Study on Antioxidants, Myocardial Infarction, and Breast Cancer," *Cancer Epidemiology, Biomarkers and Prevention,* 6(9), 1997, pages 705–710.

42. Van Dam, R.M., Willett, W.C., Rimm, E.B., et al., "Dietary Fat and Meat Intake in Relation to Risk of Type 2 Diabetes in Men," *Diabetes Care,* 25(3), 2002, pages 417–424.

43. Kim, Y.I., "Diet, Lifestyle, and Colorectal Cancer: Is Hyperinsulinemia the Missing Link?" *Nutrition Reviews,* 56(9), 1998, pages 275–279.

44. Bruce, W.R., Wolever, T.M., Giacca, A., "Mechanisms Linking Diet and Colorectal Cancer: The Possible Role

of Insulin Resistance," *Nutrition and Cancer*, 37(1), 2000, pages 19–26.

45. Franceshi, S., Favero, A., La Vecchia, C., et al., "Food Groups and Risk of Colorectal Cancer in Italy," *International Journal of Cancer*, 72(1), 1997, pages 56–61.

46. Biesalski, H. K., "Meat and Cancer: Meat as a Component of a Healthy Diet," *European Journal of Clinical Nutrition*, 56 (S1), 2002, pages S2-S11.

47. Franceschi, S., Dal Maso, L., Augustin, L., et al., "Dietary Glycemic Load and Colorectal Cancer Risk," *Annals of Oncology*, 12(2), 2001, pages 173–178.

5. Putting It All into Practice

1. Putnam, J., Economic Research Service, USDA, "U.S. Food Supply Providing More Food and Calories," *Food Review*, 22(3), 1999, pages 2–3.

6. Get Moving!

1. Manson, J. E. Greenland, P., LaCroix, A. Z., et al., "Walking Compared with Vigorous Exercise for the Prevention of Cardiovascular Events in Women," *The New England Journal of Medicine*, 347(10), pages 716–725.

2. Hakim, A. A., Curb, J. D., Petrovitch, H., et al., "Effects of Walking on Coronary Heart Disease in Elderly Men: The Honolulu Heart Program," *Circulation*, 100(1), 1999, pages 9–13.

3. American Heart Association Web site: http://www.americanheart.org/presenter.jhtml.

4. Myers, J., Prakash, M., Froelicher, V., et al., "Exercise Capacity and Mortality Among Men Referred for Exercise Testing," *The New England Journal of Medicine*, 346(11), 2002, pages 793–801.

5. Loehr, J., Schwartz, T., "The Making of a Corporate Ath-

lete," *Harvard Business Review*, 79(1), 2001, pages 120–128.

8. Looking Forward

1. Sensi, M., Pricci, F., Andreani, D., et al., "Advanced Nonenzymatic Glycation Endproducts (AGE): Their Relevance to Aging and the Pathogenesis of Late Diabetic Complications." *Diabetes Research.* 16(1), 1991, pages 1–9.
2. Cerami, A., Vlassara, H., Brownlee, M., et al., "Protein Glycosylation and the Pathogenesis of Atherosclerosis," *Metabolism*, 34(12 suppl), 1985, pages 37–42.
3. Cerami, A., Vlassara, H., Brownlee, M., "Glucose and Aging," *Scientific American*, 265(5), 1987, pages 90–96.
4. Riviere, S., Birlouez-Aragon, I., Vellas, B., "Plasma Protein Glycation in Alzheimer's Disease." *Glycoconjugate Journal*, 15(10), 1998, pages 1039–1042.
5. Lyons, T.J., "Glycation and Oxidation: A Role in the Pathogenesis of Atherosclerosis," *American Journal of Cardiology*, 71(6), 1993, pages 26B–31B.
6. McDonough, P.G., "The Randomized World Is Not Without its Imperfections: Reflections on the Women's Health Initiative Study," *Fertility and Sterility*, 78(5), 2002, pages 951–956.
7. Heaney, R.P., "Excess Dietary Protein May Not Adversely Affect Bone," *Journal of Nutrition*, 128(6), 1998, pages 1054–1057.
8. Spencer, H., Kramer, L., Osis, D., "Do Protein and Phosphorus Cause Calcium Loss?" *Journal of Nutrition*, 118(6), 1998, pages 657–660.
9. Dawson-Hughes, B., Harris, S.S., "Calcium Intake Influences the Association of Protein Intake with Rates of Bone Loss in Elderly Men and Women," *American Journal of Clinical Nutrition*, 2002, 75(4), pages 773–779.
10. Liu, S., Willett, W.C., Stampfer, M.J., et al., "A Prospective Study of Dietary Glycemic Load, Carbohy-

drate Intake, and Risk of Coronary Heart Disease in U.S. Women," *The American Journal of Clinical Nutrition*, 71, 2000, pages 1455–1461.

11. Abassi, F., McLaughlin, T., Lamendola, C., et al., "High Carbohydrate Diet, Triglyceride-Rich Lipoproteins, and Coronary Heart Disease Risk," *American Journal of Cardiology*, 85, 2000, pages 45–48.

12. Sondike, S. B., Copperman, N. M., Jacobson, M. S., "Low Carbohydrate Dieting Increases Weight Loss but Not Cardiovascular Risk in Obese Adolescents: A Randomized Controlled Trial," *Journal of Adolescent Health*, 26, 2000, page 91.

13. McManus, K., Antinoro, L., Sacks, F., "A Randomized Controlled Trial of a Moderate-Fat, Low-Energy Diet Compared with a Low-Fat, Low-Energy Diet for Weight Loss in Overweight Adults," *International Journal of Obesity and Related Metabolic Disorders*, 25(10), 2001, pages 1503–1511.

14. Volek, J. S., Gómez, A. L., Kraemer, W. J., "Fasting Lipoprotein and Postprandial Triacylglycerol Responses to a Low-Carbohydrate Diet Supplemented with N-3 Fatty Acids," *Journal of the American College of Nutrition*, 19(3), 2000, pages 383–391.

15. Westman E. C., Yancy, W. S., Edman, J. S., et al., "Effect of 6-Month Adherence to a Very Low Carbohydrate Diet Program," *American Journal of Medicine*, 113(1), 2002, pages 30–36.

16. Foster, G. D., Wyatt, H. R., Hill, J. O., et al., "Evaluation of the Atkins Diet: A Randomized Controlled Trial," *Obesity Research*, 9 (S3), 2001, abstract #01329.

17. Brehm, B. J., Seeley, R. J., D'Alessio, D. A., et al., "Effects of a Low Carbohydrate Diet on Body Weight and Cardiovascular Risk Factors," College of Nursing and College of Medicine, University of Cincinnati.

18. Stern, L., Iqbal, N., Chiceno, K., et al., "The V.A. Low Carbohydrate Intervention Diet (VALID) Study," *Journal of General Internal Medicine*, 17(S1), 2002, pages 147–148.

Index